COMPUTING SCIENCE

Peter Bishop

Nelson

Thomas Nelson and Sons Ltd
Nelson House   Mayfield Road
Walton-on-Thames   Surrey KT12 5PL

51 York Place
Edinburgh EH1 3JD

P.O. Box 18123   Nairobi   Kenya

Yi Xiu Factory Building
Unit 05–06   5th Floor
65 Sims Avenue
Singapore 1438

Thomas Nelson (Hong Kong) Ltd
Watson Estate   Block A   13 Floor
Watson Road   Causeway Bay   Hong Kong

Thomas Nelson (Nigeria) Ltd
8 Ilupeju Bypass   PMB 21303   Ikeja   Lagos

© P. J. Bishop 1982

First published by Thomas Nelson and Sons Ltd 1982
Reprinted 1982, 1983

ISBN 0-17-431267-9

NCN 200-3426-2

Designed by The New Book Factory, London
Phototypesetting by Parkway Group, London and Abingdon
Printed and bound in Hong Kong

Preface

The aim of this book is to give a broad and thorough introduction to computing science. The book is tailored to meet the requirements of all the examination boards in the United Kingdom which are offering courses in computer studies or computing science at Advanced level. Almost all the material in the syllabuses for these courses is covered in this book, which contains a number of questions from past examination papers.

Nevertheless, this book has also been written with the requirements of the computing industry in mind. A few topics, notably databases and data communications, are treated because of their significance in the world of computing. It is assumed that in due course these topics will be assimilated into the Advanced level syllabuses.

It is realised that a book of this nature is useful for a number of other purposes. These include a reference book for teachers preparing to teach computing at Ordinary or Advanced level, a textbook for students of equivalent courses at colleges of further education, and a foundation book for students embarking on computing courses at universities or polytechnics. It is not beyond the capabilities of a few general readers who want something more than superficial treatment of the subject.

This book covers five major subject areas, namely the principles of computing, the design of computer hardware, the various layers of computer software, the theory and practice of computer applications, and a brief look at the social implications and likely future of computing. Microprocessors are given due, but not undue, attention.

A model computer, named the AMC, has been designed to introduce the topics of processor architecture and operation, and low level language. The AMC is tailored specifically to the requirements of the book. In the same series as this book there is a software package which enables the AMC to be simulated on a microcomputer.

Many of the topics introduced in general terms are reinforced by case studies, drawn from various aspects of the world of computing. Case studies include processor architecture, high level languages, operating systems, data communication networks and computer applications. There is even a case study of the future of computers.

Some sections and exercise questions in the book are marked □. This indicates that they are considerably above the average level of difficulty of the material, and may be omitted without loss of continuity.

The following abbreviations are used to identify questions from past examination papers:

AEB   Associated Examining Board
OLE   Oxford Delegacy of Local Examinations
UL   University of London School Examinations Department
JMB   Joint Matriculation Board
UCLES University of Cambridge Local Examination Syndicate
WJEC   Welsh Joint Education Committee.

Acknowledgements

I am grateful to a number of people who have given their time, expertise and enthusiasm to help me with various aspects of this book.

First and foremost is Valerie Downes, from Imperial College, who has given advice on the overall structure of the book, and reviewed all the material in detail. Also at Imperial College, Derek Brough helped with the design of the AMC, and with the material on compilers and interpreters; James Jacobsen advised me on databases and Cobol; Martin Cripps gave a second opinion on the overall AMC design, and Jill Rout typed the specimen chapters.

Help with the case studies has come from a variety of sources. David Brantigan from the GLC provided the information for the traffic control system case study. Chris Long at ITN was my source for the VT 80 case study. At CBS records, Keith Simmonds and John Clarke provided a wealth of information. Mr E. Wilson from ICL supplied the material for the ICL 2900 series architecture, and its operating system, VME/B. Dr B. J. Ralston provided the information for the Cray 1 architecture, and its Cray Operating System. All the case studies are included with the permission of the organisations mentioned above. My thanks go to these organisations for giving this permission.

At Logica VTS, Justin Brunt reviewed the PL/M case study, and Pat Coen was the source for the material on the VTS 100 word processor. My thanks go to Logica VTS for permission to include this material.

Thanks are due to the following examination boards, who kindly gave permission to reproduce questions from past examination papers: the Associated Examining Board, the Joint Matriculation Board, the University of London, University Entrance and School Examinations Council, the Oxford Delegacy of Local Examinations, and the University of Cambridge Local Examinations Syndicate.

And last, but by no means least, thanks to Ruth Bush, who typed the entire manuscript.

Peter Bishop
7th February 1981

Contents overview

Contents

Computer Software

26 Applications case studies

Computing in Context

1 Introduction

A study of computing at Advanced level is no mean undertaking. At the commencement of such a study, it is essential to give some thought to the objectives to be borne in mind, the skills which will be developed along the way, and the ground which will be covered. This brief introductory chapter covers these three areas. It discusses the objectives of a study of computing at this level, lists some of the skills which are taught, and concludes with an overview of computing.

This chapter looks at the subject in broad, general terms. It makes no assumptions of previous knowledge of the subject. For those who do have previous knowledge of computing, it acts as a concise review of what is already known. In either case, it paves the way for the following chapter, which discusses a few fundamental concepts of computing in some detail.

1.1 Objectives of the Book

The overall objective of this book is to provide a grounding in all the major aspects of computing which is both sufficiently broad and sufficiently thorough for the courses for which the book is intended. Thus the book covers a wide range of material, each aspect being treated in a fair amount of detail.

More specifically, the objectives of the book are as follows:

1. To introduce and develop some fundamental concepts which form the basis of computing and the design of computers;

2. to introduce the essential features of the design of computers, and of associated devices which make up a computer system;

3. to introduce the various types of instructions which govern the way in which computers work, and discuss in some detail the functions performed by sets of these instructions at various levels;

4. to introduce the techniques used in the application of computers to specific tasks, and discuss the range of tasks currently performed by computers;

5. to provide an introduction to the computing industry;

6. to place computing in its proper perspective, both in terms of the wider implications of the use of computers, and from the point of view of the likely future of computing.

These objectives indicate a mixture of theory and practice, of abstract and concrete. Broadly speaking, the overall structure of the book is based on these objectives, in the order stated above.

1.2 Skills Taught

Closely related to the objectives of the book are the skills which are acquired and developed during its use. It is unrealistic to assert that all the skills mentioned here will definitely be acquired; nevertheless these do represent directions in which efforts should be directed. It must be emphasised that these skills can only be developed through practice. Working through the exercises at the end of each chapter of the book is a vital first step.

The skills are listed below, not in any particular order of importance. Some are related specifically to computers, others are more general.

1. The ability to perceive structures in collections of information, and manipulate these information structures.

2. A familiarity with the theory of logic which underlies much of the theory of computing.

3. An appreciation of the principles of computer design.

4. An ability to reproduce manually many of the processes commonly done on computers.

5. An ability to write simple programs in a low level programming language.

6. A thorough grounding in the principles of information processing.

7. An appreciation of the concept of a system, and an ability to use this concept in practical situations.

8. An ability to apply concepts of computing to practical situations.

9. Clear thinking.

10. Clear, concise use of language, particularly in communicating technical information.

This might seem rather a daunting list, but the benefits of possessing some or all of these skills are considerable. The last skill mentioned, the clear, concise use of language, cannot be overemphasised. A poor performance here can obscure capabilities in all the other areas.

1.3   An Overview of Computing

This chapter concludes with a broad, general overview of the field of computing, and a few comments on the nature, capabilities and limitations of a computer. These ideas pave the way for a more detailed discussion in the next chapter.

The word 'computing' is used very frequently in this book. It is an old word which has begun to acquire a new meaning. Computing is the study, design, manufacture and use of computers. It encompasses all activities relating to computers in any way. Other terms, such as 'informatics' and 'information technology' have been used in a similar context, but the word 'computing' is now becoming the accepted term.

Computing, as it is now understood, is a young, optimistic and sometimes aggressive activity. Like nuclear energy, radar and jet propulsion, it had its origins in the Second Word War. Although the beginnings of computing were much less spectacular than those of the other activities, the computing industry is now one of the world's largest single industries. In spite of the prevailing adverse economic conditions, computing continues to grow and prosper.

Computing is an activity which provides employment for millions of people, directly and indirectly. It affects, directly or indirectly, hundreds of millions of others. Although its effects are generally beneficial, this is by no means always the case.

1.4   What is a Computer?

Regrettably, the concept of a computer is the subject of much confusion by the public at large. Exaggerated and distorted statements in newspapers, films and in radio and television broadcasts have added to the confusion. In this chapter, the nature of a computer is discussed in a fairly general way. In the next chapter, a more concise definition is introduced.

A computer may be described as an automatic, electronic information processing machine.

Automatic implies that a computer carries out all the steps of a task by itself. In order to do this, a computer is loaded with a set of instructions which determine its step-by-step operation.

Electronic implies that a computer is built up around a number of solid-state electronic components, the notorious 'chips'.

Information processing is a general term which describes the range of work which computers can do. Almost everything we do, from writing a letter to landing spacecraft on the moon, involves information processing in some way. Computers can be of assistance in any information processing activity.

Machine is a reminder that computers are in the same broad line of descent as windmills, printing presses, steam locomotives and electric toothbrushes. Machines can work well or badly, and no machine is infallible.

1.5 Capabilities and Limitations of Computers

It is important at this stage to give some general indication of the capabilities and limitations of computers. The key to these capabilities and limitations is the phrase 'information processing'.

Information processing implies storing and retrieving, sorting, selecting and arranging information, and, of course, performing calculations. In addition, computers interact with their environment. This interaction is in the form of information accepted by the computer from its environment, and information supplied by the computer to its environment. In an increasing number of cases, the environment of the computer involves a communication network.

Information processing does not imply taking initiatives, responding to unforseen circumstances or making moral judgements. All these are beyond the scope of computers.

1.6 Conclusion

This chapter has outlined the objectives of the book, given an indication of some of the skills which may be acquired during its study, and taken a general look at the field of computing, and at the nature, capabilities and limitations of computers.

The next chapter takes some of the ideas introduced here, and re-states them in a much more precise way. Towards the end of the book is a further examination of the broader implications of computing.

2
Concepts of computing

The previous chapter introduces computers and computing in a fairly general way. It gives some idea of the extent of computing, and of the capabilities and limitations of computers. This chapter is more specific. It introduces a small number of key concepts of computing. Each concept is discussed, and, without being too formal, a working definition of the concept is stated. This working definition is adequate for the purposes of this book.

The concepts introduced in this chapter are fundamental to an understanding of the rest of the book. It is essential that they are considered carefully at this stage, before studying any subsequent sections.

2.1 Information and Data

The concept of **information**, not to be confused with knowledge or wisdom, is used in this book in its generally accepted sense of 'what is told'. Information may be vital or trivial, true or false. That is of no concern here.

Data, on the other hand, has a much more precise meaning. Data is information in a coded form, acceptable for input to, and processing by, a computer system. In other words, data is a representation of information.

An important point to realise is that data, on its own, has no meaning. Only when some interpretation is placed on the data does it acquire meaning. In other words:

data + interpretation = meaningful information.

Furthermore, computers cannot place interpretations on data. Only people are capable of interpretation of data. This is an important point to bear in mind when considering the concept of a computer.

2.2 System

The idea of a **system** is often mentioned in connection with computers. A computer is often referred to as a computer system. Essentially, a system is a collection of parts working together towards some common goal. Those of you who play team sports will perhaps find the idea of a system easy to understand in these terms – a well-trained team is a system, a poorly trained team is not.

Just as goals have sub-goals, so do systems have **subsystems**. A subsystem is a part of a system which accomplishes a part of the goals of the system. For example, the braking system of a motor car is a subsystem of the car. It accomplishes one aspect of the goals of the car.

A computer is a system, containing a number of subsystems. Computers in use are always part of larger systems.

2.3 Computer and Program

In the previous chapter, a computer is described as an automatic, electronic information processing machine. In this chapter, a more precise definition is discussed.

The word '**computer**' generally implies the phrase 'digital electronic computer'. The electronic aspect has already been discussed, but a few words of explanation of the term 'digital' are required at this point.

Digital implies that information is stored in discrete quantities. At the lowest level, information is represented by the presence or absence of a pulse of electricity, symbolised by a 0 or a 1. All information and instructions are stored in a computer as combinations of 0's and 1's.

Making use of the concept of data, introduced in a previous section, a concise definition of a computer is as follows:

A computer is a machine which, under the control of a stored program, automatically accepts and processes data, and supplies the results of that processing.

Although a slightly broader definition of a computer will be considered in a moment, several points in this definition deserve closer study.

Firstly, a computer is controlled by a stored **program**. A program is a set of instructions to a computer. The instructions which a computer is using at a particular time are stored inside the computer. The computer works through the instructions automatically. Furthermore, instructions and data are stored together, and no distinction is made between them. Under some circumstances, instructions are manipulated like data.

Secondly, computers process data. In a previous section it was pointed out that data is a representation of information, without any inherent meaning. Processing is manipulating this data in a number of ways. It follows that processing does not have any inherent meaning. In other words, a computer does not understand what it is doing.

Computers are sometimes called intelligent machines. The word 'intelligent' in this context must be treated with caution. What it means is that computers can be instructed to manipulate data in a way which people interpret as intelligent. It is also possible (and extremely easy) to instruct computers to process data in ways which are anything but intelligent.

Finally, computers accept data from their environment (known as **input**) and supply the results of processing to their environment (known as **output**). In many cases, much of the effort of the computer is devoted to input and output, which can be extremely sophisticated.

The above definition of a computer, as a single processing device controlled by a single program, although adequate for many purposes, is somewhat out of date. An extended definition, more in line with contemporary computer design, is now developed.

Many modern computers contain more than one processing element, and most require several programs for their operation. The functional units, programs and sets of data, are sometimes referred to as the **resources** of the computer. The management of its own resources is one of the tasks performed by a computer.

Accordingly, the working definition of a computer used in this book is as follows:

A computer is a collection of resources, including digital electronic processing devices, stored programs and sets of data, which, under the control of the stored programs, automatically inputs, processes and outputs data, and may also store and retrieve data.

One final point about computers is implied in this definition. It is that a computer is a **general-purpose** machine. The phrase 'inputs, processes and outputs data' encompasses a very wide range of activities. Processing includes sorting and selecting data, performing calculations and making decisions based on the data. These functions can be put to use in a great number of applications. Furthermore, any particular computer is usually capable of a wide variety of tasks. In contrast to general-purpose computers there are **dedicated** computers; these are discussed in Section 2.8.

2.4   Hardware and Software

In theory, the distinction between the terms hardware and software is quite clear:

> **Hardware is the physical components, solid-state and otherwise, which make up a computer;**

and

> **Software is the programs which direct the operation of a computer.**

In practice, the distinction becomes rather blurred. For example, in some computers multiplication is done directly by hardware, while in others it is done by repeated addition, controlled by software. As long as the hardware of a computer can do a small number of essential operations, more sophisticated operations can be done either by special hardware elements, or by software.

Furthermore, many computers have software permanently stored in read-only memory (ROM). This is sometimes known as **firmware**, being somewhere between hardware and software.

2.5   Algorithm

In order that a task can be carried out on a computer, a method, or technique, for the task must be described very precisely, in terms of all its different steps. An **algorithm** is a description of the steps of a task, using a particular technique. Writing an algorithm is the first step taken in preparing a task to be done by a computer.

For it to be of any use to a computer, an algorithm must express a task as a finite number of steps. No matter how fast a computer works, there comes a point at which it must be told to stop, even if it means giving up.

A number of different ways of writing algorithms have been developed, including a series of programming languages called Algol. One of the commonest methods is also the simplest. It is to use clear, concise English, and simple algebra where necessary. This method will be adopted in this book.

Below is an example of a very simple algorithm, for adding up a set of numbers in a particular way.

> **Set total to zero.**
> **While there are more numbers,**
> **Repeat**
>   **Add next number to total.**

Notice that the algorithm is written in plain, concise English. This practice is continued throughout this book.

2.6   Module and Interface

Computers are extremely complex. The concepts of **module** and **interface** are essential in reducing this complexity, and making computers possible to design, program and understand.

A **module** is an interchangeable unit. It performs a specific function, and has specific connections with its environment. For example, in many hi-fi sets, the amplifier, turntable, cassette deck and speakers are separate modules.

An **interface** is a point of contact between one module and another, or between a module and its environment.

The benefits of the concepts of module and interface are as follows: if the function and interfaces of a module are known, it is seldom necessary to understand how the module performs its function. It will make no difference if a module is replaced by another one which works differently, but performs the same task using the same interfaces.

Modules and interfaces are used in the design and construction of hardware and software of computers. In both cases, the task to be performed is split up into a number of sub-tasks. A module is specified for each sub-task, together with its interfaces to other modules. The task can be understood in terms of these sub-tasks and interfaces, without knowing the details of how each sub-task is performed. This makes the designing of the hardware and software of computers, and the understanding of them, much easier.

2.7   Design and Implementation

In computing, as in most activities, there is a certain gap between theory and practice. In theory, ideas are efficient, clean and neat, and programs always work. In practice, things are seldom so rosy. Nevertheless, it is important to formulate ideas in theory before worrying about how they can be put into practice.

For these reasons, a distinction is made between the **design** of a computer, a program or a programming language, and its **implementation**. The design is theoretical, free of the awkward constraints so often found in practice. The implementation of a design is the way it is put into practice under a certain set of circumstances. Most designs have several implementations. For example, many computer languages are implemented on a number of different types of computers. In general, no two implementations are exactly alike.

Several key chapters of this book contain the design of a model computer. This computer has been designed to illustrate a number of important concepts of the course, free of the restrictions imposed by implementations.

2.8   General-purpose and Dedicated Computers

Historically, computers evolved as calculating machines. Once the general principles of computer design had been established, it became evident that they could do far more than just calculate. The phrase 'information processing' was chosen to describe the capabilities of computers. A **general-purpose** computer conforms to this description. It can do a very wide range of information processing tasks, from scientific 'number crunching' to commercial file processing.

A **dedicated** computer is designed for a specific task, or narrow range of tasks. A common example is a computer dedicated to controlling a machine. The introduction of very cheap, small, microprocessor-based computers has led to a resurgence of dedicated computers.

In practice, dedicated and general-purpose computers must be regarded as two extremes. Most computers are somewhere between the two extremes, though the emphasis is strongly on general-purpose machines.

2.9   The Theory of Computing

The fundamental principles behind the design and construction of digital electronic computers have been developed over a period of nearly a century. Although a large number of people have contributed in various ways to the development and understanding of these principles, the work of four people is of particular significance. These people are **Charles Babbage, George Boole, Alan Turing** and **John von Neumann**.

Although Babbage's ideas were conceived in relation to mechanical computers, many of them apply to electronic machines. Babbage identified the stages of a computing task as input, processing and output, and originated the idea of a program as a set of instructions to a computing machine.

George Boole is the founder of the theory of the mathematical logic. He devised an algebra for representing logical quantities, and investigated the operations which can be performed on these quantities. Boolean logic is the theoretical basis both for the design of the circuits in digital computers, and for many techniques in programming.

Turing confronted the general concept of a computing machine. He formulated his ideas in terms of an abstract computer, called a Turing Machine. Although a Turing Machine can only carry out one simple operation at a time, he identified a very wide class of problems which it could solve in a finite number of steps. Turing's work has been particularly valuable in understanding the capabilities and limitations of computers, and in the design of programming languages.

Von Neumann assisted in the design and development of several early electronic computers at the end of the Second World War. In 1946 he published a paper outlining the general design principles of an electronic digital computer. The two main points in the paper relate to the concept of a stored program:

1. all data and instructions are represented in a binary code, and are stored together in the computer memory;
2. the computer makes no distinction between data and instructions.

There is some dispute about how many of the ideas in this paper are von Neumann's own, but nevertheless it is a vital contribution to the theory of computing. Although the principles set out in this paper have been enhanced in modern computer designs, they remain to this day the theoretical basis of the design of all digital electronic computers.

2.10 Conclusion

The concepts introduced in this chapter are the foundations upon which an understanding of the rest of the book is built. If, after working through the exercise which follows, any of the concepts are not clear, it is recommended that the relevant portion of the chapter be read a second time. This chapter should also be consulted if, at any later stage in the book, confusion arises over any of the key concepts.

The main points made in this chapter may be summarised as follows:

- Data is information in a coded form, acceptable for input to, and processing by, a computer system:
  data + interpretation = meaningful information.
- A system is a collection of parts working together towards some common objectives. A computer is a system, part of a larger system in any particular application.
- A program is a set of instructions to a computer.
- A computer is a set of resources, including digital electronic processing devices, stored programs and sets of data, which, under the control of the stored programs, automatically inputs, processes and outputs data, and may also store and retrieve data.
- Hardware is the physical components, solid-state and otherwise, which make up a computer.
- Software is the programs which direct the operation of a computer.

- An algorithm is a description of the steps of a task, using a particular technique.
- A module is an interchangeable unit, which performs a specific function, and has specific connections with its environment.
- An interface is the point of contact between one module and another, or between a module and its environment.
- The implementation of a design is the way it is put into practice under a particular set of circumstances.
- A general-purpose computer is capable of a wide range of applications.
- A dedicated computer is designed for a specific task, or narrow range of tasks.

Exercise 2

1 The discussion of each concept in this chapter includes a working definition of the concept. Identify these working definitions.

2 List some examples of systems, and some things which are not systems. In each case, justify your choice.

3 State, with reasons, which of the following devices satisfy the definition of a computer introduced in this chapter, and which devices do not satisfy this definition: slide rule; automatic washing machine; programmable pocket calculator; television game; motor car electronic ignition system.

4 Make a list of devices which are programmable. In each case state what distinguishes the device from a computer, as defined in this chapter.

5 Make a collection of statements from the press or the media about computers, which contradict the definition of a computer contained in this chapter. Discuss your findings.

6 A hi-fi set is quoted in the chapter as an example of modular construction. For each module of a hi-fi set state:
    a) its function;
    b) its interface(s) with other modules;
    c) its external interface(s), i.e. those to its environment.

7 Write down two examples of modular construction, other than computers and hi-fi sets. For each example, work through parts (a) to (c) of Question 6.

8 List the advantages of modular construction.

9 Find out more about the work of Babbage, Turing, Boole and von Neumann. Write a report on the contributions of one or more of them to the theory of computing, expanding the ideas presented in the text.

☐ 10 Other people who have made contributions to the theory of computing are:
    Noam Chomsky   (a classification of languages, applicable to programming languages)
    Marshall McLuhan (originator of the phrase 'information processing')
    Claude Shannon   (the relationship between electrical circuits and Boolean algebra)
    Ada Byron   (the first computer programmer)
    Find out about, and write reports on, the work of one or more of these people.

3
Data

This chapter covers ways in which data is represented in computer systems, both in the internal storage of a computer, and on external media accessed by a computer. Data storage is discussed in general terms. The techniques introduced here are implemented in a variety of ways on different computers.

The material introduced in this chapter is fundamental to an understanding of most of the rest of the book. In particular, it relates closely to the next chapter, on data structures, to chapters concerned with computer architecture, and to later chapters on data processing.

A certain amount of computer arithmetic is considered in this chapter. This is because the method of coding the numbers determines the way in which some arithmetic operations are performed. However, most of the discussion of computer arithmetic is in Chapter 5.

3.1   Binary Coding of Data

All data used by computers is in code. Different computers use different codes, and different codes are used in various parts of the same computer. But all these codes have one thing in common – they are based on two characters, the digits 0 and 1 only.

The reason for the use of two digits only is that all the devices used in computer systems, and all the data storage media they access, have two **states** only.

For example, switches are on or off, transistors are conducting or non-conducting, magnetic tape is magnetised in one or the other direction, a punched card has a hole or no hole at a particular place, etc. This has several advantages, notably simplicity, and wide tolerances. As long as it is clear whether a device is in a 0 or a 1 state, a high level of precision does not matter. For this reason, the electronic components of a computer are much more crudely (and cheaply) constructed than those in, for example, a hi-fi set.

Most of the numeric codes used in computers are based on the **binary** (base two) number system, which also uses the digits 0 and 1 only. A binary digit is called a **bit**.

3.2   Place Value

Much of what is to follow in this chapter depends on the concept of **place value**. A reminder of this concept is in order at this point.

In all modern number systems, the value of any digit depends on its position in the number. The place values for decimal integers are units, tens, hundreds, etc. For binary integers they are units, twos, fours, eights, etc. Similarly, 'decimal' fractions have place values tenths, hundredths, etc., and binary fractions halves, quarters, eighths etc.

The digit with the highest place value in a number is called the **most significant digit**, or, in binary, the **most significant bit**. If the digits of a number can be grouped, then the phrase **high order** is used to describe the group with higher place values than others.

3.3   Some Codes Commonly Used by Computers

Some of the commonest data coding techniques used in computing are introduced in the next few sections. Although most computers use some or all of the principles described below, details vary in implementation.

Character	Bit pattern	Decimal equivalent	Hexadecimal equivalent	Character	Bit pattern	Decimal equivalent	Hexadecimal equivalent
space	0100000	32	20	P	1010000	80	50
!	0100001	33	21	Q	1010001	81	51
"	0100010	34	22	R	1010010	82	52
#	0100011	35	23	S	1010011	83	53
$	0100100	36	24	T	1010100	84	54
%	0100101	37	25	U	1010101	85	55
&	0100110	38	26	V	1010110	86	56
'	0100111	39	27	W	1010111	87	57
(	0101000	40	28	X	1011000	88	58
)	0101001	41	29	Y	1011001	89	59
*	0101010	42	2A	Z	1011010	90	5A
+	0101011	43	2B	[	1011011	91	5B
,	0101100	44	2C	\	1011100	92	5C
−	0101101	45	2D	]	1011101	93	5D
.	0101110	46	2E	↑	1011110	94	5E
/	0101111	47	2F	←	1011111	95	5F
0	0110000	48	30	.	1100000	96	60
1	0110001	49	31	a	1100001	97	61
2	0110010	50	32	b	1100010	98	62
3	0110011	51	33	c	1100011	99	63
4	0110100	52	34	d	1100100	100	64
5	0110101	53	35	e	1100101	101	65
6	0110110	54	36	f	1100110	102	66
7	0110111	55	37	g	1100111	103	67
8	0111000	56	38	h	1101000	104	68
9	0111001	57	39	i	1101001	105	69
:	0111010	58	3A	j	1101010	106	6A
;	0111011	59	3B	k	1101011	107	6B
<	0111100	60	3C	l	1101100	108	6C
=	0111101	61	3D	m	1101101	109	6D
>	0111110	62	3E	n	1101110	110	6E
?	0111111	63	3F	o	1101111	111	6F
@	1000000	64	40	p	1110000	112	70
A	1000001	65	41	q	1110001	113	71
B	1000010	66	42	r	1110010	114	72
C	1000011	67	43	s	1110011	115	73
D	1000100	68	44	t	1110100	116	74
E	1000101	69	45	u	1110101	117	75
F	1000110	70	46	v	1110110	118	76
G	1000111	71	47	w	1110111	119	77
H	1001000	72	48	x	1111000	120	78
I	1001001	73	49	y	1111001	121	79
J	1001010	74	4A	z	1111010	122	7A
K	1001011	75	4B	{	1111011	123	7B
L	1001100	76	4C	|	1111100	124	7C
M	1001101	77	4D	}	1111101	125	7D
N	1001110	78	4E	~	1111110	126	7E
O	1001111	79	4F				

Figure 3.1
ASCII code

3.4 Character Code

Input, output and backing store media and devices generally store and manipulate data in a **character code**. Characters include letters, digits and characters such as punctuation marks. These are called **alphabetic, numeric** (together known as **alphanumeric**) and **special** characters respectively. The set of characters which can be coded is called the **character set** of the computer, or programming language.

Character code is one in which each character is coded separately as a set of binary digits. Six, seven or eight bits per character are most commonly used. Figure 3.1 shows a very common character code, the seven bit **American Standard Code for Information Interchange (ASCII)** code.

Alphabetic data generally remains in character code during processing by a computer, but numeric data is usually converted to one of the numeric codes described below. All conversion from one to another is carried out by hardware, firmware or software within the computer system.

3.5 Binary Coded Decimal

Binary coded decimal (BCD) is a simple and increasingly popular way of representing numbers within a computer. In this system, each decimal digit is coded separately in binary. For example:

379 = 0011   0111   1001.

Four bits are the minimum needed to code one decimal digit, since $9 = 1001$. BCD numbers using four bits per decimal digit are sometimes called **packed decimal** numbers. In many implementations more than four bits are used per decimal digit, with the remaining bit positions filled with zeros.

3.6 Sign-and-Magnitude Code

This section, and the two which follow it, introduce the three commonest ways of dealing with negative numbers. The first method involves representing the sign of a number, and its magnitude (or modulus), separately. This is called **sign-and-magnitude** (or sign-and-modulus) code.

If one bit is used for the sign, the convention is 0 for positive and 1 for negative. For example:

$+13 = \underline{0}1101,$
$-13 = \underline{1}1101.$

The sign bit is underlined.

3.7 Twos Complement Numbers

Twos complement coding is the commonest way of representing integers during processing on a computer. In this code, the normal binary place values are used, except that the most significant bit represents a negative quantity. For example, the place values for six bit twos complement integers are:

$-32 \quad 16 \quad 8 \quad 4 \quad 2 \quad 1.$

Some numbers coded this way are as follows:

-32	16	8	4	2	1		
0	1	1	1	1	1 =		31
0	0	0	0	0	1 =		1
0	0	0	0	0	0 =		0
1	1	1	1	1	1 =	$-32 + 31$	$= -1$
1	0	0	0	0	0 =		$-32.$

This example shows the range of numbers which can be stored (31 to -32), and the coding for 1, 0 and -1.

The reason for using twos complement storage is that it is very easy to change from a positive to the corresponding negative number (and vice versa). Consequently, subtraction can be performed by negating the second number and then adding it to the first number. For example, $7 - 5$ is the same as $7 + (-5)$.

The method of changing from a positive to the corresponding negative number is as follows: Change all the 0s to 1s and all the 1s to 0s, and then add 1. For example:

		-32	16	8	4	2	1	
19	=	0	1	0	0	1	1	
interchange bits		1	0	1	1	0	0	
add 1	+						1	
		1	0	1	1	0	1	$= -19.$

This method will also change a negative number to the corresponding positive number. For example:

	-32	16	8	4	2	1
-23 =	1	0	1	0	0	1
interchange bits	0	1	0	1	1	0
add 1 +						1
	0	1	0	1	1	1 = 23.

Two examples of subtraction using this technique follow.

Example 1
$29 - 7 = 29 + (-7)$

	-32	16	8	4	2	1
store 7:	0	0	0	1	1	1
interchange bits:	1	1	1	0	0	0
add 1, gives -7:	1	1	1	0	0	1
store 29:	0	1	1	1	0	1 +
add -7 and 29	0	1	0	1	1	0 = 22.

1 carry

Note that there is a 1 carried from the most significant bit. Most computers have a **carry bit** which is set to 1 if this occurs. The significance of this is discussed in Chapter 5, on computer arithmetic.

Example 2
$5 - 18 = 5 + (-18)$

	-32	16	8	4	2	1
store 18:	0	1	0	0	1	0
interchange bits:	1	0	1	1	0	1
add 1, gives -18	1	0	1	1	1	0
store 5	0	0	0	1	0	1 +
add -18 and 5	1	1	0	0	1	1 = -13.

Problems arise when the result of a calculation is outside the permitted range of numbers (-32 to 31 in the base of six bit, twos complement integers). For example:

$14 + 19$

	-32	16	8	4	2	1
store 14:	0	0	1	1	1	0
store 19:	0	1	0	0	1	1 +
	1	0	0	0	0	1 = -31.

The result, -31, is not correct. This problem is examined further in Section 5.9.

3.8 Ones complement numbers

Similar to twos complements, but somewhat less popular, is the method of storing integers called **ones complements**. In this system, the most significant place value is one less (in magnitude) than the corresponding twos complement place value. For example, the place values for six bit, ones complement integers are:

$$-31 \quad 16 \quad 8 \quad 4 \quad 2 \quad 1.$$

Some numbers coded this way are as follows:

−31	16	8	4	2	1		
0	1	1	1	1	1 =		31
0	0	0	0	0	1 =		1
0	0	0	0	0	0 =		0
1	1	1	1	1	1 = −31 + 31 =	0
1	1	1	1	1	0 = −31 + 31 =	−1
1	0	0	0	0	0 =		−31.

Notice the range of numbers (31 to −31) and the two different codes for 0. Notice also the codes for 1 and −1.

The advantage of using ones complements is that the negative of a number is produced simply by reversing the bits. For example:

	−31	16	8	4	2	1	
20 =	0	1	0	1	0	0	
interchange bits:	1	0	1	0	1	1 = −31 + 11 = −20.

This technique is used in subtraction. However, any carry produced by the most significant bit of the result must be added at the least significant end to produce a correct answer. The examples of the previous section are repeated using ones complement coding.

Example 1
$$29 - 7 = 29 + (-7)$$

	−31	16	8	4	2	1	
store 7:	0	0	0	1	1	1	
reverse bits, gives −7:	1	1	1	0	0	0	
store 29	0	1	1	1	0	1 +	
add −7 and 29:	0	1	0	1	0	1	
add carry:						1 +	
	0	1	0	1	1	0	= 22.

This technique is called **wrap-around carry**.

Example 2
$$5 - 18 = 5 + (-18)$$

	−31	16	8	4	2	1	
store 18:	0	1	0	0	1	0	
reverse bits, gives −18:	1	0	1	1	0	1	
store 5:	0	0	0	1	0	1 +	
add −18 and 5:	1	1	0	0	1	0	= −13.

In this example, no wrap-around carry is generated.

3.9 Fractions

Fractions may be coded in ways very similar to those introduced above for coding integers. For example, using sign-and-magnitude coding:

sign	$\frac{1}{2}$	$\frac{1}{4}$	$\frac{1}{8}$	$\frac{1}{16}$	$\frac{1}{32}$

$-\frac{13}{32} =$ | 1 | 0 | 1 | 1 | 0 | 1 | .

Twos complement coding may also be used. For example:

-1	$\frac{1}{2}$	$\frac{1}{4}$	$\frac{1}{8}$	$\frac{1}{16}$	$\frac{1}{32}$

$-\frac{13}{32} = -1 + \frac{19}{32} =$ | 1 | 1 | 0 | 0 | 1 | 1 | .

These methods of coding fractions, and the methods of coding integers introduced previously, are called **fixed point** codes. In these codes, the binary point is at a fixed position, though it is seldom coded explicitly.

The problem with fixed point codes is that the range of values that can be represented is limited. Many computers allocate 16 bits to store integers. Using twos complement notation, this gives a range of $-32\,768$ to $32\,767$, which is not sufficient for many applications.

3.10 Floating Point Numbers

The concept of **floating point numbers** is used to extend the range of numbers that can be represented by a given number of bits. Floating point numbers are similar to the scientific method of representing base ten numbers, called **standard form**.

A standard form number is the product of two parts. The first is a number between 1 and 10, and the second is a power of ten. Some examples follow:

$$57\,500 = 5.75 \times 10^4$$
$$0.000\,067 = 6.7 \ \times 10^{-5}.$$

Note that the size of the number is determined by the power of ten, and the number of significant figures, or precision of the number, is determined by the number of decimal places in the first part.

Floating point numbers apply the same principles in base two. A number is expressed as the product of two parts. The first part is a fraction between $\frac{1}{2}$ and 1, and the second is a power of two. The following are some examples, written entirely in base two:

Fixed point		Floating point
101 000·0	$= 0.101 \times 1\,000\,000$	$= 0.101 \times 10^{110}$,
0·001 1	$= 0.11 \times 0.01$	$= 0.11 \times 10^{-10}$,
$-$ 110·11	$= -0.11011 \times 1000$	$= -0.11011 \times 10^{11}$.

These probably require a few moments of study. Remember that all the numbers are in base two.

Notice how the binary point 'floats' to the front of the first part of the number, hence the name floating point. The bit following the binary is a 1, unless the whole number is zero. This is to ensure that the fraction part lies between $\frac{1}{2}$ and 1, and is called **normalisation**. Normalisation ensures that the maximum number of bit positions are available to store the fraction part of the number. It allows for maximum precision of a number within the available number of bits.

The power of two is determined by counting the number of places that the binary point has to move from the fixed point to the floating point representation of the number (the same rule applies to standard form numbers). The fraction part of a floating point number is called the **mantissa**, and the power of two the **exponent**.

Ways of implementing floating point numbers differ considerably between different types of computer. The mantissa is generally coded in sign-and-magnitude or twos complement form. The exponent is sometimes coded in one of these forms, but other methods of coding are also used.

The number of bits allocated to each part of a floating point number also differs widely between computers. The general principle is that between two and three times as many bits are allocated to the mantissa as to the exponent. There follows an example using sixteen bits for a floating point number, with eleven bits for the mantissa and five bits for the exponent. Sign-and-magnitude coding is used for both parts of the number.

					mantissa								exponent			
sign	$\frac{1}{2}$	$\frac{1}{4}$	$\frac{1}{8}$	$\frac{1}{16}$	$\frac{1}{32}$	$\frac{1}{64}$	$\frac{1}{128}$	$\frac{1}{256}$	$\frac{1}{512}$	$\frac{1}{1024}$	sign	8	4	2	1
0	1	0	1	1	0	0	0	0	0	0	0	1	1	0	0

$$= 0{\cdot}1011 \times 10^{1100} = \tfrac{11}{16} \times 2^{12} = \tfrac{11}{16} \times 4096 = 2816.$$

Arithmetic using floating point numbers, and errors which can arise in this arithmetic, are discussed in Chapter 5.

3.11 Bits, Bytes and Words

As mentioned previously, a bit is a binary digit. For most purposes, a bit is too small a unit of data to be manipulated separately. Hence bits are generally handled in groups. **Bytes** and **words** are the two commonest groupings.

A **byte** is a set of bits containing the code for one character. A byte is now generally accepted as comprising eight bits. The data on most input, output and backing store media is grouped in bytes. Many modern microprocessor-based computers do all their processing in units of bytes. These are the 8 bit microcomputers, of personal and educational computing fame.

A **word** is a larger grouping of bits, from 16 to 512 bits depending on the size of the computer. Roughly speaking, a word is a set of bits which can be manipulated by a computer in one operation. The **wordlength** is the number of bits in one word. In most computers, the registers, which store one data item during processing, can contain one word.

However, in many modern computers, the concept of a word is not very useful, as the number of bits which are manipulated in one operation can vary. The phrase **variable wordlength** is used in this context. Whether a word is of fixed or variable length, it almost always contains an integral number of bytes, i.e. 16, 24, 32 or 64 bits.

3.12 Octal and Hexadecimal Numbers

Binary numbers and codes suffer from the disadvantage of being very long for the amount of information they represent. Decimal numbers are much more concise, but are difficult to convert to binary. As a compromise, **octal** (base eight) and **hexadecimal** (base sixteen) numbers are often used to represent binary quantities. These numbers have the advantages of conciseness and ease of conversion to binary.

Octal

To convert from base eight to base two, convert each octal digit to its binary equivalent, using three bits. For example:

$725_8 = 111\,010\,101_2$.

Converting from binary to octal is done by grouping the bits in threes from the least significant end, and converting each group to an octal digit. For example:

$11\,110\,000_2 = 3\;6\;0_8$.

Hexadecimal

Conversion between binary and hexadecimal numbers is similar, except that groups of four bits are used. The hexadecimal digits A to F are generally used for the decimal quantities 10 to 15. For example:

$3A7_{16} = 0011\,1010\,0111_2$
and
$1111\,10010_2 = 1F2_{16}$.

It must be remembered that octal and hexadecimal digits are a shorthand way of representing binary codes, which themselves may represent non-numeric data. For example, the ASCII code for the symbol ? is 0 1 1 1 1 1 1. This may be represented by the octal digits 077, or the hexadecimal digits 3F.

Octal and hexadecimal numbers are used for writing certain types of computer programs, for representing data stored in a computer during processing, and for recovering from errors. They are very seldom used for input or output data. Hexadecimal numbers have the advantage that two hexadecimal digits represent eight bits, or one byte. For this reason they are more commonly used than octal numbers.

3.13 Self-checking Codes: Parity

Considerable attention is devoted, in the design of computers, to the detection and correction of errors. One valuable technique, of great assistance in achieving this objective, is the concept of a **self-checking code**. A self-checking code is one which contains enough information within the coded form of a data item, to determine whether that data item has been coded (or transmitted) correctly.

The simplest and commonest self-checking code requires the inclusion of a **parity bit** in the code of a data item. The parity is set to a 0 or a 1 so that the total number of 1s in the data item is even, for **even parity,** or odd, for **odd parity**. For example, using even parity:

0 1 1 0 1 0 1

is correct, with four 1s, but

1 0 0 1 1 0 0

is incorrect, with three 1s. The parity bit is in italics.

Parity checks are used to determine whether the parity of a data item is correct. These are most commonly carried out after a data item has been transmitted to or from an input, output or backing store device, as this is where errors are most likely. Odd parity is slightly more useful than even parity, as it will detect the failure of a transmission line, which will result in all the bits of a data item being zero. Other self-checking codes, notably the use of check digits, are discussed in Section 23.12.

3.14 Conclusion

This chapter has introduced some fundamental concepts of data storage. It is essential to become familiar with these concepts, as many aspects of computing depend on them. Many of the words and phrases introduced in this chapter occur very frequently in the language of computing.

The most important points made during this chapter are as follows:

- All codes used for data storage are based on the binary digits 0 and 1 only.
- A major reason for the use of binary codes in computers is that all the devices used in the construction of computers have two states only.
- Character code is one in which each character is coded separately as a set of binary digits.
- The set of characters which can be coded by a particular computer or programming language is the character set of that computer or language.
- Binary coded decimal is a numeric code in which each decimal digit is coded separately. Packed decimal is a variant of this code, with four bits per decimal digit.
- Sign-and-magnitude code involves coding the sign and the magnitude of a number separately.
- Twos complements is a binary code, using the usual place values, except that the most significant bit represents a negative quantity.
- Ones complements is a binary code, similar to twos complements, except that the most significant place value is one less in magnitude.
- Fixed point codes are numeric codes in which the (assumed) binary point is in a fixed position in the number.
- Floating point codes are numeric codes in which a number is expressed as the product of a fraction between $\frac{1}{2}$ and 1 (the mantissa) and an integral power of two (the exponent).
- A byte is a set of bits containing the code for one character. A byte is generally eight bits.
- A word is a set of bits which can be manipulated by a particular computer in one operation.
- Octal (base eight) and hexadecimal (base sixteen) numbers are often used as 'shorthand' representations of binary numbers.
- A common self-checking code includes a parity bit which adjusts the total number of 1s in the data item to an even (for even parity) or odd (for odd parity) number.

Exercise 3

1 Why are all data codes used by computers based on two digits only? List the advantages of this system.

2 Name a number system still in use which does not use the concept of place value.

3 What is the distinguishing feature of character code?

4 Write an informal algorithm for the process of adding two BCD digits, and producing the sum in the form of a BCD digit together with a carry bit.

□ 5 Using the algorithm from Question 4, write an informal algorithm for the process of adding two complete BCD numbers. State any additional assumptions you make, such as the lengths of the numbers.

6 Write the decimal numbers 3 and −3 in twos complement form, using (a) four bits, (b) six bits, (c) eight bits. In the light of your answers, state how a twos complement number can be extended to a larger number of bits without altering its value.

7 Repeat Question 6 using ones complement numbers.

8 In two complement notation, what is the range of integers which can be represented by (a) 4 bits, (b) 6 bits, (c) 8 bits, (d) 16 bits, (e) n bits?
    What are the corresponding ranges using ones complements?

9 Change the following (decimal) fractions into six bit, twos complement notation: $\frac{3}{8}$, $-\frac{5}{16}$, $-\frac{17}{32}$, $\frac{1}{3}$.
    Hint: in the last case, change the numerator and denominator to binary, and divide the denominator into the numerator. The result is a recurring fraction.

10 Change these fixed point binary numbers into floating point form:

$$11000, \quad 0{\cdot}011, \quad -10{\cdot}11, \quad 0{\cdot}101.$$

11 Change these floating point binary numbers into fixed point form:

$$0{\cdot}110 \times 10^{11}, \quad -0{\cdot}1011 \times 10^{110}, \quad 0{\cdot}1101 \times 10^{-111}.$$

12 The following numbers are in floating point form, with bits allocated as in the text:

sign	$\frac{1}{2}$	$\frac{1}{4}$	$\frac{1}{8}$	$\frac{1}{16}$	$\frac{1}{32}$	$\frac{1}{64}$	$\frac{1}{128}$	$\frac{1}{256}$	$\frac{1}{512}$	$\frac{1}{1024}$	sign	8	4	2	1
						mantissa							exponent		
0	1	0	1	0	0	0	0	0	0	0	0	0	1	0	0
0	1	1	1	1	0	0	0	0	0	0	0	1	1	1	0
1	1	0	0	0	0	0	0	0	0	0	0	0	0	0	1
0	1	1	1	0	0	0	0	0	0	0	1	0	1	0	0
1	1	0	1	0	0	0	0	0	0	0	1	0	1	1	1

   a) Convert the five numbers to base ten.
   b) Express the decimal numbers 80, -3072, $-\frac{1}{2}$, $1{\cdot}5$ in this form.
   c) Bearing in mind that floating point numbers must be normalised, what is the range of positive numbers which can be expressed in this form?

13 A computer has a 64 bit wordlength.
   a) How many bytes are contained in one word?
   b) How many packed decimal digits can be stored in one word?
   c) Suggest a way in which a word may be used to contain a floating point number. Justify your allocation of bits.

14 Convert the following decimal numbers (a) to binary, (b) to octal, (c) to hexadecimal: 45, 21, 32, 4097.

15 The main store of a particular computer has an extra parity bit for every byte stored. Furthermore, after every eight bytes, there is an additional parity byte, where each bit adjusts the parity of the corresponding 'column' in the eight bytes. Odd parity is used throughout.
    Below is the contents of a portion of the main store of this computer:

	bytes							parity bits	
1	0	0	1	0	0	1	0	0
0	0	0	0	0	0	0	0	1
1	1	1	1	1	1	1	1	1
1	0	1	1	0	1	0	1	0
1	1	0	1	1	0	1	1	0
0	1	1	0	1	1	0	1	0
0	0	0	0	0	0	0	0	1
1	0	1	1	1	1	0	1	1

parity byte   0   0   1   0   1   1   1   0   1

   a) Check the parity of each byte.
   b) Check the parity of each column against the parity byte.
   c) Assuming that only one bit has been stored incorrectly, identify this bit.

16 a) A data item and its parity bit are copied from one part of a computer to another. A subsequent parity check fails. Is it certain that the data item is now incorrect? Explain your answer.
   b) If, in the above case, the parity check does not fail, is it certain that the data item is now correct? Explain your answer.
   c) In the light of your answers to parts (a) and (b), comment on the usefulness of parity checks.

4
Data
structures

The previous chapter showed how items of data may be represented on computer systems. This chapter extends the concept of data in a different way. It shows how individual items of data may be associated in various ways to form **data structures**.

The concepts introduced in this chapter are both simple and powerful. They show how large and potentially unwieldy collections of data can be managed by relatively simple operations. Concepts associated with data structures have led to advances in computer architecture, and in the design of computer programs.

Ideas introduced in this chapter form the basis of several subsequent chapters. It is essential that the material in this chapter be studied thoroughly before subsequent chapters are contemplated.

4.1 The Concept of Structured Data

The structure of a set of data is created by **relationships** between individual data items. These relationships can be formally expressed by a set of rules, although this will not generally be done in this book.

The essential properties of most data structures can be expressed by specifying how to insert and delete items of data, while preserving the structure. Together with a description of an empty data structure, this is sufficient for a structure to be created and used. The data structures introduced later in this chapter are described in this way.

4.2 Structured Information in Everyday Life

Most of the information we encounter in everyday life is structured in some way. The commonest example is probably the words of our language, which are linked together in phrases, sentences and other more complex structures. The rules for constructing these structures are extremely complicated, yet we apply them almost by intuition.

Other common examples of structured information include dictionaries, telephone directories and encyclopaedias. These are all large stores of information which would be useless if the information were not strictly arranged according to a few simple rules.

The structure of a collection of information makes it easy to locate individual items of information, and to insert new items, or delete items. The same reasoning applies to structured information stored in computers.

4.3 Structured Data in Computers

A distinction can be made between data structures in the main store of a computer, and those on external media such as magnetic tapes and discs which can be accessed by a computer. This chapter is concerned with data structures held in the main store of a computer. A later chapter, Chapter 23, is concerned with structures stored on magnetic tapes and discs.

The structures introduced in this chapter have a wide variety of uses. These include applications programs, language translation programs and programs which regulate the way in which a computer operates. Some of the structures are associated with the architecture of the processing unit of a computer.

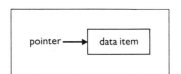

Figure 4.1
A pointer

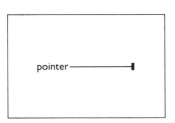

Figure 4.2
A null pointer

4.4 Pointers

Before describing some common data structures, it is necessary to introduce a type of data called a **pointer**. A pointer is a data item which indicates the location of another data item. It may be thought of as an arrow, as shown in Figure 4.1.

Pointers are frequently used in data structures. They provide the links which join elements of the structure. Of particular significance are pointers to the front and back of a data structure. Occasionally it is required that a pointer does not point to anything; in this situation, the pointer is said to have a **null** value. Figure 4.2 shows the way a null pointer is generally represented in this book.

4.5 The Fundamental Data Structures

Six data structures are now introduced, namely **strings, arrays, stacks, queues, lists** and **trees**. They are the most important data structures used in the main stores of computers (in Chapter 23, the structures discussed are **files, records, fields** and **hash tables**).

4.6 Strings

A **string** is a set of characters 'strung' together. Sometimes a string is regarded as a single data item. Strings may be of fixed or variable length. The length of a string is indicated either by the number of characters in the string placed at the front of the string, or by a special character called an **end-of-string marker** at the end. The following example shows these two methods of representing the same string:

```
10CAPITAL194    CAPITAL194#.
```

Operations on strings are of two types, namely operations which join two or more strings to produce a single string, and operations which divide a string to produce two or more sub-strings.

4.7 Arrays

An **array** is a set of data items of identical types, stored together. The number of elements in the array is fixed when the array is created. Each element may be accessed by an **index**, which indicates the position of the element in the array.

For example, if the array **BEATLES** has elements as follows:

```
BEATLES:  JOHN
          PAUL
          GEORGE
          RINGO
```

then the element with index value 3, **BEATLES (3)** is the name **GEORGE.** Occasionally it is more useful to use the index value 0 for the first array element. Under this arrangement, **BEATLES (3)** is the name **RINGO.** In some ways, the entire main store of a computer may be regarded as an array. The index of each storage space is known as the **address** of the space. The address is a number which locates a storage space within the main store.

Arrays can have more than one **dimension**. A two-dimensional array may be thought of as having rows and columns like a matrix. Two indices are required to locate an item in the array, corresponding to row and column indices in a matrix.

For example, the state of a game of noughts and crosses may be represented by a two-dimensional array, **GAME**, with three rows and three columns:

GAME:

If the top left element is **GAME** (1,1), then the O in the third column of the second row is **GAME** (2,3) and the blank element is **GAME** (3,1).

When the word 'array' is used on its own, it is generally understood to mean a one-dimensional array. Arrays with more than two dimensions are occasionally used.

4.8   Static and Dynamic Data Structures

Strings and arrays are **static data structures**, that is to say, they stay the same size once they have been created. Data structures which change in size once they have been created are called **dynamic data structures**. The structures introduced in the remainder of this chapter are dynamic data structures.

4.9   Stacks

You have probably seen the way in which plates are sometimes stored in restaurants. A pile of plates is supported on a spring. As a new plate is put on top of the pile, it pushes the rest down. When a plate is taken from the pile, the next plate pops up.

Such a structure is a **stack** in the computing sense of the word. A stack is a collection of data items which may only be accessed at one end, called the **top** of the stack.

Only two operations may be carried out on a stack. Adding a new item, called **pushing** or **stacking** the item, involves placing it on the top of the stack. The new item becomes the new top of the stack. Removing an item, called **popping** the stack, involves removing the item at the top of the stack.

If a number of items are pushed onto a stack, and then popped from the stack, the last item added will be the first one removed. For this reason, a stack is sometimes called a **last-in–first-out (LIFO) stack**. Other names for a stack are **push-down stack** and **push-down list**.

When a stack is stored in a computer memory, the elements do not move up and down as the stack is pushed and popped. Instead, the position of the top of the stack changes.

A pointer called a **stack pointer** indicates the position of the top of the stack (in some applications, the stack pointer indicates the first free space above the top of the stack). Another pointer is sometimes used to indicate the base of the stack. This pointer, called the **stack base**, keeps the same value as long as the stack is in existence. Figure 4.3 shows a stack pointer and stack base in use. If the sequence of operations **pop, pop, push 5·9**, is carried out on this stack, the result is shown in Figure 4.4.

Representing an empty stack is important. If the stack pointer indicates the first available space above the top of the stack, then this is quite simple, as shown in Figure 4.5. When the stack is empty, the stack pointer has the same value as the stack base.

The stack is one of the most important data structures in computing. Stacks are used in calculations, translating from one computer language to another, and transferring control from one part of a program to another, to mention just a few applications. Most modern processors include a stack pointer as an architectural feature. The concept of a stack is the most prominent feature in the architecture of a few computers.

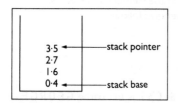

Figure 4.3
A stack

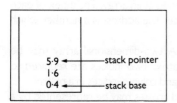

Figure 4.4

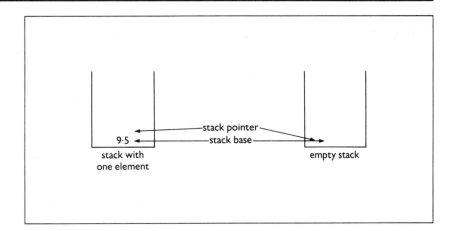

Figure 4.5

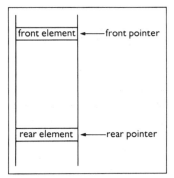

Figure 4.6
A queue

4.10 Queues

In spite of the American origins of many ideas associated with computers, that great British institution, the **queue**, has found its way into the theory of computing. Everyone knows how a queue works: newcomers join at the rear, service is provided at the front, and no pushing-in is allowed. Exactly the same rules apply to queues of data stored in a computer memory. A queue is a **first-in–first-out (FIFO)** data structure.

There are several ways of implementing the storage of a queue in a computer memory. A particularly simple way involves storing the queue elements in adjacent memory locations, and providing pointers to the front and rear of the queue. This implementation is illustrated in Figure 4.6.

When an element is added to the queue, the rear pointer is adjusted to point to the new element. Similarly, when an element is removed from the queue, the front pointer is adjusted to point to the new front element.

The problem with this method of storage of a queue is that the queue moves down the store as elements are added and removed. One solution is to allocate a fixed area of store for the queue, and then let the rear of the queue 'wrap around' to the start of the area. This is illustrated in Figure 4.7. An area of store used in this way is sometimes called a **circular buffer**.

It must be emphasised that a circular buffer is not the only method of

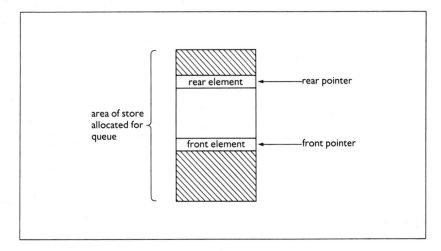

Figure 4.7
A queue 'wrapped around' in a fixed area of store

implementing a queue. Another method involves the use of pointers from one element to the next. This is explained in the context of lists in the next section.

Although queues are used slightly less frequently than stacks, they do have a variety of applications. These include queuing items from a processor for storage or output by peripheral devices, and queuing programs which are ready to be run by the computer.

4.11 Lists

A **list** is a set of data items stored in some order. Data items may be inserted or deleted at any point in the list. In this respect, a list is less restrictive than a stack or a queue.

The simplest way of implementing a list makes use of a pointer from each item to the one following it in the list. There is also a pointer to the start of the list, while the last item in the list has a null pointer. This is illustrated in Figure 4.8.

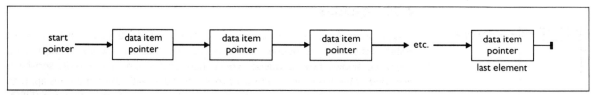

Figure 4.8
A list

A data structure of this type is also known as a **linked list**. A **list element** consists of a data item and its pointer. In many applications a list element contains a number of data items. Since elements can easily be added to the rear or removed from the front of a linked list, this structure may also be used to implement a queue.

Inserting an element into a list is achieved by adjusting various pointers to include the new element. This is illustrated in Figure 4.9. Removing an element is achieved in a similar way, as shown in Figure 4.10.

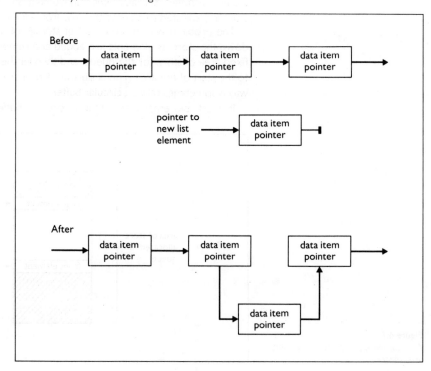

Figure 4.9
Inserting an element into a list

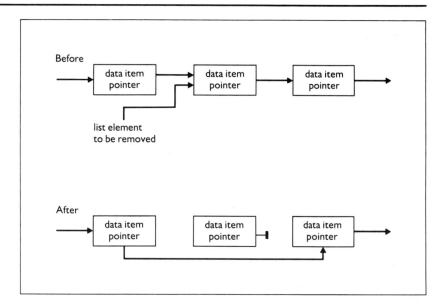

Figure 4.10
Removing an element from a list

A variation on the idea of a list is the case where the pointer from the end of the list is linked to the front of the list. This creates a **circular list**, as shown in Figure 4.11.

Data items in a list are in order, in the sense that one data item is behind another in the list. Lists are, however, frequently used in cases where the data items are in numerical or alphabetical order. Such lists are called **ordered lists**. Lists are very useful for storing ordered sets of data, if insertions and deletions of data items are frequent.

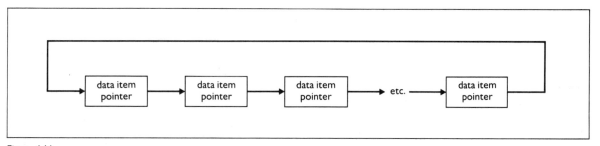

Figure 4.11
A circular list

4.12 Trees

We are all familiar with the phrases 'family tree' and 'getting to the top of the tree'. In this sense, a **tree** is a structure implying a hierarchy, with each element of the tree being linked to elements below it. For example, the family tree in Figure 4.12 shows the immediate descendants of Queen Elizabeth II (next page).

Data structures of this nature are used extensively in computing. A few more concepts are required in order to define a tree precisely. These are now introduced.

Each data item in a tree is at a **node** of the tree. The node at the top of the tree is called the **root**. Each node may be connected to one or more **subtrees**, which have the same structure as a tree. A node at the bottom of the tree, which has no subtrees, is called a **terminal node**, or a **leaf**. Figure 4.13 illustrates these concepts.

A slightly more restrictive form of tree is commonly used in computing. This is a **binary tree**, in which each node may have at most two subtrees. These are called the **left** and **right subtrees** and are binary trees in their own right. Figure 4.14 shows a binary tree. Notice how each node has zero, one or two subtrees.

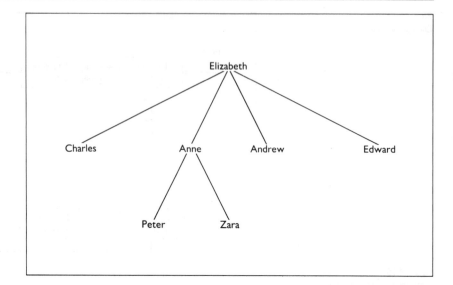

Figure 4.12
A family tree

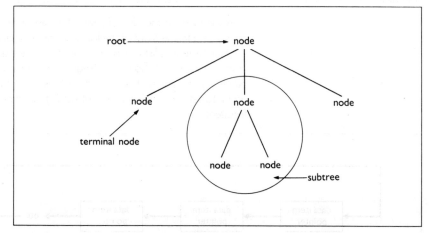

Figure 4.13
Tree concepts

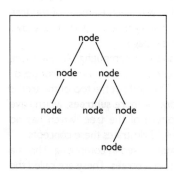

Figure 4.14
A binary tree

The most common way of representing a tree involves the use of pointers. For a binary tree, each node consists of a data item plus two pointers. One or both of the pointers may have null values if they have no subtrees to point to. Figure 4.15 shows how pointers may be used to construct the same tree as illustrated in Figure 4.14. Notice how terminal nodes have null values of both pointers.

A number of operations may be carried out on trees. Two binary trees may be **joined** to an additional node, which becomes the root of a larger binary tree, with the original trees as subtrees. A tree may be **traversed** in several ways. Traversing a tree is accessing its elements in a systematic way. Tree traversal is dealt with briefly in the exercise at the end of this chapter.

Trees have a number of applications in computing. The modules of many programs are linked together in a tree structure. Trees are also used to represent arithmetic expressions. Some computers regard their entire memory as if it were partitioned into a tree structure.

In conclusion, the essential feature of a tree is that each node is connected to subtrees, which themselves have the structure of trees. In other words, wherever you are in a tree, the structure 'below' you is a tree. This is the property of trees which makes them so useful from a computing point of view.

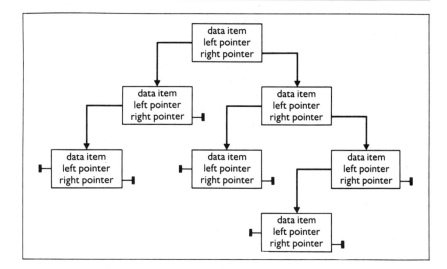

Figure 4.15
Pointers used to construct a binary tree

4.13 Data Types

A concept which links this chapter with the previous chapter is that of a **data type**. Data types include both individual data items and data structures. For many purposes it is convenient to treat entire data structures as single objects. Many program languages allow complete structures to be manipulated as if they were single data items. Data structures and individual items are often identified in the same way.

Many program languages require that the type of each data item be **declared** before the data item is used in a program. A data item may be an integer, an array, or a list, to name just a few examples. The concept of data types is discussed further in the chapters on high level languages, Chapters 16 and 17.

4.14 Implementation of Data Structures

The data structures introduced in this chapter have been described in general terms. In these terms they are sometimes known as **abstract data types**, with essential properties defined completely independently of computers. This is necessary to preserve the simplicity of these structures, and to investigate what further properties they possess.

A number of problems arise when representing any of these structures on a computer. In almost all cases the method of representation interferes with the properties of the structure. Some of the cleanness and simplicity of the abstract structure is lost. The commonest problem is that computer memory does not have an unlimited capacity. All the dynamic data structures introduced in this chapter have no theoretical limits on the size to which they can grow. In practice, a limit has to be placed on their size, and checks carried out whenever a new data item is added.

Another problem occurs when the computer or program language in use cannot deal with pointers. This causes severe difficulties. It usually means that one or more arrays are needed to represent a dynamic data structure. Manipulating these structures can become very cumbersome.

4.15 Conclusion

In conclusion, the significance of data structures cannot be stressed too much. The title of an important book on computer programming states the case very succinctly:

Algorithms + Data Structures = Programs. Data structures are one of the fundamental building blocks in constructing programs. Data structures are also fundamental to the architecture of computers. One of the frontiers of computing science is research into new data structures and further properties of existing ones.

The most important points made in this chapter are as follows:

- A data structure is a set of data items which are related to each other in a particular way.
- The essential properties of a data structure can be described by specifying how data items are added and removed, and how an empty structure is created.
- A pointer, which is a data item indicating the location of another data item, is frequently used in the implementation of data structures.
- A string is a set of characters stored together and generally regarded as a single data item.
- An array is a fixed number of data items of identical type, stored together. Each element in an array may be accessed by one or more indices, the number of indices indicating the dimension of the array.
- Static data structures are ones which stay the same size once they have been created, whereas dynamic data structures can vary in size.
- A stack, or last-in–first-out (LIFO) structure, is a collection of data items which can only be accessed at one end, the top of the stack.
- A queue, or first-in–first-out (FIFO) structure, can have items added at the rear and removed from the front.
- A list is a set of data where items may be inserted and deleted at any point.
- A tree is a data structure in which each element may be linked to one or more elements below it.
- The concept of data types includes individual data items, which may, for example, be literal or numeric, and data structures, which may be stacks, queues, lists or trees.
- In most cases when data structures are implemented, some restrictions on their properties have to be imposed. This has given rise to the concept of abstract data types, which retain their 'pure' features.

Exercise 4

1 Briefly define the following terms: data structure; pointer; null pointer; string; array; index; dimension; static and dynamic data structures; stack; top of stack; push; pop; LIFO; stack pointer; stack base; queue; FIFO; circular buffer; list; circular list; ordered list; tree; node; root; subtree; leaf; binary tree; tree traversal; data type; declaration, and abstract data type.

2 Give at least three reasons for the use of data structures in computing.

3 a) Name some examples of structured data encountered in everyday life, in addition to those mentioned in the text.
   b) Describe a collection of data occurring in everyday life which could not be called structured. Give reasons for your choice of the particular collection.

4 Briefly state the requirements that a set of data must satisfy in order to be called structured.

☐ 5 Three different data structures have been mentioned in this chapter as models for a computer memory.
   a) Name the structures
   b) In the light of your knowledge of data structures, suggest why each of them might have been chosen.

6 Mention three examples of the use of null pointers.

7 A text editing program allows strings of characters to be inserted into the middle of other strings. For example, the string **THE CAT SAT ON MAT** can be edited to become **THE CAT SAT ON THE MAT**.

   Give an informal algorithm, using separating and joining operations only, for this insertion operation.

8 An algorithm for setting all the elements of an array X to zero is as follows:

1: Let index $I = 1$
2: If $I > 10$, halt.
3: Let $X(I) = 0$
4: Increase I by 1
5: Go to step 2

Write similar algorithms for each of the following processes:

a) Adding each element of array X to the corresponding element of array Y, which also has ten elements, to produce array Z.

b) Adding up all the elements of array X to produce a single total.

☐ c) Producing the 'product' of array X and array Y, defined as follows:

$$P = X(1) . Y(1) + X(2) . Y(2) + \ldots + X(10) . Y(10)$$

(the dot means multiplication in this case).

9 The elements of the two-dimensional array A, with three rows and three columns, are to be copied into the one-dimensional array B, with nine elements, one row at a time. The first few elements are transferred as follows:

A(1,1) into B(1)
A(1,2) into B(2)
A(1,3) into B(3).

a) Continue the above list, showing how all the elements of A are transferred.

☐ b) Derive a formula for the index of array B in terms of the indices of array A.

☐ c) Repeat the question with all indices starting from 0 instead of from 1. Comment on your results.

10 A stack is often used to do calculations on a computer in the manner introduced in the following examples:

Example 1

$6 + 7 \times 4$:	Stack 6	6

	Stack 7	7
		6

	Stack 4	4
		7
		6

	Multiply 4 by 7, stack result	28
		6

	Add 28 and 6, stack result	34

Example 2

$6 \times 7 + 4$:	Stack 6	6

	Stack 7	7
		6

	Multiply 6 and 7, stack result	42

	Stack 4	4
		42

	Add 4 and 42, stack result	46

In other words, load the numbers onto the stack until an operation can be performed on the top two numbers. These two numbers are replaced by the result of the operation. The process continues until the final answer is left on the stack.

Using this method, show the steps of the following calculations. Make sure that you know the order in which the calculations must be performed before you start.

a) $21 - 10 \div 5$

b) $39 \div 13 - 2$

c) $6 \times 4 + 5 \times 3$

d) $6 \times (4 + 5) \times 3$

e) $7 + 9 + 15 - 2$

Another way of writing calculations, called **reverse Polish notation**, is introduced later in the book. It is intended for use when calculations are to be carried out using a stack.

11 One method of representing a queue is to store the elements next to each other, with a pointer to the front of the queue, and a pointer to the space behind the rear of the queue. Figure 4.16 shows an example. The data items are names of programs waiting to be run on a computer.

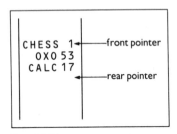

Figure 4.16

a) Draw a diagram of the queue after the programs **CHESS1** and **OXO53** have been run, and the program **STRM5** has joined the queue.

b) If no further programs are added, draw diagrams of the queue when there is one program left to run, and when the queue is empty.

c) Mention a disadvantage of storing a queue in this way in a computer memory.

12 An alternative method of implementing a list is to have two pointers associated with each element. One pointer points to the list element in front, the other to the element behind.

a) Draw a diagram of a list implemented in this way.

b) Draw diagrams to show the process of inserting a new data item into a list, using pointers in both directions.

c) Labelling the relevant pointers, specify precisely what operations are performed to accommodate the new item.

13 Draw a diagram of a circular list using pointers in both directions.

14 A set of names is stored, in alphabetical order, in an array. The last few elements of the array contain free spaces. Write informal algorithms showing the principal steps of inserting and deleting elements of this array, while preserving its alphabetical ordering and keeping the free spaces at the back. (Write the algorithms as brief English sentences. Do not specify index values in detail.)

From your results, comment on the suitability of arrays for storing ordered data.

15 Trees can be used to describe the structure of arithmetic or algebraic expressions, as shown in the following examples:

Example 1

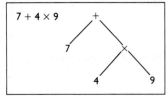

Figure 4.17

Example 2

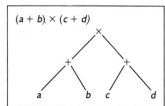

Figure 4.18

The parts of the calculations which are to be performed first form the lowest branches of the tree.

Represent the following expressions in a similar manner to the above examples:

a) $8 - 5 \div 7$

b) $(x - y) - (p \times q)$

c) $((x + y) \times 2) \div (a - 7)$

d) $a + b + c$

e) $(s + t) \times (u - v) \div (p + q)$

16 Two arrays are used to represent a tree, in the following manner. One array stores the data items in the tree. The other array contains blocks of pointers, one for each node. The first pointer in a node is the index of the data item at that node. Subsequent pointers point to blocks for nodes branching from the node. The blocks ends with a zero.

For example, the tree showing the component subjects of computing science is shown in Figure 4.19. The arrays corresponding to this tree are shown below.

	pointers array		data array	
index	item		index	item
1	2		1	applications
2	7		2	computing
3	9		3	data
4	11		4	hardware
5	13		5	software
6	0			
7	3			
8	0			
9	4			
10	0			
11	5			
12	0			
13	1			
14	0			

Arrows have been drawn to show the effects of the first few pointers.

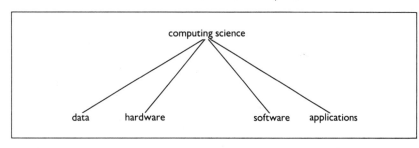

Figure 4.19

Construct similar arrays to represent the following trees:

a)

Figure 4.20

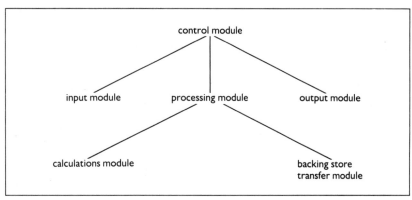

b)

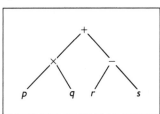

Figure 4.21

17 An array can be used to store the elements in a binary tree in a fairly simple manner. The correspondence of array indices and nodes in the tree is shown in Figure 4.22.
   a) Store the tree in part (b) of Question 16 in this manner.
   b) The array: $\begin{bmatrix} a \\ - \\ b \end{bmatrix}$ stores the binary tree: a $\searrow$ b.

   Represent the binary tree in Figure 4.23 in an array in this way.
   c) Compare this method of representing trees by arrays with the one introduced in Question 16. Comment on the suitability of this method for storing binary trees.

☐ 18 Traversing a tree is accessing its elements in a systematic way. The commonest order is 'from left to right', i.e. left subtree, node, right subtree. This way might be described by the following algorithm:

> **traverse** tree
>
> > if tree not null
> >
> > > then   **traverse** left subtree
> > > output   node
> > > **traverse** right subtree

This algorithm is recursive, in the sense that it 'calls' itself. Applied to the tree in Figure 4.15, it produces the elements in the order $7 + 4 \times 9$.

a) Apply this algorithm to the trees in Figures 4.22 and 4.23, and list the elements in the order in which they are output.

b) Change the algorithm so that it traverses both subtrees before the node is output.

c) Write down the output produced by applying the revised algorithm to the trees in Figures 4.15, 4.22 and 4.23.

19 A general way of indexing the elements of an array is the use of an **enumeration literal**.

For example, if the variable named **day** has values mon, tues, wed, thurs . . . sun, it can be used in conjunction with the array **hours worked**.

Here

> hours worked (mon)   is   the hours worked on Monday
> hours worked (tues)   is   the hours worked on Tuesday

and

> hours worked (day)   is   any particular element of the array.

In this example, the variable **day** is used as an enumeration literal for the array **hours worked**.

For each of the following arrays, write down the name and a set of values of a suitable enumeration literal.

a) **days in**, containing the number of days of each month of the year.

b) **height**, containing the heights of the significant mountain peaks in Britain.

c) **wavelength**, storing the wavelengths of a number of radio stations.

d) Comment on the advantages and disadvantages of describing arrays in this manner.

20 The rules for sorting a list of integers using a binary tree are as follows:

i) take the first integer as the data element at the root,

ii) compare the next integer with the element at the root; if it is greater it is placed on the right at the next level, otherwise on the left,

iii) for each subsequent integer in the list the process described in (ii) is repeated, with comparisons continuing through the tree until a vacant position is found.

a) Using these rules, construct a sort tree for the list 36, 75, 26, 92, 36, 23, 20, 46, 33.

b) Describe an algorithm which will retrieve the sorted list of data from the tree.

c) If it is known that the data contains many repeated items, suggest an improvement to the rules above.

d) What characteristics of the initial data list would cause this sorting method to become particularly inefficient?

UCLES 81 1 (specimen)

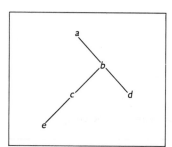

Figure 4.22

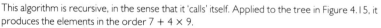

Figure 4.23

5
Computer arithmetic

This chapter concerns one aspect of the processing carried out by computers, namely **computer arithmetic.** It must be stressed that arithmetic is only one of the many ways in which a computer can process data. The days of computers being used for 'number crunching' only have long passed. On the other hand, all computers do a certain amount of simple arithmetic during the running of all programs, whether they are for numerical applications or not.

This chapter introduces some of the theory of computer arithmetic. Pencil and paper calculations are done here in a manner similar to the way in which they are done on computers. Some of the electronic circuits which actually carry out the various arithmetic operations are introduced in Chapter 7.

This chapter builds on foundations laid in Chapter 3, concerning data representation. Ways of representing numbers, and some elementary operations of computer arithmetic, are introduced in that chapter. From time to time it will be necessary to refer to material in Chapter 3 during the study of this chapter.

5.1   Characteristics of Computer Arithmetic

The arithmetic carried out by computers differs from our customary way of doing arithmetic in a number of ways. Although arithmetic operations are implemented differently on different computers, they all have a few common characteristics. These are a binary representation of numbers, a finite range of numbers, a finite precision of numbers, and some operations done in terms of other operations. Each of these characteristics is now briefly discussed.

5.2   Binary Representation of Numbers

Various binary representations of numbers have been discussed in Chapter 3. The most important point to remember at this stage is that numbers can be represented in several ways, such as in binary coded decimal form, as integers or fractions, or as floating point numbers. Furthermore, integers and fractions can be in sign-and-magnitude form, or as twos complement or ones complement numbers.

This chapter is confined to a discussion of twos complement integers and floating point numbers, as these are by far the commonest ways of representing numbers on computers. In many programming languages the programmer can choose which of these two forms is to be used for each numeric data item.

5.3   Finite Range of Numbers

Whichever way numbers are represented on a computer, there is always an upper and a lower limit on their size. These limits depend on the number representation used, and on the number of bits allocated to the number. The term **overflow** is used if an operation results in a number which is outside these limits (the term **underflow** is sometimes used in relation to the lower limit). The question of overflow is discussed again later in this chapter.

5.4   Finite Precision of Numbers

When a base ten number is written as a decimal fraction, the number of decimal places reflects the precision of the number. Most fractions cannot be represented exactly in a finite number of decimal places. The precision of a decimal fraction is a measure of how closely it comes to representing the number exactly.

In computers, fractions and floating point numbers are stored in a finite number of binary places. Just as in the case of decimal fractions, this limits the precision of these numbers. This means that a calculation using floating point numbers seldom gives exactly the right answer. The question of loss of precision in floating point numbers is discussed again later in this chapter.

5.5   Some Operations Done in Terms of Other Operations

As mentioned in Chapter 3, most computers do not have separate processing circuits for all arithmetic operations. One of the reasons for using complementary numbers is that subtraction can be done by complementation and addition. On many computers multiplication is done by a process of shifting and addition. Division is done by shifting and subtraction. An algorithm for doing multiplication in this way is included later in this chapter.

The roles of hardware and software in computer arithmetic are important. Operations such as integer addition, which are carried out directly, are done by hardware. Operations done in terms of other operations are supervised by software. If this software is permanently stored in read-only memory, it is given the name **firmware**.

Each type of computer has its own mixture of hardware and software implementation of arithmetic operations. In general, the larger the computer, the more operations which are done directly by hardware.

5.6   Some Aspects of Computer Arithmetic

The rest of this chapter contains a discussion of some aspects of computer arithmetic. Integer arithmetic and floating point arithmetic are examined separately.

5.7   Integer Arithmetic

In this section, integers are assumed to be represented in twos complement form. This form is introduced in Chapter 3, where it is explained how subtraction can be carried out by complementation and addition. Three further aspects of integer arithmetic are now discussed, namely, overflow, multiplication and division.

5.8   Overflow

Overflow occurs when the result of a calculation is outside the range of numbers which can be represented. There is no way of preventing overflow, all that a computer can do is detect it when it occurs.

In twos complement arithmetic, overflow is related to the numbers carried into and out of the most significant place value during addition. Four examples are introduced in the next section to illustrate this point, after which some general conclusions are drawn. Six bit, twos complement numbers are used throughout.

5.9   Carry and Overflow

Consider the following calculations in twos complement arithmetic. Notice carefully the numbers carried into and out of the most significant bit of the calculation, and whether or not the result is correct.

	−32	16	8	4	2	1	

Example 1: 14 + 9

	−32	16	8	4	2	1	
14 =	0	0	1	1	1	0	
9 =	0	0	1	0	0	1	+
	0	1	0	1	1	1	= 23
	0	0					
	carry out	carry in					

Carry in = 0, carry out = 0, answer correct.

Example 2: 25 + 18

	−32	16	8	4	2	1	
25 =	0	1	1	0	0	1	
18 =	0	1	0	0	1	0	+
	1	0	1	0	1	1	= −21
	0	1					
	carry out	carry in					

Carry in = 1, carry out = 0, answer incorrect.

Example 3: 17 − 13 = 17 + (−13)

	−32	16	8	4	2	1	
17 =	0	1	0	0	0	1	
−13 =	1	1	0	0	1	1	+
	0	0	0	1	0	0	= 4
	1	1					
	carry out	carry in					

Carry in = 1, carry out = 1, answer correct.

Example 4: −8 − 31 = −8 + (−31)

	−32	16	8	4	2	1	
−8 =	1	1	1	0	0	0	
−31 =	1	0	0	0	0	1	+
	0	1	1	0	0	1	= 25
	1	0					
	carry out	carry in					

Carry in = 0, carry out = 1, answer incorrect.

Examining the four results, it can be seen that the answer is correct when the number carried in to the most significant place is the same as the number carried out. This is true in general.

In other words, overflow occurs when, at the most significant bit, carry in is not equal to carry out. Most computers have a special **overflow bit** which is set to 1 when overflow is detected in this manner. These examples use six bit arithmetic. The situation is the same, in twos complement arithmetic, however many bits are used.

5.10 Integer Multiplication

If multiplication is not performed directly by computer hardware, the commonest technique is to use a process of **shifting** and **addition**. It is very similar to the method of doing binary multiplication by hand.

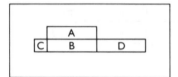

Figure 5.1

You will recall that there are various rules for determining the sign of a product from the signs of the two numbers which are multiplied. These rules are generally applied separately from the actual multiplication process. Accordingly, this section considers the multiplication of positive integers only.

An algorithm is presented below for the multiplication of two positive binary integers, by a process of shifting and addition. It is not the only one used by computers, but is representative of them.

5.11   A Multiplication Algorithm

This algorithm requires a **working area**, which might be imagined as shown in Figure 5.1.

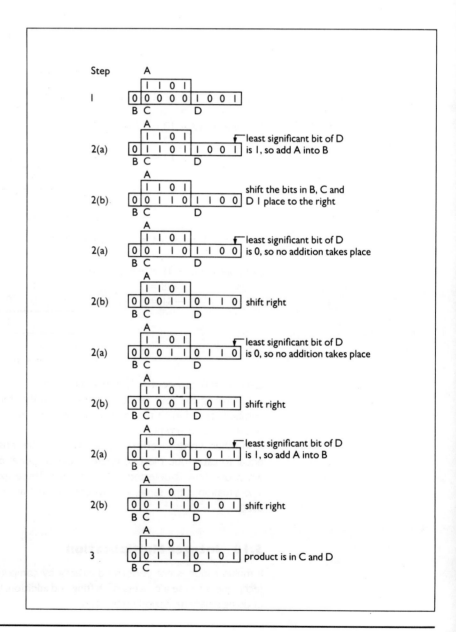

Figure 5.2
1101 × 1001

There are three storage spaces for binary integers, labelled A, B and D. The storage space labelled C is for the carry bit resulting from an addition.

The algorithm is as follows:

1 Initially, B and C contain zeros, while A and D contain the two numbers to be multiplied.
2 Repeat, for each bit of the numbers:
   If the least significant bit of D is 1, then add A to B, placing the sum in B and the carry in C.
   Shift the bits in C, B and D together one place to the right. Thus C passes into B, a bit passes from B to D and the least significant bit of D is lost.
3 When this process is complete, the product of the two numbers is in B and D.

An example of this process is now given. For simplicity, four bit integers are used. Thus step 2 is repeated four times.

Example
Multiply 1101 by 1001 using the above algorithm. See Figure 5.2.

The product of the two numbers, namely 01110101, is in B and D. The result can be checked by converting the numbers and the product to decimal.

You will notice that the product is twice as long as the original numbers. Overflow can occur if this number must be stored in the space for a single integer. Four bit numbers are used in the above example for simplicity. The steps of the algorithm are the same if longer numbers are used.

5.12 Integer Division

Integer division is done by a process of shifting and subtraction, very similar to the process of integer multiplication. The result is obtained as a quotient and a remainder. In most computers the result of the division is taken to be the quotient, without any rounding up being done. In other words, the result of dividing 20 by 7, using integer arithmetic, is 2.

5.13 Floating Point Arithmetic

Methods of representing floating point numbers are discussed in Chapter 3. You will recall that a floating point number consists of a fraction part, or mantissa, multiplied by a power of two, or exponent. For simplicity, all floating point numbers used in this section are of the following form:

		mantissa					exponent	
sign	$\frac{1}{2}$	$\frac{1}{4}$	$\frac{1}{8}$	$\frac{1}{16}$	sign	2	1
0	1	1	0	1	0	1	0

$$= 0{\cdot}1101 \times 10^{10} = \tfrac{13}{16} \times 2^2 \times \tfrac{13}{16} \times 4 = 3\tfrac{1}{4}.$$

This form is far shorter than any actual floating point representation, but serves to illustrate the principles involved.

Three aspects of floating point arithmetic are now discussed. These are **overflow**, **addition** and **multiplication**. Loss of precision is investigated in the context of addition and multiplication.

5.14 Overflow in Floating Point Arithmetic

As in the case of integers, there is an upper and a lower limit on the size of floating point numbers which can be represented by a particular number of bits. These limits are determined by the number of bits allocated to the exponent. For the above allocation of bits, the limits on the exponent are -3 and 3. This gives an approximate range of the size of the numbers of 2^{-3} to 2^3, i.e. $\frac{1}{8}$ to 8. In practice, this range is of course much wider.

If a number exceeds the upper limits of the range, **overflow** is said to occur. If a number exceeds the lower limit, some computers will set the number to zero. The word **underflow** is sometimes used in this context.

5.15 Floating Point Addition

An algorithm for the addition of two floating point numbers is as follows:

1 If the exponents of the two numbers are not equal, then, for the number with the smaller exponent, repeat:

> Shift the mantissa one place to the right
> and increase the exponent by 1
> until the exponent equals that of the other number.

2 Add the mantissas of the two numbers.

3 If the addition results in a carry from the most significant place, shift this carry bit into the mantissa and the rest of the mantissa one place to the right. Increase the exponent by 1.

This is quite a complicated procedure just for the addition of two numbers. The example below shows how it works.

Example

	mantissa				exponent			
sign	$\frac{1}{2}$	$\frac{1}{4}$	$\frac{1}{8}$	$\frac{1}{16}$	sign	2	1	
0	1	1	0	1	0	1	0	$(= 3\frac{1}{4})$
+ 0	1	0	0	1	0	0	1	$(= 1\frac{1}{8})$

The second number has the smaller exponent, so the mantissa is shifted one place to the right and the exponent is increased by 1. One bit of the mantissa is lost. The result is as follows:

$$0 \quad 0 \quad 1 \quad 0 \quad 0 \quad 0 \quad 1 \quad 0$$

As the exponents are now equal, the mantissas can be added:

```
  0 1 1 0 1
+ 0 0 1 0 0
  ─────────
  0 0 0 0 1
carry: 1
```

The carry bit is shifted into the mantissa, and the exponent is increased by 1. Again one bit of the mantissa is lost. The result is as follows:

	mantissa				exponent			
sign	$\frac{1}{2}$	$\frac{1}{4}$	$\frac{1}{8}$	$\frac{1}{16}$	sign	2	1	
0	1	0	0	0	0	1	1	

$$= \cdot 1000 \times 10^{11} = \tfrac{1}{2} \times 2^3 = \tfrac{1}{2} \times 8 = 4.$$

Adding the decimal values of the original numbers gives the result as $4\frac{3}{8}$. An error has been introduced, due to the finite number of bits allocated to the mantissa. This type of error is sometimes called a **truncation error**.

A remedy for this kind of error is to allocate more bits to the mantissa. This increases the precision of the numbers. Although it reduces this kind of error, it will never eliminate it.

Subtraction of floating point numbers is carried out by a very similar process, and can result in the same kind of errors.

5.16 Floating Point Multiplication

An algorithm for the multiplication of two floating point numbers is as follows:

1 Multiply the mantissa's of the numbers, and add their exponents.
2 Shift the bits of the product to the left until there is a 1 in the most significant place. Reduce the exponent by 1 for each place shifted.
3 Truncate the product to the number of bits allocated to the mantissa of a floating point number.

The following example, using the same floating point numbers as before, shows how this algorithm works.

Example

		mantissa				exponent		
sign	$\frac{1}{2}$	$\frac{1}{4}$	$\frac{1}{8}$	$\frac{1}{16}$	sign	2	1	
0	1	1	0	1	0	1	0	$(= 3\frac{1}{4})$
× 0	1	0	0	1	0	0	1	$(= 1\frac{1}{8})$

Multiplying the mantissa and adding the exponents gives the following results:

product of mantissas : 0 1 1 1 0 1 0 1
sum of exponents   : 1 1 .

The product is shifted one place to the left, and the exponent is reduced by 1. This gives:

product of mantissas : 1 1 1 0 1 0 1
sum of exponents   : 1 0 .

Truncating the product into the mantissa gives the following floating point result:

		mantissa				exponent		
sign	$\frac{1}{2}$	$\frac{1}{4}$	$\frac{1}{8}$	$\frac{1}{16}$	sign	2	1	
0	1	1	1	0	0	1	0	

$$= \cdot 1110 \times 10^{10} = \tfrac{7}{8} \times 2^2 = \tfrac{7}{8} \times 4 = 3\tfrac{1}{2}$$

Multiplying the decimal values of the original numbers gives the result $3\frac{21}{32}$. Once again a truncation error has been introduced. As before, this error can be reduced, but not eliminated, by increasing the number of bits allocated to the mantissa. Floating point division suffers similar limitations.

5.17 Conclusion

This chapter has introduced some of the techniques of computer arithmetic, and demonstrated, by means of a few simple examples, some of the errors which can arise. Although the number representations used in this chapter are much shorter than those used by any actual computer, the principles and the problems are the same.

The main points raised during this chapter are as follows:

- The characteristics of computer arithmetic are a binary representation of numbers, generally in more than one code, a finite range and a finite precision of numbers, and some arithmetic operations done in terms of other operations.
- In integer arithmetic, overflow is related to the numbers carried into and out of the most significant place value during addition. Integer multiplication can be carried out by a process of shifting and addition. Integer division results in a quotient and a remainder.
- In floating point arithmetic, the range of numbers which can be represented depends on the number of bits allocated to the exponent. Overflow or underflow occurs if this range is exceeded. Floating point addition and multiplication can lead to truncation errors, as can subtraction and division. These errors can be reduced, but not eliminated, by allocating more bits to the mantissa of a floating point number.

Having read this chapter, you will realise that, as far as arithmetic is concerned, a computer will not always produce the right answer.

Exercise 5

1 Briefly define the following terms: overflow; precision; firmware; overflow bit; truncation error.
2 For a number of different computers, find out what arithmetic operations are carried out by hardware and what operations are supervised by software.
3 Verify the rule established in the chapter relating carry to overflow, by carrying out the following calculations, using four bit, twos complement numbers: $2 + 5$; $6 + 3$; $4 - 5$; $-2 - 7$.
4 Do the four calculations in the examples from the section on carry and overflow, using ones complement representation. From your results, state under what conditions overflow occurs in this representation.
5 Use the algorithm for integer multiplication to multiply 1101 by 1110.
☐ 6 Design an algorithm for integer division by a process of shifting and subtraction. A similar layout of working areas can be used to that for integer multiplication. Test your algorithm with some suitable numbers.

7

		mantissa				exponent		
	sign	$\frac{1}{2}$	$\frac{1}{4}$	$\frac{1}{8}$	$\frac{1}{16}$	sign	2	1
Let $A =$	0	1	1	0	0	0	1	0
$B =$	0	1	1	0	1	0	0	1
$C =$	0	1	0	1	0	0	0	0

Perform the following calculations on these numbers, using floating point arithmetic: $A + B$; $B + C$; $A \times B$; $A \times C$. In each case, comment on any errors which arise.

8 A particular computer allocates 24 bits to a floating point number. Six of these bits are for the exponent, the first of which is a sign bit. What is the approximate range of numbers which can be represented this way?

9 Errors can be reduced in computer arithmetic by the technique of **rounding**. Rounding is carried out when bits of a number, generally the mantissa of a floating point number, are discarded. The remaining bits are rounded by adding 1 to the least signficant retained bit if the most significant discarded bit is 1.

For example, if the eight bit mantissa 01011011 is rounded to four bits, the result is 0110.

a) Round each of the following numbers, discarding the rightmost bits:

01101101	to four bits
01111011	to four bits
10011001	to six bits

b) Round the results of the floating point addition and multiplication examples in this chapter. Convert the numbers obtained to decimal, and comment on your results.

6

Boolean logic

This chapter introduces the theory behind the way in which computers manipulate data. This theory has been given the name **Boolean logic** after the English mathematician George Boole (1810–1864). In 1847, Boole published the first thorough investigation of the principles of mathematical logic.

This chapter relates to the rest of the book in a number of ways. It builds on ideas introduced in earlier chapters, particularly Chapter 3, on data representation and storage. Concepts introduced in this chapter form the basis of a number of subsequent chapters, particularly Chapter 7, on logic circuits, and the part of the book devoted to computer architecture, Chapters 8 to 13.

The chapter starts with an introduction to the elementary ideas of Boolean logic. This material is essential to an understanding of the rest of the book. However, the second part of the chapter considers one aspect of Boolean logic in more detail, namely the simplification of combinations of logic operations. This material is not essential to an understanding of the rest of the book, and may be omitted if desired.

A problem arising in a study of Boolean logic is the set of symbols to be used. Several different sets are in current use. The set of symbols used here may be unfamiliar to some, but is becoming the most widely accepted set in the computing industry. It is essential to remember that the concepts of Boolean logic are more important than the particular symbols used. Included in the chapter is a table comparing the most common sets of logic symbols.

6.1 Two-state Representation of Data

Boolean logic includes a set of operations which manipulate logical, or Boolean variables. A **Boolean variable** is a quantity which can have either of two values, or states only. Depending on the context, these states may be called **true** and **false, set** and **clear, high** and **low,** or **0** and **1**.

As mentioned in Chapter 3, all data inside a computer is represented in terms of two states only. In other words, all data is made up of Boolean variables. Furthermore, all processing of this data by the computer is carried out in terms of Boolean operations. The elementary operations of Boolean logic are introduced in this chapter. The following chapter shows how these operations are combined in various functional circuits of a computer.

6.2 The Elementary Logic Operations

This section introduces the elementary **operations** of Boolean logic. These operations transform one or more Boolean variables, producing a further Boolean variable. The value of the resulting variable depends on the values of the original variables.

Each logic operation is characterised by an **operation table**, sometimes called a **truth table**. This table shows values of the resulting variable for all combinations of input variables. Two symbols associated with each logic operation are also introduced. The first symbol is the **logic circuit** symbol. This symbol indicates the logic operation in a logic circuit, which is rather like an electrical circuit. The other symbol is the **Boolean algebra** symbol for the operation. Boolean algebra is a way of representing logic operations, similar to the way ordinary algebra represents arithmetic operations.

Later in the chapter, combinations of logic operations are introduced. Like individual operations, these combinations can be described by truth tables, logic circuits or expressions in Boolean algebra.

The six commonest operations of Boolean logic are now discussed. In the context of logic circuits, these operations are sometimes referred to as **gates**.

NOT

The NOT operation has one input variable and one output variable. The value of the output variable is the opposite of that of the input variable. Figure 6.1 shows the logic circuit symbol for a NOT gate.

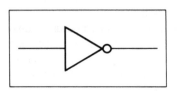

Figure 6.1
A NOT gate

Operation table

Input	Output
P	Q
0	1
1	0

Boolean expression $Q = \bar{P}$

AND

The AND operation has two or more input variables and one output variable. The output variable is 1 if *all* input variables are 1, otherwise it is 0. Figure 6.2 shows the logic circuit symbol for an AND gate.

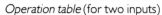

Operation table (for two inputs)

Input		Output
P	Q	R
0	0	0
0	1	0
1	0	0
1	1	1

Figure 6.2
An AND gate

Boolean expression $R = P.Q$

The operation table for an AND operation may be extended to three or more input variables using the rule for the AND operation quoted above.

OR

The OR operation has two or more input variables and one output variable. The output variable is 1 if *any* of the input variables are 1, otherwise it is 0. Figure 6.3 shows the logic circuit symbol for an OR gate.

Operation table (for two inputs)

Input		Output
P	Q	R
0	0	0
0	1	1
1	0	1
1	1	1

Boolean expression $R = P + Q$

It turns out that combinations of the NOT gate and either the AND or the OR gate are sufficient to carry out any logical operation on any number of inputs. However, three other logic gates are in common use. These are now introduced.

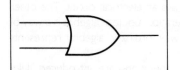

Figure 6.3
An OR gate

Exclusive OR

The **exclusive OR** or **non-equivalence** operation has two input variables and one

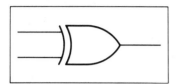

Figure 6.4
A Exclusive OR gate

output variable. Considered as an exclusive OR, the rule for its operation is as follows: the output variable is 1 if either, but not both, inputs are 1. This is shown in the following operation table:

Operation table

Input		Output
P	Q	R
0	0	0
0	1	1
1	0	1
1	1	0

Boolean expression $R = P \oplus Q$

Looking at the operation table in another way, one can see that the output is 1 if the two inputs are different. This is the non-equivalence rule for the operation. Figure 6.4 shows the logic circuit symbol for an exclusive OR gate.

NAND

The NAND operation may be considered as an AND operation followed by a NOT operation. It has two or more input variables and one output variable. The output variable is 0 if *all* the input variables are 1, otherwise it is 1. Figure 6.5 shows the logic circuit symbol for a NAND gate.

Operation table (for two inputs)

Input		Output
P	Q	R
0	0	1
0	1	1
1	0	1
1	1	0

Boolean expression $R = \overline{P.Q}$

NOR

The NOR operation may be considered as an OR operation followed by a NOT operation. It has two or more input variables and one output variable. The output variable is 0 if *any* of the input variables are 1, otherwise it is a 1. Figure 6.6 shows the logic circuit symbol for a NOR gate.

Operation table (for two inputs)

Input		Output
P	Q	R
0	0	1
0	1	0
1	0	0
1	1	0

Boolean expression $R = \overline{P + Q}$

6.3   Logic Operation Symbols

As mentioned at the beginning of this chapter, there are several sets of symbols for logic operations in current use. Figure 6.7 shows the relationship between these various sets.

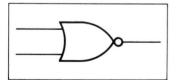

Figure 6.5
A NAND gate

Figure 6.6
A NOR gate

Operation	Boolean algebra symbols		Logic circuit symbols	
NOT	$\bar{P}$	$\sim P$		NOT
AND	$P \cdot Q$	$P \wedge Q$		AND
OR	$P + Q$	$P \vee Q$		OR
Exclusive OR	$P \oplus Q$	$P \not\equiv Q$		EOR
NAND	$\overline{P \cdot Q}$	$\sim (P \wedge Q)$		NAND
NOR	$\overline{P + Q}$	$\sim (P \vee Q)$		NOR

Figure 6.7
Different sets of logic symbols

6.4 Combinations of Logic Operations

The logic operations introduced in the previous section are seldom used on their own. Combinations of these operations may be imagined as connecting the output of one gate to the input of another gate. Some of the logic circuits of even the simplest computers are extremely complex. Such complexity is deliberately avoided here. The objective of this section is to show how logic elements can be combined, and how the operation table for a combination can be determined from the operation tables of the individual gates. Boolean expressions for the combinations of operations are also shown.

The three examples discussed in this section are not particularly useful to computers. Their intention is to illustrate the objectives mentioned above.

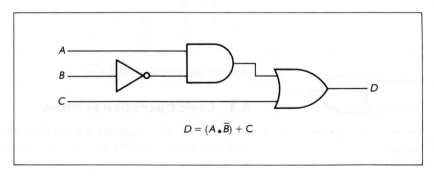

$$D = (A \cdot \bar{B}) + C$$

Figure 6.8
Logic circuit example 1

Example 1

The logic circuit shown in Figure 6.8 combines an AND, an OR and a NOT gate. The Boolean expressions for this combination is

$$D = (A.\bar{B}) + C.$$

There are two ways of obtaining the operation table for a circuit such as this. One is to follow all possible combinations of inputs through the circuit, and obtain the value of the output for each input. The other is to build up the operation table through a series of intermediate columns. There is a column for each part of the Boolean expression. The columns are combined according to the rules for Boolean operations, until a column for the whole expression is obtained. This process is shown in the following table.

Input					Output
A	B	C	$\bar{B}$	$A.\bar{B}$	$(A.\bar{B}) + C$
0	0	0	1	0	0
0	0	1	1	0	1
0	1	0	0	0	0
0	1	1	0	0	1
1	0	0	1	1	1
1	0	1	1	1	1
1	1	0	0	0	0
1	1	1	0	0	1

Example 2

The logic circuit shown in Figure 6.9 combines a NAND and a NOR gate. The Boolean expression for this combination is:

$$S = \overline{(P + Q)}.R.$$

As before, the operation table for the circuit is obtained by using intermediate columns for parts of the Boolean expression.

Input				Output
P	Q	R	$\overline{P + Q}$	$\overline{(P + Q).R}$
0	0	0	1	1
0	0	1	1	0
0	1	0	0	1
0	1	1	0	1
1	0	0	0	1
1	0	1	0	1
1	1	0	0	1
1	1	1	0	1

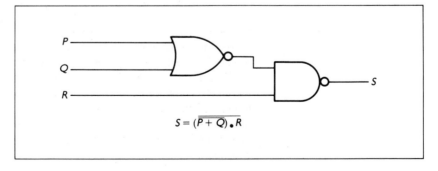

$$S = \overline{(P + Q)}.R$$

Figure 6.9
Logic circuit example 2

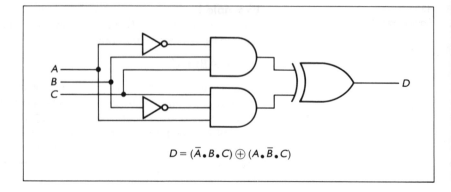

$$D = (\bar{A}.B.C) \oplus (A.\bar{B}.C)$$

Figure 6.10
Logic circuit example 3

Example 3

The logic circuit shown in Figure 6.10 combines two 3 input AND gates, two NOT gates and an exclusive OR gate. The Boolean expression for this combination is

$$D = (\bar{A}.B.C) \oplus (A.\bar{B}.C).$$

The operation table for the circuit is obtained by the same method as before.

Input							Output
A	B	C	$\bar{A}$	$\bar{B}$	$\bar{A}.B.C$	$A.\bar{B}.C$	$(\bar{A}.B.C) \oplus (A.\bar{B}.C)$
0	0	0	1	1	0	0	0
0	0	1	1	1	0	0	0
0	1	0	1	0	0	0	0
0	1	1	1	0	1	0	1
1	0	0	0	1	0	0	0
1	0	1	0	1	0	1	1
1	1	0	0	0	0	0	0
1	1	1	0	0	0	0	0

These examples show how the operation table for a logic circuit can be obtained from the expression for the circuit. It must be remembered that, in designing the logic circuits of a computer, one starts with a required operation table, and derives the Boolean expression and logic circuit to produce this table.

6.5 Simplification of Combinations of Logic Operations

One of the properties of Boolean operations is that more than one combination of operations will produce the same result. In other words, the same operation table can be implemented by more than one logic circuit. The main objective of **simplifying** logic circuits is to determine the combinations of logic operations which will produce the desired result, using the minimum number of gates. This reduces the cost and power consumption of logic circuits, and increases their speed. A second objective is sometimes to produce a logic circuit using certain types of gates only.

There are a number of ways of achieving these objectives, some of which are extremely sophisticated, and beyond the scope of this book. The simplification technique introduced here relies on a few algebraic properties of Boolean operations. These are introduced below. For simplicity, only AND, OR and NOT operations are considered in these sections. AND and OR gates are restricted to two inputs.

6.6 Some Properties of Boolean Operations

A few elementary algebraic properties of Boolean operations are listed below. You will notice how several of these resemble the algebraic properties of ordinary arithmetic operations.

Double negative:	$\bar{\bar{A}} = A$
Associative:	$(A + B) + C = A + (B + C)$
	$(A . B) . C = A . (B . C)$
Distributive:	$A + (B . C) = (A + B) . (A + C)$
	$A . (B + C) = (A . B) + (A . C)$
Absorption:	$A . A = A$
	$A + A = A$
De Morgan's laws:	$\overline{A + B} = \bar{A} . \bar{B}$
	$\overline{A . B} = \bar{A} + \bar{B}$

These properties may be proved by writing out the operation table for each side of the equation. This is done below, as an example, for the first of the distributive rules.

				Left hand side			Right hand side
A	B	C	$B . C$	$A + (B . C)$	$A + B$	$A + C$	$(A + B) . (A + C)$
0	0	0	0	0	0	0	0
0	0	1	0	0	0	1	0
0	1	0	0	0	1	0	0
0	1	1	1	1	1	1	1
1	0	0	0	1	1	1	1
1	0	1	0	1	1	1	1
1	1	0	0	1	1	1	1
1	1	1	1	1	1	1	1

The columns for the left hand side of the equation, and that for the right hand side, can be seen to be the same.

6.7 Some Examples of Simplifying Logic Circuits

Three examples of simplifying logic circuits are introduced below. In each case, a logic circuit and its Boolean expression are given. The Boolean expression is then simplified by means of the equations introduced above. The logic circuit of the resulting expression is then drawn. In each case the objective is to reduce the number of gates in the circuit.

Example 1

Figure 6.11 shows a logic circuit containing three NOT gates and an AND gate. Its Boolean expression is as follows:

$$z = \overline{\bar{X} . \bar{Y}}.$$

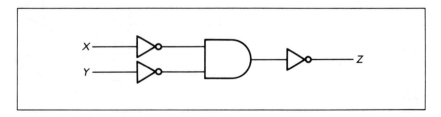

Figure 6.11
Simplification example 1 (before)

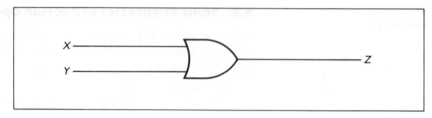

Figure 6.12
Simplification example 1 (after)

Simplification consists of using the rules from the previous section to replace parts of the given expression. To some extent, it is a process of trial and error.

Examining the rules, you will notice that the right hand side of the first of De Morgan's laws matches part of the above expression. Substituting the left hand side of this law gives the following expression:

$$Z = \overline{\overline{X + Y}}.$$

Now the double negative rule may be used to give

$$Z = X + Y.$$

This is the simplest possible form of the expression. Four gates in the original expression have been reduced to a single gate. The resulting logic circuit is shown in Figure 6.12.

Example 2
Figure 6.13 shows a logic circuit containing three AND gates and two NOT gates:

$$S = \overline{(P.Q)} \ . \ \overline{(P.R)}$$

Applying the second of De Morgan's laws to the terms in brackets gives the following:

$$S = (\bar{P} + \bar{Q}).(\bar{P} + \bar{R}).$$

The first of the distributive rules may now be used, giving

$$S = \bar{P} + (\bar{Q}.\bar{R}).$$

Using the first of De Morgan's laws on the second part of the expression gives

$$S = \bar{P} + \overline{(Q + R)}.$$

Finally, the second of De Morgan's laws can be used on the whole expression. This gives

$$S = \overline{P.(Q + R)}.$$

The circuit for this expression is shown in Figure 6.14. It contains three gates, as opposed to five in the original circuit.

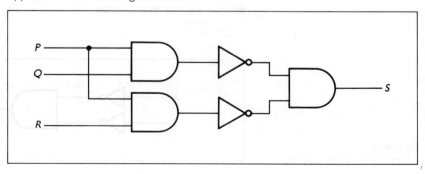

Figure 6.13
Simplification example 2 (before)

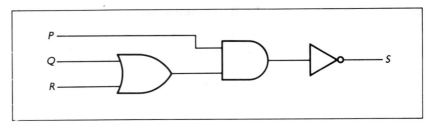

Figure 6.14
Simplification example 2 (after)

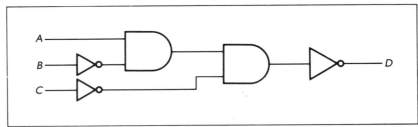

Figure 6.15
Simplification example 3 (before)

Example 3

Figure 6.15 shows a logic circuit containing two AND gates and three NOT gates. Its Boolean expression is

$$D = \overline{(A . \bar{B}) . \bar{C}}$$

The associative rule is first used to collect the two negated inputs together. This gives

$$D = \overline{A . (\bar{B} . \bar{C})}$$

The first of De Morgan's rules can be used on the term in brackets. This results in the following expression:

$$D = \overline{A . \overline{(B + C)}}$$

Remembering that A is the same as $\bar{\bar{A}}$, the first of De Morgan's rules can be used on the whole expression. This gives

$$D = \overline{\bar{\bar{A}} + \overline{(B + C)}}$$

The double negative rule simplifies this to

$$D = \bar{A} + (B + C)$$

The circuit for this expression is shown in Figure 6.26. Once again, five gates in the original circuit have been reduced to three gates in the simplified circuit.

To conclude this section, it must be emphasised that these examples are far simpler than the problems encountered in practice. Sophisticated techniques, some involving the use of computers, are used to simplify the logic circuits used in computers. Nevertheless, the principles of simplifying logic circuits are the ones introduced here. These principles form the basis of all simplification techniques.

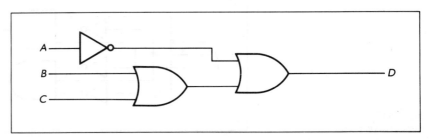

Figure 6.16
Simplification example 3 (after)

6.8 Conclusion

This chapter has introduced the operations which form the basis of all processing done by computers. Ways of combining these operations have been demonstrated, together with some ways of simplifying these combinations. In the process, some of the properties of logic operations have been noted.

The concepts which have been introduced here form the basis of the next few chapters of this book. These chapters cover some of the more important logic circuits used in computers, and how the structure of a computer is built up from these circuits.

The most important points made in this chapter are as follows:

- The theoretical basis for the operation of computers is Boolean logic. It consists of a number of operations which can be applied to Boolean, or logical variables, having two states only.
- Boolean operations can be represented by symbols in Boolean algebra, logic circuits, in which they appear as gates, or operation tables.
- All logic operations can be expressed as a combination of the elementary operations AND, OR and NOT. However, three other operations, NAND, NOR and non-equivalence, are in common use.
- Logic expressions can be simplified, in order to reduce the number of operations, or use only certain operations, while still achieving the same results.

This chapter concludes the first part of the book, concerning the principles of

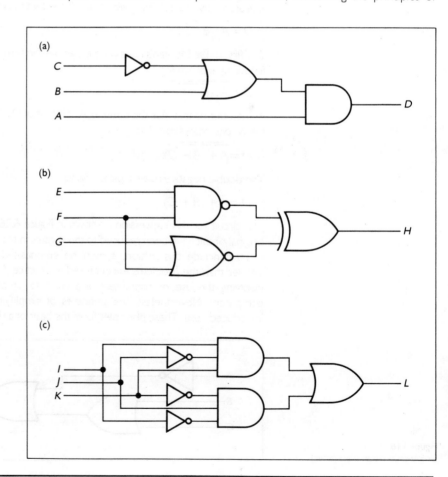

Figure 6.17
Logic circuit exercises

computing. This part has introduced the basic concepts of computing, the nature and representation of data, fundamental data structures, and the principles of computer arithmetic and Boolean logic. The stage is now set to apply this knowledge to the hardware of computers.

Exercise 6

1 Briefly define the following terms: Boolean logic; Boolean variable; operation table; logic circuit; Boolean algebra; Boolean operation; gate.

2 Draw the truth tables for three-input AND, OR, NAND and NOR gates.

3 Summarise the connection between two-state representation of data and Boolean logic.

4 a) Write Boolean expressions for each of the logic circuits in Figure 6.17.
   b) Obtain the operation table for each of these logic circuits.

5 Draw logic circuits for each of the following Boolean expressions:

$$V = \bar{K}.\bar{L}$$

$$W = \overline{K.L}$$

$$X = P.Q + \bar{P}.R$$

$$Y = A.\overline{(B + C)}$$

$$Z = \overline{(D + E).(\bar{D} + F)}$$

☐ 6 Express the exclusive OR operation in terms of AND, OR and NOT operations.

7 a) Draw logic circuits for each of the following Boolean expressions:

$$K = \overline{\bar{A} + \bar{B}}$$

$$L = (C + \bar{D}).(C + \bar{E})$$

$$M = (P.(\bar{Q}.\bar{R})) + (P.(Q.R))$$

   b) Simplify these expressions to reduce the number of operations they contain.
   c) Draw logic circuits for the simplified expressions.

☐ 8 Write a Boolean expression and draw a logic circuit for the following operation table:

Input			Output
A	B	C	D
0	0	0	0
0	0	1	0
0	1	0	0
0	1	1	1
1	0	0	0
1	0	1	0
1	1	0	0
1	1	1	0

9 Express the AND operation in terms of the OR and NOT operations.

10 a) Draw a diagram to show how a two-input NAND gate can be used as a NOT gate.
   b) Hence show how the AND and OR operations can be expressed in terms of the NAND operation only.
   c) What conclusion can you draw from these results?

7

Logic circuits

This is the first chapter in the part of the book concerned with computer hardware. It examines some of the essential processing circuits inside a computer. The electronic components of these circuits are briefly considered, but the emphasis is on their logical structure and properties. The circuit designs presented here are independent of any actual computer, but nevertheless they form the basis of the circuits commonly used.

This chapter relates closely to a number of other chapters. It is an application of the theory of Boolean logic introduced in the previous chapter. The logic gates introduced in the previous chapter are used extensively here. This chapter also relates to earlier chapters on data representation and computer arithmetic. Many of the circuits introduced here show how ideas from these chapters are put into practice. Finally, this chapter paves the way for the rest of this part of the book, which is a study of various aspects of computer hardware.

This chapter starts with a brief look at the implementation of logic operations, using transistors, integrated circuits and microprocessors. Then a number of commonly used circuits are introduced. The logic gates making up each circuit are shown, and the contribution the circuit makes to the running of the computer is explained.

7.1 Hardware Implementation of Logic Operations

The previous chapter introduced a number of operations which manipulate Boolean variables. You will recall that a Boolean variable can take on the values 0 and 1 only.

It turns out that solid-state electronic components can be made to behave like Boolean operations. The 'variables' which they manipulate are voltages. In many, but not all, cases, a high voltage represents the value 1, and a low, or zero, voltage represents the value 0. In the old days of computing, these electronic components were valves. Contemporary computers use transistors, and, more commonly, integrated circuits.

7.2 Transistors

You will recall from the previous chapter that a logic operation can be regarded as a gate. The most general gate combines one or more inputs to produce a single output. Its behaviour is governed by a truth table.

A **transistor** is an electronic component with three connections. These can be arranged so that two are for input and one is for output. Furthermore, the behaviour of the transistor, or a simple combination of transistors, can be made to correspond to the truth table of the gate. This is the basis of the way in which logic circuits are constructed. Figure 7.1 shows a logic gate and a transistor.

7.3 Integrated Circuits

For about ten years, from 1955 to 1965, logic circuits of computers were constructed using individual transistors for logic gates, as described above. Then it was realised that circuits could be constructed containing a number of transistors and other components as a single, solid-state unit. These **integrated circuits** perform the function of a number of logic gates. The principle on which they work is, however, the same as that for an individual transistor.

The design of integrated circuits has evolved through several stages. The first integrated circuits were equivalent to approximately ten transistors. Then came **medium scale integration** (MSI), with hundreds of components on one circuit. The

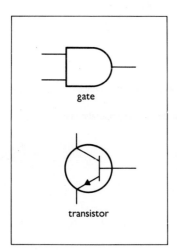

gate

transistor

Figure 7.1
A gate and a transistor

word 'chip' came into use to describe an integrated circuit. Today we are in the era of **large scale integration** (LSI), with thousands or even hundreds of thousands of components on one chip. Chips contain complete computer memories, or all the processing circuits of a computer. The latter type of chip is called a **microprocessor**.

There are several reasons for the rapid acceptance of very large scale integrated circuits. These circuits are small, consume very little electrical energy (and therefore do not produce much heat), and are generally very reliable. However, the overriding consideration is cost. As the capabilities of individual chips have increased, their costs have continued to decrease.

The logic circuits introduced in this chapter are explained in terms of Boolean operations. Most of them are implemented as integrated circuits, or as parts of microprocessors or memory chips.

7.4   Gate Delay

One property of transistors and integrated circuits must be mentioned at this point. This is that, after the input voltages have been altered, there is a delay before the output voltage stabilises at its new value. This property is called **gate delay**. It is one of the factors which limits the speed of a computer, and it affects the design of some logic circuits.

7.5   Some Logic Circuits

A number of common logic circuits are introduced in the next few sections. They serve two purposes, namely, to demonstrate how Boolean operations are applied, and to familiarise you with some of the basic building blocks of computers.

7.6   Control Switches

Data, addresses and control signals are sent from place to place inside a computer by means of data **channels**, also known as data **highways** or **buses**. Data channels are parallel connections, with one wire for each bit of the data item. **Control switches** regulate the flow of data in a channel. A control switch is opened to allow a data item to pass, or closed to block the passage of the data.

A control switch uses a set of AND gates, one for each bit of the data item, arranged in parallel. Figure 7.2 shows a four bit control switch. You will notice that each AND gate has one input from the data channel, and one from the common control input.

A control switch works in the following manner. If the control input is 0, then all outputs are 0, no matter what the data inputs are. The switch is open, and no data pass. However, if the control input is 1, then each output has the same value as the corresponding data input. This can be checked from the operation table of an AND gate. The switch is closed, and data pass along the channel.

All computers contain a large number of control switches of this type. They regulate the flow of data between the various functional circuits, and into and out of the various storage elements.

7.7   Masks

More general-purpose than a control switch, but still using parallel AND gates, is a **mask** circuit. It can be imagined as a set of control switches, with a separate switch for each bit of the data. Figure 7.3 shows a four bit mask circuit.

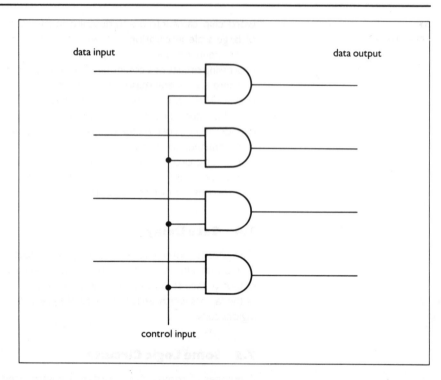

Figure 7.2
A four bit control switch

The purpose of a mask is to select certain bits of a data item, and 'mask out' the remaining bits. If a particular bit of the data item is required, then the corresponding control input is set to 1. If the bit is to be masked out, then the corresponding control input is set to 0. The operation table of an AND gate can be used to verify this. The control input is sometimes referred to as a mask. For example, if the three most

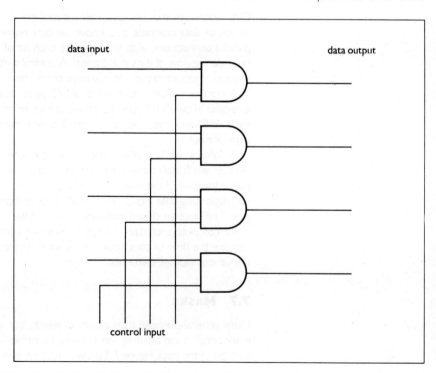

Figure 7.3
A four bit mask circuit

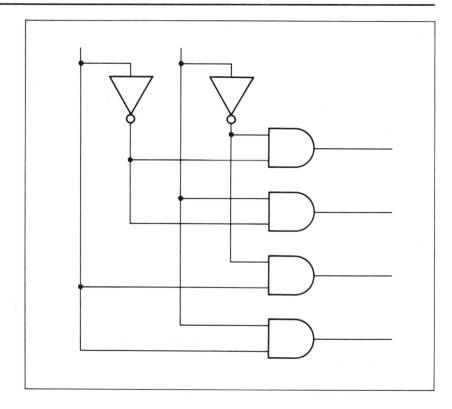

Figure 7.4
A decoder

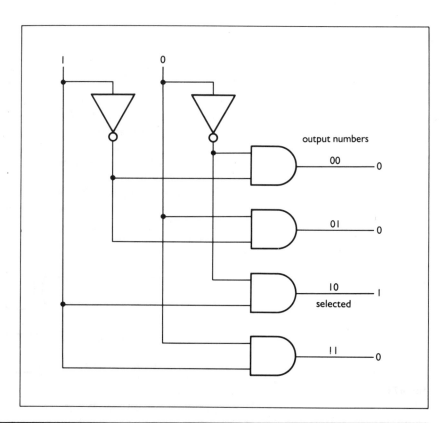

Figure 7.5
A decoder in operation

significant bits of an eight bit data item are required, then a mask of 11100000 is used. Most computers have at least one mask circuit, but they are not as common as control switches.

7.8 Decoders

A **decoder** is a circuit which selects one of a number of outputs according to the code of an input data item. Working in base ten for a moment, the principle is as follows: if there are 20 outputs, then an input number between 1 and 20 will cause the corresponding output to be selected. For example, the number 13 will cause the thirteenth output to be selected.

The decoder shown in Figure 7.4 has two inputs and four outputs. The outputs may be numbered (in binary) 00, 01, 10 and 11. The circuit works in such a way that any binary number input will cause the output with the corresponding number to be selected. Figure 7.5 shows the number 10 causing the output numbered 10 to be selected.

The decoders used in most computers contain more inputs and far more outputs than those illustrated here. They are used to locate memory cells, and in carrying out program instructions.

7.9 Addition Units

As mentioned in Chapter 5, all computers do addition by hardware. The logic circuits forming the **addition units** of a computer are now discussed.

The rules for adding two binary digits are expressed in the following table:

Inputs		Sum	Carry
0	0	0	0
0	1	1	0
1	0	1	0
1	1	0	1

You will notice that the sum column can be produced by an exclusive OR gate, and the carry column by an AND gate. A logic circuit containing these gates is shown in Figure 7.6. It is called a **half adder**.

If two complete binary numbers are added, the carry from the previous column must also be taken into account. A **full adder** is a circuit which adds two bits, together with a previous carry, to produce a sum and a carry. A full adder may be constructed from two half adders, as shown in Figure 7.7, or it may be implemented directly. This latter method is discussed in the exercise at the end of the chapter.

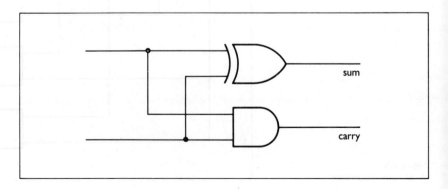

Figure 7.6
A half adder

sum

carry

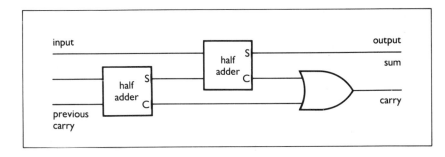

Figure 7.7
A full adder, made from two half adders

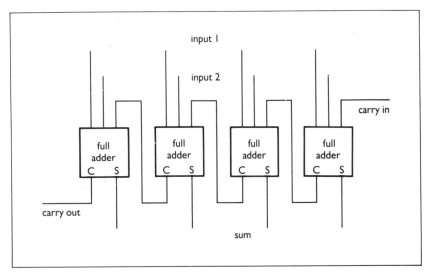

Figure 7.8
A four bit parallel adder

There are two approaches to adding complete binary numbers. One is to have a full adder for each pair of bits. All the additions take place at the same time. A circuit of this type is called a **parallel adder**, shown in Figure 7.8. The other approach is to add one pair of bits at a time. This approach gives rise to a **serial adder**, which is discussed in the exercise at the end of the chapter.

Returning to the parallel adder for a moment, several further points must be made. You will notice from Figure 7.8 that a parallel adder has a **carry out** and a **carry in**. The carry out is the same as the carry bit discussed in Chapters 3 and 5. The carry in is very useful, as it enables a number to be increased by 1. One application of this which has already been discussed is the process of obtaining the twos complement of a number, by negating the bits and then adding 1. Figure 7.9 shows a combined addition/subtraction unit based on this principle.

As mentioned earlier in this chapter, there is a delay associated with data passing through each logic gate in a circuit. Although Figure 7.8 depicts a parallel adder, you will realise that a carry might have to be passed across all the full adders in the circuit. This involves a considerable delay, and addition is not quite 'in parallel'.

To minimise this delay, some parallel adders include **carry prediction circuits**, which determine the value of each carry directly from the inputs. Such circuits are, however, beyond the scope of this course.

7.10 Flip-flops

The logic circuits introduced up to now are all concerned with the processing of data. Attention is now focused on an important class of circuits used to **store** data.

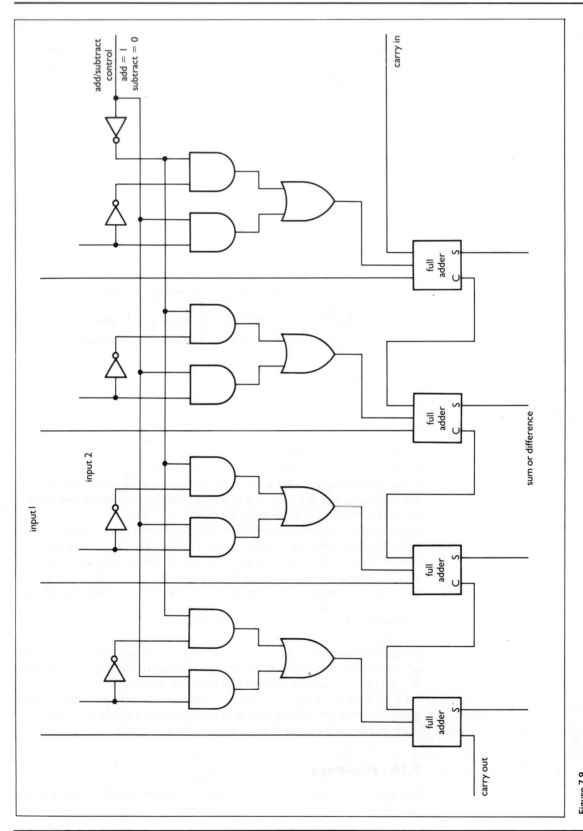

Figure 7.9
A four bit combined addition/ subtraction unit

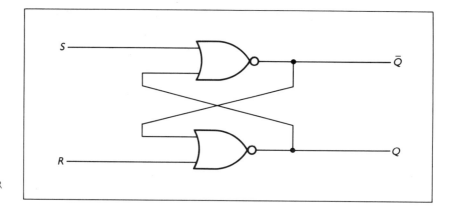

Figure 7.10
An RS flip-flop made from two NOR gates

Storage circuits differ from processing circuits in one important respect. The output of a processing circuit is determined by the state of its inputs at the time, but the output of a storage circuit is determined by its inputs and also its previous output state. This is because storage circuits always contain connections which 'feed back' from output to input.

Several types of storage circuits are used in computers. Two of the commonest ones are discussed here; a further type is introduced in the exercise at the end of the chapter.

7.11 The RS Flip-flop

The simplest storage circuit is called an **RS flip-flop** or **bistable**. One way of constructing it is to use two NOR gates, connected as shown in Figure 7.10. Notice how the outputs are 'fed back' into the inputs.

This circuit has acquired its name because it can be made to 'flip' from one stable output state to the other by a signal at the inputs. One input is called the **set** input, the other is called the **reset** input. The two outputs are always in opposite states, hence their labels Q and $\bar{Q}$.

The operation table for an RS flip-flop is given below. It shows the current output Q in terms of the inputs R and S, and the previous value of Q.

R	S	previous Q	current Q
0	0	0	0
0	1	0	1
0	0	1	1
1	0	1	0
0	0	0	0
1	0	0	0
0	1	1	1
1	1	0	0 or 1
1	1	1	0 or 1

The rows of the table have been written in an unusual order, to illustrate the way the circuit is used. The rows are considered one at a time.

The first row shows that if both inputs are zero, the output does not change. The second row shows that a 1 at the S input changes the output from 0 to 1. The flip-flop is set. The third row shows that if S now returns to zero, the output stays at 1.

The first three rows indicate that a **pulse** at input S, i.e. a change from 0 to 1 and back to 0, causes the output to flip from 0 to 1 *and stay there*. In other words, the pulse at S is 'remembered'.

Rows 3, 4 and 5 of the table illustrate the reverse process. Row 3 shows the circuit in the set state. If input R becomes 1, as shown in the fourth row, then the output changes from 1 to 0. The fifth row, which is a copy of the first row, shows that input R can return to 0 without affecting the output state. These rows show that a pulse from R causes the output to flip from 1 to 0 *and stay there*. The flip-flop is reset.

The next two rows show that a pulse at R will not affect the output if it is already 0, and a pulse at S will not change the output if it is already 1.

The last two rows show the problem associated with this circuit. If both inputs become 1 at the same time, then the output is not known. It can be either 0 or 1.

From this description of the way in which an RS flip-flop works, you will realise that it can be used to store one bit of data. A pulse at S causes a 1 to be stored, and a pulse at R causes a 0 to be stored.

7.12   The JK Flip-flop

There are a number of problems associated with RS flip-flops, in particular the undefined state when both inputs are 1. Accordingly, a more sophisticated circuit, known as a **master-slave** or **JK flip-flop** is commonly used to store data. Figure 7.11 shows the circuit for a JK flip-flop. You will notice that it contains two RS flip-flops and a **clock input**. The clock input is used to control the timing of the storage of data.

The operation table for a JK flip-flop is shown below. It is written in the same order as the table for an RS flip-flop. You will notice that the only difference between the two is in the last two lines. For simplicity, the clock signal and the set (S) and reset (R) inputs are omitted.

Figure 7.11
A JK flip-flop

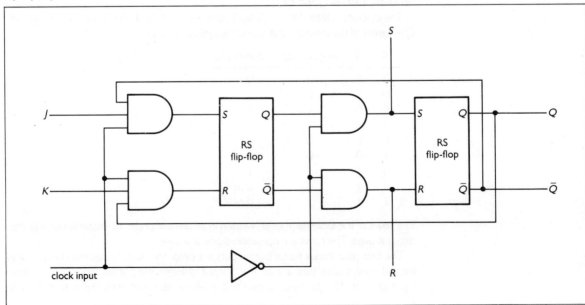

K	J	previous Q	current Q
0	0	0	0
0	1	0	1
0	0	1	1
1	0	1	0
0	0	0	0
1	0	0	0
0	1	1	1
1	1	0	1
1	1	1	0

It must be emphasised that RS and JK flip-flops are not the only circuits used to store data on computers. However, all data storage circuits have the property that a pulse at one input causes the output to change from one state to the other and stay there. All computers use large numbers of data storage circuits.

7.13 Registers

The previous section described how one bit of data can be stored by a logic circuit. These circuits are seldom used on their own. Several of them are generally combined to form a **register**, which stores a complete data item. Figure 7.12 shows one possible arrangement of a register. Notice how all the bits can be cleared from one input, and how the storage of input data is timed by a clock input.

Figure 7.12
A four bit register, made from JK flip-flops

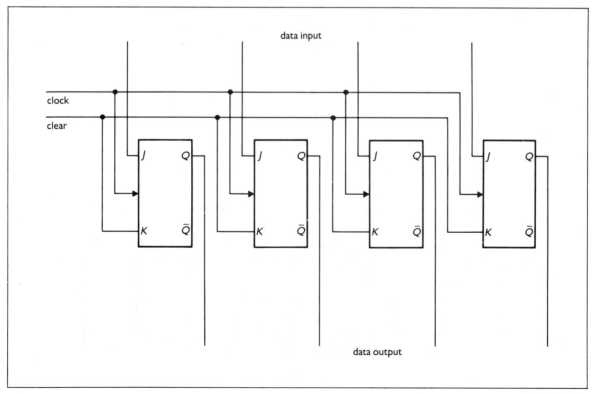

Most computers contain a number of registers to store, among other things, data items which are currently being processed, and instructions which are currently being carried out.

7.14 Shift Registers

One type of register which deserves special mention is a **shift register**. Such a register enables bits of a data item to be shifted from one position to the next. Figure 7.13 shows how a number of JK flip-flops can be combined to form a shift register. Every time the clock line is pulsed, each bit of the data item moves one place to the right.

Shift registers have a number of uses. These include playing a part in multiplication, division and serial addition, and accepting input from serial input devices. One significant application, known as a **USART**, is discussed in the exercise at the end of this chapter.

7.15 Conclusion

This chapter has shown how the operations of Boolean logic can be applied to some of the fundamental processing and storage functions of computers. It has introduced a number of logic circuits which are essential building blocks in the construction of computers.

The material introduced here is used in a number of subsequent chapters, notably Chapters 9 to 13, on processor architecture and operation, and peripheral devices.

The most important points made in this chapter are as follows:

● The electronic components used to implement logic operations are transistors and integrated circuits.
● Solid-state circuits have now reached the stage of large scale integration, including complete processors on a single chip, called microprocessors.
● Control switches regulate the flow of data on data channels.
● A mask is a logic circuit which selects certain bits in a data item.
● A decoder selects one of a number of outputs according to the code of an input data item.

Figure 7.13
A four bit shift register, made from JK flip-flops

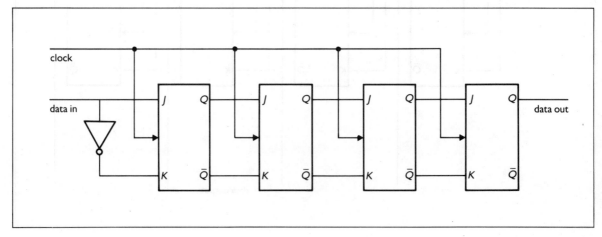

• Addition is generally carried out by means of a serial or parallel adder, containing a number of full adders which add pairs of bits.
• The basic storage element in a computer is a flip-flop, which has two stable output states. A signal at either of its inputs can cause it to flip from one state to another.
• A register is a storage element for a complete item of data.
• A shift register enables bits of a data item to be shifted from one position to the next.

Exercise 7

1 Briefly define the following terms: integrated circuit; microprocessor; gate delay; data channel; control switch; mask; decoder; full adder; parallel adder; bistable; register; shift register.

2 The first, third and fifth bits (counting from the left) of an eight bit data item are to be examined. The remaining bits are not required.
   a) What arrangement of mask bits will enable this to be done?
   b) What is the result of masking the data item 11011010 in this way?

3 The decoder shown in Figure 7.4 has two inputs and four outputs.
   a) How many outputs does a three-input decoder have?
   b) How many outputs does an n-input decoder have?
   c) Design a three-input decoder similar to the one in Figure 7.4. Number the outputs from 000 to 111. Show how the input bit pattern 101 will cause the 101th output to be selected.

☐ 4 a) Draw up the operation table for a full adder. Label the inputs A, B and C (for carry in), and the outputs S (sum) and T (carry out).
   b) Use this table to verify that the logic expressions for S and T are as follows:

$$S = A.B.C + A.\bar{B}.\bar{C} + \bar{A}.B.\bar{C} + \bar{A}.\bar{B}.C$$

$$T = A.B + B.C + A.C$$

   c) Use the above expressions to design a logic circuit for S and one for T. The circuit for S requires three NOT gates, four 3-input AND gates and one 4-input OR gate. The circuit for T uses three 2-input AND gates and one 3-input OR gate.

☐ 5 Figure 7.14 shows the processing part of a serial addition unit. If two bits are supplied at the inputs, and the clock line at the carry hold flip-flop is pulsed, it will add the input bits and the previous carry, producing a sum bit and storing the carry bit in the carry hold. It is now ready to repeat the process for the next pair of bits.

Figure 7.14
Part of a serial addition unit

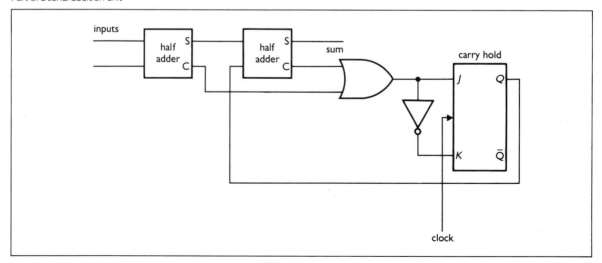

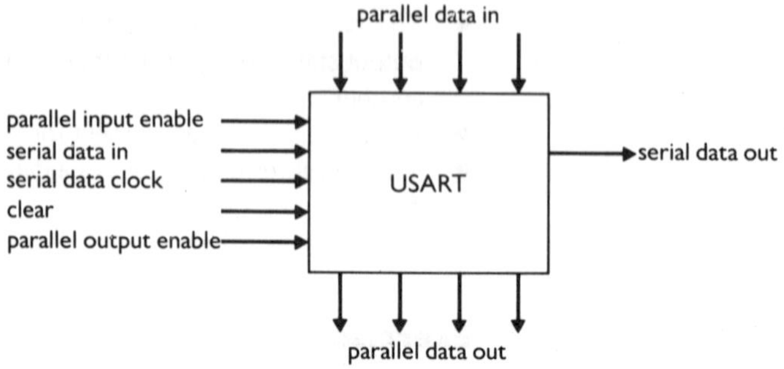

parallel data in

parallel input enable
serial data in
serial data clock
clear
parallel output enable

USART

serial data out

parallel data out

Figure 7.15
A USART

a) Connect three 4-bit shift registers to this circuit, to supply the input numbers and store the sum. Draw a diagram showing the complete serial addition unit.

b) Draw two extra connections onto your diagram, showing how a carry in and a carry out can be included.

☐ **6** At the beginning of this book, the concept of a **module** is introduced (Section 2.6). Although it has not been explicitly mentioned, this concept has been used a number of times in this chapter. Explain, with examples, how the concept of a module is used in the context of logic circuits.

7 Combine two of the diagrams in this chapter to show how data can be passed from one register to another, using a control switch.

8 A commonly used data storage element is the **D type flip-flop**. It has the following properties:

- Inputs are a single data line and a clock line.
- A NOT gate and an RS flip-flop are used.
- The flip-flop takes the value at its input when a clock pulse appears, and remains in the same state until the next clock pulse appears.
- Outputs are the same as those for an RS flip-flop.

From this information, draw a diagram of a D type flip-flop.

☐ **9** A circuit frequently used for serial input and output is a Universal Synchronous/Asynchronous Receiver/Transmitter, or **USART**. It is a register which can be loaded with either serial or parallel data, and which will output either serial or parallel data.

A 'black box' view of a four bit USART is shown in Figure 7.15. Notice that there are control signals for parallel data in and parallel data out, a clear signal and a clock signal for serial data in and out.

Using JK flip-flops, AND gates and a NOT gate, construct the internal circuits of this black box.

Hints: Use the S inputs of the flip-flop for parallel data in, and the R inputs for the clear signals. Also see Figures 7.12 and 7.13.

10 a) Explain what is meant by a truth table. Illustrate your answer by means of a truth table for the logical function NAND.

b) Given a decimal integer in the range 0 to 127, construct either a logical function or a flow diagram to decide whether there are just three ones in the binary equivalent.

c) Show why the logical function AND can be described as multiplication modulo two.

OLE 801

11 A **multiplexer** is a logic circuit with a number of data inputs, a number of control inputs and a single data output. Its purpose is to select a single data input which is copied to the data output.

Using the design of a four bit decoder (Figure 7.4) draw a logic circuit diagram of a four bit multiplexer. It has four data inputs, two control inputs and a data output. The binary number formed by the control inputs determines which data input is copied to the output.

8
Computer structure

This chapter takes an overall view of the hardware of a computer system. The units making up typical computer configurations of various sizes are discussed. Brief descriptions of the functions of these units are given, and some problems arising from their different characteristics are mentioned.

It is worth remembering at this stage that a computer is a system, a collection of parts working towards some common objectives. This chapter considers a computer as a total system. It paves the way for later chapters which consider various parts of a computer, notably the processor, in a considerable degree of detail.

8.1 The Functional Units of a Computer

The definition of a computer, quoted in Section 2.3, is as follows:

> **A computer is a collection of resources, including digital electronic processing devices, stored programs and sets of data, which, under the control of the stored programs, automatically inputs, processes and outputs data, and may also store and retrieve data.**

From the hardware point of view, the essential features of this definition are 'a collection of . . . digital electronic processing devices'.

Computers vary enormously in size, processing power and cost. Nevertheless, all computers consist of one or more functional devices, each carrying out one or more of the tasks described above. Each carries out a precisely specified task, and connects to other modules via defined interfaces. Modules of the same type of computer may be exchanged, and new modules added, without modification to their internal workings. The phrase **plug-compatible** is used in this context.

The modules which make up typical computer configurations of various sizes are now discussed. It must be emphasised that these configurations are no more than convenient examples. In practice there is a continuous variation in size and complexity from very small to very large systems.

8.2 Mainframes, Minis and Micros

Very broadly speaking, there are three overall classes of computers, according to their size and complexity. These classes are known as **mainframes, minicomputers** (or **minis**) and **microcomputers** (or **micros**).

Mainframes are large computers, comprising a number of free-standing units. Mainframes are generally housed in specially designed, air-conditioned rooms. Connections between the units are made by wires running beneath the floor of the room. Mainframes are generally very powerful, supporting a number of applications running concurrently. Examples of mainframes are the ICL 2900 series, the IBM 370 series, the Burroughs B6700 series and the Cray 1.

Minicomputers are smaller than mainframes, with several functional devices mounted in a rack in a single unit. Minicomputers do not generally require an air-conditioned environment. They are often to be found in laboratories, factories and offices. Minicomputers can generally support more than one application running concurrently, though not as many as mainframes. The PDP-11 series is the most popular minicomputer. Other examples are its descendants, the LSI-11 and VAX computers, and the Digico M16.

Microcomputers are the newest addition to the computer family. They are small and cheap, and are generally contained in a few small units. Their distinguishing feature is that processing is carried out on a single processor chip. Although they are very versatile, microprocessors can only support one application at any one time.

Examples of microcomputers are the Research Machines 380Z, the Commodore Pet, the Apple 2 and the North Star Horizon.

It must be emphasised that the classification of computers into mainframes, minis and micros is only very approximate. Computers are getting smaller and more powerful all the time. Micros are being introduced with the capability of minis only a few years old. Minis are incorporating microprocessors to assume the capability of mainframes. In Section 30.6 there is a case study of a **micro mainframe**.

8.3 A Typical Medium Sized Computer

With such a wide variety of computers now available, the most obvious place to start an overall description is in the middle of the range. Figure 8.1 shows the units of a typical medium sized computer, and the flow of data between them. The computer could be a small mainframe or large mini. The function of each type of unit is now discussed.

Processing of data takes place in the **central processing unit**, or CPU, now becoming more commonly known simply as a **processor**. This consists entirely of solid-state electronic components, in circuits such as those introduced in Chapter 7. Some processors, particularly in mainframes, have a **front panel** which contains switches and lights which indicate the current state of the processor. Linked to the processor are a number of **peripheral** devices.

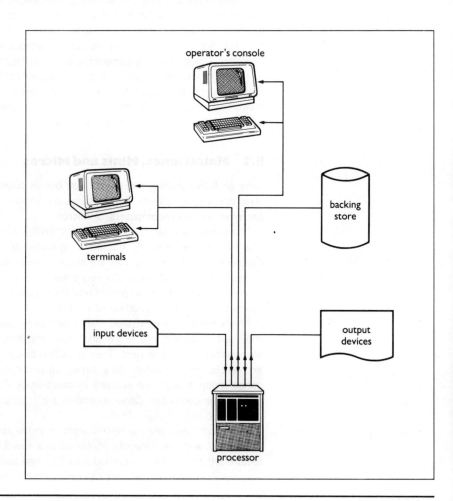

Figure 8.1
The units of a typical medium sized computer

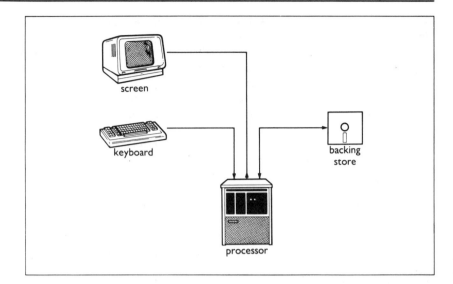

Figure 8.2
The structure of a typical
microcomputer

Input devices supply data to the processor. Data is read from a variety of media such as punched cards, paper tape, magnetic ink characters and bar codes, and sent in a binary code to the processor.

Output devices print or display data from the processor. These include various types of printers, plotters and devices which reproduce data or microfilm.

Terminals are general-purpose input/output devices. They consist of a keyboard for input, and a printer or display screen for output. Terminals may be linked to the processor from long distances.

Backing store is storage of large quantities of data for rapid access by the processor. Magnetic discs and magnetic tapes are the most common storage media.

The **operator's console** allows the person operating the computer to interact with the computer. In appearance and structure it resembles a terminal.

Although it is made up of separate units, it must be remembered that a computer is a system. In other words, the individual units work together to achieve some common objectives. The step-by-step control of the system is in the hands of the processor. Overall control, however, rests with the person operating the computer.

8.4 A Microcomputer

At the bottom end of the size and price range is the microprocessor-based computer, or **microcomputer**. They are the most recent addition to the family of computers, and already outnumber their larger relations.

Figure 8.2 shows the structure of a typical microcomputer. In some models, the units are separate, as shown in the diagram. In others, the processor and backing store or the processor and keyboard are combined in a single unit. Many micros include a character printer.

Backing store media are either small, flexible magnetic discs, called **floppy discs** or cassette tapes. In newer models, hard, high capacity **Winchester** discs are used.

8.5 A Typical Large Mainframe

At the other end of the scale, with processing power (and cost) tens of thousands of times that of a microcomputer, is the large mainframe system. As can be seen from

Figure 8.3, large computers are characterised by multiple processing units, and a number of different types of peripheral devices.

At the centre of the system is a **front-end processor**. This controls the flow of data between the two central processors and the various peripheral devices in the system.

A separate **communications processor** is required to control the flow of data to and from the terminals and data communications links. There may be hundreds of terminals.

A **backing store control** unit controls the passage of data to and from the various backing store units.

The front-end processor, communications processor and backing store control unit each have considerable processing power in their own right. They have facilities for storing a certain amount of data, routing data to the required channel, and transferring data from one code to another.

An essential unit in all mainframe computers, although it has no data links to other units, is an **uninterrupted power supply** unit. This device smoothes the flow of

Figure 8.3
The units of a typical large mainframe

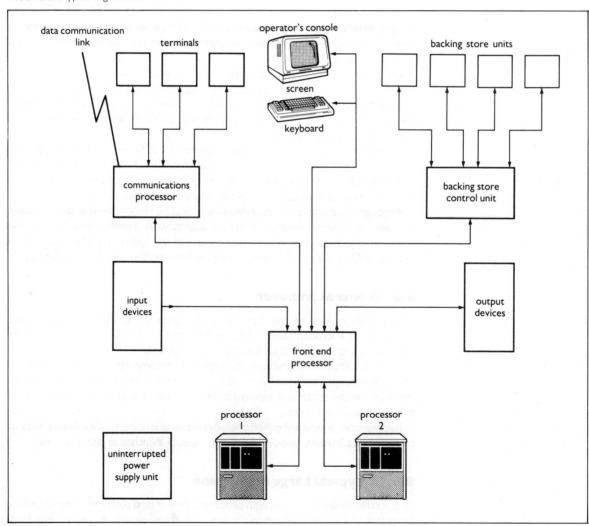

electricity to the computer. It 'irons out' any fluctuations in voltage, and has batteries to ensure that there is no break in the electricity supply to the computer should there be a power failure. The batteries are sufficient to keep the computer going until standby generators can be started.

8.6 Conclusion

This chapter has introduced the overall structure of computers of various sizes. Various units making up the computers have been introduced, and their relationships to the rest of the system indicated.

Although these units are all part of the same system, it must be noted that they have very different operating characteristics, particularly with regard to speed. In general, processors are many times as fast as peripheral devices. This causes considerable problems in the co-ordination of the devices in an efficient way.

In the next five chapters, aspects of the devices introduced in this chapter are discussed in more detail.

Exercise 8

1 Discuss the concept of a module in relation to the structure of a computer system.
2 Briefly define the following terms: plug-compatible; peripheral; microcomputer; front-end processor; front panel; mainframe; minicomputer.
3 Extend the lists of mainframes, minis and micros quoted in Section 8.2.
4 Note the overall structure of one or more computers known to you. In each case, make a sketch of the units and their inter-connection, similar to the diagrams in this chapter.
5 It is becoming increasingly common for manufacturers to produce peripheral devices which are plug-compatible with processors made by other manufacturers. Find out the names of some companies producing such equipment, and discuss the advantages and disadvantages of this practice.

9
Processor architecture

This chapter is concerned with the architecture of the processor of a computer. The objectives of a processor are discussed, together with various aspects of the structure of a typical processor. To simplify this discussion, a model computer is used. This model computer has been specially designed for this course.

This chapter is closely related to the following chapter, which describes the way in which a processor operates. These chapters provide as close a look at the detailed workings of a computer as is possible in this course.

While studying these chapters, it is important to distinguish between general principles and implementation details, as the latter vary from computer to computer. This chapter is generally concerned with the principles of processor architecture. A later chapter, on processor case studies, shows some of the ways in which these principles are put into practice.

It must be mentioned at this point that the word 'processor' is used rather loosely in computing circles. In some contexts it means the whole processing unit of a computer. In other cases, it means one chip within a processing unit. Such a chip is also known as a **microprocessor**.

9.1 Objectives of a Processor

The primary objective of a processor is to carry out the steps of a data processing task. In order to become familiar with the level at which a processor operates, this objective needs some clarification.

You will recall from previous chapters that data is a representation of information, in some binary code. You will also recall that data and instructions are stored and processed together, and no distinction is made between them.

Accordingly, a step of a data processing task involves the manipulation of one or more items of data, in a binary code, in response to an instruction, also in a binary code. The manipulation is carried out by logic circuits, discussed in a previous chapter, on individual bits of the data items. This, then, is the level at which a processor operates.

In addition to accomplishing its primary objective, a processor must work as quickly as possible, using as little electricity as possible, while avoiding errors and breakdowns. These objectives sound rather a tall order, but in practice they are attained to a remarkable extent. Thirty years of intensive research and development have led to processors which are fast, powerful, efficient and cheap. Nevertheless, the basic design principles of processors, formulated just after the Second World War, have remained the same. It is these design principles which are the subject matter of this chapter.

9.2 The Structure of a Processor

As explained in the previous chapter, computers come in all shapes and sizes. Although the design principles are similar in most cases, these principles are implemented in a variety of ways. It is therefore impossible to choose one computer as a representative, and discuss various features of the structure of its processor.

To overcome this problem, a model computer has been designed, specifically for this course. It is used in this chapter to introduce the important features of a processor. It is also used in subsequent chapters, to help explain how a processor operates, and to introduce the program languages used to control a computer.

The following sections introduce the overall structure of a processor, using the model computer as an example.

9.3 A Model Computer – the AMC

The **A-level model computer**, or **AMC**, has been designed to assist in the teaching of a number of topics in this book, the first being processor architecture. The design of the AMC reflects a compromise between the requirements of A-level computing science syllabuses and the features of a number of actual computers. Design principles are implemented in as straightforward a manner as possible.

9.4 The Overall Structure of the AMC

In common with most processors, the AMC may be thought of as a number of functional units, connected by one or more **buses**, as well as control links. Figure 9.1 shows the overall block structure of the AMC. Control links are omitted for simplicity.

A bus is a pathway along which data, address and control signals pass within a processor. The two buses in the AMC are both 16 bits wide, and are used for both data and addresses. The input and output ports are, however, 8 bits wide, as most input/output devices work in units of 8 bits.

The AMC is a **16 bit processor**. This means that all operations are performed on 16 bit quantities and internal transfers of data are in units of 16 bits. In the context of the AMC, a 16 bit quantity is called a **word**, and an 8 bit quantity a **byte**.

The four functional units in Figure 9.1 each contain a number of **registers** (introduced in Section 7.13) and other logic circuits. Most of the registers are 16 bits wide, and most logic circuits process 16 bit quantities in parallel.

Each of the functional units of the AMC is described in a subsequent section in this chapter.

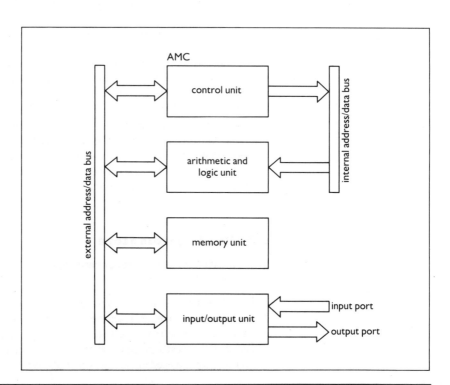

Figure 9.1
AMC block structure

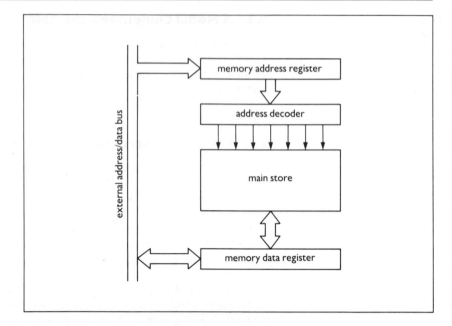

Figure 9.2
AMC memory unit

9.5   The AMC Memory Unit

The AMC memory unit consists of the **memory address register**, **address decoder**, **main store** and **memory data register**. Figure 9.2 shows these components. The function of the memory unit is to store and retrieve data and instructions. The interface between the memory unit and the rest of the AMC is the external address/data bus.

The **main store** of the AMC is an **immediate access store**. The store is partitioned into a number of locations, each of which is identified by a number called an **address**. Each location stores one byte. Given its address, any location may be accessed immediately.

Like most AMC registers, the **memory address register** holds 16 bits. This means that there are 2^{16} (= 65 536) distinct addresses. A unit of memory size commonly used is the **K** unit, where $1K = 2^{10} = 1024$. Thus the AMC memory contains $65\,536 \div 1024 = 64K$ locations.

The 16 bit **memory data register** holds data during transfer to or from main store. Data may be stored or retrieved in units of bytes or words. A word occupies two consecutive store locations. The lower byte address is always used to locate a word.

The concept of addressing is fundamental to the way a computer works. Several techniques of addressing are used in the AMC. These are discussed in the next chapter.

9.6   Reading from Store

When a data item is accessed, or **read from** main store, the following sequence of actions takes place:

1 The address of the data item is placed in the memory address register.
2 The address decoder accesses the store location addressed.
3 If a word is being read, the byte addressed by the memory address register is placed in the most significant half of the memory data register, and the byte at the next address is placed in the least significant half.

4 If a byte is being read, it occupies the least significant half of the memory data register, and the most significant half of the register is filled with copies of the most significant bit of the byte. This process is called **sign extension**.

9.7 Writing to Store

When a data item is placed in, or **written to** main store, the following sequence of actions takes place:

1 The address of the store location to be used is placed in the memory address register.
2 The data item is placed in the memory data register.
3 If a word is being written to store, the most significant byte of the memory data register is placed in the store cell addressed by the memory address register, and the least significant byte in the next store location.
4 If a byte is being written to store, it is taken from the least significant half of the memory data register.

9.8 A Memory Cycle

You will notice that the sequences of actions for reading from or writing to store are very much the same. One such sequence is called a **memory cycle**. The complexity of an operation often depends on how many memory cycles it involves, and the time taken for a memory cycle is an important factor in determining the overall speed of a processor.

9.9 Construction of Immediate Access Store

Until a few years ago, the main store of most computers was constructed from **ferrite cores**. A ferrite core is a small ring of soft iron, which can be magnetised in one direction or the other to store a 0 or a 1.

Contemporary computers use solid-state electronic circuits for main store. Such stores are called **random access memory**, or **RAM**. A number of different types of circuits are used, which fall into two groups, namely **static** memory and **dynamic** memory.

Static memory has the property that data is retained for as long as power is supplied to the memory circuits. In the case of dynamic memory, data gradually 'leaks away', and must be **refreshed** periodically. Memory refresh is accomplished by reading an item from the store and writing it back into the same location. Locations are refreshed in rotation all the time that the computer is running.

Some areas of a computer memory may be loaded with data or instructions which must be permanently stored. This type of memory is called **read-only memory**, or **ROM**. Accessing data from read-only memory has the same steps as in the case of random access memory, but an attempt to write data to ROM has no effect. Certain types of ROM can, however, be cleared and loaded with different data or instructions. These are called **programmable read-only memory**, or **PROM**.

9.10 The AMC Arithmetic and Logic Unit

The AMC **arithmetic and logic unit**, or **ALU**, consists of an **accumulator**, a set of **logic circuits**, a **result register** and four **condition codes**. These form the part of the

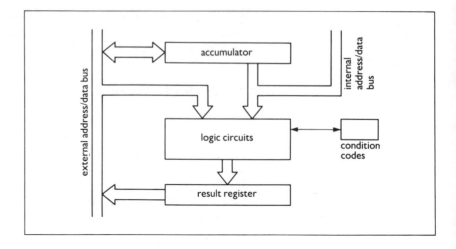

Figure 9.3
AMC arithmetic and logic unit

processor concerned with the actual manipulation of data. Figure 9.3 shows this portion of the AMC.

The **accumulator** is the principal 'working area' of the computer. It contains the data item being processed at any time.

The **logic circuits** carry out various operations on one or two data items. The logic circuits have two inputs and one output, as well as a connection to a register containing a number of condition codes (explained below). Figure 9.4 shows the internal arrangement of the logic circuits of the AMC. They can be seen to contain a set of NOT gates, an addition unit, sets of AND, OR and non-equivalence gates, and a shift register. All processing is in units of 16 bits.

Rather surprisingly, this seemingly limited set of logic circuits is quite sufficient to perform all the various data processing operations carried out by the computer. The reason for this is that operations are expressed as a large number of small steps, each step involving one or two of the logic circuits of the ALU. Ways in which this can be done for various arithmetic operations are discussed in Section 5.5.

The **result register** is a temporary store for the output from the logic circuits.

The **condition codes** are four bits which provide information about the most recent operation carried out by the ALU. These codes are also known as **program status bits**. The AMC has four condition codes, as follows:

Zero (Z) is set to 1 if the output from the current operation is zero.

Negative (N) is set to 1 if the output from the current operation is negative, i.e. the most significant bit is 1.

Carry (C) is set to 1 if there is a carry out of the most significant bit during shifting or addition.

Overflow (V) is set to 1 if an addition results in an overflow. The method of determining whether overflow has occurred is discussed in Section 5.9.

Values of condition codes are used in the control of programs, and in carrying out certain operations. This is discussed in more detail in the next chapter.

9.11 The AMC Input/Output Unit

Communication between the AMC processor and peripheral devices is via an **input** and an **output register**, and a **peripheral device selection register**. Unlike the storage, processing and control registers, these registers are only 8 bits wide. They are connected to the least significant 8 bits of the external address/data bus. Figure 9.5 shows the AMC input/output unit.

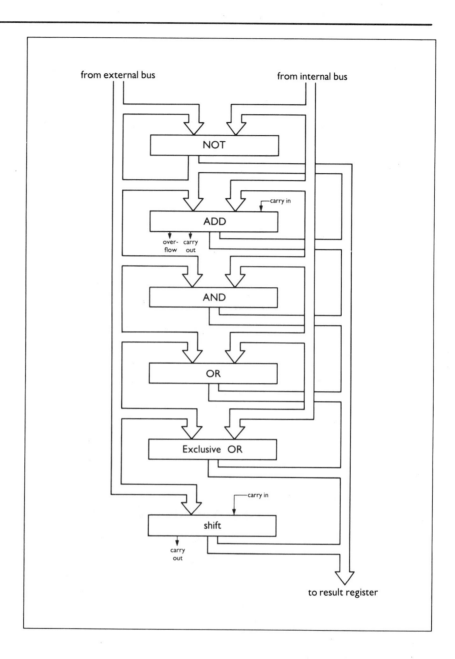

Figure 9.4
AMC logic circuits

All input and output to and from the AMC is assumed to be in character form. This is the case for the majority of peripheral devices. For this reason, input and output registers contain one byte, or one character.

When a character is input to the AMC, the sequence of events is as follows:

1 The identification of the input device is placed in the peripheral device selection register.
2 The input device thus selected is requested to send a character to the input register.
3 When the input register has been loaded, a signal is sent to the AMC control unit.
4 The character is then copied from the input register into the AMC.

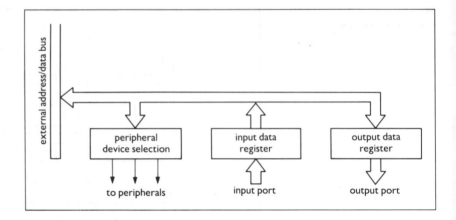

Figure 9.5
AMC input/output unit

Similarly, when a character is output by the AMC, the sequence of events is as follows:

1 The character to be output is placed in the output register.
2 The identification of the output device is placed in the peripheral device selection register.
3 The output device thus selected is requested to copy the character from the output register.
4 When the character has been copied, a signal is sent to the AMC control unit.

It can be seen that there are several steps involved in the input or output of a single character. Furthermore, each step requires one program instruction. Although this is a very cumbersome process, it is fairly representative of the way many actual computers work.

9.12 The AMC Control Unit

The **control unit** of the AMC comprises the **program counter, instruction register** and **decoder, stack pointer** and **index register**. Figure 9.6 shows these components. The control unit also contains a **clock pulse generator** which controls the timing of the whole processor.

The task of the control unit is to direct the step-by-step working of the processor as it carries out each instruction of a program. More specifically, the functions of the control unit are:

1 To control the sequence on which instructions are executed.
2 To control access to the main store of the processor.
3 To regulate the timing of all operations carried out within the processor.
4 To send control signals to, and receive control signals from, peripheral devices.

The part played by each register in the control unit in carrying out these tasks is now discussed.

The **program counter** contains the address of the current program instruction. After the instruction has been fetched from main store, the contents of the program counter is increased, ready for the next instruction. AMC instructions occupy 2, 3 or 4 bytes, thus the amount of the increase varies from one instruction to another. If an instruction transfers control to another part of the program, the address to which control is transferred is loaded into the program counter.

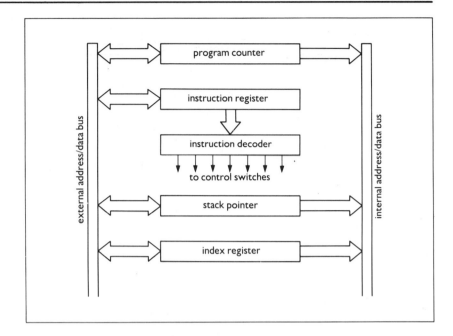

Figure 9.6
AMC control unit

The **instruction register** stores a copy of the current program instruction. This register is connected to an **instruction decoder**, which in turn connects with control switches at various points throughout the processor. In this way, control switches are opened or closed according to the instruction in the instruction register.

In common with most modern processors, the AMC organises part of its main store as a stack. The stack serves a number of purposes, most of which are introduced in the next chapter. The **stack pointer** stores the current address of the top of the stack.

The **index register** is used to implement a particular type, or **mode**, of addressing. Address modes are explained in the next chapter.

Not shown in the diagram is the **clock pulse generator**. This produces signals in a number of control lines, at regular intervals. These signals switch on, or **enable** various components of the AMC. In this way, co-ordination of the timing of the whole processor is achieved.

To complete the description of the AMC at register level, Figure 9.7 shows the register layout of the whole AMC processor.

9.13   The AMC and Real Processors

A reminder is necessary at this stage that the AMC is a model computer. It implements a number of concepts of processor architecture in as simple and direct a way as possible. Among the differences between the AMC and real processors are the following:

1 In many processors, the program counter, index register, stack pointer and accumulator are not specific **dedicated** registers, but can be any one of a set of **general-purpose** registers. In other words, any register in the set can be used as an accumulator, index register, etc.
2 Some processors have restrictions on the storage of words in memory. In many cases words may only be stored at even addresses.

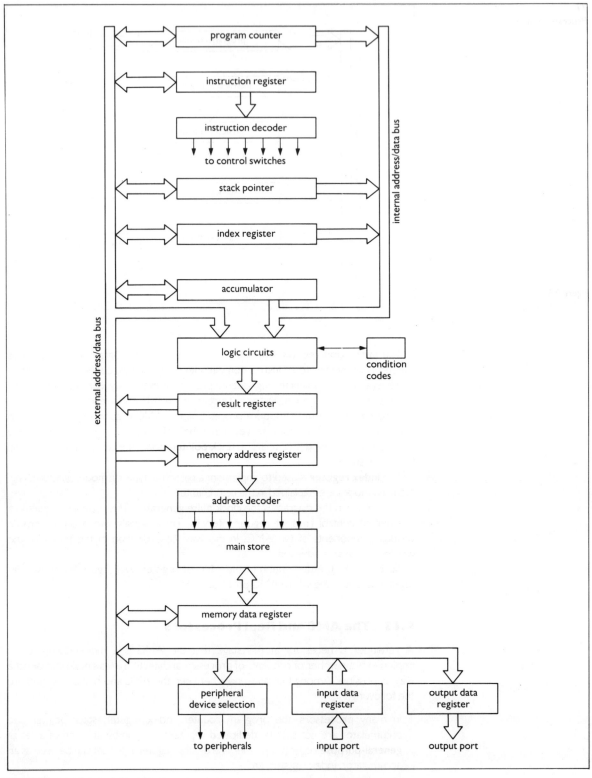

Figure 9.7
AMC register layout

3 In many processors, particularly microprocessors, input and output is done via store locations, rather than input and output registers.

4 Many processors have far larger main stores than the AMC. To describe the capacity of these stores, the **M** unit, where $1M = 1024K = 2^{20}$, is coming into use.

More about the architecture of the processors of real computers is to be found in Chapter 13, which contains a number of case studies of processor architectures.

9.14 Conclusion

This chapter has introduced the architecture of a simple processor, described at the level of registers, decoders and other logic circuits. The objective is to give a 'feel' for the structure of a computer at this level.

Several general points can now be made about the structure of a processor, namely:

- The structure of a processor, at register level, is quite simple.
- The range of operations which can be carried out directly by the hardware of a processor is fairly limited.
- In order to be carried out by a device of this sort, a data processing task must be expressed as a large number of simple steps, each step being an operation within the capabilities of the hardware of the processor.
- All the circuits of the processor are devoted to carrying out one program instruction at a time.
- The most important concept introduced in this chapter is the idea of an **address**. Addresses are used to locate instructions and data.

The next chapter shows how the registers and other functional circuits of a processor are put to work. It again uses the AMC as an example.

Exercise 9

1 Briefly define the following terms: main store; ALU; bus; control unit; immediate access store; address; RAM; ROM; PROM; memory cycle; accumulator; condition codes; program counter; enable; dedicated register; sign extension; program status bits.
2 a) In your own words, explain the concept of an address.
   b) State why addresses are so important to the functioning of a processor.
3 In a particular type of computer, addresses are 24 bits.
   a) Calculate the number of locations which can be addressed.
   b) A unit of memory size gaining increasing popularity is the M unit. $1M = 2^{20} = 1048\,576$. Express the answer to part (a) in M units.
   c) Express the M unit in terms of the K unit introduced in the chapter.
4 Discuss the concept of a **module** in relation to the architecture of a processor.
5 Briefly distinguish between static and dynamic memory.
6 Draw a logic circuit to show how the zero (Z) condition code is determined from the output of the AMC logic circuits. The output carries 16 bits.
7 The integrated circuits which make up the processing and storage components of a computer can be made in several different ways. Popular types include **metal oxide semiconductor** (**MOS**), **transistor-transistor logic** (**TTL**) and **emitter coupled logic** (**ECL**). Write short notes on each of these types and their relative advantages and disadvantages.

10
Processor operation

This chapter describes the way in which a processor operates. The instructions which control the step-by-step working of a processor are introduced, and the sequence of actions needed to carry out one instruction is explained. Once again, the AMC is used as an example throughout the chapter. Some features of actual computers, which are not found in the AMC, are outlined at the end of the chapter.

This chapter relates closely to the previous chapter, which describes the structure of a processor. It extends the material presented in the previous chapter, and is essential to an understanding of several subsequent chapters, notably the following chapter, on advanced processor features, and a later chapter on assembly languages.

10.1 Machine Language

The instructions which control the step-by-step working of a processor are in a language called **machine language**. Machine language instructions are closely related to the architecture of a computer. There is one machine instruction for each operation performed directly by the hardware of the computer. Consequently, each type of computer has its own machine language.

The length and composition of machine language instructions vary considerably from one computer to another, but all have a few features in common. These include the following:

1 Machine instructions are in a binary code.
2 Machine instructions relate directly to various registers and functional units of the computer.
3 Every machine instruction includes an **operation code**. This specifies the type of operation to be carried out.
4 Some machine instructions refer to the main store of the computer. Ways of doing this are discussed in the next section.
5 All the instructions in the machine language of a computer make up the **instruction set** of the computer.

10.2 Addressing

As mentioned previously, some machine instructions refer to the main store of a computer. This is accomplished by specifying, in some manner, the **address** of the particular memory location. Addressing can be done in a number of ways, some of which are quite complex. Only the essential features of addressing are dealt with here.

10.3 The Number of Addresses

The number of addresses in a single machine instruction can vary. Computers can be classified according to the maximum number of addresses they permit in a machine instruction. One- and two-address computers are the most common, but three- and four-address computers have been constructed as well as zero-address computers, where the entire main store is regarded as a stack.

Examples of machine instructions with various numbers of addresses are given below. They are not taken from the instruction sets of any actual computer, and are written in English, rather than in machine code.

One-address instruction
ADD J   Add the number in memory location **J** to the number in the accumulator, and store the sum in the accumulator.

Two-address instruction

A D D J , K   Add the numbers in memory locations **J** and **K**, and store the sum in location **J**.

Three-address instruction

A D D J , K , L   Add the numbers in memory locations **J** and **K**, and store the sum in location **L**.

Zero-address instruction

A D D   Pop the top two numbers from the stack, add them together, and push the sum onto the stack.

It must be emphasised that the instruction set of a particular computer can contain more than one of the above types of instructions. A common combination in microcomputers is zero- and one-address instructions.

10.4 Addressing modes

Each address in a machine instruction may refer to a memory location in one of several different ways. These methods of addressing are called **addressing modes**. Part of the machine instruction is a specification of the addressing mode used.

Addressing modes vary between different types of computers. The following modes are, however, common to most types.

Absolute or direct address

This is the simplest address mode to understand. The number in the address part of the machine instruction is the number of the required location in the memory.

Indexed address

The number in the address part of the machine instruction is added to the contents of a register, called the **index register**, in order to obtain the address of the memory location. This mode is particularly useful when a set of data items is stored in consecutive memory locations. The machine instruction contains the address of the first element in the set, and the index register contains the number (or **offset**) of the particular element in the set.

Indirect address

The address in the machine instruction does not locate a data item, but the address of the data item. The latter address is used to locate the data item. In theory, this principle can be extended to several layers of indirect addresses, although this is not very common. Indirect addressing is particularly useful if data is structured into linked lists or trees. The address of the data item, which is located by the machine instruction, is sometimes called a **pointer** to the data item.

Relative address

The address in the machine instruction indicates the offset of the data item from the machine instruction, i.e. the address of the data item relative to the machine instruction. In order to locate the data item, the value of the program counter is added to the relative address (you will recall that the program counter stores the address of the current instruction). Relative addresses are used if a block of instructions and data must be moved from one place to another in the computer memory, without alteration to the addresses being needed. Such a block is called **relocatable code**. Addresses within it are valid wherever it is in memory.

Immediate operand

An immediate operand is a data item located in the address part of a machine instruction. In this case, the memory is not accessed at all. Immediate operands are a useful way of including constants in a program.

The above are the most common addressing modes, implemented on most types of computers. The phrases **address modification** or **address transformation** are used to describe indexed, indirect and relative addressing. Other, more complex, addressing modes may be formed by combining two or more of the above modes. An example is indexed indirect addressing. Such addressing modes are, however, beyond the scope of this course.

The reason for having these various addressing modes is that they enhance the power of a computer, and make it easier to program at machine language level. On the other hand, complex addressing modes mean that several memory cycles and passes through the addition unit are needed before the data item required by a machine instruction is obtained. This slows down the computer.

10.5   AMC Machine Language

The machine language of the AMC is now introduced, together with some examples

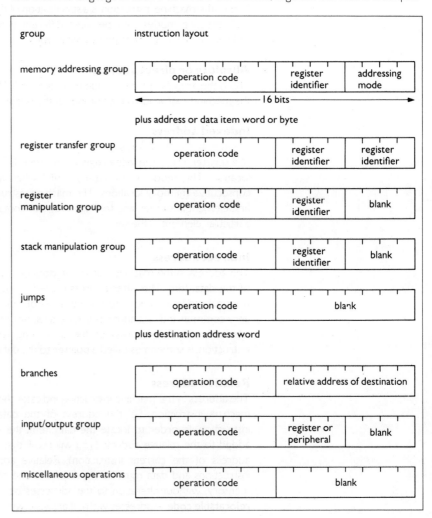

Figure 10.1
Bit layout of AMC machine instructions

of programs in machine language. The intention is to clarify the concepts introduced in the first part of this chapter.

10.6   General Features

The AMC is a one-address computer. In other words, instructions which refer to the main store contain at most one address. Addressing modes available are immediate operand, absolute, indirect and indexed.

AMC machine instructions occupy one word (16 bits), followed, in some cases, by a word containing an address, or a word or byte containing a data item. Hexadecimal notation is used to describe the instructions, being far more compact than binary. You will recall from Chapter 3 that one hexadecimal digit represents four bits. Thus four hexadecimal digits will describe an AMC instruction.

The AMC instruction set is divided into groups. All the instructions within a group perform similar operations. The first hexadecimal digit of the instruction identifies the group. The second hexadecimal digit of an AMC instruction identifies the operation within the group. Taken together, the first two hexadecimal digits of the machine instruction form the **operation code**. The interpretation of the remaining two hexadecimal digits in an instruction depends on its group.

Three of the AMC registers are under program control. They are the **accumulator**, **index register** and **stack pointer**. These registers are numbered 1, 2 and 3, respectively, in machine instructions. In most cases the third hexadecimal digit of the machine instruction identifies the register used. The fourth digit indicates the addressing mode.

Figure 10.1 shows the layout of the different groups of AMC instructions. The table in Figure 10.2 contains the complete AMC instruction set. You will notice how the instructions in a group perform similar operations, and have the same layout. Figure 10.2 also specifies the effect of each instruction on the condition codes. This is explained in more detail later.

Each group of instructions in the AMC instruction set is discussed in the next few sections.

10.7   Memory Addressing Group

All the instructions which refer to the AMC memory are in this group. You will notice that each operation can be applied to a word or a byte of data. An instruction in this group consists of an operation code, register identifier, and addressing mode, followed by an address word, or a data word or byte. Some examples are:

1312 423B	operation code **13**:	add word
	register identifier **1**:	accumulator
	addressing mode **2**:	absolute address
	address **423B**	

All this means: add the word (i.e. 16 bit number) at (absolute) address **423B** to the accumulator.

2234 17B5	operation code **22**:	store byte
	register identifier **3**:	stack pointer
	addressing mode **4**:	indexed
	address **17B5**	

This means: store the (least significant) byte from the stack pointer at memory address **17B5** plus contents of index register.

M	addressing mode:	1	immediate operand
		2	absolute address
		3	indirect address
		4	indexed address
R	register identifier:	1	accumulator
		2	index register
		3	stack pointer
P	peripheral device:	1	terminal
XX	relative address of destruction of branch		
	Effects on condition codes:	S	set (becomes 1)
		C	cleared (becomes 0)
		N	no effect
		D	conditional upon result
	condition codes:	Z	zero
		N	negative
		C	carry
		V	overflow

Figure 10.2
AMC instruction set

2 1 1 1 BB	operation code **2 1**:	load byte
	register identifier **1**:	accumulator
	addressing mode **1**:	immediate operand
	data item **BB**	

Because the addressing mode indicates an immediate operand, the instruction is followed by a data item, rather than an address. This instruction means: load the byte **BB** into the accumulator.

All the instructions in this group affect the Z (zero) and N (negative) condition codes. For example, if an addition results in a negative number, then Z becomes 0 and N becomes 1. Addition, subtraction and comparison operations affect the C (carry) and V (overflow) codes as well. The three logic operations clear these codes, while load and store operations leave them unchanged.

10.8 Register Transfer Group

The single instruction in this group copies the contents of one register into another register. For example:

3 1 2 3	operation code **3 1**:	move
	register identifiers **2**:	index register
	3:	stack pointer

This means: copy the contents of the index register into the stack pointer. This instruction affects the zero and negative condition codes, but does not alter the carry and overflow codes.

10.9 Register Manipulation Group

This group of instructions operates on the contents of one of the registers. The clear, increment, decrement and negate instructions are obvious enough, but a word or two of explanation is needed about the others.

The complement instruction forms the twos complement of the contents of the

machine instruction (hexadecimal)	interpretation	effect on condition codes			
		Z	N	C	V
memory addressing group					
11 RM	load data word to register	D	D	N	N
21 RM	load data byte to register	D	D	N	N
12 RM	store register word in memory	D	D	N	N
22 RM	store register byte in memory	D	D	N	N
13 RM	add data word to register	D	D	D	D
23 RM	add data byte to register	D	D	D	D
14 RM	add data word and carry bit to register	D	D	D	D
24 RM	add data byte and carry bit to register	D	D	D	D
15 RM	subtract data word from register	D	D	D	D
25 RM	subtract data byte from register	D	D	D	D
16 RM	subtract (data word plus carry bit) from register	D	D	D	D
26 RM	subtract (data byte plus carry bit) from register	D	D	D	D
17 RM	AND data word with register	D	D	C	C
27 RM	AND data byte with register	D	D	C	C
18 RM	OR data word with register	D	D	C	C
28 RM	OR data byte with register	D	D	C	C
19 RM	NEQ (exclusive OR) data word with register	D	D	C	C
29 RM	NEQ (exclusive OR) data byte with register	D	D	C	C
1ARM	compare register with data word	D	D	D	D
2ARM	compare register with data byte	D	D	D	D
register transfer group					
31 $R_1 R_2$	move word from register 1 to register 2	D	D	N	N
register manipulation group					
01 R0	clear register	S	C	C	C
02 R0	increment register (increase by 1)	D	D	D	D
03 R0	decrement register (decrease by 1)	D	D	D	D
04 R0	rotate register right, 1 bit, via carry bit	D	D	D	D
05 R0	rotate register left 1 bit, via carry bit	D	D	D	D
06 R0	arithmetic shift right, 1 bit	D	D	C	C
07 R0	arithmetic shift left, 1 bit	D	D	C	C
08 R0	complement register	D	D	D	D
09 R0	negate register (NOT operation)	D	D	C	C
stack manipulation group					
41 R0	push register word onto stack	D	D	N	N
42 R0	pop top of stack word to register	D	D	N	N
jumps					
51 00	unconditional jump to specified address	N	N	N	N
52 00	jump to subprogram, stack return address	N	N	N	N
branches					
61 XX	unconditional branch	N	N	N	N
62 XX	branch if zero (Z = 1)	N	N	N	N
63 XX	branch if non-zero (Z = 0)	N	N	N	N
64 XX	branch if greater than or equal to zero (Z = 1 or N = 0)	N	N	N	N
65 XX	branch if greater than zero (Z = 0 and N= 0)	N	N	N	N
66 XX	branch if less than or equal to zero (Z = 1 or N = 1)	N	N	N	N
67 XX	branch if less than zero (N = 1)	N	N	N	N
68 XX	branch if carry clear (C = 0)	N	N	N	N
69 XX	branch if carry set (C = 1)	N	N	N	N
6A XX	branch if overflow clear (V = 0)	N	N	N	N
6B XX	branch if overflow set (V = 1)	N	N	N	N
6C XX	branch if input not complete	N	N	N	N
6D XX	branch if output not complete	N	N	N	N
input/output group					
71 P0	signal peripheral device to load input register	N	N	N	N
72 R0	copy byte from input register to register R	D	D	N	N
73 P0	signal peripheral device to unload output register	N	N	N	N
74 R0	copy byte from register R to output register	D	D	N	N
miscellaneous operations					
31 00	set carry bit	N	N	S	N
82 00	clear carry bit	N	N	C	N
83 00	return from subprogram (unstack return adddress)	N	N	N	N
84 00	no-operation	N	N	N	N
85 00	halt	N	N	N	N

Figure 10.2
(continued)

register. As explained in Chapter 3, this is done by negating the bits and then adding 1.

The rotate operations include the carry bit, and are best explained by means of a diagram. See Figure 10.3.

The arithmetic shift operations preserve the most significant bit of the word (the sign bit) and shift the rest. The arithmetic shift left has the effect of multiplying by 2,

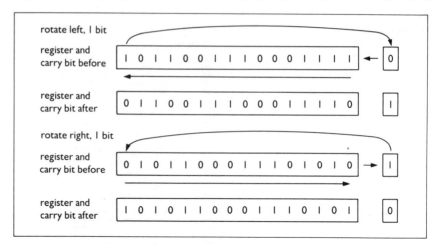

Figure 10.3
Rotate instructions

and the arithmetic shift right has the effect of dividing by 2. In the latter case the sign bit is copied into the next position. These operations are illustrated in Figure 10.4.

An example of a machine instruction in this group is:

0320   operation code **03**:   decrement
                           register identifier **2**:   index register

This means: decrease contents of index register by 1. All the instructions in this group affect all the condition codes.

10.10 Branches

The branches and input/output groups of instructions are discussed next, as they enable a complete example program to be given in the following section.

The branching instructions transfer control to another part of the program, using relative addressing. The first instruction in the set is an unconditional branch, the remaining 13 transfer control depending on the value of one or more condition codes. These enable a branch to be made depending on the outcome of some previous operation.

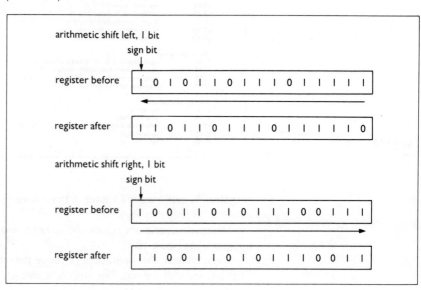

Figure 10.4
Arithmetic shift instructions

For example, suppose that a branch has to be made if two numbers are equal. One number is loaded into the accumulator, and compared with the other. The compare operation in the memory addressing group is used. It subtracts the numbers, sets the condition codes depending on the result, but does not retain the result. If the numbers are equal, the difference is zero, and the Z code is set to 1. The branch if zero instruction is then used.

The address of the destination of the branch is contained in the second byte of the instruction word. This byte is interpreted as a twos complement integer, and can thus have a value in the range -128 to 127. This limits the range of the branches, which are sometimes called 'short' branches. This address is relative to the current value of the program counter. By the time the branch instruction is executed, the program counter has been reset to contain the address of the next instruction. Thus the destination of the branch is the address of the next instruction plus the relative address contained in the branching instruction.

For example:

678A   operation code **67**: branch if less than zero
relative address **8A**: 138 in base ten

If this instruction is at address 0049 ($= 73$ in base ten), then the program counter contains 004B ($= 75$ in base ten), the address of the next instruction. The destination address of the branch is $138 + 75 = 213$ in base ten, or 00D5 in hexadecimal. Accordingly, if condition code $N = 1$ (i.e. less than zero), control will be transferred to the instruction at address 00D5. If $N = 0$, control passes to the next instruction, at address 004B.

The reason for having this rather awkward addressing mode in branching instructions is to save memory space. Instructions of this type occupy only one word, whereas a jump to an absolute address occupies two words. Although these instructions depend on values of various condition codes, they do not alter these values in any way.

10.11 Input/Output Group

The input/output instructions control the transfer of data between the AMC processor and peripheral devices. Two branching instructions are also concerned with input/output.

Communication between the AMC processor and peripheral devices is via input and output registers, each with a capacity of one byte. In other words, all input and output is done one character at a time.

An example of the sequence of instructions to input a character is given below:

7110   operation code **71**: input request
peripheral device **1**: terminal
This instruction requests the terminal to load a character into the input register.

6CFE   operation code **6C**: branch if input not complete
relative address **FE** $= -2$ in base ten.
This instruction branches back to itself until the character has been loaded.

7210   operation code **72**: copy character from input register
register identifier **1**: accumulator
This instruction copies the character from the input register to the accumulator.

You will now realise how much effort is needed for the input of a single character. The second instruction causes the processor to wait until the input has taken place. Although it is very inefficient, it is one way of synchronising a processor with a slower peripheral device.

The instructions in this group which relate to peripheral devices have no effect on condition codes. The instructions which move data to or from input/output registers affect the zero and negative condition codes.

10.12   Example Program 10.1

Sufficient AMC machine instructions have now been introduced for a complete example program to be presented. Although it is simple, and fairly short, it illustrates a number of important techniques of machine language programming.

The objective of this program is to input a sequence of characters and store them in consecutive memory locations. The end of the input is marked by a special character, with hexadecimal code FF. The address of the memory location to contain the first character is known when the program is written.

The program uses the technique of indirect addressing. The address of the first character is loaded into a convenient memory location. A character is input, and compared with the end-of-input marker. If the character is not the marker, it is stored at the address specified in the memory location, using indirect addressing. This address is then increased by 1, and the next character is input. When the end-of-input marker is found, the program ends. For convenience, the program is written starting at address 0000.

Program

Address	Instruction		Comments
0000	001F		Address of first character, later of current character.
0002	7110		Signal terminal to load character into input register.
0004	6CFE		Branch back to this instruction if input not complete.
0006	7210		Copy character from input register to accumulator.
0008	2A11	FF	Compare character with end-of-input marker.
000B	6210		Branch if equal, to address 001D.
000D	2213	0000	Store character at address in location 0000.
0011	1112	0000	Load address of current character to accumulator.
0015	0210		Increase contents of accumulator by 1.
0017	1212	0000	Store address of next character in location 0000.
001B	61E5		Branch to address 0002, to input next character.
001D	8500		Halt.
001F			First character.

Points to notice

Location **0000** initially contains the address of the first character, namely **001F**. After each character has been input, the contents of this location is increased by 1. In this way, characters are stored in consecutive memory locations.

The first program instruction is at address **0002**, the previous word is used for data.

Program instructions occupy 2, 3 or 4 store locations. The length of an instruction determines the address of the next instruction.

The relative address in the first branching instruction is **FE** (= −2 in base ten).

This instruction has the effect of branching back to itself repeatedly, until a character has been input. In this way, the processor 'waits' for the terminal.

Three different addressing modes are used in this program. They are immediate operand (at address **000B**), indirect address (at address **000D**) and absolute address (at addresses **0011** and **0017**).

The characters are stored immediately after the program. If a different memory area is required for them, all that needs to be changed is the address in location **0000**.

The portion of program from address **0002** to address **001B** is repeated, one for each input character. A portion of a program which is repeated is called a **loop**.

Notice how the relative addresses in branching instructions are the difference between their destination addresses and the addresses of the following instructions.

10.13 Further AMC Machine Instructions

The remaining groups of AMC machine instructions are introduced in the next few sections.

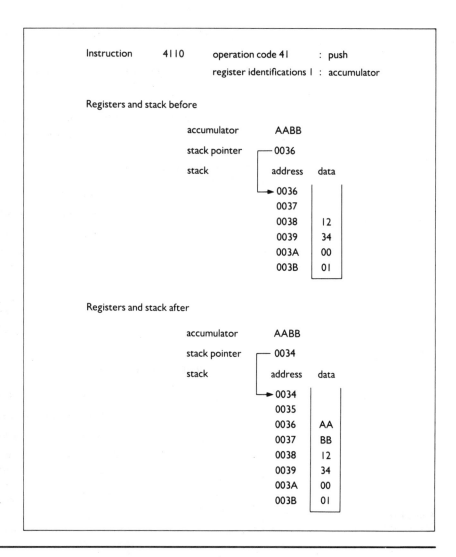

Figure 10.5
The push instruction

10.14 Stack Manipulation Group

The two instructions in this group implement the push and pop operations introduced in Chapter 4.

Any part of the AMC memory may be used for the stack. Early in a program, the stack pointer is loaded with the address of the stack base. During the program it points to the next available space above the stack top. The stack grows 'upwards' in the memory, from high addresses to low addresses. Stack elements are words, occupying two memory locations.

The **push** operation involves the following steps:

1 The data item is copied from the register specified in the push instruction, into the two memory locations addressed by the stack pointer.
2 The contents of the stack pointer is reduced by 2, so that it again contains the address of the memory location into which the next stack element is to be pushed.

Figure 10.5 contains an example of the push instruction.

The **pop** operation contains the following steps:

1 The contents of the stack pointer is increased by 2. It now addresses the top element of the stack.
2 The word addressed by the stack pointer is copied into the register specified in the pop instruction.

Figure 10.6 contains an example of the pop instruction.

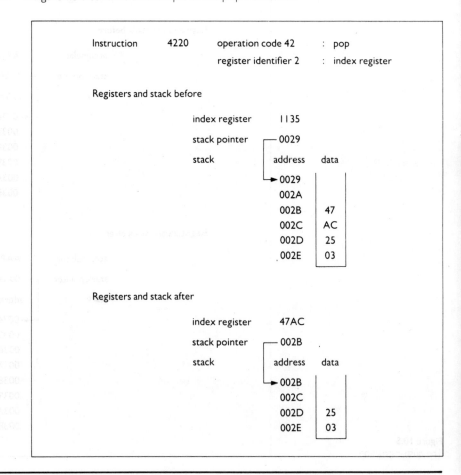

| Instruction | 4220 | operation code 42 | : pop |
| | | register identifier 2 | : index register |

Registers and stack before

index register	1135
stack pointer	0029
stack	address	data
	0029	
	002A	
	002B	47
	002C	AC
	002D	25
	002E	03

Registers and stack after

index register	47AC
stack pointer	002B
stack	address	data
	002B	
	002C	
	002D	25
	002E	03

Figure 10.6
The pop instruction

10.15 Jumps and Subprogram Calls

The two instructions in this group transfer control to another part of the program. Unlike the branching instructions, these instructions are followed by the (absolute) address of the destination of the jump, in a separate word. For example:

5100 341A operation code **51**: jump
destination address **341A**

This instruction transfers control to the instruction at address 341A. Because a complete word is used for the destination address, any location in the AMC memory can be reached.

The second instruction in this group introduces the idea of a **subprogram**. A subprogram is a set of instructions, carrying out a specific task, which is called from any other part of the program. When the subprogram is complete, control returns to the point in the program from which the subprogram was called. Figure 10.7 illustrates the idea of a subprogram.

From a machine language point of view, the problem with subprograms is how to remember the address to which control returns after the subprogram is complete. In the AMC, and in many other modern computers, this problem is solved by means of the system stack.

When a jump to subprogram instruction is executed, the program computer contains the address of the next instruction (it has already been reset). This is the required return address. It is loaded onto the stack, and the stack pointer is updated. Control then passes to the subprogram, by loading the destination address of the jump to subprogram instruction into the program counter.

The last instruction in the subprogram is a return instruction. Although it is in the miscellaneous instructions group, it is discussed here. This instruction causes the return address to be popped from the stack to the program counter. Control thus returns to the instruction following the jump to subprogram instruction. Although the stack may be used by the subprogram, it is important that the return address is at the top of the stack when the subprogram ends.

Dealing with return addresses in this way means that subprograms may contain

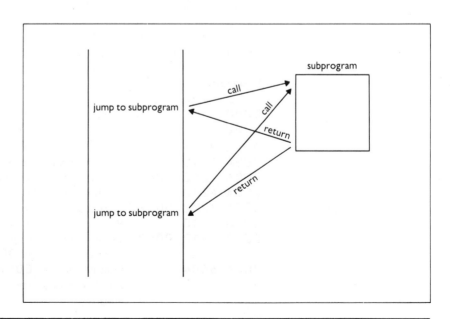

Figure 10.7
Calls to and returns from a subprogram

calls to other subprograms, or even calls to themselves, a technique known as **recursion**. The use of the stack ensures that control returns in the reverse order to that of the subprogram calls.

10.16   Miscellaneous Instructions

The remaining few AMC machine instructions are grouped together in the miscellaneous instructions group. Only the operation code part of the instruction word is used.

Apart from the return from subprogram instruction, which is discussed in the previous section, the only instruction which deserves special mention is the no-operation instruction. This causes the AMC processor to 'idle'. It may be used to slow down a program, to synchronise the processor with a peripheral device, or to reserve space in a program so that other instructions can be inserted later.

10.17   The AMC Instruction Set Reviewed

A few general points about the AMC instruction set can usefully be made here.

Although the AMC is a simplified model computer, its instructions are fairly typical of the type of operations carried out at machine level by a wide range of computers. Studying programs in AMC machine language should give a 'feel' for programming at this level. It should become evident how painstaking such programs are, and how every last detail must be taken care of. This part of the chapter concludes with another example program in AMC machine language.

10.18   Example Program 10.2

This program illustrates the use of a subprogram, and shows how information can be passed to and from a subprogram by means of the stack.

The purpose of the subprogram is to decide which of two given numbers is larger. The numbers are passed to the subprogram on the stack, and the larger number is returned on the stack.

You will recall that the return address is placed on the stack when the subprogram is called. This address must be stored in the memory during the running of the subprogram, as the numbers are beneath it on the stack. Just before the subprogram ends, the return address is again placed on the stack.

Program

Address	Instruction		Comments
0000			Temporary storage for return address.
0002			Temporary storage for one number.
Start of subprogram			
0004	4210		Pop return address to accumulator.
0006	1212	0000	Store return address in location **0000**.
000A	4210		Pop first number to accumulator.
000C	1212	0002	Store first number in location **0002**.
0010	4210		Pop second number to accumulator.
0012	1A12	0002	Compare second number (in accumulator) with first number (in location **0002**).
0016	6404		Branch to address **001C** if greater than or equal to zero (i.e. second number is larger, or numbers are equal).

```
0018  1112  0002    Load first number to accumulator.
001C  4110          Stack larger number.
001E  1112  0000    Load return address to accumulator.
0022  4110          Stack return address.
0024  8300          Return from subprogram.
```

End of subprogram, start of main program

```
0026  1131  007F    Initialise stack pointer (to 007F).
002A  1111  4135    Load second number (4135) to accumulator.
002E  4110          Stack second number.
0030  1111  62A4    Load first number (62A4) to accumulator.
0034  4110          Stack first number.
0036  5200  0004    Jump to subprogram.
003A  4210          Pop larger number to accumulator on return.
003C  8500          Halt.
```

Points to notice

The return address is stored in location **0000** for the duration of the subprogram.

In the main program, the numbers are stacked in reverse order. The last number pushed onto the stack is the first number popped from the stack in the subprogram.

10.19   The Instruction Cycle

Two aspects of the hardware of a processor have so far been introduced, namely the register layout and machine instructions. To complete the picture of a computer at this level, the sequence of actions required to carry out one machine instruction is now outlined. This sequence is called the **instruction cycle**.

The instruction cycle of a computer depends on its register architecture and the nature of its machine instructions. Consequently, the actions carried out for a machine instruction vary from computer to computer. Nevertheless, the overall pattern is much the same in all cases. The overall pattern of the instruction cycle is discussed below. A more detailed discussion follows, once again using the AMC as an example.

10.20   The Overall Pattern of an Instruction Cycle

Whatever the machine instruction, the sequence of actions required to carry it out follows the same overall pattern in all computers. The overall stages are outlined below.

Fetch

The first action is to fetch the machine instruction from the memory. The program counter contains the address of the instruction. This address is used to locate the instruction. If the instruction occupies more than one memory location, several memory cycles are needed to fetch it. The instruction is loaded into the instruction register.

Reset

As soon as the current instruction has been fetched, the contents of the program counter is updated so that it contains the address of the next program instruction. The amount by which it must be increased depends on the length of the current instruction.

Locate operand

If the instruction contains an address, or an immediate operand, the data item, or **operand**, referred to by the instruction must be located. Details of the way this is done depend on the addressing mode of the instruction. Apart from the immediate operand mode, all modes require at least one access to the memory. The number of memory locations occupied by the operand also influences the number of memory cycles required.

Execute

The operation required by the machine instruction is carried out. In most cases, one or more registers are involved, as well as the operand from memory. The arithmetic and logic unit generally carries out the process involved. Condition codes are generally set or cleared according to the result of the operation.

Store

If a store operation is required, this is the point in the cycle at which it is done. Furthermore, in many computers, if a data item has been read from memory, it is written back into the same locations at this point. This is always the case with computers having ferrite core memories, as the memory locations are cleared when the data item is read.

Some general points about the instruction cycle

You will notice that an instruction cycle involves at least one memory cycle, to locate the instruction itself. If a long data item is used, located by means of a modified address, several more memory cycles are involved. The speed of a memory cycle, and the number of memory cycles per instruction cycle, are important factors in determining the duration of an instruction cycle.

The steps of an instruction cycle are controlled, partly by the timing circuits of the computer, and partly by outputs from the instruction decoder. Another important way of controlling these steps is mentioned in Section 10.24.

The duration of an instruction cycle varies from one type of computer to another, and also depends on the particular machine instruction. This duration is typically from 10 microseconds (μs) to 100 nanoseconds (ns), over the range of computers currently in operation (1 μs = 1 millionth of a second, 1 ns = 1 thousand millionth of a second).

10.21   The AMC Instruction Cycle

Figure 10.8 shows the AMC instruction cycle. It must be studied in conjunction with the AMC register layout, Figure 9.7. The flow of instructions, addresses and data items between the main store and various registers can be followed.

Below are a few general points about the AMC instruction cycle:

1 The fetch and reset phases are combined. The program counter (PC) is updated more than once if the instruction comprises more than one word.
2 The locate operand phase results in the operand in the memory data register (MDR), no matter what addressing mode is in the instruction.
3 Accordingly, execution of the operation only involves the memory data register, and one of the program-controlled registers (accumulator, index register or stack pointer).
4 The last part of the cycle is only carried out if a store word or a store byte instruction is being executed.

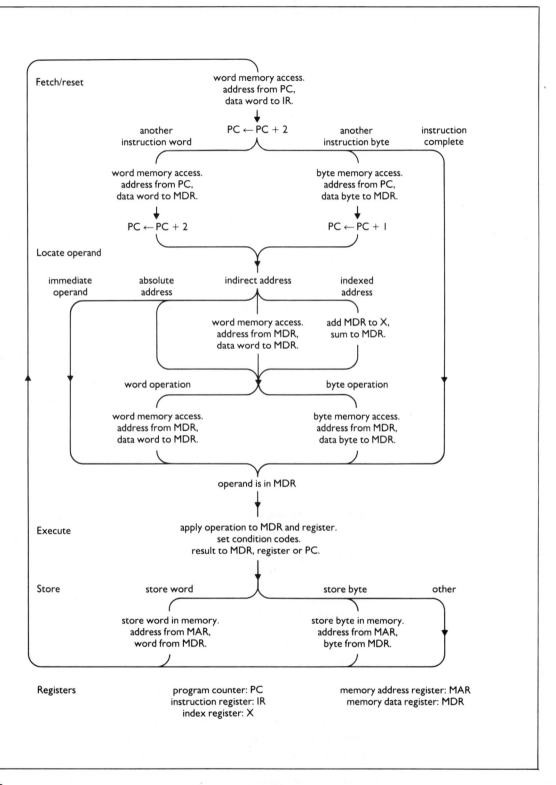

Figure 10.8
The AMC instruction cycle

10.22   Other Features of Processor Operation

A very brief mention must be made of two features of processor operation which have been excluded from the AMC in order to keep it simple. These features are **interrupts** and **microcode**.

10.23   Interrupts

At the beginning of this book, it was mentioned that modern computers are seldom controlled by one program. Rather, they are controlled by a hierarchy of programs. At the top of the hierarchy is a program called an operating system, which forms the subject of a later chapter.

In order for control to be transferred from one of these programs to another, it is necessary to provide a mechanism whereby the running of a particular program can be **interrupted**. An interrupt is an external event or signal which causes the running of a program to be suspended. This interrupt signal is generally placed on one or more **interrupt lines**, which are part of the bus connecting the processor to peripheral devices.

When an interrupt occurs, the current contents of all the registers are saved and control passes to an **interrupt service routine**, generally part of the operating system. The interrupt service routine determines the source of the interrupt, generally by examining a number of **flags**, and transfers control to a routine to handle the particular type of interrupt which has occurred. At a later stage, running of the interrupted program is resumed, from the point at which it was interrupted. This is achieved by restoring the values of all the registers which were saved when the interrupt occurred.

Common causes of interrupts include the input or output of data, the detection of an error in a program, or the fact that a program has exceeded the time allocated to it. The instruction sets of most computers include instructions which **disable** interrupts, effectively switching them off, and **enable** interrupts, switching them on.

10.24   Microcode

In the AMC, and a number of actual computers, the step-by-step control of each instruction cycle is carried out directly by the instruction decoder and the timing circuits of the control unit. Such computers are said to have **hard-wired** control.

In contrast to this method of control, many other computers have another level of instructions, beneath that of machine language. These are **micro-instructions** or **microcode**. Micro-instructions are stored in a special read-only memory known as the **control memory**, and control the detailed steps of each machine instruction. Each machine instruction accesses a set of micro-instructions, which control the opening and closing of various control switches as the machine instruction is carried out.

There are several advantages of microcode. One is that the instruction set of a computer does not have to be 'frozen'. Changes at microcode level enable different instruction sets to be used. In this way one type of computer can be made to **emulate** another type of computer, by adopting its machine code. Another advantage is cost. Control circuits of microcoded computers are generally simpler, and therefore cheaper, than those of hard-wired computers.

The major disadvantage of the use of microcode is speed. Microcoded computers are generally slower than hard-wired computers with similar instruction sets.

10.25 Conclusion

This somewhat lengthy chapter has shown, in a fair amount of detail, the way in which the processor of a computer operates. Here are the main points of the chapter again:

- The program language which controls the step-by-step working of a computer is called machine language.
- Machine language instructions refer directly to the hardware of the computer.
- All machine instructions include an operation code, which specifies the type of operation to be carried out.
- Some machine instructions refer to the main store of the computer. Data is located by specifying the address of the required store location.
- A number of different addressing techniques are in common use. Some require a considerable amount of address transformation before the data item, or operand, is located.
- In some computers, machine instructions may contain more than one address.
- The AMC is a one-address computer. AMC machine instructions occupy one word, sometimes followed by a word containing an address, or a word or byte containing an operand.
- AMC machine instructions are divided into groups. The instructions in each group have the same bit layout, and perform similar operations. The operation codes of instructions in the same group have the same initial hexadecimal digit.
- The sequence of actions required to carry out one machine instruction is called an instruction cycle.
- Instruction cycles include fetch, reset, locate operand, execute and store phases.
- All computers have a mechanism to enable the running of a program to be interrupted by some external signal.
- Two ways of controlling the steps of an instruction cycle are hard-wired control, and micro-instructions.

Taken together, this and the previous chapter describe what might be called a traditional computer architecture. A distinguishing feature of this type of architecture, which you may have already noticed, is that only one step takes place at a time. This severely limits the speed and processing power of the computer.

The next chapter introduces some advanced processor features. Most of these are ways of permitting various operations inside a processor to take place in parallel.

Exercise 10

1 Briefly define the following terms: machine language; operation code; instruction set; addressing mode; offset; pointer; address modification; subprogram; recursion; instruction cycle; interrupt; micro-instruction; hard-wired control; emulate; loop.

2 Describe one use for each type of addressing mode mentioned in this chapter.

3 Consider the following three locations of AMC main store:

Address	Contents	
2A61	1113	49B6
3521	AB02	
49B6	3521	

State clearly the result of carrying out the instructions in location 2A61.

4 For each of the following numbers: 16, 56, −128
   a) Express the number as a 16 bit two complement integer.
   b) Apply the operation **arithmetic shift left** to the 16 bit integer, and convert the result to a decimal number.

c) Apply the operation **arithmetic shift right** to the 16 bit integer, and convert the result to a decimal number.

Comment on your findings.

5 Calculate the destination addresses (in hexadecimal) of these AMC branching instructions:

Address	Instruction
0024	6120
0120	61E4

6 Show the contents of the AMC stack after the following sequence of instructions:

Address	Instruction	Comments
0100	1131 0200	Initialise stack pointer (to **0200**).
0104	1111 AABB	Load **AABB** to accumulator.
0108	4110	Push contents of accumulator to stack.
010A	1111 CCDD	Load **CCDD** to accumulator.
010E	4110	Push contents of accumulator to stack.

Also write down the value of the stack pointer after the instructions.

7 If the byte **80** (hexadecimal) is copied into a sixteen bit AMC register, the contents of the register is **FF80** (hexadecimal). Explain why this is so (convert both of the above quantities, regarded as twos complement integers, via binary to decimal to assist your explanation).

8 The program shown below, written in AMC machine language, is designed to add up the corresponding numbers in two arrays, and store the results in a third array. In other words, the first number in the third array is the sum of the first number in the first array, and the first number in the second array.

In the program, each number occupies one word, i.e. two storage locations, and each array contains four numbers. The length of each array is thus eight bytes.

The index register serves a dual purpose. It is used to locate array elements via the indexed addressing mode, and also to count the number of additions which have been made. Processing starts at the back of the arrays, working towards the front. Because the numbers occupy two storage locations, the index is decreased by two for each addition.

The part of the program which adds together two array elements is repeated four times. Such a portion of a program is called a **loop**.

Program

Address	Instruction	Comments
0000	08	Length of arrays, 8 bytes or 4 words.
0001		Array 1, assumed
to 0008		already loaded.
0009		Array 2, assumed
to 0010		already loaded.
0011		Array 3
to 0018		

Start of program

| 0019 | 2122 0000 | |

Start of loop to add each pair of numbers

001D	0320	
001F	0320	
0021	670E	
0023	1114 0001	
0027	1314 0009	
002B	1214 0011	
002F	61EC	

End of loop

| 0031 | 8500 | |

a) Copy down the program, and write an appropriate comment next to each instruction. The comment must state clearly, in a few words, precisely what the instruction does.
b) What is the value of the index register at the end of the program?
c) Will the program instructions need to be altered if arrays of a different length are to be added? If so, what changes must be made?

d) Replace one instruction in the program, so that array elements are subtracted rather than added.

You will see in a later chapter that some computers have a single machine instruction to add corresponding elements of two arrays.

9 Write a program in AMC machine language to output a set of characters, stored in consecutive memory locations. The character with hexadecimal code 7E is used to mark the end of the set. The memory area used to store the characters can be immediately after the output program. Next to each machine instruction write a comment which explains clearly what the instruction does.

10 The following extract is taken from the manufacturer's literature accompanying a popular range of minicomputers. Read the extract carefully and then answer the questions.

MAJOR REGISTERS
Accumulator (AC)
The AC is a 12-bit register in which arithmetic and logic operations are performed. Under
5 program control the AC can be cleared or complemented or its contents can be rotated right or left. The contents of the Memory Buffer Register can be added to the contents of the AC (via the adder circuit), and the result stored in the AC. The contents of both of these registers can be combined by the logical AND operation with the result remaining in the AC. The inclusive OR may be performed between the AC and the switch register (on the
10 programmer's console), and the result left in the AC. The AC also serves as an input/output register; all programmed information transfers between the core memory and an I/O device are passed through the AC to data lines located on the (input/output) bus line.

Program Counter (PC)
15 The PC is a 12-bit register that is used to control the program sequence; that is, the order in which instructions are performed is determined by the PC. The PC contains the address of the core memory location from which the next instruction is taken. Information enters the PC from the core memory via the memory buffer register and from the memory address register. Information in the PC is transferred into the memory address register to determine
20 the core memory address from which each instruction is taken.

Memory Address Register (MAR)
The MAR is a 12-bit register that contains the address in core memory that is currently selected for reading or writing. All of core memory can be directly addressed by the MAR.
25 Data can be transferred into the MAR from the memory buffer register, from the program counter and from the switch register on the operator's console.

Memory Buffer Register (MBR)
The MBR is a 12-bit register that is used for all information transfers between the central
30 processor registers and the core memory. Information can be transferred and temporarily held in the MBR from the AC or the PC . . .

i) What is the difference between an arithmetic operation and a logic operation (line 3)?
ii) The program counter receives information from core memory or from the MAR (lines 21, 22). Under what circumstances will the PC be loaded from each of these two sources? How else would the PC contents normally be altered?
iii) The MAR can receive data from the switch register (line 31). How could this facility be of use?
iv) Draw a diagram of the registers described above, showing the flow of data between them.
v) Describe how an indirectly-addressed unconditional transfer of control makes use of the registers described above.

UL 78 l

11 Figure 10.9 includes five of the registers found in the central processor of a computer. Explain the function of each of the named registers:

i) AC: Accumulator,
ii) SCR: Sequence control register,
iii) SAR: Store address register,
iv) SDR: Store data register,
v) IR: Instruction register.

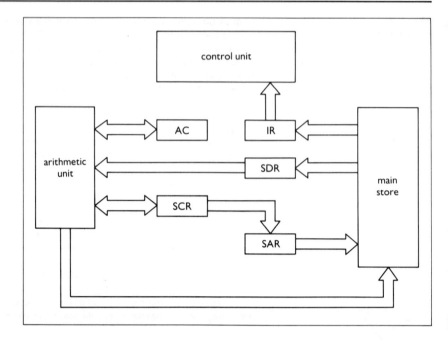

Figure 10.9

Describe how these registers are used in the execution of the 'fetch-cycle' when an instruction is retrieved from store.

In principle, it is necessary to have information about *four* storage addresses, in order to execute an add instruction:

   i) and ii) the addresses of the two operands,
  iii) the address where the result is to be placed,
  iv) the address from which the next instruction is to be taken.

Explain how the registers in Figure 10.9 above, and a re-organisation of the computation, enable addition of two numbers to be carried out in a computer that can only hold *one* address in each instruction word.

UL 80 I

11
Advanced processor features

The principles of the design of digital electronic computers were first set out in 1946, by John von Neumann. These principles lead to a computer architecture like that described in the previous two chapters. A great many computers have been built in accordance with these principles, and no doubt many more will be built in the future.

The advantages of the 'traditional' von Neumann design are its simplicity and versatility. The major disadvantage is that only one action is performed, inside a processor, at any one moment. By and large, advanced processor features are attempts to introduce a measure of **parallelism** into the design of computers. Parallelism means that several actions can be performed simultaneously within a processor.

This chapter briefly examines a number of advanced processor features. Each is an attempt to enhance the processing power of a computer in some way. Some are only suitable for special-purpose computing, particularly scientific computing. Others are suitable for computers of all types. The features are discussed in broad outline only, as the details of some of them are extremely complicated.

11.1 Duplicate Processing Circuits

The most obvious way to achieve a measure of parallelism is to duplicate some of the processing circuits in a processor. A common example is a simple addition unit which resets the value of the program counter while an instruction is being executed. In a few computers, the entire mechanism which deals with the address part of an instruction is separate from the circuits which execute the instruction. This involves a considerable amount of duplication.

11.2 Distributed Array Processing

In scientific computing, the situation is frequently encountered where large arrays of data items must be processed. The operations carried out on each element of an array are identical.

In such situations, a considerable amount of time can be saved by carrying out the operations on all the elements of an array simultaneously. This can be done by a computer with a large number of arithmetic and logic units, and circuits which can supply the required data to each ALU at the same time, and similarly deal with the outputs from all the ALUs. This kind of processing is called **distributed array processing**.

The problem with distributed array processing is to ensure that the processing power of the computer is used effectively. Sophisticated programming techniques are required if this is to be achieved.

11.3 Direct Memory Access

One of the slowest aspects of the operation of a computer is the transfer of data between processing units and peripheral devices. In a conventional computer, such as the AMC, all the steps of such transfers are controlled directly by the program. This often involves 'idling' a processor while a peripheral device completes the transfer of a data item.

Several techniques have evolved to deal with this problem. The most common is **autonomous peripheral operation**, with the peripheral having direct access to the main store of the processor. This technique is also known as **direct memory access** or **DMA**. It requires hardware known as **DMA controllers**.

Data is input or output under DMA, not as individual characters, but in blocks of characters. The DMA controller is supplied with the start address of the data in main store, and the number of characters to be transferred. The controller then proceeds independently of the processor, until the transfer of the data is complete.

Memory cycles are 'stolen' from the processor whenever they are required by the DMA controller. Because the processor works much faster than the peripheral which governs the speed of the DMA controller, this does not slow the processor down very much. A further development, which eliminates the need for cycle stealing, is the **multi-port** memory. This enables several data items to be stored or accessed simultaneously through a number of ports.

11.4 Pipelining

The feature which has probably contributed the most towards improving the performance of a processor is a technique known as **pipelining**. Pipelining is widely used, even among fairly small computers.

Pipelining can be used whenever an operation can be expressed as a sequence of actions. A functional unit is constructed for each action. These are connected by storage areas, or **buffers**, which hold the items as they pass through the pipeline. Figure 11.1 shows the general idea of a pipeline.

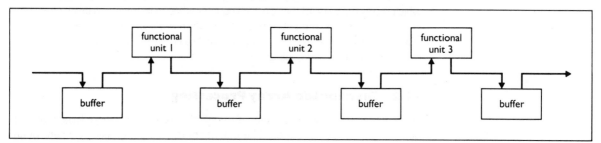

Figure 11.1
A pipeline

A fundamental requirement of a pipeline is that each action takes the same length of time. During this time interval, called a **beat**, each item in the pipeline moves from a buffer, through a functional unit, into the next buffer. At any one time, a number of items are at different stages of processing, each only one beat behind the previous item.

Another fundamental requirement of a pipeline is that each stage of the process is independent of all the other stages. This means that separate functional circuits can be constructed for each stage, and items are not held up at any stage because information from some other stage is not available. This requirement of independence of stages is not always met in practice, and causes considerable problems in the design and operation of pipelines.

The concept of pipelining is implemented in two ways in computers. These are **instruction pipelines** and **arithmetic pipelines**. In an instruction pipeline, each functional unit carries out one stage of the instruction cycle of the computer. Items moving through the pipeline are instructions. Each instruction is only one beat behind the previous instruction.

Problems arise when the results from one instruction are needed by the next instruction, and when a branching instruction is encountered. Details of the way in which these problems are dealt with are beyond the scope of this course.

An arithmetic pipeline is especially useful when dealing with floating point numbers, and for multiplication of all types of numbers. In this case items in the pipeline are numbers, and each functional unit carries out one step of the calculation.

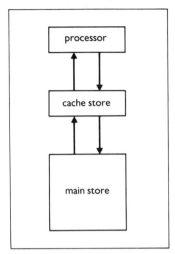

Figure 11.2
A cache store

11.5 Cache Stores

One of the slowest activities taking place within a processor is access to memory. As a memory access can occur a number of times during one instruction cycle, the speed of memory access is a major factor in determining the speed of the processor.

One way of improving the speed of memory access is to use a **cache store**, also known as a **slave store**. This is a small store, with a very fast access time, situated between the main store and the rest of the processor. See Figure 11.2.

The use of the cache store is based on the assumption that, for most of the time, processing requires data and instructions close to each other in main store. Areas of main store surrounding the current machine instruction and data item are loaded into the cache store. This is generally done independently of the operation of the processor, at the maximum speed of the main store. Data and instructions required by the processor are then accessed from the cache store. From time to time the processor is slowed down when an item it requires is not in the cache store. A cache store is frequently used in conjunction with an instruction pipeline.

11.6 Content-addressable Memory

The fundamental principle of the operation of a computer memory is that an address is used to locate a data item. However, for certain operations it is very useful to have a portion of store which works the other way round – a data item is used to locate an address. A portion of store which works in this way is called a **content-addressable memory**, or **associative store**.

The most common application for a content-addressable memory is looking up an item of data in a table. What is required is the position of the item in the table. The table is loaded into content-addressable memory, and the data item is compared, simultaneously, with all the entries. The address of the location at which a match is found is returned. This process is illustrated in Figure 11.3.

It must be emphasised that only a small portion of the store of a computer can be content-addressable memory. This portion is almost always part of a cache store, as described in the previous section.

11.7 Network Architecture

One of the latest developments in computer architecture is the idea of combining several processors to form a network. The intention is that each processor is a simple, cheap microprocessor, but the network as a whole has considerable power. The problem with this concept, which is currently the subject of intensive research, is the overall control of the system, and the regulation of the flow of data between the processors.

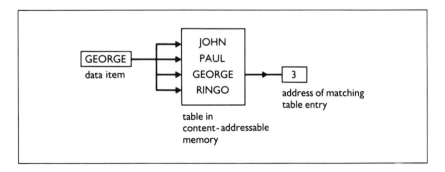

Figure 11.3
A content-addressable memory

One promising implementation of a network architecture is the concept of a data **ring**. A number of processors and peripherals are connected to the ring, which is the central data path of the system. This is discussed in more detail in Chapter 25.

11.8 Conclusion

This chapter has shown, in a very brief survey, some of the ways in which computer architecture is evolving away from the traditional 'one step at a time' concept. Some of the ideas presented, such as pipelining and cache stores, are fairly well established, while others, such as distributed array processing and network architecture, are relatively recent. In all cases, the motivation for these new developments is the same, namely faster, more powerful and more versatile computer systems at a lower cost.

Exercise 11

1 Briefly define each of the following terms: parallelism; distributed array processing; direct memory access; DMA controller; multi-port memory; pipelining; cache store; content-addressable memory; network architecture.

2 The overall steps of the AMC instruction cycle are fetch, locate operand, execute and store. Briefly describe how an instruction pipeline could be used to implement these steps, and some of the problems which would be encountered.

3 A particular computer has an instruction cache with a capacity of 256 instructions. Explain the benefits of this facility when executing program loops of less than 256 instructions.

4 A multiplication pipeline has a beat time of 10 μs, and contains 32 stages.
   a) How long does it take for one complete multiplication operation?
   b) How long does it take for 32 multiplication operations?
   c) How long does it take for *n* multiplication operations?

5 To what extent, if at all, do the advanced CPU features in this chapter alter the concept of a computer, discussed in Chapter 1?

6 Example program 10.1 can be generalised to input data from any peripheral device, to AMC main store. Assume that it is used to read data from a disc drive, and the speed of the disc drive is such that the instruction at address **0004** must be executed 10 times per data item.
   a) Count the number of memory cycles per data item transferred.
   b) Use this figure to estimate the number of memory cycles needed to transfer 1K of data from the disc drive.
   c) If a DMA controller requires 32 memory cycles to set up, and thereafter steals one memory cycle per data item, calculate the number of memory cycles needed for 1K of data.
   d) Comment on your results from parts (b) and (c).

12
Peripheral devices

This chapter is a brief investigation of the variety of peripheral devices which, together with one or more processors, make-up the hardware of a computer system. Some general points about the objectives of peripherals are first made. There follows a very brief description of the essential features of a number of popular peripherals. The chapter concludes with a section on the way in which peripherals are linked to, and controlled by, processing units.

Detailed information about the working of various peripheral devices is deliberately avoided in this chapter, for a number of reasons. The two most significant reasons are that such details are not relevant to a course of this nature, and the technology of peripheral devices is constantly changing. For the same reasons, precise figures of speeds and storage capabilities are not given.

This chapter relates closely to the material in Chapter 8, on computer structure, and is particularly relevant to later chapters on the applications of computers.

At the start of this chapter it is important to clarify the terms **medium** and **device**. A medium is a material used for the storage of data. An example of a medium is magnetic tape. A device is a machine responsible for the transfer of data, generally to or from a storage medium.

12.1 Objectives of Peripherals

As their name implies, peripheral devices are in some sense on the outside of a computer system. As such, they act as an interface between the processor of a computer and the outside world.

Peripheral devices have one or more of the following objectives:

a) the transmission of data from an external medium, or from the environment of the computer, to a processing unit of the computer (**input**);
b) the transmission of data from a processing unit of the computer to an external medium, or to the environment of the computer (**output**);
c) the storage of data on some backing store medium, and the retrieval of data from this medium (**storage**).

Peripheral devices may be physically close to a processor, or linked to it from long distances by radio, telephone or satellite communication systems. However, the objectives of peripherals remain the same in all cases.

In the early days of computing, the CPU was the largest, most important and most expensive item of equipment in a computing installation. In many cases, the current-day situation is almost the opposite. The processor is the smallest and cheapest item of equipment in a computer configuration, and may in some situations be regarded as merely a control device for the peripherals. In the study of peripheral devices, it is important to bear in mind the concept of a **module**. The majority of peripheral devices may be regarded as modules. What they do is important, whereas how they do it is less significant. A peripheral may be unplugged and replaced by one which achieves the same objectives in a different way without affecting the computer system as a whole in any way at all.

The concept of an **interface**, as a link between two modules, is also important in the study of peripherals. This point is dealt with in some detail at the end of the chapter.

12.2 Some Common Peripheral Devices

Some of the more common peripheral devices are outlined in the next few sections. The list of devices is by no means exhaustive, but does give an overall picture of the current situation, and some indication of the trends in the use of peripherals.

The most common peripheral device, the visual display terminal, is discussed first. Other devices are grouped under the headings input, output and backing store. If a device relates to a storage medium, then the two are discussed together.

12.3   Terminals

A **terminal** is the simplest and most common way of gaining access to a computer. A terminal may be an integral part of the processing unit, as in the case of microcomputers, or be linked to a computer by telephone or radio from a very long distance. A terminal is used for both input and output.

The most popular form of terminal includes a keyboard, resembling that on a typewriter, and a display screen, similar to a television screen. A terminal of this type is called a **visual display unit**, or **VDU**. Input is typed on the keyboard, and output appears, in character form, on the display screen.

A more sophisticated variation of a VDU is a **graphics terminal**. In addition to characters, a graphics terminal allows a variety of shapes and patterns to be displayed on the screen. Diagrams, maps, animated cartoons and graphs may be generated by these patterns. Many graphics terminals work in colour, and some permit **high resolution graphics**, with a much finer level of detail. Graphics terminals are currently a major growth area in peripheral devices. Another type of terminal does not have a display screen, but produces printed output. These are called **teletypewriters**, or teletypes.

A terminal may perform a variety of tasks in a computer system. In an application such as word processing, a terminal is a **work station** where text is entered, edited, stored and retrieved. The processor is dedicated to the support of the terminal. In a number of computing systems, terminals are used for **direct data entry**. Data input at the terminal are stored on magnetic discs until ready for processing. In most modern computers the **operator's console** is in the form of a terminal. A **software front panel** enables the contents of registers and key memory cells to be displayed when necessary. Finally, in most microcomputers, a terminal has the role of input/output device and operator's console.

12.4   Input Devices

Input devices transfer data from an external medium to a processor. In many cases, data is stored on the external medium in a code. The code may be formed by patterns of holes punched in paper, or thick or thin stripes of ink or paint. In most cases this external code is not the same as the code used by the processor. However, translation is generally done by the processor and not the peripheral.

12.5   Card Readers

Dating back to the turn of the century, card readers are the traditional type of input device for automatic data processing systems. Card readers were the most important input device from the inception of electronic computers until the mid-1970s, but have gradually been superseded since then by direct data entry and other input methods. However, punched cards seem assured of a small but significant part in computing in the foreseeable future. Cards survive on direct data entry systems as **card images**.

The data storage medium used by card readers is **punched cards**. These are made of stiff paper, with patterns of holes to code the data. A small number of standard card sizes are commonly used. A set of cards for one program or collection of data is called a **deck**. A card reader uses a light and a set of photo-electric cells to determine the pattern of holes on a card. Fibre optics are used in newer models. In most cases, all the characters (generally eighty) on one card are read at the same time. Reader speeds vary between 300 and 1000 cards per minute.

12.6   Paper Tape Readers

The use of paper tape as a data storage medium was already well established in the field of data communications when electronic computers arrived on the scene. Computers have inherited the storage medium and some of the data codes (notably the ASCII code) from the telecommunications field.

Paper tape has a number of **tracks** running along the length of the tape. Holes may be punched in these tracks to make up the codes for the data. The code for one character is in a **frame**, running across the tracks. Six, seven or eight track tapes are used, often including a **parity track**.

A paper tape reader uses metal strips which make electrical contact through the holes, or a light and a set of photo-cells to sense the pattern of holes in the tape. One character is input at a time, and speeds vary between ten and a thousand characters per second.

12.7   Direct Input from Source

One problem with the use of punched cards and paper tape is that the data they contain has to be copied from some other document, called a **source document**. To save time and paper, several methods of data input have been devised to accept data directly from its source. These include optical character recognition, magnetic ink character recognition and the use of bar codes.

Optical character recognition makes use of a data input device which can recognise printed or typed characters by a light scanning process. A simpler variation of this system is **mark sensing**. Mark sense equipment can recognise whether certain areas of a document have been shaded in pencil. These input methods have the advantage of being able to read directly from source documents, but are relatively slow and error-prone by comparison with other methods.

Magnetic ink character recognition is the process of reading characters which are printed in magnetic ink. It is used almost exclusively within the banking system for the automatic clearing of cheques, and is fairly fast and relatively error-free.

Bar codes are a relatively new input medium. They are rapidly gaining wide popularity as a way of displaying machine-readable information on merchandise, particularly in supermarkets. A bar code consists of a number of vertical stripes, in black ink or paint on a white background. Characters are coded by combinations of thick and thin stripes, and check characters are always included.

A **bar code reader** interprets the pattern of stripes and produces the equivalent character code. Laser beams are used in the most recent bar code readers. Experience to date indicates that bar code input is fairly fast and acceptably reliable.

12.8   Voice Recognition

Voice recognition has been the subject of intensive research for a considerable period of time. Although success has been limited, this is a fairly promising growth area for the future.

Current voice recognition systems can respond to a fairly small number of words or phrases from a person whose voice has been 'learned'. Recognition rates are fairly high, but not yet adequate for a wide variety of applications. Speed of input is, of course, limited by the rate at which a person can speak coherently.

12.9   Output Devices

Output devices transfer data from a processor to an external medium. As in the case of input devices, the data code used by the output device is sometimes different from the internal code used by the processor. Again, changing to the output code is generally done by the processor.

12.10   Printers

Printers are the commonest form of output device, with a wide variety currently available. The largest and fastest printers are **line printers** which print all the characters in an entire line in one operation. Lines generally contain 120 characters, and speeds vary from 300 to 1200 lines per minute. At the top of the range are **laser beam printers**, which achieve an incredible 17000 lines per minute.

More suited to minicomputers and microcomputers are **character printers**, which print one character at a time. Some models speed up the operation by printing alternate lines in alternate directions. The commonest character printers are **dot matrix printers** and **daisy wheel printers**. Dot matrix printers form characters by combinations of dots. Their major advantage is their quietness. Daisy wheel printers have a print wheel with one or two characters on each 'petal'. The wheel is rotated in order to select the character to be printed. Character printers are slower but cheaper than line printers.

12.11   Computer Output on Microfilm

Computer output on microfilm (COM) is an output technique gaining wide acceptance. It avoids the bulk and expense of the large quantities of paper produced by printers.

A 'page' of output is displayed on a screen and photographed by a special camera. The film image of one page measures less than a quarter of an inch square. The film is generally cut into postcard-sized **microfiches**, which contain the images of approximately 100 pages. A **microfilm reader** is used to project the enlarged image of a page onto a screen.

12.12   Digital Plotters

Computer applications in areas such as engineering and architecture use **digital plotters** to produce plans, engineering drawings and maps. A digital plotter has a pen whose motion across the surface of the paper is controlled by a computer. Digital plotters are very slow output devices, and require special software to control them. In some applications they have been replaced by graphics terminals.

12.13   Speech Synthesis

Speech synthesis output is the counterpart of voice recognition input. Like voice recognition, speech synthesis is currently the subject of intensive research. A few speech synthesis output devices have been implemented, but the full potential of this technique is far from being realised.

Speech synthesis works by storing a digitally coded form of a number of key sounds. Words are constructed by combining these codes, and then decoding the digital patterns through a suitable set of circuits connected to a speaker.

12.14 Backing Store

The data storage capacity of a computer is greatly enhanced by the use of **backing store** devices. In some computer applications, a 'bank' of stored data is the most important element in the system. Backing store technology is being developed all the time. Improvements in speed and storage capacity, and reductions in cost, are frequently announced.

12.15 Magnetic Discs

Magnetic discs are the most popular backing store medium. A magnetic disc is made of metal or plastic, coated with a layer of a magnetisable substance. Data is stored as small spots of magnetisation in one direction or the other. The layout of data on a magnetic disc is discussed in Chapter 23.

Magnetic discs occur in a number of different sizes. At the top end of the range are **exchangeable disc packs**, with a number of large discs mounted on a common shaft. In the middle of the range are **single disc cartridges**, used mainly by minicomputers. Microcomputers generally use **floppy discs**, which are small, flexible discs made of plastic. Storage capacities range from hundreds of **megabytes** for disc packs to a few megabytes for floppy disc (1 megabyte = 1 million characters).

A recent development of some significance is the **Winchester** hard mini-disc. A Winchester is a small, high precision hard disc, with an extremely high storage capacity.

The device which transfers data to or from a magnetic disc is called a **magnetic disc drive**. A **read–write head** moves very close to the surface of the disc to detect magnetised areas, or create them. Speeds of data transfer vary from a few hundred characters per second for floppy disc drives to nearly a million characters per second for large disc drives. There is, however, a delay in locating the data before transfer can commence. Transfer is always in blocks of characters.

The biggest problem affecting the use of magnetic discs is dust. Large discs are made of metal, machined to a very high precision. The gap between the surface of the disc, which rotates at a high speed, and the read–write head is very small. If a speck of dust is caught in the gap, it can cause a **disc crash**, damaging both the disc and the read–write heads. Floppy disc drives have read–write heads which rub against the surface of the disc. Dust can cause the disc to be scratched.

12.16 Magnetic Tape

Magnetic tape is the cheapest medium for storing large quantities of data. The tape is made of plastic, coated with a magnetic substance, and resembles ordinary sound recording tape.

Magnetic tapes vary in length from several hundred to a few thousand feet. The longest tapes can store several million characters. **Cassette tapes**, resembling ordinary sound cassettes, are used by many microcomputers. **Magnetic tape units** transfer data to and from magnetic tape. They include spools for the tape, a read–write head, and, in many cases, **vacuum columns** to allow the tape to be started and stopped rapidly. Many magnetic tape units can read from or write to a tape when it is running in either direction.

Data can only be transferred to or from a magnetic tape when it is running at full speed. Data is always transferred in blocks, not in single characters.

A recent development is simple, cheap magnetic tape units called **streamers**, whose sole purpose is to provide backup copies of magnetic disks.

12.17 Serial and Random Access to Data

There is one significant difference between magnetic discs and magnetic tape, which determines which is more suitable for a particular application. Magnetic tape is a **serial** access medium, while magnetic discs are a **random** or **direct** access medium. These terms are explained below.

Serial access means that the order of the data on the storage medium is significant. In the case of magnetic tape, this means that the time taken to locate a block of data depends on the position of the block on the tape. The quickest way to access all the data on a tape is in the order in which it occurs on the tape.

Random access means that the order of the data in the storage medium is not significant. In the case of magnetic discs, this means that the time taken to locate a block of data is more or less independent of the position of the block on the disc. Furthermore, each location on the disc or disc pack is identified by an **address**, similar to the address of a location in main store.

12.18 Interfacing Processors to Peripherals

The previous few sections have introduced some of the wide variety of peripheral devices in common use. It must be emphasised that the devices discussed here are not the only ones. In many cases, the same processor supports a number of peripheral devices, with very different characteristics.

Accordingly, linking or interfacing peripherals to a processor can be quite a complicated business. Several characteristics of a peripheral must be taken into account, in particular:

i) the character code used by the peripheral;
ii) the rate of transfer of data;
iii) the number of characters transferred in one operation.

Precise details of interfaces between peripherals and processors vary considerably from one system to another, but two features, namely **buffers** and **flags**, are very commonly used. These are discussed below.

A **buffer** is an area of main store set aside for data in the process of being transferred to or from a peripheral device. The size of the buffer generally corresponds to the number of characters passed to or from the peripheral in one operation. For example, the buffer for a line printer generally contains the number of characters in one line. The buffer is loaded by the processor and unloaded by the printer.

A **flag** is a single bit register or store location used for the synchronisation and control of a peripheral device. A flag may be **set** (value 1) or **cleared** (value 0). For example, two flags may be used in the control of a line printer in the following way. When the printer buffer has been filled by the processor, one flag is set, to signal to the printer to start printing the contents of the buffer. When the printing is complete, the printer sets the other flag. The flags are cleared once the signal has been noted.

Most microprocessor-based computers deal with input and output in the following way. There is a special **parallel input–output** (PIO) chip to deal with all peripheral devices except for the visual display screen. The visual display screen is linked directly to a certain area of main store. The characters on the screen are copies of the characters in this memory area, which is known as a **map** of the screen. In other words, when a character is to be displayed on the screen, it is written into the memory location corresponding to the desired position for the character on the screen. This is a simple but extremely powerful method of interfacing the display screen to the processor.

Interfacing many modern peripherals is simplified by the fact that a number of peripheral devices now include a microprocessor dedicated to the control of the device and to the transfer of data to and from the CPU. Many disc drives are controlled by a **disc control unit**, which supervises all data transfers, and organises access to the discs in such a way that the time taken to locate each block of data is minimised.

12.19   Automatic Checking During Data Transfer

Transfer of data between peripheral devices and processors, and to and from backing store media, is a relatively error-prone operation. Accordingly, a number of checks are carried out automatically during these operations, on most computer systems.

In addition to **parity checks**, discussed in Chapter 3, these checks include the use of **check sums** and **block sums**, and self-correcting codes such as **Hamming codes**. The latter methods are discussed below.

When a set of data items, such as the elements of a record, is transferred, a **check sum** is formed from the numeric value of the code for each data item. After the set of data and its check sum have been received, the check sum is again calculated. If the new value does not match the transmitted value of the sum, then an error has occurred during transmission. In some cases, an error is recorded as soon as this occurs. In other cases, the set of data is re-transmitted, and checked again. If a number of re-transmissions are all unsuccessful, then an error is reported.

A block sum is similar to a check sum, except that it is used in conjunction with a block of data transferred from a magnetic tape or magnetic disc.

Hamming codes are binary codes, used to represent data items, which have a number of extra bits for checking purposes. The check bits are assigned in such a way that it is possible to detect and correct an error in the transmission of a single bit, and detect errors in the transmission of more than one bit. Question 7 of Exercise 25 investigates Hamming codes in more detail.

12.20   Conclusion

This chapter has provided a very brief description of the general features of the commonest input, output and backing store devices. Ways of linking these devices to processing units have also been discussed.

The most important point to be made is that input or output of data, or transfer of data to or from backing store, is a very complicated process. In many computer applications, it is the most time-consuming activity carried out by the system. The speed of input and output is very often the limiting factor in the performance of a system.

In most cases, the details of the transfer of data to and from peripheral devices are taken care of by a layer of software called an **operating system.** Operating systems are discussed in some detail in Chapter 19.

Exercise 12

1 Briefly define the following terms: medium; device; interface; terminal; deck; track; frame; source document; microfiche; disc crash; serial access; random access; buffer; flag.

2 Give some reasons for the replacement of punched cards and paper tape by direct data entry and direct input from source techniques.

☐ 3 Bearing in mind the nature of a computer, as outlined in Chapter 2, do you think that computers will ever be able to interpret continuous passages of spoken input in ordinary language?

4 A set of data contains one million characters.
   a) How many punched cards will the data occupy, at 50 characters per card?
   b) How long will the cards take to punch, at 7·5 seconds per card?
   c) How long will the cards take to be read, at 400 cards per minute?
   d) If 2 per cent of the cards are found to contain errors, and it takes 30 seconds to locate an error and re-punch the card, how long will the process of correction take?
   e) If it takes 6 seconds to key in one card image on a direct data entry system, how long does input take?
   f) Errors are detected by the DDE system as a card image is entered. If 3 per cent of the card images are found to contain errors, and correction takes 10 seconds per card image, how long does the correction process take?
   g) Comment on your results for the punched card system and for the direct data entry system.

5 A line printer outputs 600 lines per minute, each line comprising 120 characters. What is the average rate of output in characters per second?

6 A 20 megabyte disc is to be dumped onto magnetic tape, i.e. the entire contents of the disc is to be copied onto a magnetic tap. The data is in blocks each containing 1K of characters.
   a) How many blocks are there on the disc? (Assume that 1 megabyte = 1000K of characters.)
   b) A 1K buffer is used for the transfer. At a transfer rate of 500K characters per second, how long does it take to fill the buffer from the disc? (Give your answer in microseconds, where 1 second = 1000 microseconds.)
   c) At a transfer rate of 20K characters per second to the magnetic tape, how long does it take to empty the buffer to the tape?
   d) If there is an additional 15 μs overhead on the transfer of each block, how long does the whole copying operation take?

7 The transfer of a data item from a processor to a peripheral device is controlled by three flags, labelled A, B and C. The data item is loaded into a buffer by the processor, and removed from the buffer by the peripheral.
   Algorithms for the functioning of the processor and of the peripheral are as follows:

   Processor
   Repeat
      If flag A = 1, then set it to zero and continue else wait.
      If flag B = 1, then set it to zero and continue else wait.
      Load data item into buffer.
      Set flag B to 1.
      Set flag C to 1.

   Peripheral
   Repeat
      If flag C = 1, then set it to zero and continue else wait.
      If flag B = 1, then set it to zero and continue else wait.
      Copy data item from buffer.
      Set flag B to 1.
      Set flag A to 1.

   Initially, flags A and B are 1, and flag C is zero.
   a) Write down the steps involved in transferring one character from the processor to the peripheral. State the values of the flags at each step.
   b) By studying the algorithms, and from your answer to part (a), you will realise that the purpose of flag B is to protect the buffer while it is being loaded or unloaded. Briefly state the purposes of flags A and C.

c) If the peripheral works much more slowly than the processor, at which point will most of the waiting occur?

☐ **8** Write a program, in AMC machine language, to accept ten characters as input, and store them in consecutive memory locations. The first eight characters are data, the last two together are the check sum of the numeric value of the previous eight characters.

Having input the data, re-calculate the check sum and compare it with the input value. Output 1 if the check is successful, and 0 if the check fails.

9 Find out more details about some of the peripheral devices mentioned in this chapter, particularly ones which are relatively recent, such as voice recognition and synthesis systems, and Winchester discs.

10 A method of checking data, in addition to those mentioned in the text, is the **cyclic redundancy check** (CRC). Find out how this checking method works, and how it is used.

13

Processor case studies

This chapter examines the topic of computer hardware from a fresh point of view. Whereas the previous six chapters have dealt with the topic from a theoretical standpoint, this chapter looks at more practical aspects, by presenting case studies of a number of currently used processors.

In view of the ever increasing number of processors in current use, the choice of a representative sample is not easy. In making the choice, an attempt has been made to give an idea of the range in size and complexity of processors, while selecting ones which are up-to-date, widely used and regarded as having a sound architecture.

Accordingly, the following four processors have been selected:

Zilog Z80 microprocessor,
PDP-11 minicomputer,
ICL 2900 series mainframe computer,
Cray 1 megacomputer.

In the sections which follow, each processor is described in general terms, and then its register layout and machine language are discussed further. Of necessity, the discussion is fairly brief. The intention is to present the overall design features of each processor, without going into too much detail, and to show how the principles of processor architecture are put into practice in each case.

13.1 Zilog Z80 microprocessor

The **Zilog Z80 microprocessor** was first introduced in 1976. It is a general-purpose 8 bit microprocessor, constructed on a single chip. It has become one of the most widely used microprocessors, forming the CPU of, amongst others, Research Machines 380Z and Sinclair ZX80 microcomputers.

13.1.1 Register Structure

Figure 13.1 shows the overall layout of the processor, and Figure 13.2 shows the processor registers. You will notice that there are two sets of general-purpose registers. Control can be transferred from one set to another, for example, when an interrupt occurs. In addition to an accumulator and a flag register, each set contains six general-purpose registers. These registers are 8 bits wide, and can be paired to form three 16 bit registers.

Data items can occupy 8 or 16 bits, though individual transfers to or from main store are in units of 8 bits. Addresses are, however, 16 bits wide, giving an address space of $2^{16} = 64K$. The special purpose registers (index registers, stack pointer and program counter) associated with addressing are 16 bits wide. The Z80 processor chip is designed to be used with separate memory and peripheral interface chips.

13.1.2 Instruction Set

Z80 machine instructions may be 8, 16, 24 or 32 bits long. The instruction set comprises the following groups:

Load and exchange,
Block transfer and search,
Arithmetic and logical;

Bit manipulation,
Jump, call and return,
Input and output,
Processor control.

Significant features of each group are discussed below.

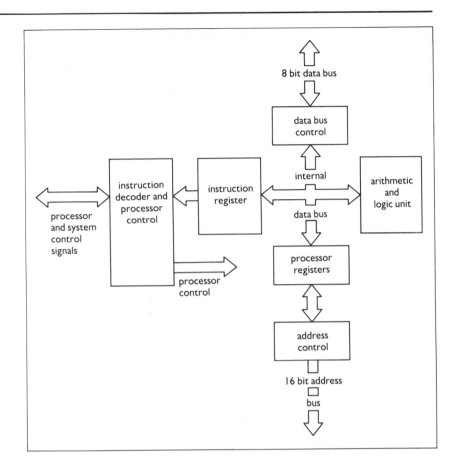

Figure 13.1
Z80 processor block structure

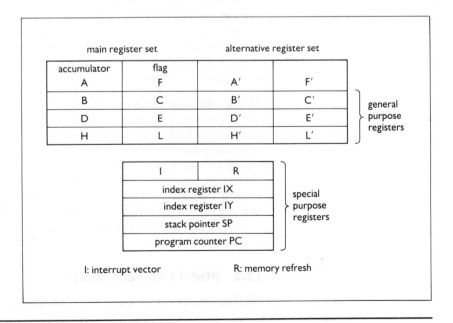

Figure 13.2
Z80 processor registers

Load and Exchange

The load instructions move an 8 or 16 bit data item between registers, or between a register and one or two main store locations. The exchange instructions interchange data items.

Block Transfer and Search

These are extremely powerful instructions for a processor of this size. The block transfer instruction moves a block of data, of any size, from one place in main store to another. The block search instruction searches block of store, of any size, for a given 8 bit data item.

Arithmetic and Logical Instructions

These instructions operate on data items in registers or store locations, placing the result in the accumulator, and setting the flag bits accordingly. Addition and subtraction can be applied to 8 or 16 bit quantities, but the remaining operations (which include AND, OR, exclusive OR, shifts and rotates) are all carried out in units of 8 bits only. Special provision is made for the manipulation of numbers in BCD form. Multiplication and division are not implemented directly as single machine instructions.

Bit Manipulation

These instructions allow any bit in a register or store location to be set, cleared or tested.

Jump, Call and Return

A wide variety of instructions are available to transfer control from one point in a program to another. These include 'short' relative jumps and long jumps to an absolute address.

13.1.3 Addressing Modes

In order to keep Z80 machine instructions as short as possible, no less than ten addressing modes are used. Examples of these modes include **immediate** (one byte operand) and **immediate extended** (two byte operand), as well as **absolute, relative, indexed** and **register indirect** addressing.

The majority of the instructions refer to two operands, but are one-address instructions with respect to main store. Notable exceptions are block transfer and search instructions, which are two-address instructions. Each instruction has its own set of permitted addressing modes.

13.1.4 An Assessment of the Z80

The Z80 is one of the most successful microprocessor chips produced to date. Its architecture is based on a combination of special- and general-purpose registers, and it can manipulate both 8 and 16 bit data items. Notable features include the block transfer and search facilities, and the alternative register set.

Although only certain combinations of operations and addressing modes are available, the Z80 instruction set is both powerful and versatile. A number of high level languages can be translated fairly efficiently into Z80 machine language.

The Z80 processor has been incorporated into a wide variety of digital electronic systems, including computers, control devices and remote sensing equipment.

13.2 PDP-11 Minicomputer

Manufactured by Digital Equipment Corporation, the **PDP-11** is probably the

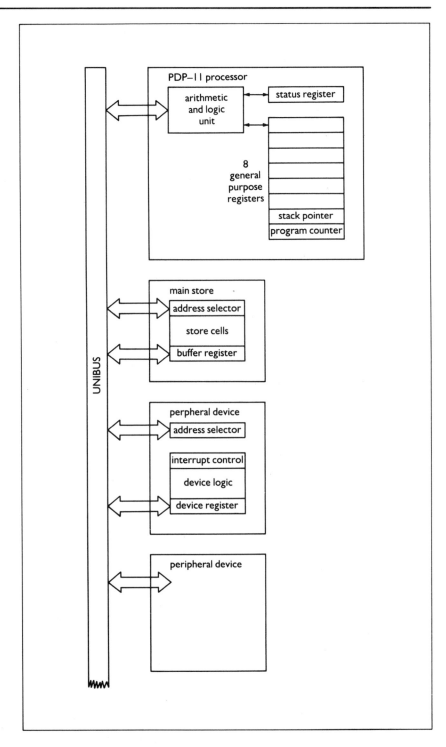

Figure 13.3
PDP-11 block structure

world's most popular minicomputer. It is a general purpose computer, capable of a wide range of applications. Its processor architecture is very highly regarded.

13.2.1 The UNIBUS
The hardware and software 'backbone' of the PDP-11 series is a communication

path known as a UNIBUS. It is the connection between a processor, main store and peripheral devices, as shown in Figure 13.3. Any device wishing to use the UNIBUS first requests control of it, and then uses it to transfer data or instructions.

13.2.2   Register Structure

Figure 13.4 shows the register and main store structure of the PDP-11 processor. It can be seen to be a 16 bit processor, based on the principle of general-purpose registers. The eight registers, labelled R0 to R7, can be used as accumulators, index registers or for indirect addressing. Although R6 is used as a stack pointer, and R7 as the program counter, all registers are treated in the same manner by program instructions.

Registers used for input and output, such as the teletype status and data registers, are treated as if they were memory locations, with octal addresses 177560 to 177566. The main store is addressed in units of bytes (8 bits). Words (16 bits) occupy two consecutive bytes, starting at an even address.

13.2.3   Instruction Set

The PDP-11 has a concise, yet powerful instruction set. Both one- and two-address instructions are available. One-address instructions include increment, decrement, negate, rotate and shift operations. Two-address instructions include move, compare, add, subtract, AND, and OR operations.

There is a 'long' unconditional jump instruction and a wide variety of 'short' relative conditional branching instructions. Other instructions enable condition codes to be set or cleared, and control to be transferred to or from subprograms. Most models of PDP-11 computers do not have machine instructions for multiplication or division.

There are no specific instructions for input or output, as registers which interface with peripheral devices are regarded as main store locations. Data items in these registers may be processed by any instructions which refer to main store. In this way, input and output may be very closely co-ordinated with processing.

13.2.4   Addressing Modes

Eight addressing modes are available, some of which are extremely powerful. Any addressing mode can be used in conjunction with any register, including the stack pointer and program counter. Although all instructions are one word (16 bits) long, various addressing modes enable the word following the instruction code to be used as a data item or an address.

Addressing modes include **immediate operand, absolute, relative, indexed, register indirect** and combinations of indexed and indirect addressing. There are also modes which increase or decrease the contents of a register before or after it has been used as an index or indirect address register. These make manipulation of stacks and arrays of data a simple matter.

One of the most significant features of the PDP-11 architecture is that any addressing mode can be used in conjunction with any one- or two-address instruction. This considerably simplifies the programming of the computer and enhances the power of its instruction set.

13.2.5   An Assessment of the PDP-11

The most significant features of the PDP-11 are its clean, simple architecture, general-purpose registers which are all treated equally by machine instructions, and the fact that all addressing modes are available to all instructions.

For these reasons, the PDP-11 is very widely used in teaching computer

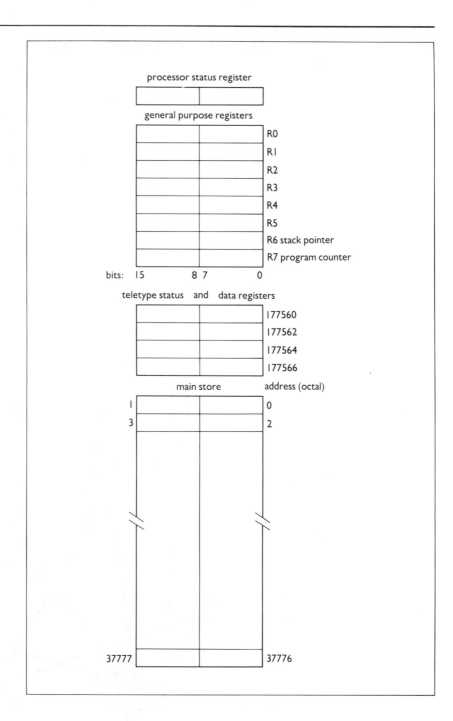

Figure 13.4
PDP-11 register and main store
structure

architecture and low level languages. Furthermore, its architecture, particularly the UNIBUS feature, has influenced the design of many other processors, particularly single-chip microprocessors.

In spite of increasing competition from microprocessor-based computers, the popularity of the PDP-11 is undiminished. In commercial terms, it is one of the most successful computers ever produced.

13.3   ICL 2900 Series Computers

Designed and manufactured by International Computers Limited, the **ICL 2900** series is an attempt to create an architecture which is the basis of a powerful, versatile hardware and software system. A particular objective is the efficient processing of machine code translated from a program in a high level language.

The design principles of the processor are implemented over a range of models in the 2900 series. The largest computers in the range are many times as powerful as the smallest. The largest models use hard-wired control, cache stores and pipelining, while smaller models make extensive use of microprogramming.

Computers in the series can be configured in a number of ways. Large configurations have more than one processor. In all cases, peripheral devices and processors have independent access to main store, via devices called **store multiple access controllers**. Figure 13.5 shows a large 2900 series configuration, including two processors.

13.3.1   Register Structure

Figure 13.6 shows the processor register structure and logical main store layout of

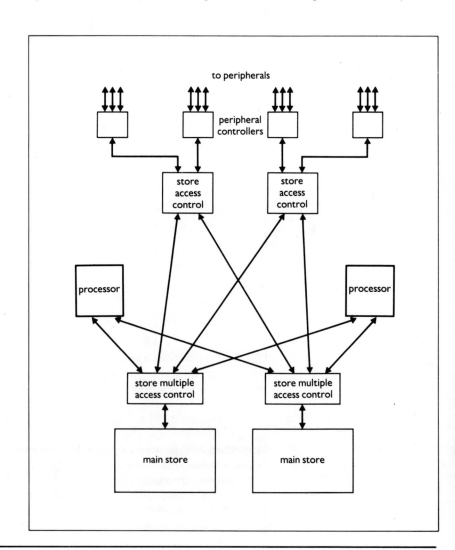

Figure 13.5
ICL 2900 series multiprocessor configuration

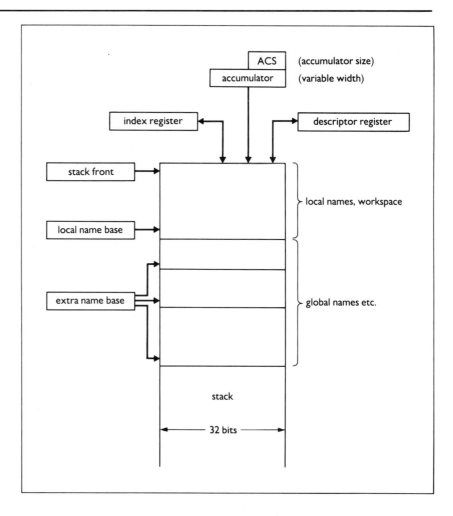

Figure 13.6
ICL 2900 register and main store
structure

the ICL 2900 series. The single accumulator can store 32, 64 or 128 bits, other registers are 32 bits wide. 32 bits is the wordlength of the ICL 2900 series.

The main store is partitioned in a fairly complex manner, because it is designed to be occupied by a number of programs (more properly called **processes** in this context) at the same time. Each process is allocated a separate portion of store, structured as a stack. Most addressing is relative to the base of the stack belonging to the particular process. Stacks are 32 bits wide.

13.3.2   Instruction Set

An ICL 2900 is basically a one-address computer, though a few two-address instructions are available to move data from one store location to another. Most addressing modes refer to various portions of the stack allocated to the particular process. Any data items not in this stack are accessed via a **descripter register**. All addressing modes are available to all instructions. In this way, the address transformation hardware is kept separate from the instruction decoding hardware in the instruction pipeline.

Machine instructions are available for a wide range of fixed and floating point operations, including multiplication and division. Floating point numbers can occupy up to 128 bits. Packed decimal representation, using four bits per BCD digit, may also be used for the storage and processing of integers.

13.3.3 Protection

Because the ICL 2900 main store is designed to be occupied by a number of processes at any time, it incorporates a sophisticated protection mechanism. This allows portions of processes to be shared, under strictly controlled conditions, while preventing errors in one process from corrupting the store area allocated to other processes, and making it almost impossible to 'break into' an unauthorised process.

The question of protection is discussed further in Chapters 19 and 20, on operating systems.

13.3.4 An Assessment of the ICL 2900

The most significant features of the ICL 2900 processor architecture are its single accumulator, stack-oriented addressing and extensive use of cache stores and pipelining.

The 2900 series architecture is an attempt to design a 'high level language' processor, suitable for multi-purpose configurations and interfacing to data communication networks. It reflects some of the most advanced concepts in computer design.

13.4 Cray I Series Large Computers

The **Cray I** series is a family of large computers, designed for scientific and engineering applications. First marketed in 1976, Cray computers are used for such diverse activities as weather forecasting, nuclear physics research, defence systems, structural analysis and electrical power distribution.

Although they are amongst the largest and fastest computers in the world, Cray processors use only medium scale integrated circuits, mounted on standard sized printed circuit boards which are connected by miles of wire. Because of the close packing of components, Cray processors are liquid cooled, using cooling systems similar to those in domestic refrigerators.

13.4.1 Register Structure

Figure 13.7 shows the register, functional units and main store of a Cray I processor. The processor can be seen to be divided into an **instruction section**, an **address section**, a **scalar section** for individual data items, and a **vector section** for arrays of data items. In general, each section has its own cache store, registers and functional units, providing a considerable degree of parallelism. All functional units operate independently of each other, and all are internally pipelined.

The distinguishing feature of the Cray I architecture is the vector processing circuits. Each of the 8 vector registers holds an array of 64 data items, each 64 bits in length. Successive elements from a vector register enter a functional unit in successive clock periods.

Each of the four buffers in the instruction cache can contain 64 consecutive 16 bit instructions. This means that program loops, provided that they are reasonably short, can be executed without reference to main store.

A Cray I main store varies in size between 256K and 4M words. A word is 64 data bits, together with 8 check bits. The check bits enable a single error to be corrected and a double error to be detected in the word.

13.4.2 Instruction Set

Instructions which transfer data to or from main store are one-address instructions, though in most cases blocks of data are transferred. Instructions which process data refer to registers only. Again, many instructions process arrays of data from

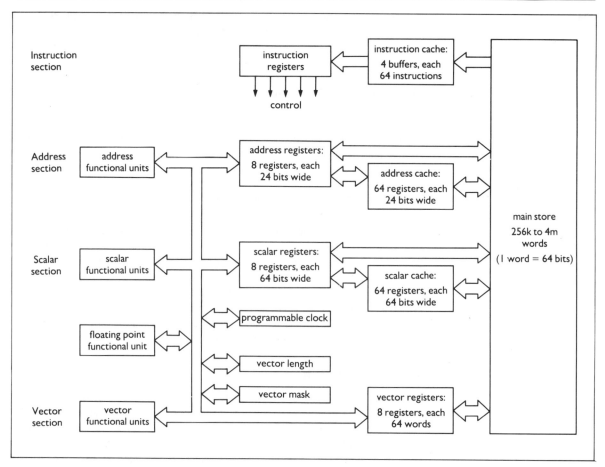

Figure 13.7
Cray 1 register and main store
structure

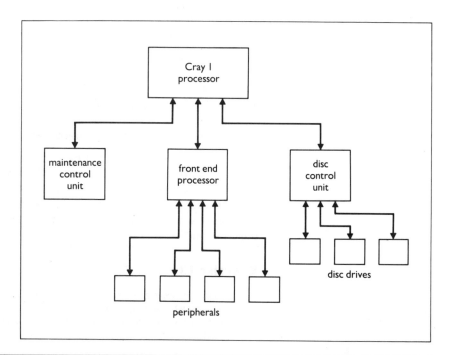

Figure 13.8
A computer system using a Cray 1
processor

registers. Arithmetic operations include addition, subtraction, multiplication and calculation of reciprocals, on integers and floating point numbers. For example, a single instruction can add corresponding elements in two vector registers, and return the sums to a third vector register.

13.4.3 Links to Peripheral Devices

A Cray 1 processor requires a separate **front-end processor** to control the flow of data to and from peripheral devices, with the exception of disc drives, which can be controlled directly. In addition, another processor is required as a **maintenance control unit**, to monitor the performance of the main processor. Figure 13.8 shows the configuration of a computer system using a Cray 1 processor.

13.4.4 An Assessment of the Cray 1

Distinguishing features of the Cray 1 processor are its vector registers and processing circuits, the high degree of parallelism in its design, and its extensive use of pipelining and cache stores. The Cray 1 is a specialised 'number crunching' computer. Static data structures like arrays can be handled directly at machine level, but there is hardly any provision for dynamic structures such as stacks.

The Cray 1 is one of the largest, fastest and most complex processors currently available. Although only small numbers of them have been sold (and each takes several months to assemble by hand), they have made a significant contribution to the development of computer architecture.

13.5 Conclusion

This rather brief survey of a few selected computer architectures has given some idea of the wide variety of ways in which the principles of computer design are put into practice. It shows the range in size and complexity, from a microprocessor to a mega-computer. It also brings to light a few differences of opinion on issues of computer design. For example should registers be dedicated to a specific task, or general-purpose?

However, there are a number of underlying similarities, common to these (and most other) processor architectures. These include the following:

● A centralised main store, from which both instructions and data can be drawn.
● A place where instructions are decoded, to become sequences of pulses along control lines.
● An addressing mechanism, whereby instructions and data items are located in main store.
● Functional circuits which perform arithmetic and logical operations.

This chapter concludes the part of the book concerned with computer hardware. This part has described the structure and functioning of a computer at the very lowest level, namely registers, processing circuits and machine language. The next part of the book works outwards from this 'core' level, describing the various layers of software which surround the hardware of a computer, transforming it into a useful machine.

Exercise 13

1 Distinguish between general-purpose and dedicated registers. List the computers described in this chapter which use each type of register.
2 Classify the case study computers in the groups one-address computers and two-address computers.

3 Which features of the case study computers are also to be found in the AMC? In the light of your study of the AMC, state why you think each feature is included in its architecture.

4 Which of the case study computers use pipelining?

5 Consider the following Cray 1 machine instruction:

Instruction (octal)	Interpretation
155123	Add corresponding integers in vector register 1 and vector register 2, and store the sums in vector register 3.

In Exercise 10 there is a program, in AMC machine language, which performs an equivalent process on vectors in the AMC memory.

a) How many AMC instructions are equivalent to this Cray 1 instruction?

b) The Cray 1 instruction takes (number of array elements $+3$) clock periods to execute. Assume that AMC instructions take 8 or 16 clock periods to execute, depending on whether they occupy 1 or 2 words.

If each array contains 32 elements, work out the number of clock periods required by each processor. Comment on your results, bearing in mind that a Cray 1 clock period is about one hundredth of the length of a feasible AMC clock period.

6 Which of the case study computers makes the most extensive use of a stack in its memory arrangement? Suggest which of the design objectives of the particular computer is the reason for this.

☐ **7** By obtaining manufacturers' literature, carry out a case study of your own on a suitable processor. Write a report on the processor, in about as much detail as the ones in this chapter. Some suggested processors are:

Eight bit microprocessors: Intel 8080, Motorola M6800, Rockwell 6502.
Sixteen bit microprocessors: Intel 8086, Zilog Z8000.
Minicomputers: Digico M16, PDP-8.
Mainframes: IBM 370 series, Burroughs 6500, 6700 or 7700 series, CDC Star 100.

14
Assembly languages

This is the first chapter in the part of the book devoted to computer software. As mentioned at the beginning of the book, software is another word for programs. A program is a set of instructions to a computer, which sets it up to do a particular task. As you will see during this and the following chapters the task of some programs is to set up a computer to be able to run other programs. Accordingly, software may be regarded as layers, surrounding the hardware of a computer, and bridging the gulf between the hardware and a user-oriented machine. Figure 14.1 illustrates this idea.

This chapter concerns a class of programming languages called **assembly languages**. It explains their nature and objectives, and outlines their development. Features of assembly languages are introduced, using the assembly language of the AMC as an example. After you have studied this chapter, you should be able to write simple programs in AMC assembly language. The chapter concludes with a discussion of the role of assembly languages in practice.

This chapter relates closely to material in the previous part of the book, particularly to areas concerned with machine languages. It is also linked closely to the following chapter, which introduces programs called assemblers, which translate from assembly language to machine language.

14.1   The Nature and Objectives of Assembly Languages

In Chapter 9, a class of programming languages called machine languages was introduced. The step-by-step control of a computer is achieved through instructions in the particular machine language of the computer. Having studied the chapter, and having tried out some machine language programs, you will realise how slow and difficult it is to program a computer in its machine language.

Assembly languages have come into being to overcome these difficulties. Broadly speaking, the objective of an assembly language is to simplify the programming of a particular computer, while still remaining closely related to the architecture of the computer.

From this it follows that each type of computer has its own assembly language, which is not too far removed from its machine language. An assembly language may be defined as a programming language whose data structures correspond to the physical structure of the registers and main store of its host computer, and whose instructions are closely related to the machine instructions of the computer.

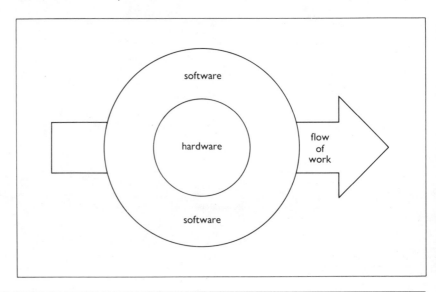

Figure 14.1
Hardware and software

Machine languages and assembly languages are together known as **low level languages**. This is because they are both close to the architecture of the computer which supports them.

14.2 The Development of Assembly Languages

In their most primitive form, assembly languages are almost as old as electronic digital computers. The first computers, produced in the period 1945 to 1950, could initially only be programmed in machine language. Although programming in those days was confined to a small group of specialists, writing out programs in binary code and personally allocating each memory cell soon proved far too cumbersome and error-prone.

Assembly languages quickly began to evolve out of machine languages, with additional features being added as time went by. At first they were just a character representation of machine code. Then features such as symbolic addressing, automatic conversion of data, directives and macro-instructions were added, in different ways on different computers. The confusion caused by the piecemeal development of assembly languages was one of the incentives for the development of high level languages starting in about 1955. Since then, the nature and objectives of assembly languages have become better understood. These languages have generally been simplified and their structure improved.

14.3 Features of Assembly Languages

Although assembly languages differ considerably from one type of computer to another, they generally have the following features in common: **mnemonic operation codes, symbolic addresses, automatic data conversion, directives** and **macros**. These features are discussed in the next five sections.

14.4 Mnemonic Operation Codes

To preserve a close relationship to the architecture of its host computer, an assembly language includes a set of instructions which are in one-to-one correspondence with the machine language of the computer. In other words, for every machine language instruction, there is an assembly language instruction.

Whereas machine language instructions are written in binary, octal or hexadecimal notation, assembly language instructions use a group of letters for the operation code. This group of letters is known as a **mnemonic**. For example, the instruction to stop a program in AMC machine language and assembly language is as follows:

AMC machine language   AMC assembly language
    8500   **HLT**

14.5 Symbolic Addresses

In machine language, the address of a data item or instruction is expressed as a number, in binary, octal or hexadecimal notation. This involves considerable inconvenience, particularly when indexed or relative addressing is used, or when the location of the program in the computer memory is not known. Assembly languages overcome this problem by the use of **symbolic addresses**. A symbolic address is a group of characters which represents the address of an instruction or data item. For example:

AMC machine language	AMC assembly language	Interpretation
1312 00AB	**ADD A NUM**	Add the number at address **00AB**, symbolic address **NUM**, to the accumulator.

Notice how the accumulator is also identified by a symbol, the letter A.

In order to associate the symbolic address with the data item or instruction to which it refers, the address is used to **label** the data item or instruction. The following program segment illustrates the idea of a label.

AMC machine language	AMC assembly language	Interpretation
	NM1 WRD	Location storing a number.
1A12 0002	**CMP A NM1**	Compare number in accumulator with number at address **NM1**.
6404	**BGE DWN**	Branch to instruction labelled **DWN** if greater than or equal to zero.
1112 0002	**LOA NM1**	Load number at **NM1** to accumulator.
4110	**DWN PSH A**	Push number in accumulator onto stack.

Notice how the symbolic address **NM1** labels the memory location storing the number, and the symbolic address **DWN** labels the instruction to which control is transferred by the **BGE** instruction.

The above program segment compares a number in the accumulator with one at address **NM1**, and pushes the larger of these numbers onto the stack.

14.6   Automatic Data Conversion

If the value of a data item is used in a machine language program, for example, as an immediate operand, then this value must be in the same notation as the rest of the machine language, namely binary, octal or hexadecimal code. In assembly languages, the value of a data item can generally be expressed as a decimal number, or as a set of characters. The characters are interpreted in a character code such as ASCII. For example:

AMC machine language	AMC assembly language	Interpretation
1121 0010	**LOA X N + 16**	Load the number 16 to the index register.
1111 4243	**LOA A N/BC/**	Load the characters **BC** to the accumulator.

Notice how the letter N is used to denote an immediate operand.

14.7   Directives

In addition to instructions which correspond directly to the machine instruction set of the particular computer, assembly languages have certain instructions which operate at a slightly higher level. These are known as **directives**, or **pseudo-operations**, and have no direct counterpart in machine language. Directives generally enhance the power of the assembly language, making the computer easier to program at this level.

Among the tasks performed by directives are marking the end of a program, which may be nowhere near a halt instruction, and reserving space for data items.

AMC assembly language used the directives **BTE** and **WRD** to reserve space for a byte and a word of data. For example:

AMC assembly language   Interpretation
NM1 WRD +35   Reserve a word for a data item, loaded with the value 35, and with symbolic address **NM1**.

14.8 Macros

A macro, more properly called **macro-instruction**, is a single instruction which represents a group of instructions. A macro-instruction is defined at the start of a program by listing the set of instructions which it is to represent. Whenever the macro-instruction is subsequently used in the program, it represents the entire set of instructions previously defined.

For example, supposing a certain assembly language does not have instruction which negates the number in the accumulator, but that the following two instructions would achieve this:

STO A TMP   Store number in accumulator in location **TMP**.
NEG A TMP   Negate the number in location **TMP** into the accumulator.

A macro-instruction **NGA**, negate accumulator, could be defined in terms of these instructions, as follows:

NGA MCD   Define a macro instruction named **NGA**.
   STO A TMP
   NEG A TMP
   EDM   End of macro definition.

The two directives **MCD** and **EDM** are used to start and end the macro definition. Whenever the instruction **NGA** is subsequently used in the program, it is replaced by the instruction in the above definition.

Macros are an extremely powerful feature of most assembly languages, but are not implemented in AMC assembly language. Macros are also used in some operating system command languages. See Section 19.17.

M addressing mode:	N immediate operand (blank) absolute address	
	I indirect address	
	D indexed address	
R register identifier:	A accumulator	
	X index register	
	S stack pointer	
ADR	symbolic address	
OPD	operand	
P peripheral device	T terminal	
effects on condition codes:	S set (becomes 1)	
	C cleared (becomes 0)	
	N no effect	
	D conditional upon result	
condition codes:	Z zero	
	N negative	
	C carry	
	V overflow	

Figure 14.2
AMC assembly language

instruction			interpretation	effect on condition codes			
				Z	N	C	V
memory addressing group							
LOA	R M OPD		load data word to register	D	D	N	N
LOB	R M OPD		load data byte to register	D	D	N	N
STO	R M OPD		store register word in memory	D	D	N	N
STB	R M OPD		store register byte in memory	D	D	N	N
ADD	R M OPD		add data word to register	D	D	D	D
ADB	R M OPD		add data byte to register	D	D	D	D
ADC	R M OPD		add data word and carry bit to register	D	D	D	D
ACB	R M OPD		add data byte and carry bit to register	D	D	D	D
SUB	R M OPD		subtract data word from register	D	D	D	D
SRB	R M OPD		subtract data byte from register	D	D	D	D
SBC	R M OPD		subtract (data word plus carry bit) from register	D	D	D	D
SCB	R M OPD		subtract (data byte plus carry bit) from register	D	D	D	D
AND	R M OPD		AND data word with register	D	D	C	C
ANB	R M OPD		AND data byte with register	D	D	C	C
ORR	R M OPD		OR data word with register	D	D	C	C
ORB	R M OPD		OR data byte with register	D	D	C	C
NEQ	R M OPD		NEQ (exclusive OR) data word with register	D	D	C	C
NQB	R M OPD		NEQ (exclusive OR) data byte with register	D	D	C	C
CMP	R M OPD		compare register with data word	D	D	D	D
CPB	R M OPD		compare register with data byte	D	D	D	D
register transfer group							
MOV	R_1 R_2		move from register 1 to register 2	D	D	N	N
register manipulation group							
CLR	R		clear register	S	C	C	C
INC	R		increment register (increase by 1)	D	D	D	D
DEC	R		decrement register (decrease by 1)	D	D	D	D
ROR	R		rotate register right, 1 bit, via carry bit	D	D	D	D
ROL	R		rotate register left, 1 bit, via carry bit	D	D	D	D
ASR	R		arithmetic shift right, one bit	D	D	D	D
ASL	R		arithmetic shift left, one bit	D	D	D	D
COM	R		complement register	D	D	D	D
NEG	R		negate register (NOT operation)	D	D	C	C
stack manipulation group							
PSH	R		push register word onto stack	D	D	D	N
POP	R		pop top of stack word to register	D	D	N	N
jumps							
JMP		ADR	unconditional jump to specified address	N	N	N	N
JSR		ADR	jump to subprogram, stack return address	N	N	N	N
branches							
BRN		ADR	unconditional branch	N	N	N	N
BZE		ADR	branch if zero (Z = 1)	N	N	N	N
BNE		ADR	branch if non-zero (Z = 0)	N	N	N	N
BGE		ADR	branch if greater than or equal to zero (Z = 1 or N = 0)	N	N	N	N
BGT		ADR	branch if greater than zero (Z = 0 and N = 0)	N	N	N	N
BLE		ADR	branch if less than or equal to zero (Z = 1 or N = 1)	N	N	N	N
BLT		ADR	branch if less than zero (N = 1)	N	N	N	N
BCC		ADR	branch if carry clear (C = 0)	N	N	N	N
BCS		ADR	branch if carry set (C = 1)	N	N	N	N
BVC		ADR	branch if overflow clear (V = 0)	N	N	N	N
BVS		ADR	branch if overflow set (V = 1)	N	N	N	N
BIN		ADR	branch if input not complete	N	N	N	N
BON		ADR	branch if output not complete	N	N	N	N
input/output group							
IRQ	P		signal peripheral device to load input register	N	N	N	N
INP	R		copy byte from input register to register R	D	D	N	N
ORQ	P		signal peripheral device to unload output register	N	N	N	N
OUP	R		copy byte from register R to output register	D	D	N	N
miscellaneous operations							
STC			set carry bit	N	N	S	N
CLC			clear carry bit	N	N	C	N
RTS			return from subprogram (unstack return address)	N	N	N	N
NUL			no - operation	N	N	N	N
HLT			halt	N	N	N	N

Figure 14.2
(continued)

14.9 AMC Assembly Language

Most of the rest of this chapter is taken up with an introduction to AMC assembly language. This language has been specifically designed for this course. It is simple, but fairly powerful, and illustrates the principal features of assembly languages. The presentation is sufficiently detailed for you to be able to write programs in AMC assembly language by the end of the chapter.

The general features of AMC assembly language are now discussed, after which some example programs are given.

14.10 Mnemonic Operation Codes

The operation code for an AMC assembly language instruction consists of three letters. A complete list of these codes is in Figure 14.2. If the operation refers to a register, a further letter is used to identify the register, as follows:

A   accumulator
X   index register
S   stack pointer

For example:

CLR A   Clear accumulator
MOV X S   Copy from index register to stack pointer

14.11 Symbolic Addresses

In AMC assembly language, a symbolic address consists of up to three characters. The first character must be a letter, the others can be letters or numbers. In addition, there is a letter for the addressing mode, as follows:

N   immediate operand
     (blank) absolute address
I   indirect address
D   indexed address

For example:

LOB A D CHR   Load the byte at address (CHR + Index) to the accumulator.
STO S I RES   Store the contents of the stack pointer at the address contained in the location with address RES.
ADD A   NM1   Add the number at address NM1 to the accumulator.

14.12 Automatic Data Conversion

The value of a data item can be included in an AMC assembly language program in one of two ways, as follows:

1 an integer may be written as a signed decimal number;
2 a literal data item may be written as one or two characters, between the symbols //, e.g. /I T/. (Remember that one character occupies a byte, and two characters occupy a word.)

Data items written in this way in a program are called **immediate operands**, or **constants**. Some examples of instructions using constants are as follows:

ADD X N +32   Add 32 to the contents of the index register.
LOB A N /J/   Load the character J to the accumulator.

Note that if a constant is used in a program instruction, the addressing mode must be immediate operand.

14.13 Directives

AMC assembly language has three directives, with mnemonics BTE, WRD, and END. They are used as follows:

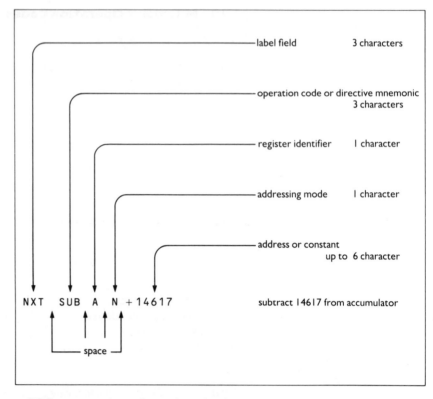

Figure 14.3
AMC assembly language instruction format

BTE reserves a byte of store for a data item.
WRD reserves a word of store for a data item.

In each case, the value of the data item may be included as a constant, as described in the previous section.

END marks the end of the program. It must be placed after all the other directives and instructions in the program.

14.14   Instruction Format

The spacing of an AMC assembly language instruction is important. There is a specific **field** for each part of the instruction. These fields are shown in Figure 14.3. If a field is not required in a particular instruction, it is left blank.

14.15   Example Programs

A number of example programs in AMC assembly language are now introduced. The first one is a program which is written in AMC machine language in Chapter 10.

Each example program is designed to illustrate one specific programming technique. As separate programs, the examples are not very useful, but in practice the same techniques are used to construct modules of large programs.

14.16   Example Program 14.1

The objective of this program is to input a sequence of characters, and store them in consecutive location in the AMC memory. The end of the input is marked by the character ∗.

Apart from the end-of-input marker, this program is identical to the first program example in Chapter 10, in AMC machine language. It enables a comparison to be made between the two levels of language. For details of the method, see Chapter 10.

Program

```
PTR WRD        CHR    Address of first character, later of current character.
```

Start of loop

```
AGN IRQ T              Signal terminal to load character into input register.
HRE BIN        HRE     Branch back to this instruction if input not complete.
    INP A              Copy character from input register to accumulator.
    CPB A N /*/        Compare character with end-of-input marker.
    BZE        OUT     Branch if equal, to instruction labelled OUT.
    STB A I PTR        Store character at address in location PTR.
    LOA A · PTR        Load address of current character to accumulator.
    INC A              Increase contents of accumulator by 1.
    STO A   PTR        Store address of next character in location PTR.
    BRN        AGN     Branch to instruction labelled AGN, to input next
                       character.
```

End of loop

```
OUT HLT                Halt.
```

Start of data area

```
CHR BTE                Space for first character.
    END                End of program.
```

Points to Notice

It is most likely that this program is much easier to follow than its machine language equivalent.

The address of the current character is in a location labelled **PTR**, short for **pointer**. This address may be said to point to the current character.

Notice how the assembly language program is set out in columns.

Apart from the directives, there is a one-to-one correspondence between instructions in assembly language and instructions in machine language.

14.17   Example Program 14.2

As mentioned in Chapter 4, one method of constructing a list of data items is as follows:

Each element of the list consists of a data item and a pointer. The pointer holds the address of the next list element. The last element in the list has an end-of-list marker for its pointer value.

This example program assumes that a list, structured in this way, has been loaded into the AMC memory. Each list element consists of a byte storing the data item (one character), and a word storing the pointer to the next list element. The end-of-list marker is a zero pointer.

The objective of the example program is to output the data items in the list, given the address of the start of the list. The method is to output a data item, and then use the next word in store as an indirect address to locate the next data item.

Program

```
PTR WRD         LE1    Address of first list item, later address of current list
                       item.
```

Start of program loop

```
NXT LOB A I PTR        Load current list item to accumulator, using location
                       PTR as an indirect address.
HRE BON         HRE    Branch to this instruction if output not complete.
    OUP A              Copy current list item to output register.
    ORQ T              Request terminal to output current list item.
    LOA A       PTR    Load address of current list item to accumulator.
    INC A              Increment accumulator, to become address of
                       pointer part of current list item.
    STO A       PTR    Store address of pointer part of list item.
    LOA A I     PTR    Load pointer part of list item to accumulator.
    BZE         OUT    Branch to end of program if pointer is zero.
    STO A       PTR    Store pointer part of list item, i.e. address of next list
                       item.
    BRN         NXT    Branch to instruction labelled NXT to continue.
```

End of program loop

```
OUT HLT                Halt.
```

Data area

```
LE2 BTE         /B/    Second list element.
    WRD         LE3
LE1 BTE         /A/    First list element.
    WRD         LE2
LE3 BTE         /C/    Third list element.
    WRD         +0     End-of-list marker.
    END                End of program.
```

Points to notice

Notice carefully how indirect addressing is used to go from one list item to the next.

The pointer part of each list element contains the address of the next list element.

The portion of program from the instruction labelled **NXT** to the instruction **BRN NXT** is repeated once for each list element. This loop is ended when a zero pointer is found in a list element.

14.18 Example Program 14.3

In Chapter 5, an algorithm is given for the multiplication of two unsigned integers, by a process of shifting and addition. This program puts the algorithm into practice.

The algorithm is written again below, using slightly different notation. The layout of the working areas used by the program is shown in Figure 14.4. Three words of store are used for these working areas in the program, but it is helpful to imagine them set out as in the diagram.

Algorithm

1 Initially, the carry bit and working area 1 contain zeros, while integer 1 and working area 2 contain the two numbers to be multiplied.

2 Repeat, for each bit of the numbers
   a) Mask out all but the least significant bit of working area 2. If this bit is 1, then

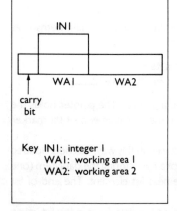

Figure 14.4
Working areas for multiplication algorithm

add integer 1 to working area 1, placing the sum in working area 1, and the carry in the carry bit.
b) Shift all the bits in the carry bit, working area 1 and working area 2 one place to the right.
3 When this process is complete, the product of the two numbers is in working area 1 and working area 2.

Program

```
IN1 WRD      +31465    Integer 1, with value declared.
WA1 WRD      +0        Working area 1: initially zero, finally most
                       significant word of product.
WA2 WRD      +15437    Working area 2: initially integer 2, finally least
                       significant word of product.
```

Start of program

```
    LOA X N  +16       Initialise index register to 16. The index register
                       is used to count the number of bits processed.
    LOA A    WA2       Load accumulator with working area 2.
```

Start of loop

```
NXT AND A N  +1        Mask all but least significant bit of accumulator.
    BZE      OVR       Branch if result is zero, to instruction labelled
                       OVR.
    LOA A    WA1       Load accumulator with working area 1.
    ADD A    IN1       Add integer 1 to accumulator.
    BRN      DWN       Branch to instruction labelled DWN.
OVR LOA A    WA1       Load accumulator with working area 1.
    CLC               Clear carry bit.
DWN ROR A             Rotate accumulator right, 1 bit, via carry bit.
    STO A    WA1       Store new value of working area 1.
    LOA A    WA2       Load working area 2 to accumulator.
    ROR A             Rotate accumulator right, 1 bit, via carry bit.
    STO A    WA2       Store new value of working area 2.
    DEC X             Decrease index register by 1.
    BGT      NXT       Branch if index is still positive, to continue
                       shifting and adding.
```

End of loop

```
    HLT               Halt.
    END               End of program.
```

Points to notice

The carry bit is used to pass a bit from working area 1 to working area 2 during the rotation operation. In the first rotation operation, the least significant bit of working area 1 moves into the carry bit. In the second rotation, the same bit moves from the carry bit into the most significant bit position of working area 2.

This program contains a loop from the instruction labelled **NXT** to the instruction **BGT NXT**. The index register is used to count the number of times the loop is repeated.

14.19 Example Program 14.4

This program scans a set of characters, and counts the number of occurrences of a given character. It is assumed that the set of characters is already loaded into the AMC memory, and is terminated by the character ★.

The program is written as a subprogram, called from a main program. The address of the start of the set of characters is passed from the main program to the subprogram, together with the character whose occurrences are to be counted. On return from the subprogram, the number of occurrences of the character is passed back to the main program. Registers are used to pass the information to and from the subprogram.

Within the subprogram, indirect addressing is used to locate each character in the set. The algorithm for the subprogram is as follows:

1 Set the number of occurrences of the character to zero.
2 Load a character from the set to the accumulator.
3 If the character is the end-of-set marker, then return to the main program.
4 If the character is the required character, increase the number of occurrences of the character by 1.
5 Go to step 2.

Program

CHR	BTE		Character whose occurrences are to be counted.
LOC	WRD		Address of current character in set.
CNT	WRD		Number of occurrences of character.

Start of subprogram

SBP	STB	X	CHR	Store required character, passed to subprogram in index register.
	STO	A	LOC	Store address of first character in set, passed to subprogram in accumulator.
	CLR	A		Clear accumulator.
	STO	A	CNT	Set character count to zero.

Start of loop to inspect one character

BGN	LOB	A I	LOC	Using indirect addressing, load current character to accumulator.
	CPB	A N	/★/	Compare with end-of-set marker.
	BZE		OUT	Branch to end of subprogram if equal.
	CPB	A	CHR	Compare with required character.
	BNE		DWN	Branch to instruction labelled **DWN** if not equal.
	LOA	A	CNT	Load character count to accumulator.
	INC	A		Increment character count.
	STO	A	CNT	Store new value of character count.
DWN	LOA	A	LOC	Load address of current character to accumulator.
	INC	A		Increment address of current character.
	STO	A	LOC	Store new address of current character.
	BRN		BGN	Branch back to repeat loop.

End of loop

OUT	LOA	A	CNT	Load character count to accumulator.
	RTS			Return to main program.

End of subprogram, start of main program

	LOB	X N	/T/	Load character to be counted, T, to index register.
	LOA	A N	SET	Load start address of character set to accumulator.
	LOA	S N	+127	Initialise stack pointer to 127.

	JSR	SBP	Jump to subprogram.
	HLT		Halt on return to main program.

End of main program, start of data area

SET	BTE	/T/	
	BTE	/H/	
	BTE	/E/	
	BTE	/ /	
	BTE	/C/	
	BTE	/A/	
	BTE	/T/	
	BTE	/*/	
	END		End of program.

Points to notice

The accumulator and index register are used to pass data to the subprogram. The accumulator is also used to pass data back from the subprogram.

The branching instruction **BNE DWN** is designed to skip the next three instructions if the current character is *not* the one which is being counted. Branching in this manner, on a negative condition, is an efficient way of constructing a portion of a program such as this.

The test for the end-of-set marker must be made before the test for the required character.

14.20   Example Program 14.5

This program adds together two numbers which are stored in character form. This is a fairly common process in non-scientific computing. Many modern computers have various 'decimal adjust' instructions in their assembly languages to enable such addition to be done fairly easily. As the AMC does not have these facilities, the process is fairly laborious. However, it does illustrate several programming concepts, notably indexed addressing.

The program assumes that the numbers to be added, and the sum, are stored as ASCII characters in consecutive bytes. The numbers are five digits long, and thus occupy five bytes each, with six bytes allocated to the sum.

The ASCII codes for the digits 0 to 9 have hexadecimal values 30 to 39. Thus, if the codes for two digits are added, the result is no longer in the correct range. For example, if the codes for 1 (31) and 2 (32) are added, the result is 63. To obtain the correct result, the code for 0 (30) must be subtracted.

If the result of an addition exceeds 9, then 10 must be subtracted, and 1 carried into the next addition. In the program, a byte of store holds the value of the carry from one addition to the next, as the ordinary carry bit cannot be used.

The program adds one pair of digits at a time, using the index register as a loop counter.

Program

NM1	BTE	/9/	First number to be added (= 98274).
	BTE	/8/	
	BTE	/2/	
	BTE	/7/	
	BTE	/4/	
NM2	BTE	/4/	Second number to be added (= 45342).

```
                    BTE         /5/
                    BTE         /3/
                    BTE         /4/
                    BTE         /2/
          CDS BTE                       Carry digit of sum.
          SUM BTE                       Sum.
                    BTE
                    BTE
                    BTE
                    BTE
          CRY BTE               +0      Carry from one addition to the next.

Start of program
                    LOA X N +4          Initialise index register to 4, one less than the number
                                        of digits in each number.

Start of loop
          AGN LOB A D NM1               Load digit of first number to accumulator, using
                                        indexed addressing.
                    ADB A D NM2         Add digit of second number, using indexed
                                        addressing.
                    SBB A N /0/         Subtract the code for 0 to adjust sum.
                    ADB A   CRY         Add carry from previous addition.
                    CPB A N /9/         Compare sum with code for 9.
                    BGT         GTR     Branch if greater to instruction labelled G T R.
                    STB A D SUM         Store digit in sum, using indexed addressing.
                    CLA A               Clear accumulator.
                    STB A   CRY         Store zero in carry byte.
                    BRN         NXT     Branch to instruction labelled N X T.
          GTR SBB A N +10              Subtract 10 from accumulator.
                    STB A D SUM         Store digit in sum, using indexed addressing.
                    LOB A N +1          Load I to accumulator.
                    STB A   CRY         Store I in carry byte.
          NXT DEC X                     Decrease index register by I.
                    BGE         AGN     Branch if greater than or equal to zero, to continue
                                        loop.

End of loop, deal with carry digit of sum
                    LOB A N /0/         Load the code for zero to accumulator.
                    ADB A   CRY         Add carry byte to accumulator.
                    STB A   CDS         Store result in carry digit of sum.
                    HLT                 Halt.
                    END                 End of program.
```

Points to notice

The index register is used as a loop counter, and also to address the digits of the numbers. Its values run from 4 to 0. In this way, it counts from the least significant digits of the numbers, at addresses NM1+4, NM2+4 and SUM+4, to the most significant digits, at addresses NM1+0, NM2+0, SUM+0.

Using a loop counter which decreases in value simplifies the condition for continuing the loop. It is a very common practice.

14.21 Uses of Assembly Languages

With the development of high level languages (discussed in Chapter 16), there has been a gradual reduction in the relative importance of assembly languages. However, they still have a variety of uses, notably in the writing of **systems software**, and in programming of microcomputers.

Systems software is a name given to the layers of software which transform the raw hardware of a computer into a useful machine. Systems programs include operating systems and language translation programs, both of which are discussed in later chapters. Most system software is written in a low level language, though high level languages are becoming increasingly popular in this area.

The advent of microcomputers has given low level languages a new lease of life. Many microcomputers are too small to support anything but the most primitive subset of a high level language. Furthermore, a significant proportion of micro-processors are dedicated to the performance of a single task, such as controlling a camera. The only program which these microprocessors require is permanently stored on read-only memory. Such programs are almost always written in a low level language.

14.22 Conclusion

This chapter has introduced the concept of an assembly language, outlined the objectives and features of assembly languages, and then used AMC assembly language to demonstrate a number of techniques of low level language program-ming. The main points of the chapter are as follows:

- The objective of an assembly language is to simplify the programming of a particular computer, while still remaining closely related to the architecture of the computer.
- An assembly language is a programming language whose data structures correspond to the physical structure of the registers and main store of its host computer, and whose instructions are closely related to the machine instructions of the computer.
- Characteristic features of assembly languages include mnemonic operation codes, symbolic addresses, automatic data conversion, directives and macros.
- Assembly languages are used principally in the writing of systems software and in the programming of microcomputers.

The material in this chapter is carried a stage further in the next chapter, which concerns the process of translating a program from assembly language to machine language.

Exercise 14

1 Briefly define the following terms: assembly language; mnemonic; symbolic address; label; directive; macro-instruction; low level language; immediate operand; pointer.
2 Write short sequences of instructions, in AMC assembly language, for each of the following operations:
   a) Set a store word, labelled DT1, to zero.
   b) Store the decimal value 16291 in a word labelled CS1.
   c) Increase the contents of a byte of store, labelled CTR, by 1.
   d) Test whether the contents of two store locations with addresses AB1 and AB2 are equal.
   e) Create a stack containing the code for the following ASCII characters:

| AB |
| CD |
| EF |

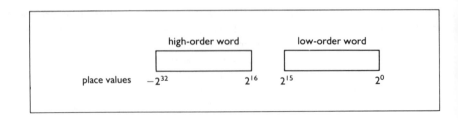

place values -2^{32} 2^{16} 2^{15} 2^{0}

Figure 14.5
A double length integer

3 Rewrite Example Program 10.2 in AMC assembly language.

4 Rewrite the program in Exercise 10, Question 8, in AMC assembly language.

5 A 'double length' integer may be stored in two consecutive words of AMC store, as follows:

The first word stores the high-order part of the number, with the most significant bit representing a negative quantity. The place value of this bit is $-2^{31} = -2\ 147\ 483\ 648$. The least significant bit in this word has the place value of $2^{16} = 65\ 536$.

The second word stores the low-order part of the number, with all bits representing positive quantities. Place values range from $2^{15} = 32\ 768$ to $2^0 = 1$.

For example, if the high-order part of the word contains the decimal value 10 000 and the low-order part contains the decimal value 8 763, then the double length number represented is $2^{16} \times 10\ 000 + 8\ 763 = 655\ 368\ 763$.

Figure 14.5 illustrates the storage of a double length integer.

Addition of two double length integers is fairly straightforward. The low-order words of the two numbers are added first, and the sum stored. The high-order words are then added, together with the carry from the low-order addition. The program shown below carries out this process:

Program
Data areas
```
    HI1 WRD    +10000    High-order word of integer 1.
    LI1 WRD    +  8763   Low-order word of integer 1.
    HI2 WRD    +20000
    LI2 WRD    +14261
    HSM WRD              High-order word of sum.
    LSM WRD
```

Start of program
```
        LOA  A  LI1
        ADD  A  LI2
        STO  A  LSM
        LOA  A  HI1
        ———  —  ———
        STO  A  HSM
        HLT
        END
```

Make a copy of this program, and
a) Fill in the missing instruction in the program.
b) Write suitable comments next to each program line.
c) Write a program to add three double length integers.
□ d) Write a program to subtract two double length integers.

6 Write a program in AMC assembly language to locate the end of a list of data, structured as in Example Program 14.2. The program is given the address of the first list element, and scans the list until the last element is located. The program halts with the address of the last list element in the accumulator.

7 Write a program in AMC assembly language which subtracts two numbers which are stored in character form. It is suggested that five digit numbers are used, as in Example Program 14.5.

8 Write a program in AMC assembly language to divide two unsigned integers by a process of shifting and subtraction.

9 The simplest form of integer multiplication is by a process of repeated addition. For example, to multiply 4 by 9, add 4 nine times. This process was used on early computers. An algorithm for this method of multiplication is as follows:

To multiply integers **IN1** and **IN2**, using working areas **WA1** and **WA2**,

1 Clear **WA1**, and load **IN2** to **WA2**.
2 If **WA2** is zero, halt.
3 Add **IN1** to **WA1**.
4 Reduce **WA2** by 1.
5 Go to step 2.

Write a program in AMC assembly language to implement this algorithm. Either use data numbers which are small enough for the product to be accommodated in one word (**WA1**), or use a double length word for **WA1**, and add the carry arising in step 3 into the high-order word.

10 Integer division may be carried out by a process of repeated subtraction. For example, to divide 40 by 7, count the number of times 7 may be subtracted from 40.
   a) Write an algorithm for division by this method.
   b) Write a program in AMC assembly language to implement your algorithm.

11 Explain what is wrong with the following AMC instruction

   STO A N /AB/

12 The least significant bit of a 16 bit word is an even parity bit. This means that the parity of the word is correct if the total number of 1s is an even number.

   Write a program, in AMC assembly language, to check the parity of the word. Use repeated shifting, masking and addition to obtain the total number of 1s in the word.

   Assume that, at the start of the program, the word to be checked is loaded into the accumulator. At the end of the program, the accumulator contains 0 if the parity is correct, and 1 if it is not correct.

13 a) Describe briefly what is meant by indexed addressing.
   b) A certain computer has one accumulator and one index register, and no indirect addressing capability. Thirty small integers are stored in addresses **ARRAY, ARRAY+1,** ... Show, by means of a description, a flowchart or a section of assembly code (use a real or an imaginary language, explaining the notation used) how the sum of the thirty values may be evaluated and stored in the address **SUM**.

UCLES 81 Specimen 1

15
Assemblers

This chapter concerns the process of translating a program written in an assembly language to an equivalent program in machine language. The item of software which performs this task is called an **assembler**. The nature and objectives of an assembler are discussed, together with a brief examination of some of the techniques of assembly used in practice. As in previous chapters, AMC machine and assembly language are used as examples. This chapter relates closely to material in previous chapters, especially areas concerned with machine languages and assembly languages.

15.1   Nature and Objectives of an Assembler

Briefly stated, the objective of an assembler is to translate a program from the assembly language to the machine language of a particular computer. An assembler is thus an integral part of the systems software of a computer. Each type of computer has its own assembler.

A slightly more general objective of an assembler is to assist in the development of low level language programs for a particular computer. Thus, in addition to their translation function, assemblers perform other tasks, notably the detection and reporting of errors in programs which they are required to translate.

An even more general objective of an assembler is to provide a programmer-oriented interface to the hardware of a particular computer. In other words, the assembler enables a programmer to 'see' the hardware of a computer in a simple, useful way. It must enable the hardware of the computer to be used in the most effective manner.

In addition to these general objectives, an assembler must be acceptably short, and carry out its tasks quickly and efficiently. In practice, this objective must be balanced against the desire to include a large number of non-essential features in an assembler.

Bearing in mind these objectives, an assembler may be described in the following terms:

> An assembler is a program which translates from the assembly language to the machine language of a particular computer, and provides additional facilities to assist in the development of low level language programs for the computer.

15.2   Tasks Performed by an Assembler

This section examines some of the tasks carried out by an assembler in the process of translating from assembly language to machine language. Many of these tasks are associated with features of assembly languages, mentioned in the previous chapter. Although the details of the ways these tasks are performed vary from one assembler to another, the general nature of the tasks is common to all assemblers. The tasks are analysis of the structure of an assembly language program, decoding mnemonic operation codes, dealing with symbolic addresses, automatic data conversion, interpreting directives and macro expansion.

15.3   Analysis of the Structure of an Assembly Language Program

The first task of an assembler is to analyse the structure of an assembly language program, and determine the nature of each part of the program.

Each assembly language has a set of rules which govern the structure of programs written in the language. These rules determine both the overall structure of a program, and the detailed structure of each program line. In most cases these rules are fairly simple. Programs generally consist of one instruction or directive per line. Lines either have fixed length fields for specific purposes, or use punctuation marks to separate fields. AMC assembly language is an example of the first case.

The assembler uses these rules in the analysis of a program. The rules enable each group of characters to be interpreted as a mnemonic operation code, symbolic address, etc. Once the nature of a group of characters has been determined, more detailed work can be done, as outlined in the following sections.

If the structure of any portion of a program does not match the requirements of the rules, then an error is detected by the assembler. An error message is displayed.

15.4   Decoding Mnemonic Operation Codes

This is a very straightforward procedure. As there is a one-to-one correspondence between assembly language mnemonics and machine instruction codes, a table is used to store each mnemonic together with its equivalent machine language operation code. Each mnemonic operation code in a program is looked up in this table, and the corresponding machine language operation code placed in the machine language program. If a mnemonic operation code is not in the table, then an error is recorded, and a suitable error message is displayed.

15.5   Dealing with Symbolic Addresses

The objective here is to replace each symbolic address by a machine language address. The procedure is more complicated than decoding operation codes, and several stages are generally involved.

Every symbolic address used in a program must occur in one, and only one, position in the program as a label. As the assembler works through a program, the address of each instruction or directive is determined. If the instruction or directive has a label, then the address is associated with that label. Part of the task of an assembler is to build up a table of all the labels used in a program, together with the addresses at which they occur. If identical labels are encountered at different addresses, then an error is reported.

The table thus created is used to relate each symbolic address in a program to a machine address. If a symbolic address is not in the table, then an error is detected. In some assemblers, the process of creating the table is completed before symbolic addresses are looked up in it. In others, the two processes occur concurrently. This point is dealt with again in the section on the structure of assembler programs.

In some cases, the machine addresses allocated to symbolic addresses at this stage are the final ones which are used when the machine language is run. In other cases, they are relative addresses, generally relative to the start of the program. They are changed into absolute memory addresses at a later stage, when the machine language program is loaded into its position in store for running.

15.6   Automatic Data Conversion

If an assembly language permits the representation of data values in various number bases and character codes, then conversion algorithms and tables are used to change these representations to machine code format. This is generally a very straightforward process.

15.7 Interpreting Directives

As mentioned in the previous chapter, directives are assembly language instructions which do not have a counterpart in machine code. An assembler acts upon a directive as soon as it is recognised. The nature of the action depends on the particular directive. For example, if, in AMC assembly language, the directive **W R D** is encountered, the assembler reserves a word of store.

15.8 Macro Expansion

You will recall from the previous chapter that a macro-instruction is a single instruction which is defined, within a program, to represent a set of instructions.

When an assembler encounters the definition of a macro-instruction, it decodes the set of instructions which the macro-instruction represents, and records the mnemonic of the macro-instruction in a table. When the macro-instruction is encountered in the body of the program, the set of instructions is inserted at the corresponding position in the machine language program. In this way, the macro-instruction is expanded to the full set of instructions in the machine language program.

15.9 The Structure of an Assembler Program

Having outlined the tasks carried out by an assembler, it is useful to investigate, very briefly, the way in which an assembler program is structured, in order to carry out these tasks.

Most assembler programs consist of a number of modules, one for each task mentioned previously. The structure analysis module is in overall control. Once the nature of a set of characters in an assembly language program has been recognised, the appropriate module is called to carry out whatever detailed work is required.

There are, broadly speaking, two approaches to the analysis of the structure of an assembly language program. The traditional method involves scanning the assembly language program twice. Assemblers using this method are now called **two-pass assemblers**. The more modern approach involves only one scan of the assembly language program. Assemblers of this type are called **single-pass** or **incremental assemblers**.

15.10 The AMC Assembler: a Two-pass Assembler

The program which translates from AMC assembly language to AMC machine language is an example of a two-pass assembler. A brief description of this assembler is given below, in order to clarify some of the concepts introduced earlier in the chapter.

The tasks performed during each pass through an assembly language program are as follows.

First pass

1 Break down the current assembly language program line into its constituent parts (label, operation code mnemonic, etc.).
2 If the label field is non-blank, store the label and its corresponding machine address in the symbolic address table.
3 Decode the operation mnemonic, register identifier and addressing mode, or directive.

4 Insert the operation code into the current machine language program instruction, and record the address of this instruction.
5 From the number of words used by the current machine language program instruction, calculate the address of the next machine language program instruction.

Second pass

1 If the current assembly program line contains a symbolic address, look this address up in the symbolic address table. Insert the equivalent machine code address into the current machine code instruction.
2 If the current assembly program line contains the value of a data item as a decimal number or set of ASCII characters, obtain the hexadecimal equivalent of this value and insert it into the current machine code instruction.
3 If the current assembly program line is a relative branching instruction, calculate the relative offset and insert it into the current machine code instruction.

If an error is detected during any of these steps, an appropriate error message is displayed. Assembly continues to the end of the current pass.

15.11 Language of Assemblers

Assemblers are programs which translate from the assembly language to the machine language of a particular computer. But in what language is the assembler program itself written? In the early days of computing, the answer was obvious: in the machine language of the particular computer. This is still the case for a great many current-day assemblers, particularly those used by microcomputers.

However, a significant proportion of assemblers are written in the assembly language which they translate. Others are written in high level languages, which are introduced in the next chapter. Some assemblers are designed to run on a different computer from the one whose language they translate. Such assemblers are called **cross assemblers**.

15.12 Conclusion

This chapter has introduced one of the essential items of systems software of a computer, namely the program which translates from the assembly language to the machine language of the computer. The main points of the chapter are as follows:

- An assembler is a program which translates from the assembly language to the machine language of a particular computer, and provides additional facilities to assist in the development of low level language programs for the computer.
- Tasks performed by an assembler include:

  analysis of the structure of an assembly language program
  decoding mnemonic operation codes
  dealing with symbolic addresses
  automatic data conversion
  interpreting directives
  macro expansion

- The overall control of an assembler is carried out by the structure analysis module. Other tasks are performed by modules called from this module.
- The two approaches to the analysis of an assembly language program are the two pass and single pass or incremental techniques.

Exercise 15

1 Briefly define the following terms: assembler; cross assembler.
2 Summarise, in about 150 words, the tasks carried out by an assembler.
3 In addition to language translation, what other function does an assembler perform?
4 Why can a symbolic address be used as a label in only one position in a program?
5 If the machine and assembly languages of a computer were altered to include a new instruction, what changes would have to be made to the assembler program?
6 The machine code corresponding to the following AMC assembly language program is shown after the first pass of the AMC assembler. The table of symbolic addresses is also shown.

AMC assembly language				AMC machine language		Interpretation
	LOA	X N	+1	0000	1121 _____	Use index register as loop counter, initial value 1.
NXT	CMP	X N	+27	0004	1A21 _____	Compare index register with 27.
	BGT		OUT	0008	65__	Exit loop if greater than 27.
	LOA	A N	+100	000A	1111 _____	Load 100 in accumulator.
	STB	A D	W	000E	2214 _____	Store contents of accumulator in W+index.
	INC	X		0012	0220	Increment index register.
	BRN		NXT	0014	61__	Continue loop.
OUT	HLT			0016	8500	Halt.
W	BTE			0018		Data item.

Table of symbolic addresses
```
NXT  0004
OUT  0016
W    0018
```

Make a copy of the program, and complete the machine language version by carrying out the steps of the second assembly pass. Remember that the relative address in a branching instruction is calculated from the address of the following instruction. For example, the relative address in the machine language version of **BGT OUT** is calculated from address **000A**.

7 Select a program in AMC assembly language from Chapter 15, and convert it to AMC machine language. Start the machine language version at address **0000**. Include a table of the symbolic addresses used in the program, together with their machine addresses.

16
High level languages

This chapter is concerned with a class of programming languages called **high level languages**. The chapter explains the nature of high level languages, outlines their development and discusses their objectives. Various types of high level languages are described.

The bulk of the chapter is concerned with features common to most high level languages. To conclude the chapter is an assessment of the impact of high level languages on computing.

The material in this chapter relates to the rest of the book in a number of ways. Many of the data structures introduced earlier are created and manipulated by programs in high level languages. An important section of the book which follows shortly is concerned with translation from a high level language to a machine language. Finally, many operating systems and most programs for computer applications are written in high level languages.

16.1   What is a High Level Language?

Briefly stated, a high level language is **problem oriented**, whereas a low level language is **machine oriented**. In other words, a high level language is a convenient and simple means of describing the information structures and sequence of actions required to perform a particular task.

A high level language is independent of the architecture of the computer which supports it. This has two major advantages. Firstly, the person writing the programs does not have to know anything about the computer on which the program will be run. Secondly, programs are **portable**, that is, the same program can be run on different types of computer. However, a word of caution is necessary here: this feature of machine independence is not always achieved in practice.

In most cases, programs in high level languages are shorter than equivalent programs in low level languages. However, conciseness can be carried too far, to the point where programs become impossible to understand. A more important feature of a high level language is its ability to reflect clearly the structure of programs written in it.

16.2   The Development of High Level Languages

Work started on the development of high level languages in the mid-1950s, about ten years after the emergence of electronic digital computers. During those ten years it had become evident that the major shortcoming of computers was not their hardware performance but their software performance. Writing correct, useful machine and assembly language programs for the computers of the day was a difficult, time-consuming and expensive process. It must be remembered that most computing in those days was for scientific and engineering purposes, 'number crunching' in today's language.

During this period, advances in computer languages consisted of additional features to increase the capabilities of assembly languages. Although these features provided a few short cuts, they increased the complexity of the assembly languages. The languages lacked a clear, coherent overall structure.

There was resistance to the idea of high level languages on the grounds of inefficiency. High level languages require compilers to translate the programs into machine language before they can be run. It was feared that the machine language programs produced by compilers would be extremely inefficient, compared with programs written directly in machine language. Considering the small size and low speed of computers in these days, this fear had considerable justification.

Despite these objections, the period from 1954 to 1960 saw the development of three major high level languages, namely Fortran, Algol 60 and Cobol. Some details about the development of these languages are provided in the next chapter.

In spite of the problems mentioned earlier, once high level languages become available, their use spread very rapidly. Many more languages were written, and compilers were produced to implement these languages on the various computers currently in use. It has been estimated that there were about 1700 programming languages by 1965, but the three mentioned above are still among the most popular.

Work on the development of high level languages still continues today. Existing languages are modified in the light of experience, and sometimes substantially revised. For example, a new version of Algol, Algol 68, was introduced in 1968. From time to time, new high level languages are produced, the latest prominent example being Ada, in 1979.

16.3 Types of High Level Languages

High level languages may be broadly classified as **general-purpose** or **special-purpose**. Special-purpose languages can be grouped according to the purpose they serve.

General-purpose languages are intended to be equally well suited to business, scientific, engineering or systems software tasks. The commonest general-purpose languages are Algol 68 and PL/1. The language Ada, currently under development, also falls into this category. Because of their broad capabilities, these languages are large and relatively difficult to use.

The commonest categories of special-purpose languages are commercial, scientific and educational. In the commercial field, Cobol still reigns supreme, while Fortran is still the most widely used scientific language. In the computer education field, Basic is the most popular, with Pascal gaining increasing prominence. Both Basic and Pascal are general-purpose languages in their own right, Pascal having considerable power.

Several of the languages mentioned above are described in more detail in the next chapter, on high level language case studies.

16.4 Objectives of High Level Languages

Before going on to discuss the features of high level languages, it is essential to be clear about what high level languages are trying to achieve. Some of the objectives of high level languages have been mentioned in previous sections. This section examines them in more detail.

As mentioned previously, the defining characteristics of a high level language are problem-orientation and machine independence. These are taken for granted in the following discussion.

The first objective of a high level language is to provide a convenient means of expressing the solution to a problem. There are two other common ways of doing this – mathematics, and natural languages, such as English. Most high level languages borrow, without much modification, concepts and symbols from mathematics. The problem with natural languages is that, in their full richness and complexity, they are quite impossible to use to instruct a computer. Nevertheless, high level languages use words from natural languages, and allow these words, and mathematical symbols, to be combined according to various rules. These rules create the structure of programs written in the language. The result, in a good high level language, is a clear structure, not too different from our customary ways of thinking and expressing ourselves.

This discussion leads to the second objective of high level languages – simplicity. Simplicity is achieved by a small set of basic operations, a few clear rules for combining these operations, and, above all, the avoidance of special cases.

The third objective of a high level language is efficiency. Programs in the language must be able to be translated into machine code fairly quickly, and the resulting machine code must run efficiently. This objective almost always conflicts with the first two. Most high level languages reflect a compromise between these objectives.

The final objective is readability of programs. Many languages allow for the inclusion of comments or additional 'noise' words, to make programs easier to read. However, a good high level language should enable programs to be written which are clear to read without additional comments. Regrettably, some high level languages ignore this objective altogether.

To summarise, the objectives of a high level language are:

application orientation,
machine independence,
a clear structure,
simplicity,
efficiency,
readability.

The next section, concerning features of high level languages, shows how these objectives are put into practice.

16.5   Features of High Level Languages

The next few sections outline the features common to most high level languages. These features are grouped under the headings character set and reserved words, program structure, data, operations and control structure. In this chapter, these features are discussed in general terms. The next chapter shows how these features are implemented in some popular high level languages.

16.6   Character Set and Reserved Words

The **character set** used by a language is the set of all characters which may be used in programs written in the language. Almost all languages use letters and decimal digits, differences arise in the use of special characters such as punctuation marks.

Most high level languages use **reserved words**. These are words which have a specific meaning in programs, and may not be used by the programmer for any other purpose. For example, in Basic language, reserved words include **READ**, **LET** and **PRINT**. Some languages permit abbreviations of reserved words. The size and complexity of a language can be measured by the number of reserved words it uses. For example, most simple versions of Basic language have about fifteen reserved words, while Ada uses more than sixty.

16.7   Program Structure

Perhaps the most important feature of a high level language is the way in which programs in it are structured. The structure of a program is defined at several levels: the overall construction of the program, the structure of individual statements, and the structure of parts of statements, for example arithmetic expressions.

The structure of a program is specified by a set of rules, called **rules of syntax**. Different languages have different ways of expressing these rules. In some, the rules are written in concise English. Others use diagrams, while others (notably Algol) use a notation originally called **Backus-Naur form**, now known as BNF. An example of the use of BNF notation is to be found in the exercise at the end of the chapter.

Much attention has been devoted, in the development and use of high level languages, to the way in which programs are split up into **blocks**, each block doing a specific task. In some languages, notably Fortran, these blocks are called **subroutines**, in others, notably Algol and Pascal, these blocks are called **procedures** or **functions**. Because of the careful structuring of programs into blocks which they permit, Algol, Pascal and similar languages are called **block-structured languages**.

Procedures, functions or subroutines are activated via **calls** from other parts of the program. For example, if a program contains a procedure to calculate the square root of a given number, this procedure is called every time a square root is required in the rest of the program. Some languages permit a procedure or function to call itself, a feature known as **recursion**. This is an extremely powerful feature, from the point of view of the person writing programs in the language, but causes difficulties when the language is translated into machine code. The case study of Algol 60, in the next chapter, gives an example of the use of recursion.

16.8 Data

An important aspect of high level languages is the way in which they handle the data items and data structures used in a program. Broadly speaking, data items fall into two categories: **variables**, which can change their value during the running of a program, and **constants**, which keep the same value. In most program languages, variables are given names, or **identifiers**. In some languages, such as Fortran and Basic, constants are referred to by their values, while in others, such as Algol and Pascal, constants are also given identifiers.

Some program languages require that all variables be **declared** before they are used. Generally, variables are declared by listing them at the start of the procedure or subroutine in which they are to be used. An attempt to use a variable which has not been declared results in an error.

This gives rise to the idea of the **scope** of a variable. The scope of a variable is the part of a program in which it may be used. Variables which are declared for use in one procedure only are called **local** variables. Their scope is limited to that procedure. Variables which are declared for use in the whole program are called **global** variables. Their scope is the whole program.

The intention of providing each variable with a scope is to enable a program to be broken up into 'watertight' blocks, or modules. Each block uses only the information it requires. This simplifies the task of designing, writing and testing programs, and limits the effects of errors.

Almost all high level languages include the notion of **data types**. In Basic language, the standard data types are **numeric** and **character strings**. These types can be incorporated into **arrays**, which are tables of items of the same type. In most high level languages, numbers can be **integers** or **real** numbers (generally stored in floating point form). PL/1 even permits the number of significant figures in a number to be declared. Another common standard data type is **Boolean**, with the range of values 'true' and 'false'.

A data type which is the subject of some controversy is the **pointer** type. A pointer is a data item which contains the address of another data item. Pointers can be used to construct such data structures as lists and trees. For example, a list of people's names could be constructed as follows:

Pointer types are only available in some high level languages, notably Algol and Pascal. The problem with pointers is that careless use of them can result in program errors which are very difficult to detect and correct.

Some languages permit the programmer to declare his or her own data types, built up from standard data types. **Records** can be constructed, containing data of different types. The following section of a Pascal program shows how this can be done.

```
type  name=array [1 . . . 20] of char;
      day=(mon, tues, wed, thur, fri, sat, sun);

      payrecord=record employee name: name;
                       payrate: real;
                       hours worked: integer;
                       pay: real;
                       payday: day
            end
```

In the above example, **char** is a data type. Variables of type **char** have values consisting of a single character. The data type 'name' is an array of twenty characters. Variables of the data type 'day' can have one of the values listed in the brackets.

The purpose of data types is to make programs more meaningful, and to provide additional checks for errors. For example, if an attempt is made to add an integer variable to a character variable, then an error will be caused.

16.9 Operations

The operations included in a high level language enable data items and data structures to be manipulated in various ways. Almost all program languages permit arithmetic operations. Many allow expressions of any degree of complexity to be evaluated on one statement. Most languages include the logical operations AND, OR and NOT, again combined to form expressions if necessary.

Some program languages, notably PL/I and some versions of Basic, have instructions to manipulate entire data structures such as matrices. In these languages, multiplying two matrices, for example, requires only one program instruction.

All program languages have rules of **precedence** which specify the order in which operations are carried out within the same expression. Arithmetic operations follow the usual rules: multiplication before addition, etc., but languages differ over the precedence of logic operations over arithmetic operations in the same expression.

The process whereby a variable takes on a value is called **assignment**. Different languages express assignment in different ways. For example, assigning the value of a variable Y to a variable X is expressed in Basic and Fortran as

$X = Y$

Algol 60, Algol 68 and Pascal would express it as

$x := y$

while in Cobol it would be written as

MOVE Y TO X.

16.10   Input and Output

High level languages vary considerably in their treatment of input and output. The intention in all cases is to obscure the problems which surround input and output at machine level, although in many cases these problems are taken care of by the operating system.

Most high level languages provide a simple, logical method of transferring data to or from the computer. Some languages, notably Fortran and Cobol, pay consider-able attention to the layout, or **format** of the data. Other languages deliberately 'play down' this aspect, to simplify matters for the programmer.

16.11   Control Structure

All program languages, both low level and high level, have ways of transferring control from one part of a program to another. In high level languages, there are generally three aspects of the question: **sequencing**, **looping** and **branching**.

Sequencing

Sequencing is the flow of control from one instruction to the next. In most program languages this is achieved by writing instructions one after the other, separated by semi-colons, or on consecutive lines. Basic language is an exception, with instructions being executed in order of line number.

Looping

Looping is concerned with repeating instructions or groups of instructions. Most high level languages have instructions for performing loops a certain number of times, using one variable as a counter. Some languages allow loops to be repeated while some condition is true, or until a condition becomes true.

Branching

Branching concerns transferring control to one part of a program when a condition is true, and to another part when the condition is false. The most general form of a branching instruction is as follows:

>   *if* (condition) **then** (instructions to be executed if condition is true)
>   **else** (instructions to be executed if condition is false).
>   *endif*

Basic language has a simpler conditional branching instruction, as follows:

>   **I F** (condition) **THEN** (statement number to which control is transferred if condition is true)

If the condition is false, control is transferred to the statement following the **I F** statement.

Multi-way Branching

A more sophisticated version of the conditional branching instruction is available in many languages. This is the **multi-way branch** instruction.

In Pascal, the multi-way branch is implemented as the **case** statement. For example

```
case operator of
   add       : a:=a+b
   subtract  : a:=a-b
   multiply  : a:=a*b
end
```

Depending on the value of the variable **operator**, one of the statements is executed.

In Basic, multi-way branching is implemented as the **ON..GO TO** or **ON.. GOSUB** statement. In Fortran, there is the **computed GO TO** statement.

Unconditional Branching

There is some controversy about the use of the unconditional branching instruction, of the form:

go to (statement number)

in high level languages. In languages such as Basic without the **if** .. **then** .. **else** .. construction, the use of **go to** is unavoidable. However, **go to** is regarded as a low level language feature, to be avoided in well-written high level language programs.

16.12   An Assessment of High Level Languages

A high level language is a programming language which is problem-oriented and machine independent, and has the objectives of a clear structure, simplicity, efficiency and readability. How well do high level languages match these criteria in practice?

Problem-orientation is generally well achieved, especially in special-purpose languages such as Cobol. Machine independence does not score so highly. A 'standard' version of most popular high level languages has been published, but machine-dependent features persist in most implementations. Basic language is particularly bad, with different computer manufacturers offering different enhancements to the language on their own computers.

A clear structure of programs is achieved on many high level languages. Perhaps the best example of this is the fact that several large operating systems have been successfully written in high level languages. Simplicity is certainly possible in most high level languages, but it is limited by the complexity of the problem being programmed.

With computers becoming cheaper, and programmers' time becoming more expensive, high level languages are appearing more and more efficient, at least from the point of view of the data processing system as a whole. Program readability is still very much a matter for the individual programmer.

The main success of high level languages has been their transformation of the art (or science ...) of computer programming from the domain of a few highly skilled computer experts to a much wider group of people, including school pupils and interested amateurs. This has increased the range of computer applications, and helped to dispel some of the myths which surround computers.

However, there is still a place for programming in low level languages. Systems software must still be written, at least in part, in a low level language. Many of the new microprocessor-based computers are too small to support anything more than a simple subset of a high level language. If a microprocessor is to be dedicated to a specific task, such as word processing, all the software required is usually written in assembly language.

At present there is a move towards an even higher level of programming languages, which might be called **specification languages**. These are discussed in Section 30.3.

Exercise 16

1 Briefly define the following terms: high level language; portable; general-purpose language; character set; reserved word; syntax; block; subroutine; call; recursion; variable; constant; declaration; scope; local variable; global variable; data type; Boolean variable; pointer; rule of precedence; assignment; format.

2 What are the two distinguishing features of high level languages?

3 What factors were the driving force behind the development of high level languages?

4 Summarise the objectives of high level languages.

5 What similarities and differences are there between natural languages (such as English) and high level programming languages?

6 A notation called BNF is frequently used to define the syntax of various structures in programming languages. This notation can also be used for the syntax of natural languages.

For example, a very small class of English sentences can be specified by the following BNF rules:

⟨sentence⟩ :: = ⟨noun⟩⟨verb⟩
⟨noun⟩   :: = John/Paul/George/Ringo
⟨verb⟩   :: = eats/sleeps/sings

In ordinary English, these rules are:

a sentence is a noun followed by a verb
a noun is John or Paul or George or Ringo
a verb is eats or sleeps or sings

These rules can be used to produce the sentences

John eats
Paul sings
Ringo sleeps etc.

On the other hand, the sentence

John eats George

is not in accordance with the rules.

A much larger class of sentences is obtained by adding the following rules:

⟨sentence⟩   :: = ⟨sentence⟩ ⟨conjunction⟩ ⟨sentence⟩
⟨conjunction⟩ :: = and/or

The first of these rules is called **recursive** since the same element, namely sentence, appears on the left and the right of the :: = symbol.

These rules allow the production of sentences such as

John eats and Paul sings or Ringo sleeps.

However, the sentence

John or Paul sings

is not in accordance with the rules.

a) Construct some more correct and incorrect sentences according to the above rules.

The following BNF rules specify the structure of a fairly wide class of decimal numbers:

1 ⟨decimal number⟩ :: = ⟨decimal point⟩⟨number⟩/⟨number⟩ ⟨decimal point⟩ ⟨number⟩
2 ⟨number⟩ :: = ⟨digit⟩/⟨digit⟩ ⟨number⟩

3 ⟨digit⟩ :: = 0/1/2/3/4/5/6/7/8/9
4 ⟨decimal point⟩ :: = ·

A formal way of using these rules to analyse a number is as follows:

Example 1: 97·652

	9	7	·	6	5	2
rule 3	⟨digit⟩	⟨digit⟩		⟨digit⟩	⟨digit⟩	⟨digit⟩
rule 4	⟨digit⟩	⟨digit⟩	⟨decimal point⟩	⟨digit⟩	⟨digit⟩	⟨digit⟩
rule 2	⟨digit⟩	⟨number⟩	⟨decimal point⟩	⟨digit⟩	⟨digit⟩	⟨digit⟩
rule 2		⟨number⟩	⟨decimal point⟩	⟨digit⟩	⟨number⟩	
rule 2		⟨number⟩	⟨decimal point⟩		⟨number⟩	
rule 1			⟨decimal number⟩			

Example 2: 3·

$$\frac{}{3}$$

rules 3 and 4 ⟨digit⟩ ⟨decimal point⟩

No further rules can be applied. This is not a valid decimal number as defined by the above rules.

b) Analyse the following numbers by the above rules. State whether each is a valid number in terms of these rules:

469 · 31
· 734
4325
45 · 6 · 7
846 ·

c) Extend the BNF rule for ⟨decimal number⟩ so that both 4325 and 846 · become valid numbers.

d) Write a set of BNF rules to specify the structure of a **signed integer**. The integers +4 and − 1162 are valid signed integers, but 351 is not.

7 Below is a complete program in Pascal language. It inputs a set of ten numbers and outputs them, together with their squares and reciprocals. Functions are used to calculate squares and reciprocals.

```
program   question 7 (input, output);          (*line 1*)

var    x: real;                                  (*line 2*)
     count: integer;                             (*line 3*)

function  square (y : real) : real;             (*line 4*)
          var w : real;                          (*line 5*)
          begin  w : = y*y;                      (*line 6*)
                    square : = w                  (*line 7*)
          end;                                    (*line 8*)

function  reciprocal (z : real) : real;          (*line 9*)
          var v : real                            (*line 10*)
          begin  if z = 0·0 then v : = 0·0        (*line 11*)
                          else v : = 1·0/z;       (*line 12*)
                  reciprocal : = v                (*line 13*)
          end;                                    (*line 14*)

begin     for    count : = 1 to 10 do            (*line 15*)
          begin  readln (x);                      (*line 16*)
                  writeln (x, square (x),
                  reciprocal (x))                  (*line 17*)
          end                                      (*line 18*)
end.                                               (*line 19*)
```

This program has three blocks, namely the two functions and the main program. The scope of a variable is the block within which it is declared. In Pascal, variables are declared by a **var** instruction, or in a **function** declaration.

Thus the scope of variable w is the function square, from line 5 to line 8.

a) Write down the scope of the variables x, count and v.

b) Is it permissible to refer to variable x in line 7?

c) Is it permissible to refer to variable w in line 13?

d) Which variables are local variables, and which are global variables?

e) From which program line are the two functions called?

8 Consider the following segment of a Basic program, containing two assignment statements:

105 LET Y = X
110 LET X = Y

a) If **X** and **Y** initially have the values 3 and 4, what are their values after this segment of program?

b) Write a sequence of three assignment statements which will interchange the values of **X** and **Y**.

9 In Fortran, a **FORMAT** statement specifies the layout of input and output data. It contains a number of codes, for integers, spaces, real numbers, etc.
For example, to input three integers, set out as follows:

314 2175 46629

the program segment below can be used:

```
      READ (1,100) I, J, K
100   FORMAT (I3, 1X, I4, 1X, I5)
```

where **I3** means a 3 digit integer and **1X** means a space.

a) Write a **READ** and **FORMAT** statement to input the following data:

41 23 16 4117 2234 1697

b) Write a set of data which would be read by:

```
      READ (1,120) K, L, M1, M2, N
120   FORMAT (I4, 2X, I4, 2X, I2, 1X, I2, 1X, I8)
```

c) Comment on the advantages and disadvantages of this type of input.

10 Consider this statement from a Pascal program:

```
if (x < 0) or (x > 9) then y : = 10
                      else y : = 9 − x
```

Write down the value of **y** in each of the following cases:

a) x = 4
b) x = 10
c) x = −2
d) x = 0
e) x = 9
☐ f) If you are familiar with Basic language, write a segment of a Basic language program to achieve the same effect as the Pascal statement above. Comment on similarities and differences between it and the Pascal language instruction.

11 Identify some shortcomings of many implementations of high level languages.

☐ 12 Examine the low level language introduced in Chapter 13. To what extent (if at all) does it satisfy the objectives of high level languages?

☐ 13 John Backus, leader of the team which developed Fortran, has the view that conventional programming languages are still far too closely tied to the general ideas of computer architecture, such as addresses, sequences of operations etc. In the light of your knowledge of computer architecture, and of high level languages, comment on this view.

17
High level language case studies

The previous chapter dealt with various aspects of high level languages in general terms. This chapter takes the ideas from the previous chapter and relates them to seven significant high level languages, namely Fortran, Algol 60, Cobol, Basic, Pascal, RPG and PL/M. However, this chapter does not aim to teach programming in any of these languages.

Each language is discussed separately, using the same headings as in the previous chapter, namely development, objectives, features and an assessment. Also included is a short example program in each language. The program is designed to illustrate the distinguishing features of the language. As the discussion of each language is self-contained, it is not necessary to study all seven languages.

The reasons for choosing the languages are as follows: Fortran, Algol 60 and Cobol are three of the oldest high level languages, Cobol and Fortran (in that order) being the two most popular programming languages currently in use. Algol 60 is the forerunner of a long line of high level languages, notably Algol 68 and Pascal. Pascal and Basic are more recent languages, developed in the light of earlier experience. Both are becoming extremely popular, especially in the field of education. RPG is a special purpose language, used exclusively for certain commercial data processing applications. It is a relatively recent language, becoming increasingly popular. PL/M is the first significant high level language specifically designed for the programming of microcomputers. It is rapidly gaining wide acceptance.

As a group, these case studies cover a wide spectrum of high level languages, from special-purpose to general-purpose, from simple to complex and from scientific to commercial. The group represents a class of computer languages whose members number over a thousand.

17.1   Fortran

The name Fortran comes from the **For**mula **Tran**slation. Fortran, developed between 1954 and 1957, is a programming language designed for scientific and engineering applications.

17.1.1   The Development of Fortran

In December 1953, John Backus, an employee of IBM, proposed the idea of Fortran. At the time virtually all programming was in assembly language. Although some work had been done in the direction of high level languages, there was much scepticism about the efficiency of '**automatic programming**' as it was then called.

Backus was motivated by an economic factor – the cost of programmers' time, as they laboriously wrote assembly language programs. His proposal was accepted, and in January 1954 a Fortran team was set up in New York, by IBM.

The main objective of the team was to produce a language which could be translated into efficient machine code. The details of the language were made up as the team went along. In November 1954, the team produced a preliminary report.

In early 1955, work started on the huge task of producing a Fortran compiler. The computer for which the compiler was written was the newly-released IBM 704. The compiler was reportedly 'always six months to completion', and was finally finished in April 1957.

From its first release, Fortran was very popular. From time to time, the language has been revised. The version in common use today is Fortran IV, the fourth major revision. Fortran is available on most computers. Simple versions have been written for small computers, and very powerful versions, with a significant degree of parallel processing, have been written for large computers.

17.1.2 The Objectives of Fortran

Fortran is designed for use in mathematical, scientific and engineering applications. As previously mentioned, the prime objective of Fortran is to produce programs which can be translated into efficient machine code. Other objectives include ease of use, and close resemblance to ordinary mathematical notation.

As Fortran was sponsored by IBM, not much thought was initially given to the objective machine independence. However, time has shown that Fortran is fairly easy to implement on other computers.

17.1.3 Features of Fortran

The following sections introduce the most significant features of Fortran language.

17.1.4 Character Set and Reserved Words

The character set used by Fortran includes capital letters, decimal digits and a few special characters. Fortran has a fairly large set of reserved words, including data type declarations (**INTEGER**, **REAL**, etc.) and instruction words (**READ**, **WRITE**, **CALL**, **RETURN**, etc.). All statements except calculations start with an instruction word.

17.1.5 Program Structure

A Fortran program consists of a main program and a number of subprograms, called **subroutines**. Subroutines can be called from the main program, or from other subroutines. However, recursive calls from a subroutine to itself are not permitted.

Subroutines are compiled separately from each other, and from the main program. The scope of all variables is thus limited to the subroutine in which they occur, unless they are declared to be in a **COMMON** block. Within each routine, a program consists of a number of statements, each written on a separate line, with various columns having special purposes. Line numbers are optional, and do not have to be in order.

17.1.6 Data

The data types available are integer, real, double precision, complex and logical (i.e. Boolean). Variable names consist of up to six alphanumeric characters, the first of which must be alphabetic. Unless otherwise declared, variables starting with any of the letters from I to N are integers, and the rest are real. Variables do not have to be declared at the start of the routine in which they are used.

The **DIMENSION** statement is used to create arrays. The elements of an array may be of any of the above data types. Most versions of Fortran allow at least three dimensions of arrays. For example, the statement:

```
DIMENSION LOAD(10), STRESS(10,4)
```

declares **LOAD** to be a one-dimensional array of 10 items, and **STRESS** to be a two-dimensional array of 40 items.

17.1.7 Operations

All the usual operations of arithmetic are available, with rather complicated rules for combining variables (or constants) of different types in the same expression. A number of standard arithmetic functions (sin, cos, tan, etc.) are available, as well as user-defined functions. Relational operators (greater than, less than, etc.) are included, for use in logical expressions which may appear in **IF** statements.

17.1.8 Input/Output

The methods of input and output provided are very powerful, but rather cumbersome. At the start of the program, all peripheral devices required are listed, together with their **channel number** for the duration of the program. Each input or output statement specifies a channel number, a list of variables to be transferred, and a **FORMAT** statement. The **FORMAT** statement specifies the precise layout of the data on the input, output or backing store medium. For example

```
READ (1,100) NPART, NSTOCK, PRICE
100 FORMAT (I6, 2X, I6, 2X, F6·2)
```

inputs the integers **NPART** and **NSTOCK** and real variable **PRICE** from channel 1. The integers each have six digits, and the number contains six characters, with two digits after the decimal point. The data items are separated by two spaces.

17.1.9 Control Structure
Two types of conditional branching statement are available, namely the arithmetic **IF** and the logical **IF**. The **arithmetic IF** statement includes an expression and three statement numbers. The expression is evaluated. If the result is negative, control passes to the first statement, if the result is zero, control passes to the second statement, and if the result is positive, control passes to the third statement.

For example

```
IF (X + Y)  10, 20, 30
```

branches to statement
   10 if $X + Y < 0$
   20 if $X + Y = 0$
   30 if $X + Y > 0$.

The **logical IF** statement includes a logical expression, and an unconditional statement. If the logical expression is true, the unconditional statement is executed, otherwise control passes to the statement after the **IF** statement.

For example:

```
IF (AMOUNT.LE. 20·00)  CHARGE = 5·00
```

assigns the value 5·00 to **CHARGE** if **AMOUNT** is less than 20·00. Unconditional branching (**GO TO**) is available, as is multi-way branching.

Program loops can be constructed by means of the **DO** statement. The **DO** statement includes the statement number of the end of the loop, a variable to be used as a counter, its initial and final values, and (optionally) a step size.

For example

```
DO 20 MONTH = 1, 12, 1
```

causes the program segment ending at statement 20 to be repeated for all values of **MONTH** from 1 to 12 in steps of 1.

Loops controlled by **DO** statements are always performed at least once. This is regarded by some as a shortcoming of Fortran.

17.1.10 Example Fortran Program
The subprogram shown below accepts two 10×10 matrices, and multiplies them together. The formula used is as follows:
If

   $C = A \times B$ where A, B and C are matrices
then

   $c_{ij} = a_{i1} \times b_{1j} + a_{i2} \times b_{2j} + \dots a_{i10} \times b_{10j}$.

The subprogram uses three nested loops. The outer and middle loops work through the rows and columns of the product matrix C, the inner loop adds up the terms which form the product, as shown in the formula.

Program

```
      SUBROUTINE MATMULT (A, B, C)
      REAL A(10, 10), B(10, 10), C(10, 10)
C  OUTER LOOP WORKS THROUGH ROWS OF PRODUCT
      DO 100 I = 1, 10
C  MIDDLE LOOP WORKS THROUGH COLUMNS OF PRODUCT
      DO 100 J = 1, 10
C  SET PRODUCT ELEMENT TO ZERO
      C(I, J) = 0·0
C  INNER LOOP ADDS UP TERMS OF PRODUCT
      DO 100 K = 1, 10
100   C(I, J) = C(I, J)+A(I, K) * B(K, J)
      RETURN
      END
```

Notes

1 The lines starting with the letter C are comments.
2 The statement numbered 100 is the end of all three loops.
3 The dimension of the matrices are declared in the second line of the subprogram.

17.1.11 An Assessment of Fortran

Fortran was designed as a scientific and engineering language and in general it is excellent for tasks of this nature. The only major shortcoming is the difficulty experienced by many programmers with input and output. To overcome this, some versions of Fortran have simplified input/output statements.

Fortran's weaknesses become apparent when handling non-numeric data. Input, output, storage and manipulation of data in character form is extremely cumbersome, even compared to a language such as Basic. In addition, the range of data types is limited, and user-defined data types are not allowed.

In spite of these shortcomings, Fortran remains as popular as ever. It has even survived attempts by its original sponsor, IBM, to replace it with a supposedly superior language, PL/1.

17.2 Algol 60

The name Algol comes from the phrase **Algo**rithmic **L**anguage. Algol 60 is a carefully structured general-purpose language developed between 1957 and 1962.

17.2.1 The Development of Algol 60

During the mid-1950s, the idea of a 'universal programming language' was expressed by a number of people, in Europe and in the USA. They envisaged a language which was clearly structured, general-purpose and machine independent. Fortran, which became available at this time, did not measure up to these somewhat lofty ideals.

During 1957, the first steps towards designing such a language were taken by the USA **Association for Computing Machinery (ACM)** and its European counterpart, **GAMM**. In October 1957 a letter from GAMM to ACM suggested a combined approach.

Accordingly, during May and June 1958, a joint working conference was held in

Zurich. Delegates were from computer manufacturers, users, universities and governments on both sides of the Atlantic, but did not formally represent these institutions. This conference produced a preliminary draft of the language, which became known as Algol 58.

Algol aroused considerable interest, but by 1959 it was already clear that Fortran, with IBM backing, was going to be more widely used, certainly in the USA.

As the concepts of language design became clearer, it soon became evident that Algol 58 could be improved. A meeting was held in Paris, in January 1960, at which a new version of the language was drafted, to incorporate all the improvements which had been suggested. Prominent delegates at this meeting were John Backus, of Fortran fame, and Peter Naur. Naur, with assistance from Backus, devised the notation, now known as BNF, in which the syntax of the revised language, called Algol 60, was expressed.

Algol 60 was appreciated, almost immediately, as a 'rounded work of art'. Its clear, consistent structure had a big influence on the design of subsequent high level languages, and on the architecture of many computers. Compilers were written to implement Algol 60 on a number of computers.

The finishing touches to Algol 60 were added at a meeting in Rome in 1962. At this meeting a few awkward points were clarified, and a revised report was produced.

It must be emphasised that Algol 60 was written and revised during a few short, intensive meetings attended by approximately fifteen people. There was no formal voting procedure, design decisions being reached by consensus. Algol 60 represents a degree of international co-operation hardly ever achieved in any field.

17.2.2   The Objectives of Algol 60

Algol was originally conceived as a 'universal programming language'. As various drafts were written, it acquired an algebraic bias, and thus an orientation towards scientific and engineering problems. However, it is certainly more general-purpose than Fortran.

The objective of machine independence is achieved in a very interesting way. No less than three versions of the language have been defined, namely a **reference language**, a **publication language** and various hardware **implementation languages**. The reference language is the standard, 'official' version, used in the revised Algol 60 report. It forms the basis of the other versions. The publication language permits a wider range of characters and notations, and is intended for the publication of algorithms. Each hardware version is the language implemented on some computer. It contains a set of rules for translating from the reference language to the hardware representation.

The other objective which is very well achieved is that of a simple, clear structure with a minimum of special cases.

17.2.3   Features of Algol 60

The following sections introduce the most significant features of Algol 60.

17.2.4   Character Set and Reserved Words

In any hardware representation of Algol 60, the character set depends on the computer being used. Unlike Fortran, most current representations permit the use of lower case letters.

Algol 60 has a slightly larger set of reserved words than Fortran. For example, the pair of reserved words **begin..end** are particularly important.

17.2.5 Program Structure

An Algol 60 program has the following structure, called a **block**:

```
Label: begin
          declarations;
          statements
       end
```

The **label** is a general form of a statement number, and is optional. **Declarations** are lists of the **types** and **identifiers** of all the variables used in the block.

Statements are simple statements, or complete blocks, having the same structure as above. Blocks within a program are called **procedures**, and correspond roughly to the idea of subroutines in Fortran. A procedure may be called from any other procedure, or recursively from itself.

17.2.6 Data

Data **types** are **integer**, **real**, **Boolean** and character **strings**. Arrays may be created out of these types. Identifiers are sequences of letters or digits, starting with a letter.

All variables must be declared at the start of the block in which they are used. The scope of each variable is the extent of the block in which it is declared. This includes any sub blocks declared inside the block. Any reference to a variable which has not been declared, or outside its scope, is invalid.

17.2.7 Operations

All the usual operations of arithmetic are available, with rules for combining different types in the same expression. Some standard functions (sin, cos, tan, etc.) are available on most hardware representations of the language. User-defined functions are written as procedures. Relational operations are available for use in logical expressions.

17.2.8 Input/Output

The reference language contains no provisions for input or output. Input/output operations have subsequently been standardised. These are much simpler, but less powerful, than those in Fortran.

17.2.9 Control Structure

Two conditional branching constructions are available:

```
if condition then statement,
```
and
```
if condition then statement 1 else statement 2.
```

Since each statement may be a complete block, this is an extremely powerful construction. In most cases, it eliminates the need for the **go to** statement, which is, however, available.

Loops are constructed as follows:

```
for count := m1 step m3 until m2 do statement
```

where the counter variable starts at value **m 1**, and is increased in steps of **m 3** until it reaches **m 2**. The statement may be a complete block. The counter variable is tested before each execution of the statement, and thus the loop may be repeated no times, if **m 1** is greater than **m 2** at the start.

Sequencing of instructions is achieved by placing a semi-colon between two consecutive statements. Statements do not have to start on new lines.

17.2.10 Example Algol 60 Program

The factorial of a number *n* may be written as:

factorial $(0) = 1$

factorial $(n) = n \times$ factorial $(n-1)$.

This is a recursive definition of factorials. It is used in the following program which calculates and outputs the factorials of five input numbers.

Program

```
begin
     integer number, fact, count;
          integer procedure factorial (n);
               value n; integer n;
               begin integer i;
                    if n = 0 then factorial := 1
                         else begin i := factorial (n - 1);
                              factorial := n * i
                         end
          end
     for count := 1 step 1 until 5 do
          begin
               ininteger (0, number);
               fact := factorial (number);
               outinteger (1, fact)
          end
end
```

Notes

1 The variables declared in the outer block are

   number: input number

   fact: factorial of input number

   count: counter

   Their scope is the whole program.

   Working variables **n** and **i** are declared in the inner blocks. Their scope is limited to these blocks.

2 The instructions **ininteger** and **outinteger** are for input and output respectively. The numbers 0 and 1 refer to particular input and output channels of the computer.

3 The recursive call to the factorial procedure is in the statement

   i := factorial (n − 1)

17.2.11 An Assessment of Algol 60

The original objective of Algol 60 was to be a 'universal programming language'. This objective has not been achieved, as Algol has turned out to be scientifically oriented, with virtually no character handling facilities. Machine independence has been well achieved by the use of a separate reference language. A specific criticism of Algol is that its input/output facilities are very clumsy and weak. Algol 60 has not been used very widely.

Algol's biggest contribution has been to the theory of the design of computer languages. Ideas which were first used in Algol, such as a block, the scope of a variable and the if .. then .. else construction, have been copied by many other languages. The clear structure of the language is one of its strongest points.

Algol has given rise to a whole family of computer languages, often referred to as **Algol-like languages**. These languages have influenced the design of computers, and have been used to write systems software, notably operating systems. Some of these operating systems are the most complex pieces of computer software in existence. That they have been successfully written in Algol-like languages is a tribute to these languages.

17.3 Cobol

The name Cobol comes from the phrase **Co**mmon **B**usiness **O**riented **L**anguage. Cobol is a language designed for commercial data processing, developed between 1959 and 1960.

17.3.1 The Development of Cobol

In the late 1950s, computer manufacturers and users began to realise the need for a common, machine-independent, business-oriented programming language. In April 1959 a meeting was held at the University of Pennsylvania to discuss these views. At this meeting it was agreed that the sponsorship of the new language should be independent of any computer manufacturer. Accordingly, the USA Department of Defense was asked to co-ordinate the project. In May 1959, a meeting was held at the Pentagon in Washington. Present were representatives of all major computer manufacturers, prominent users and USA government departments. The meeting agreed on the desirable characteristics of a common business language, and set up a number of committees to carry out the development work. The overall steering committee was called **Codasyl** (Conference on data systems languages).

After a short, intensive period of formal meetings, with decisions being taken by vote, the initial specification of the language was completed. It was accepted by the Codasyl committee in January 1960, and published soon afterwards under the name of Cobol 60. By the end of 1960, Cobol programs were running on several different types of computers.

Various revisions of Cobol were introduced during the 1960s. A standard version was accepted in 1968 by the American National Standards Institution (ANSI).

17.3.2 The Objectives of Cobol

The primary objectives of Cobol are machine independence, and a correspondence with current business practices. In addition, the following 'desirable characteristics' were identified at the initial planning meetings: maximum use of simple English; ease of use, even if less powerful than other languages, and 'to broaden the base of those who can state problems to computers'.

17.3.3 Features of Cobol

The following sections introduce the most significant features of Cobol.

17.3.4 Character Set and Reserved Words

The character set includes capital letters and digits, and is implementation dependent. The set of reserved words is very large, including 'noise' words which can be included to improve the readability of programs, but are not acted on by the computer.

17.3.5 Program Structure

All Cobol programs consist of four **divisions**. These are

Identification division: This identifies the program, its author and its purpose.
Environment division: This specifies the computer environment of the program, particularly peripheral devices used.

Data division: This specifies the nature and organisation of all the data used in the program. The identifiers of data items are declared, together with certain information about the data.

Procedure division: This specifies the operations to be carried out on the data.

Each division is organised into **sections**, **paragraphs**, **sentences** and **words**.

17.3.6 Data

The identifiers for data items can be up to 30 alphanumeric characters, containing hyphen (-) characters if required. For example **GROSS-PAY** and **PAY-RATE** are valid data names. Data items are declared using **picture clauses** which specify the number and type of characters in the data item. For example:

```
77 NET-INCOME IS PICTURE 999V99
```

declares a data item containing five digits, two of which are after the decimal point.

Arrays are declared as follows:

```
01 PRICE-LIST
   02 ITEM-PRICE PIC 99V99 OCCURS 20
```

declares an array named **PRICE-LIST** of twenty **ITEM-PRICES**.

17.3.7 Operations

Separate words (known as **verbs**) are used for each arithmetic operation. For example:

```
MULTIPLY ITEM-PRICE BY NUMBER-SOLD GIVING SALE-
                                             VALUE
```

However, the **COMPUTE** verb may be used if an expression is to be evaluated.

A very useful verb is the **SORT** verb which causes a set of data items to be sorted into numerical or alphabetical order.

17.3.8 Input/Output

All input and output data is structured in **files**, composed of **records**. The verbs **READ** and **WRITE** are used to input and output records. The layout of input and output data is carefully specified, including **FILLER** items for spacing.

17.3.9 Control Structure

Both **IF .. THEN** and **IF .. THEN .. ELSE** constructions are available for conditional branching. The **GO TO** statement is available for unconditional branching.

The **PERFORM** verb is used for loops. A paragraph can be repeated until a certain condition is true, or a specified number of times. Examples of each type are:

```
PERFORM WAGE-CALCULATION-PARAGRAPH UNTIL END-
                         OF-FILE MARKER = 'X'
```

and

```
PERFORM PRICE-CALCULATION VARYING ITEM-NUMBER
                FROM 1 BY 1 UNTIL ITEM-NUMBER = 20
```

17.3.10 Example Cobol Program

The following program inputs a file of names, addresses and telephone numbers from punched cards. The file is sorted into alphabetical order of names, and then output on a line printer.

Program

```
IDENTIFICATION DIVISION
PROGRAM-1D.
    DIRECTORY-SORT.
DATE WRITTEN.
    16 MAY 1980.

ENVIRONMENT DIVISION.
INPUT-OUTPUT SECTION.
FILE CONTROL.

    SELECT  DIRECTORY-FILE-IN   ASSIGN TO CARD-READER
    SELECT  DIRECTORY-FILE      ASSIGN TO WORK-DISK
    SELECT  DIRECTORY-FILE-OUT  ASSIGN TO LINE-PRINTER.
DATA DIVISION.
FILE SECTION.
SD  DIRECTORY-FILE
01  ENTRY
    05  SURNAME             PIC X(20).
    05  INITIALS            PIC X(5).
    05  ADDRESS             PIC X(60).
    05  TELEPHONE-NUMBER    PIC 9(7).

FD  DIRECTORY-FILE-IN
01  ENTRY-IN
    05  SURNAME-IN          PIC X(20).
    05  INITIALS-IN         PIC X(5).
    05  ADDRESS-IN          PIC X(60).
    05  TELEPHONE-NUMBER-IN PIC 9(7).

FD  DIRECTORY-FILE-OUT
01  ENTRY-OUT
    05  SURNAME-OUT          PIC X(20).
    05  INITIALS-OUT         PIC X(5).
    05  ADDRESS-OUT          PIC X(60).
    05  TELEPHONE-NUMBER-OUT PIC 9(7).
WORKING STORAGE SECTION.
01  MORE-ENTRIES-REMAIN-FLAG
    88  MORE-ENTRIES-REMAIN     PIC XXX VALUE 'YES'
    88  NO-MORE-ENTRIES-REMAIN          VALUE 'YES'
                                        VALUE 'NO'

PROCEDURE DIVISION.
SORTING SECTION.
    SORT DIRECTORY-FILE
        ASCENDING KEY SURNAME
        ASCENDING KEY INITIALS
        INPUT PROCEDURE LOAD-FILE
        GIVING DIRECTORY-FILE-OUT.
    STOP RUN.

LOAD-FILE SECTION.

    OPEN INPUT DIRECTORY-FILE-IN
        OUTPUT DIRECTORY-FILE-OUT.
    READ DIRECTORY-FILE-IN
        AT END MOVE 'NO' TO MORE-ENTRIES-REMAIN-FLAG.
    IF MORE-ENTRIES-REMAIN
        MOVE ENTRY-IN TO ENTRY
        RELEASE ENTRY.
```

Notes

1 There are three data files: an input file, a working file used by the **SORT** verb, and an output file. All three files have the same structure.

2 The sort is in ascending order of surnames, and ascending order of initials for the same surname.

3 The sorting section calls the loading section to input each directory entry. As soon as an entry has been loaded, it is released to the sort.

17.3.11   An Assessment of Cobol

One of Cobol's stated objectives is to 'broaden the base' of the people who can write computer programs. As Cobol is now the world's most popular programming language, there is no doubt that this objective has been achieved.

Another objective is the 'maximum use of simple English' in programs. This is indeed achieved, although it has led to criticisms that Cobol is verbose and cumbersome. Undoubtedly, the overall structure of a Cobol program is clear, though there are some awkward features, such as the construction surrounding the sort verb.

The major setback to an even wider acceptance of Cobol has been the negative view of it taken by the university-based computing science community. This has benefited neither the university nor the business community.

Cobol's future seems assured, partly through the enormous investment in existing software, and partly because simple versions of Cobol are becoming available for the new generation of microprocessor-based computers.

17.4   Basic

The name Basic comes from the phrase **B**eginner's **A**ll-Purpose **S**ymbolic **I**nstruction **C**ode. Basic is designed to introduce students, particularly non-science students, to computer programming. Basic was developed between 1963 and 1964.

17.4.1   The Development of Basic

Basic language was developed by Thomas E. Kurtz and John Kemeny at Dartmouth College, USA. Dartmouth College is a small institution, with the main teaching emphasis on the humanities. Computing is taught as a supporting subject to other disciplines. During the early 1960s, several attempts were made to produce a simple, introductory programming language.

Basic language was designed as part of an overall plan to make it easier for students to use the college's computer. In the summer of 1963, John Kemeny began work on a Basic compiler, for a General Electric 225 computer. On 1st May 1964, at 4 a.m., the first Basic program was run.

From the outset, Basic was used on an interactive, multi-access computer system. Work continued at Dartmouth on improvements and extensions to the language. Six Dartmouth editions of Basic have been released.

Basic was well received from its first release. Over the years it has established itself as the world's most popular educational programming language. Many of the new generation of microprocessor-based computers use Basic as their standard language. In addition, Basic has been extended to become a powerful scientific and commercial programming language in its own right.

17.4.2   The Objectives of Basic

The prime objective of Basic is ease of use, even at the expense of machine efficiency. In the words of Thomas Kurtz:

'The system would be designed to save the time of the user, even if it appeared that the computer was being "wasted".'

Those were very brave words in an era when computer time was much more expensive than user time. Today, in a world of cheap microcomputers, the situation has been reversed, and the objective makes very sound commercial sense.

17.4.3 Features of Basic
The following sections introduce the most significant features of Basic language.

17.4.4 Character Set and Reserved Words
The character set used by Basic includes capital letters, digits and a few special symbols. Early versions of Basic use a very small set of reserved words, a minimal set numbering about a dozen. Extended versions of Basic require much larger sets of reserved words.

17.4.5 Program Structure
A Basic program consists of a set of numbered statements, which are executed in order of statement number. Subprograms may be written, but they are not clearly differentiated from the main program, with no local variables or parameter passing.

17.4.6 Data
The data types available are **numeric** and **character string** variables and constants. Arrays may be constructed out of either variable type. Identifiers consist of a single letter, optionally followed by a single digit. Character string variable identifiers include a **£** or **$** symbol. Thus valid identifiers are:

$$X, \quad A3, \quad M\$ \text{ and } J3\$.$$

Although this is a very simple notation, it is rather restrictive. Some versions of Basic permit longer identifiers.

Data items need not be declared before use, and the scope of all variables is the whole program.

17.4.7 Operations
Arithmetic operations, standard functions and user-defined functions are available. Relational operators may be used in **IF** statements. One of the strengths of Basic is the number of character string operations and functions which are available. These make manipulation of non-numeric data extremely simple. For example, if **A$** = "CAT" and **B$** = "FISH", then the instruction:

$$\text{LET } C\$ = A\$ + B\$$$

assigns to **C$** the value "CATFISH", using the joining operator +.

17.4.8 Input/Output
The input and output operations combine simplicity with considerable power. Unless otherwise specified, output is automatically arranged in columns.

Many versions of Basic permit data transfer to or from named data **files** on backing store. This enables programs to manipulate large sets of data, and pass this data from one program to another.

17.4.9 Control Structure
Conditional branching is achieved by a simple form of the if... then construction, namely

IF (condition) THEN (statement number).

Control passes to the statement specified if the condition is true, otherwise it passes to the statement after the if statement. For example

```
IF A > 5 THEN 60
```

Passes control to statement 60 if **A** is greater than 5.

Recent versions of Basic permit compound condition joined by AND or OR, and complete statements after THEN. Some editions extend the construction to include ELSE.

A GO TO statement is available for unconditional branching.

The FOR..NEXT construction is used for program loops. A counter is used to control the number of times that the loop is repeated. For example:

```
10 FOR K = 1 TO 20 STEP 1
      part of program to be repeated 20 times.
100 NEXT K
```

In most versions of Basic, the loop is repeated zero or more times.

17.4.10   Example Basic Program

The subprogram shown below is part of a word processing program. The subprogram takes a line of text, stored as the string variable **T$**, and inserts the string **A$** into the line, immediately before the string **B$**.

For example, if the line of text **T$** is:

NOW IS THE TIME FOR ALL GOOD TO COME TO THE AID OF THE PARTY

and the character string **A$** is **MEN**, and **B$** is ▽TO (▽ indicates a space), then the result is:

NOW IS THE TIME FOR ALL GOOD MEN TO COME TO THE AID OF THE PARTY

The subprogram uses some of the string manipulation functions available in Basic.

Firstly, the position of the string **B$** in the text is located. Then the text is split into two parts, the second starting with the characters in **B$**. Finally the string **A$** is inserted between the two parts.

Program
```
1000 REM SUBPROGRAM TO INSERT STRING INTO LINE
        OF TEXT
1010 REM
1020 REM LOCATE POSITION OF STRING B$ IN
        TEXT T$
1030 LET P = POS (T$, B$)
1040 REM IF P = 0, STRING IS NOT IN TEXT, GO
        TO END OF SUBPROGRAM
1050 IF P = 0 GO TO 1130
1060 REM SPLIT LINE T$ INTO TWO PARTS
1070 LET U$ = MID$ (T$, 1, P - 1)
1080 LET V$ = MID$ (T$, P, LEN (T$))
1090 REM U$ IS THE FIRST PART, V$ IS FROM B$
        TO THE END
```

```
1100 REM INSERT STRING A$ BETWEEN THE
     TWO PARTS
1110 LET T$ = U$ + A$ + V$
1120 REM
1130 RETURN
```

Notes

1 Lines starting with the word **REM** are remarks.
2 Most of the work is done by the Basic functions **POS** and **MID$**, and the joining operator +.
3 The line numbers of the statements go up in steps of 10. This is normal practice in writing programs in Basic.
4 In some versions of Basic, the **MID$** function is called by a different name, and the joining operator is not +, but **&**.

17.4.11   An Assessment of Basic

In its primary objective of simplicity, Basic has undoubtedly been extremely successful. In 1978, one of the authors of Basic, Thomas Kurtz, estimated that five million schoolchildren had learned Basic language. This simplicity is achieved through a clear program structure, and simple yet powerful instructions, particularly for character handling and input/output.

Basic is particularly well suited to interactive computing, graphics, games and simulations, as well as to its original application area − teaching programming to beginners.

A few criticisms of Basic language can be made. The identifiers permitted for variable names are rather restrictive. Subprograms are not clearly separated from each other, with no mechanism for parameter passing. And, perhaps the most serious problem, there is no widely accepted standard version of Basic available.

However, new versions of Basic are overcoming these problems. There is still time for a consensus to be reached about a standard version of Basic.

17.5   Pascal

Pascal language is named after the French mathematician and philosopher, Blaise Pascal. It was developed between 1968 and 1971.

17.5.1   The Development of Pascal

By contrast with Fortran, Algol 60, Cobol and Basic, Pascal is the work of one person − Niklaus Wirth, a university professor in Zurich, Switzerland. Using Algol 60 as a basis, Wirth set out to design a language suitable for teaching computer programming to university students.

The first draft of the language was made in 1968. A compiler for Pascal, also written by Wirth, was operational in 1970. Pascal was first published in 1971, and a revised report appeared in 1973.

Since its publication, Pascal has gained increasingly wide acceptance at universities. Pascal is available on some microcomputers. Its use may yet spread to schools and to the business computing community.

17.5.2   The Objectives of Pascal

The primary objectives of Pascal are best expressed by its author, Niklaus Wirth:

'The development of the language Pascal is based on two principal aims. The first is to make available a language suitable to teach programming as a systematic discipline based on certain fundamental concepts clearly and naturally reflected by the language. The second is to develop implementations of this language which are both reliable and efficient on presently available computers.'

Pascal is a compromise between these aims. On the one hand, it has a concise, consistent abstract structure. On the other hand, it is sufficiently close to modern computer architectures to be easily and efficiently implemented.

17.5.3   Features of Pascal
The following sections introduce the most significant features of Pascal language.

17.5.4   Character Set and Reserved Words
Most implementations of Pascal use upper and lower case letters, digits and a number of special characters. Pascal has a fairly large set of reserved words, including a few not found in other programming languages. Some of these are introduced in the following sections.

17.5.5   Program Structure
Like Algol 60, Pascal is a block structured language. However, a Pascal block is slightly more restricted than one in Algol 60. In outline, the structure of a Pascal program is as follows:

A **program** is a **program heading** followed by a **block**.

A **block** is a number of **declarations** (of labels, constants, data types, variables, **procedures** and **functions**), followed by a set of **statements**.

A **procedure** is a **procedure heading** followed by a **block**.

A **function** is a **function heading** followed by a **block**.

A **statement** is a simple statement or a set of statements enclosed by the words **begin** and **end**.

Statements are separated by colons, and do not have to be on separate lines.

It can be seen that a program may contain a number of procedure and function blocks, which may themselves contain procedure and function blocks. A procedure or function may be called recursively from itself.

17.5.6   Data
One of the strengths of Pascal is the variety of **data types** available, and the provision of user-defined data types. This means that a person writing a Pascal program can construct data types, either by combining the standard types, or by listing all the values a data item can have. An example of user-defined data types is given in Section 16.8.

Pascal permits the use of **pointers**, which are data items storing the address of other data items. Pascal is unusual in having the operations **new** and **dispose** which create and delete data items pointed to in this way.

In addition to individual data items, **arrays**, **sets** and **records**, Pascal language contains the concept of a **file**. All input and output takes place via a few simple operations on files. **Enumeration literals** can be used in conjunction with arrays.

Like Algol 60, Pascal includes the concept of **scope**. The scope of a data item is the block within which it is declared, and any sub-blocks contained in that block.

17.5.7   Operations
Pascal contains all the arithmetic (except raising to powers), relational and logical

operations. In addition, the set operations **union**, **intersection** and **set difference** are available. In all cases, the types of the data items used must be compatible with the operations.

In addition to the usual arithmetic functions, there are a number of functions to handle non-numeric data. For example, there are functions to find the **successor** and **predecessor** of a given data item in its set of values.

17.5.8 Input/Output

All input and output, as well as transfers to and from backing store, take place via files of data. A few simple operations enable data items to be transferred to or from these files. Each file is associated with a particular peripheral device.

17.5.9 Control Structure

Like Algol 60, Pascal has both `if..then` and `if..then..else` constructions for conditional branching. The `go to` statement is available, but its use is discouraged.

Pascal has three different constructions for program loops. If a loop is to be repeated a certain number of times, the statement is:

`for count := startvalue to endvalue do statement`

The counter variable is automatically increased in steps of 1. If a loop must be repeated at least once, until a certain condition becomes true, the construction is:

`repeat statement until condition.`

If a loop must be repeated none or more times, while a certain condition holds, the construction is:

`while condition do statement.`

In this case, the condition is tested before each repetition of the loop. In the previous case, the condition is tested after each repetition. In all of the above examples, 'statement' may be a set of statements, enclosed by the words `begin..end`.

17.5.10 Example Pascal Program

The following procedure of a program shows how a list can be constructed using pointers. The program inputs the names of 25 people, and stores them in a list, structured as in Figure 17.1.

Note that there is a pointer called **first** pointing to the start of the list. The pointer at the end of the list does not point to anything – it has the value **nil**.

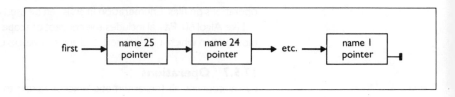

Figure 17.1

Program

```
procedure makelist;
    type   list = ↑ person;                          (*means 'pointer to'*)
           person = record
                       name : array [1..20] of char;      (*20 character array*)
                       next : list                        (*pointer to next person*)
                    end
    var    first, newperson : list;              (*front pointer and list element*)
           count : integer;                               (*loop counter*)
           newname : name
    begin  first := nil;
           for count := 1 to 25 do
               begin  readname (newname);    (*procedure, not shown, to read a name*)
                      new (newperson);  (*create storage space for new list element*)
                      newperson ↑ .next := first;   (*link pointer to existing list*)
                      newperson ↑ .name := newname;   (*fill in name of new person*)
                      first := newperson (*change front pointer to new list element*)
               end
end (*makelist*)
```

Notes

1 Diagramatically, the sequence of operations is as follows:

Create storage space for new list element: Figure 17.2.
Link pointer of new list element to existing list, and fill in new name: Figure 17.3.
Change front pointer to point to new list element: Figure 17.4.

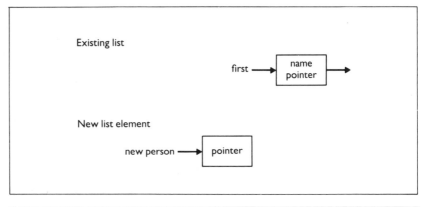

Figure 17.2

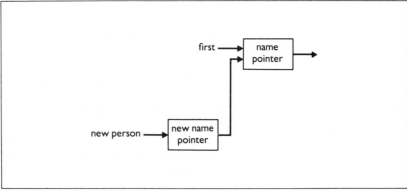

Figure 17.3

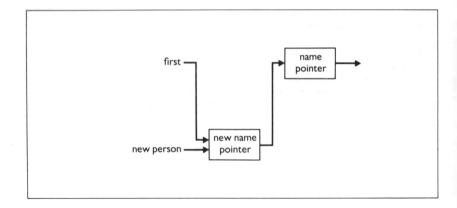

Figure 17.4

2 Notice how comments can be inserted in the program.

3 The notation 'newperson↑' means 'the data item to which the pointer newperson points'.

The notation '.next' refers to the field called 'next' in the record.

Thus 'newperson ↑ .next' means the field called 'next' in the record pointed to by 'newperson'.

17.5.11 An Assessment of Pascal

Pascal was designed to illustrate certain key concepts in programming, such as structured programming, and various types and structures of data. In general, Pascal achieves this objective very well. It combines simplicity with considerable power.

Pascal generally tries to provide one mechanism to implement each programming concept. Short cuts are deliberately discouraged. While this sometimes makes programs somewhat longer than they might be in other languages, it does help identify, isolate and eliminate program errors.

Particular strengths of Pascal are its handling of data types and structures, and its disciplined use of pointers. Some people would criticise its input/output facilities as being rather restrictive, but they do have the advantage of simplicity.

Pascal language has been developed in the light of experience in other high level languages. It has already gained wide acceptance, and is currently one of the fastest-growing computer languages in terms of numbers of users.

17.6 RPG

The letters RPG stand for **R**eport **P**rogram **G**enerator. The primary purpose of RPG is to produce reports, or summaries of information, from commercial files.

17.6.1 The Development of RPG

RPG was developed by IBM, and first introduced in 1964. It was at first only implemented on IBM computers, but its use has gradually spread to other machines. A new version of the language, RPG II, was introduced in 1971.

17.6.2 The Objectives of RPG

RPG is not an algorithmic language like Algol. An RPG program does not specify *how* processing is to be carried out. It simply specifies *what* information is required in a report. The RPG translation system generates the actual program from these specifications.

Thus the main objective of RPG is to provide a simple, machine-independent way of specifying the contents and layout of reports. A secondary objective is to allow for the updating of master files.

17.6.3   Features of RPG

The following sections introduce the most significant features of RPG language.

17.6.4   Character Set and Reserved Words

The character set includes capital letters, digits and a few special characters. The set of reserved words is fairly small, mainly the names of operations.

17.6.5   Program Structure

The structure of an RPG program specification is very strict. Each section is set out in columns, each column having a special significance. Five **specification forms** are used to complete an RPG program specification. These are:

File description specification form: defines the general characteristics of all input and output files used by the program.
Extension specification form: only used in certain cases, such as non-sequential files.
Input specification form: defines the record structure of the input files used.
Calculations specification form: describes the arithmetic and other operations to be performed.
Output specification form: describes the information content and layout of the report to be produced.

17.6.6   Data

The basic data item in RPG programming is a **field**, of fixed length, containing a numeric or literal value. Fields are contained in **records** which are contained in **files**. Names are used to identify these items. Names are up to eight alphanumeric characters, starting with a letter.

17.6.7   Operations

Like Cobol, RPG has separate words for each arithmetic operation. For example, the instruction

    AMOUNT ADD AMTTOTAL AMTTOTAL

means: add **AMOUNT** to **AMTTOTAL**, and place the result in **AMTTOTAL**.

17.6.8   Input/Output

The input file structure and output report structure are specified in great detail. The particulars are filled in at the appropriate places in the input and output forms.

17.6.9   Control Structure

Control is achieved by the concept of a **control break** which occurs when one input record differs in a particular field from the previous record. For example, if a number of records refer to the same date, the control break occurs when a new date is encountered. In most cases there are several **levels** of control breaks.

Certain actions can be specified to occur when a particular level of control break occurs. For example, when the control break occurs at the end of the records for one day, totals can be added up and output for that day.

In addition, all calculations can be specified to occur under certain conditions only. Other conditions may be set or cleared as a result of the calculations. These conditions are identified by **indicators**. Indicators have the values **ON** and **OFF**.

17.6.10   Example RPG Program

The following RPG program inputs a file of sales records from a shop. Each record comprises a date, invoice number and an amount.

The output is a report showing the total amount for each date.

```
Program
01 H
02 F* FILE SPECIFICATIONS
03 FINVOICESIPE F2000  30     READER
04 FREPORT   0   F 133 133    PRINTER
01 I* INPUT FILE FORMAT SPECIFICATIONS
02 IINVOICESAA 01            1  8 DATE    L1
03 I                         9 10 SPACE
04 I                        11 180INVNO
05 I                        19 20 SPACE
06 I                        21 282AMOUNT
01 C* CALCULATION SPECIFICATIONS
02 C* GO TO INITIALISATION STEP
13 C   NO2                   GOTO INIT
04 C* CALCULATION WHEN NO CONTROL BREAK OCCURS
05 C*           AMOUNT   ADD  TOTAL    TOTAL
06 C* CALCULATION WHEN A CONTROL BREAK OCCURS
07 CL1                       MOVE DATE      OUTDATE
08 C* INITIALISATION SECTION
09 C             INIT        TAG
10 C                         SETON          02
11 C                         MOVE 000·00    TOTAL
12 C                         MOVE DATE      OUTDATE
01 O* OUTPUT FILE FORMAT SPECIFICATIONS
02 OREPORT  H     NO2
03 O                         18 'DAILY SALES
                                TOTALS'
04 O        H     NO2
05 O                          4 'DATE'
06 O                         10 '  '
07 O                         28 'TOTAL OF
                                INVOICES'
08 O        T     L1
09 O                    OUTDATE    8
10 O                              10 '   '
11 O                    TOTAL   B 18 '    0·00'
12 O* END OF PROGRAM
```

Notes

1 There is only one control break in the program, designated L1. This occurs when a new invoice date is encountered. When L1 occurs, the current date and total are output (lines 08 to 011 of output section). The letter B in line 011 of the output section specifies that the total is then reset to zero. The new date is passed to the variable **OUTDATE** (calculation section line 07), and processing continues.

2 When no control break occurs, the invoice amount is added to the current total (line 05 of calculation section).

3 At the start of the program, various headings are printed (lines 020 to 070 of

output section). Control switch 02 is then set **ON** (line 10 of calculation section), to prevent these headings from being printed repeatedly. The total is initialised to zero and the first date moved to **OUTDATE** (lines 11 and 12 of calculation section).

17.6.11   An Assessment of RPG

By comparison with other high level languages, RPG has extremely limited objectives. It appears that it achieves these objectives well, providing a convenient means for generating reports from data files. Furthermore, RPG is the forerunner of a number of information retrieval and database management languages. Its popularity is showing a steady increase.

17.7   PL/M

PL/M, or **Programming Language/Microprocessors**, is designed for the programming of microcomputers, at both systems and applications level. It is intended to be powerful as well as easy to use and to understand. Variations of the language have been produced for different microprocessors, the one described here being for the Intel 8080 8 bit microprocessor.

17.7.1   The Development of PL/M

PL/M was originally developed within Intel Corporation in 1973. A revised specification was issued in 1976, and further development work is continuing.

17.7.2   The Objectives of PL/M

PL/M is intended to be simple, concise, and easy to learn, use and understand. It is powerful enough to make full use of the facilities of the microcomputer which supports it.

More specific objectives include:

1 to reduce the time and cost of programming;
2 to increase the reliability of software;
3 to be self-documenting;
4 to facilitate the maintenance of software.

17.7.3   Features of PL/M

Although PL/M is a block structured high level language, it includes a number of features normally found only in low level languages. These include the ability to manipulate bytes of data, as well as addresses, and to enable and disable interrupts. Operations include shift operations. These low level features are particularly useful in writing systems software.

17.7.4   Character Set and Reserved Words

The PL/M character set includes upper and lower case letters, decimal digits and a number of special characters. The **$** symbol is used to make variable names and constants easier to read. Examples of such variable names are `time$of$day` and `error$condition$1`.

The set of reserved words is fairly small, and includes a few not usually found in high level languages, such as **byte**, **interrupt**, **enable** and **disable**.

17.7.5   Program Structure

Like Algol 60 and Pascal, PL/M is a block structured language. The basic building blocks are the **procedure**, enclosed by the words **procedure** and **end**, and the **do** block, enclosed by the words **do** and **end**. Blocks may be nested within other blocks. Complete procedures can be written in assembly language, and linked to the rest of the program after compilation.

All variables used in a PL/M program must be declared before they are used. The scope of a variable is the block within which it is declared, including any nested blocks.

Procedures can be called recursively, as in the case of other block structured languages. However, PL/M differs from most other high level languages in that procedures can be **interrupted** by an external event (interrupts are discussed in Section 19.10). When an interrupt occurs, the current statement is completed, and control transfers to a procedure which handles the interrupt. When this procedure is complete, control returns to the statement following the interrupted statement. If a procedure is to be protected from interrupts, then a **disable** statement is placed in front of it. An **enable** statement after the procedure allows interrupts to resume.

Because of the recursive property of PL/M, it is quite possible that a procedure will be interrupted, and then called again from the interrupt handling routine. To cope with this situation, procedures may be declared to be **re-entrant**. This means that if they are interrupted, current variable values and working areas are pushed onto a stack. A call of the same procedure during the handling of an interrupt uses new variable values and working areas. These in turn are also stacked if the procedure is interrupted a second time. As each level of interrupt is handled, the different sets of variable values are popped from the stack.

17.7.6 Data
The basic data types are **byte** and **address**. A byte is any eight bit data item, representing a literal or numeric quantity, while an address contains sixteen bits. The concept of pointers is implemented via **based variables**. One variable is declared to be the base, or address, of another.

Constants may be expressed as decimal, binary, octal or hexadecimal integers. The numbers are suffixed by letters which identify their base: B for binary, O or Q for octal, H for hexadecimal and optionally D for decimal.

Arrays may be created of variables of the same type, and **structures** may be created of data items of different types. A structure corresponds to the concept of a record in other languages. Arrays may be contained within structures, and vice versa.

17.7.7 Operations
Arithmetic operations are provided for integer addition, subtraction, multiplication, division and determination of the remainder in integer division.

Overflow or underflow does not occur. Variable values simply 'wrap around' if they exceed their defined range. For example, a byte variable can have a range of values from 0 to 255. If it has the value 255 and 1 is added, it reverts to 0. Logical and shift operations may also be carried out.

17.7.8 Input/Output
Input and output is handled at character level by assigning eight bit values to variables from a number of **input ports**, or assigning values to a number of **output ports**.

17.7.9 Control Structure
Like Algol 60 and Pascal, PL/M has both `if..then` and `if.. then..else` constructions for conditional branching. The `go to` statement is available, but its use is discouraged, except in the case of dealing with errors.

Program loops are controlled by variations of the `do..end` block. The do..while construction allows a loop to be repeated while a certain condition remains true. The do..case construction enables one alternative to be selected from a number.

PI/M enables endless loops to be constructed quite deliberately, by means of the do..forever statement.

17.7.10 Example PL/M Program

The following program illustrates the use of PL/M in a very simple process control function. The objective of the program is to send a control signal to a machine every one fifth of a second.

The microprocessor has an internal clock which 'ticks' 1024 times per second, by causing an interrupt at level 1. This causes control to jump to location 8 when the current program instruction is complete.

The program has a procedure to which control is transferred from location 8. This is achieved by planting an appropriate machine instruction at location 8. The interrupt handling procedure increases a timing counter by 1 every time an interrupt occurs, and resets it to zero when it reaches 205, i.e. once every fifth of a second. The main program contains an endless loop which examines the value of the timing counter. Whenever it has the value zero, a signal is sent to the output port connected to the machine.

Program
```
/*EXAMPLE PROGRAM 17.7*/
/*SEND CONTROL SIGNAL TO MACHINE*/
/*EVERY 1/5 SECOND*/

MACHINE$CONTROL:

DO;
    DECLARE TIMING$COUNTER BYTE INITIAL(0);
    DECLARE LOC$8 BYTE AT (8);
    DECLARE LOC$9 ADDRESS AT(9);

/*PROCEDURE TO HANDLE TIMING INTERRUPTS*/

COUNTS$TIMING$PULSES:
PROCEDURE INTERRUPT 1;
    IF TIMING$COUNTER = 205 THEN
        TIMING$COUNTER = 0;
    ELSE
        TIMING$COUNTER = TIMING$COUNTER + 1;
END COUNT$TIMING$PULSES;

/*MAIN PROGRAM*/

DISABLE;                /*DISABLE INTERRUPTS*/
 LOC$8 = 0C3H;          /*LOAD LOCATIONS 8 AND 9 WITH*/
 LOC$9 = .COUNT$TIMING$PULSES/*JUMP TO PROCEDURE
                            COUNT$TIMING$PULSES*/
ENABLE;                 /*ENABLE INTERRUPTS*/
DO FOREVER;
  IF TIMING$COUNTER = 0 THEN
  DO;
        TIMING$COUNTER = 1;
        OUTPUT (1) = 0FFH
```

```
    END;
    END;      /*DO FOREVER*/
END MACHINE$CONTROL
```

Notes

1 Comments are contained between the symbols **/ *** and *** /**.
2 The machine code instruction **0 C 3** (Hexadecimal) is placed at location 8. The address of the procedure **COUNT$TIMING$PULSES** is placed at location 9. Together these locations contain an instruction which transfers control to the procedure **COUNT$TIMING$PULSES**.
3 Interrupts are disabled while locations 8 and 9 are being loaded.
4 The machine being controlled is connected to output port 1. The control signal has the hexadecimal value **F F**.
5 The program illustrates the use of a **DO FOREVER** loop, and the interrupt handling feature of PL/M.

17.7.11   An Assessment of PL/M

PL/M is rapidly gaining wide acceptance, both for systems programs and for applications programs. Its blend of high level and low level features makes it ideal for the programming of microprocessor-based computers. It is particularly useful for microcomputers dedicated to a specific task, such as word processing. These machines are often controlled by a single large program, which functions both as an operating system and as an applications program.

17.8   Conclusion

This small sample from the rapidly increasing population of high level languages shows some of the similarities and some of the differences that exist between these languages.

Although each language studied has its strengths and weaknesses, it is impossible to say that any one is better than all the others. Each language is best suited to a certain class of computer applications.

The idea of a universal programming language was mentioned in this chapter, in the context of Algol, but it is not taken very seriously today. As in the case of spoken languages, it seems that there will always be a multitude of programming languages. This is not as bad a situation as it sounds – once one programming language has been mastered, others are not too difficult to learn.

Exercise 17

1 Select *any two* of the languages described in this chapter. Answer the following questions, comparing the selected languages.
   a) Compare the input and output facilities provided by the languages. State, with reasons, which language is simpler and which language is more powerful in this respect.
   b) Compare the provisions for calculation provided by the languages. State, with reasons, in which language complicated calculations can be expressed more concisely.
   c) Compare and contrast the provisions for conditional and unconditional branching in the languages.
2 Of all the languages described in the chapter, Algol 60 is probably the least widely used. In the light of your studies of the chapter, suggest some reasons for this.
3 Give your own views on the idea of a universal programming language.
4 What is the main difference between the objectives of Algol 60 and those of Pascal? What difference do you think this has made in the relative popularity of the two languages?

5 Which of the languages mentioned in this chapter come closest to being a general-purpose language, suitable for scientific, commercial and educational computing? Give reasons for your choice.

6 Suggest at least two reasons for the persistent popularity of Fortran, and two for that of Cobol.

7 Select a programming language not discussed in this chapter. Using suitable references, write a concise account of the language, under the same headings as those used in this chapter. Some suitable languages are Algol 68, Simula, Lisp, RTL/2, PL/1, Snobol, and Ada.

☐ 8 Consider the problem of printing the digits of a number in reverse order. One possible method is as follows:

> output last digit of number
> if digits remain
>   then reverse remaining digits.

This method is recursive, because it uses itself repeatedly until there are no more digits to reverse. A procedure of a Pascal program to carry out this process is as follows:

```
procedure reverse (n : integer);
begin
        write (n mod 10);              (*the remainder when n is
                                         divided by 10*)
        if n div 10 <> 0              (*the integer part of n
                                         divided by 10*)
            then reverse (n div 10)  (*recursive call*)
end
```

a) Write down the steps carried out by this procedure if it is supplied with the number 8271.

A portion of a program in Basic language, to carry out the same task, is as follows:

```
1000 REM PRINT DIGITS OF NUMBER N IN REVERSE ORDER
1010 LET X = INT (N/10) : REM INTEGER PART OF N
                          DIVIDED BY 10
1020 PRINT N - 10*X      : REM REMAINDER WHEN N IS
                          DIVIDED BY 10
1030 IF X = 0 THEN RETURN
1040 LET N = X
1050 GO TO 1010
```

b) Dry run this program segment, using the number 8271.

c) In your opinion, which program segment is easier to understand? Give reasons for your answer.

d) Write an equivalent program segment in one of the other languages introduced in this chapter. Comment on similarities and differences between it and the above program segments.

9 Comment on the relative emphasis on arithmetic operations in the seven languages studied.

10 Outline the steps that would be required to write the PL/M example program in any of the other programming languages.

11 Rank the case study languages in order of ease of readability of programs. Comment on your ordering.

☐ 12 The microcomputer programming language PL/M contains certain low level language features. This idea is developed further in a set of languages designed for computers based on Z80 microprocessors. These languages are collectively known as PL/Z.

Carry out a case study on the PL/Z languages. Identify the role of each language, and the inter-relationships between them. Compare the features provided by these languages with those provided by PL/M.

18
Compilers and interpreters

This chapter concerns the process of translating a program written in a high level language to an equivalent program in a machine language. The objectives of language translation are discussed, and the two major approaches, called **compilation** and **interpretation** are introduced. The steps of compilation are outlined, and the process of interpretation is explained. The chapter concludes with an assessment of compilers and interpreters.

Language translation is a relatively difficult area of programming. It is not easy to understand some of the concepts involved. Consequently, this chapter deals with the topic in broad outline only. A more thorough study must wait for a more advanced course in computing.

This chapter is closely tied to material in previous chapters, both on high level languages and on machine languages. It covers an important area of the systems software which is available on most computers.

18.1 The Objectives of Language Translation

The prime objective of a language translation program is to convert input in a high level language to output in a machine language, sometimes via one or more intermediate languages. The input language is called the **source language**, and the output language the **object** or **target language**. The translation program itself is written in a **base language**.

A language translation program can be represented as a **T diagram**, shown in Figure 18.1. An example of the T diagram for a Basic language compiler, written in Z80 assembly language, producing Z80 machine code, is shown in Figure 18.2.

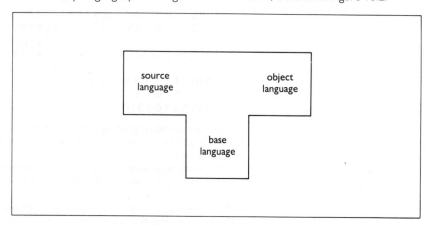

Figure 18.1
A T diagram of a language translation program

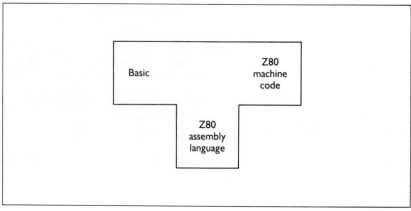

Figure 18.2
An example of a T diagram

A second objective of a translation program is to identify any errors in a source program. Suitable error messages are output, to assist the programmer to correct the errors.

Thirdly, many language translators attempt to produce object code which is as efficient as possible. The process of making the code more efficient is known as **optimisation**.

Finally, the translation program itself should be efficient. It should not take too long to translate a source program, and must not occupy too much space in the main store of the computer. This objective conflicts with the other objectives, particularly the third one. Most translation programs represent a compromise between this and the other objectives.

The objectives of a language translator may be summarised in the following terms: a language translation system makes it easy for a computer to be programmed.

18.2 Principles of Compilation and Interpretation

Compilers and interpreters represent two very different approaches to the task of enabling programs written in a high level language to be run. Distinguishing features of the two approaches are now outlined.

A compiler translates a source program in a high level language into an equivalent object program in a machine language. The object program may then be executed. The translation process is applied to the source program as a whole. Source statements may be separated or combined, and there is not always a direct correspondence between a source program statement and one or more object program instructions.

An interpreter transforms a computer into a high level language machine. Each source program statement is analysed, and then executed. Object code is not generally produced.

Thus, compilers and interpreters have in common the process of analysing the source code, though the methods they use generally differ. Having analysed the source code, compilers then generate equivalent object code, whereas interpreters execute the source code directly. Compilers are generally more sophisticated than interpreters, as the latter can do little by way of optimisation. The majority of language translation programs used by mini and microcomputers are interpreters.

The next few sections of this chapter discuss the steps of language translation, in relation to compilers. Interpreters are mentioned again towards the end of the chapter.

18.3 The Steps of Compilation

The main steps of compilation are **lexical analysis**, **syntax analysis** and **code generation**. These are now discussed, together with three other important features of compilers, namely a **dictionary**, **optimisation** and **error handling**. All compilers include these features, though in some they are more distinct than in others.

18.4 Lexical Analysis

Lexical analysis is the first stage in the processing of a source program by a compiler. It may be regarded as 'tidying up' the source program, ready for more detailed analysis.

Lexical analysis generally has to perform two tasks. These are changing the source code into a form which is independent of the input device, and removing redundant information such as spaces and comments. To illustrate the first task, a program line might be typed at a terminal as:

100 LI ← ET X = 0

where ← means backspace. The lexical analyser deals with this correction, and reproduces the line as

100LETX=0

having also removed the spaces.

An example of the removal of redundant information is as follows. Consider the following segment of a program in Basic language:

200 FOR I = 1 TO N STEP 1
210 LET X(I) = 0 : REM INITIALISE ARRAY
215 NEXT I

A lexical ânalysis might produce the following

200FORI=1TON \ 210LETX(I)=0 \ 215NEXTI

where the character \ marks the end of a line.

Rather surprisingly, lexical analysis is often one of the slowest stages in compilation. This is because each character of the source program is considered separately. Later stages of language translation deal with characters in groups.

18.5 Syntax Analysis

Syntax analysis is where the structure, and, to some extent, the meaning, of a source program is determined by the compiler. The overall source program is analysed into blocks, the blocks are analysed into instructions, and the individual items such as instruction words, variables and constants in each instruction are identified.

As mentioned in Chapter 17, the syntax of a high level programming language can be expressed as a set of rules. Each rule specifies how one structure in a program is composed of smaller structures. These rules are applied, in a systematic way, to the source program, to determine its structure. The word **parsing** is sometimes used to describe this process.

For example, one of the syntax rules of Basic language can be written, in BNF notation, as follows:

⟨program line⟩ : : = ⟨line number⟩ ⟨instruction word⟩ ⟨rest of instruction⟩

This rule analyses the line

100 LET X = 0

as follows:

⟨line number⟩	**: 100**
⟨instruction word⟩	**: LET**
⟨rest of instruction⟩	**: X = 0**
and, therefore: ⟨program of line⟩	**: 100 LET X = 0**

A common technique of syntax analysis involves the use of **state tables**. These are discussed briefly in the exercise at the end of this chapter.

18.6 The Dictionary

A considerable amount of information about a program is accumulated as compilation proceeds. This information is stored in a data structure known as a **dictionary**. The information is generally loaded during early parts of compilation and accessed during later stages.

Much of the information in the dictionary concerns the use of variables in the source language. As each variable in a source program is encountered, an entry for it is made in the dictionary. This entry includes the name of the variable, its type, and the address of the memory location where its value is to be stored.

For example, the dictionary entry for the variable X in the Basic program line previously mentioned might be as follows:

variable name	type	address
X	N	3A2F

where N represents numeric, and the address is a hexadecimal number.

The dictionary also contains information about the line numbers or labels of statements. For example, a Basic program might include the lines

70 GO TO 100

...

100 LET X = 0

An entry in the dictionary is created for the line number 100. This contains the address of the translated code for the line. It might be as follows:

variable name	type	address
100	L	2B1A

where L represents line number, and the address is a hexadecimal number. This entry enables the branching instruction in line 70 to be translated completely. It provides the destination of the branching instruction.

18.7 Code Generation

Having analysed the structure of the source program, it is now possible to translate it into object code. This step is known as code generation. Code generation generally takes place as each item in the source program is identified by the syntax analyser. For example, if a variable name is recognised in an instruction, then the dictionary is used to find its address. This address is inserted into the machine code instruction being generated.

In most cases, a statement in a high level language generates more than one machine code instruction. To give an example of this, a short section of a Basic program is shown below, together with the equivalent code in AMC assembly language. It must be remembered that compilers generally produce machine code, but assembly code, together with comments, is shown here for simplicity.

```
Basic                        AMC assembly language
200 FOR I = 1 TO N              LOA X N + 1   Use Index as loop counter.
                    NXT CMP X    N            Compare with N.
                        BGT      OUT          Exit loop if greater than N.
205 LET Y(I) = 0            CLR A             Clear accumulator.
                           STO A D Y          Store contents of
                                              accumulator in Y + index.
210 NEXT I                     INC X          Increment index.
                               BRN  NXT       Continue loop.
                    OUT
```

18.8 Optimisation

One of the objections to high level languages, when they were first introduced, was that the object code they produced would be less efficient than machine code written by hand. Accordingly, much attention has been paid, especially in the early days of compilers, to increasing the efficiency of object code.

Optimisation can take place before or after code generation, and sometimes at both places. Either the source or the object code is manipulated to produce a more efficient end product. In most cases, 'more efficient' means object code which will run more quickly when it is executed.

Optimisation can be attempted on almost any part of the code of a program, but loops are one of the most fruitful areas. Here the objective is to do as much as possible outside the loop, and reduce the number of times that the test for the end of the loop is carried out.

As an example, consider the portion of assembly code in the previous section. The instruction to clear the accumulator can be taken outside the loop. Furthermore, if the loop limit N is an even number, then the body of the loop can be performed twice before the test for the end of the loop is carried out. These optimisations lead to the following code:

```
        CLR  A              Clear accumulator.
        LOA  X  N + 1       Use index as loop counter.
NXT     CMP  X    N         Compare with N.
        BGT       OUT       Exit loop if greater than N.
        STO  A  D Y         Store contents of accumulator in Y + index.
        INC  X              Increment index.
        STO  A  D Y         Store contents of accumulator in Y + index.
        INC  X              Increment index
        BRN       NXT       Continue loop.
OUT
```

Although the object code now contains more instructions, it will be executed more quickly.

One problem with optimisation is that it considerably increases the size and complexity of the compiler. It is accordingly becoming less popular, particularly in compilers for minicomputers and microcomputers. An alternative way of optimising programs, which is gaining acceptance, is to allow machine code instructions to be combined with high level language statements in a program. This allows the programmer to optimise crucial areas of the program, and simplifies the task of the compiler.

18.9 Error Handling

In all of the previous sections it has been assumed that the source program input to the compiler is correct. Unfortunately, this is not always the case.

Errors detected during compilation are generally of two types. The first type are **syntax errors**, when a source program does not conform to the rules of syntax of the source language. The other type includes transfers of control to statements which do not exist, and duplicate labels on statements.

When an error is detected, most compilers attempt to locate the position of the error, and determine its cause. This process is called **diagnostics**. A message, called a **diagnostic error message**, is output, together with some indication of the position of the error.

In most cases, when an error is detected, compilation cannot be completed. The usual practice is to continue to the end of the syntax analysis phase, in case any more errors are encountered. Code generation does not take place. In some cases it is difficult to continue syntax analysis, as assumptions have to be made about the correctness of code near the error. Analysis generally re-commences from the start of the next source program statement.

A few compilers make an attempt to correct certain errors such as mis-spelt instruction words. This practice does not, however, meet with widespread approval.

18.10 Interpreters

As mentioned previously, an interpreter is a program which analyses and runs a source program, statement by statement. Like compilers, interpreters analyse the structure of each source program statement. However, lexical and syntax analysis are not always distinguished. Interpreters also create and maintain a dictionary of variable names and statement labels.

Instead of generating object code for each source program statement, the interpreter carries out a sequence of actions equivalent to the instructions in the statement. If object code is generated in the process, it is not retained.

As a consequence of this, optimisation is virtually impossible, and error diagnostics are limited, by comparison with compilers. However, interpreters are generally shorter and simpler than compilers. Only one copy of the program being translated is kept, in source code. For these reasons, interpreters are particularly popular on minicomputers and microcomputers.

18.11 Conclusion

This chapter has introduced a number of essential ideas related to language translation programs. The objectives of language translation programs have been discussed, and ways of achieving these objectives have been described.

Over the last twenty years, language translators have become an indispensable part of computers. Some computers, particularly microcomputers, go to the lengths of having a language translator permanently stored on read-only memory. Many of these computers can only be programmed in a high level language.

Compilers and interpreters generally achieve their prime objective of language translation very well. Error diagnostics, however, often leaves much to be desired, and optimisation is sometimes ignored.

Language translation is a very active area in computing. Work is in progress improving existing compilers and interpreters, and writing translators for new languages or new computers. Much attention is currently being paid to the problem of writing translators for large languages on small computers.

One line of development, however, might make language translation programs obsolete. This is the design of computers which have a machine instruction set in a high level language.

Exercise 18

1 Briefly define the terms source language, object language, base language, optimisation, diagnostics and parsing.
2 Compare and contrast the processes of compilation and interpretation.
3 Why is interpretation more suited to small computers than compilation?
4 What are the two tasks performed during lexical analysis?
5 A much simplified form of the Basic language **I F . . T H E N** statement is specified by the following syntax rules, written in BNF notation:

1 ⟨conditional statement⟩ : : = ⟨line number⟩ **I F** ⟨condition⟩ **T H E N** ⟨line number⟩
2 ⟨condition⟩ : : = ⟨variable⟩ ⟨relation⟩ ⟨constant⟩
3 ⟨relation⟩ : : = < / > / =

Using these rules to analyse a statement, the steps are as follows:

Example   **200 I F A > 10 THEN 300**

	200	**IF**	**A**	**>**	**10**	**THEN**	**300**
rule 3	⟨line number⟩	**I F** ⟨variable⟩	⟨relation⟩	⟨constant⟩	**THEN**	⟨line number⟩
rule 2	⟨line number⟩	**I F**		⟨condition⟩		**THEN**	⟨line number⟩
rule 1			⟨conditional statement⟩			

Use these rules to analyse the following statements. Some are valid and some are invalid.
a)   **50 IF J = 1 THEN 75**
b)   **95 IF K > L THEN 100**
c) **100 IF 100 = M THEN 50**
d)   **30 IF T < − 5 THEN 20**
e) Modify Rule 2 so that the statement in part (b) becomes a valid statement.

6 An alternative method of analysing the syntax of a program is the use of **state tables**. The program is examined character by character. The state table contains a row for each state, and a column for each character which may be encountered. An entry in the table contains either a jump to another state, an exit instruction or an error condition. An exit instruction indicates that the structure defined by the table has been recognised.

The state table below is for the recognition of signed decimal numbers. The symbol ∇ indicates that the end of the number has been reached.

state			next character		
	+	**−**	**digit**	**.**	**∇**
1	2	2	3	4	error 1
2	error 2	error 2	3	4	error 3
3	error 2	error 2	3	4	exit
4	error 2	error 2	4	error 4	exit

The use of the table is best illustrated by some examples.

Example 1   −59·6

	state	next character	new state
Start in state 1:	1	−	2
	2	5	3
	3	9	3
	3	.	4
	4	6	4
	4	∇	exit

As an exit is reached, −59·6 is a valid signed decimal number.

Example 2   7·8·9

	state	next character	new state
Start in state 1:	1	7	3
	3	.	4
	4	8	4
	4	.	error 4

An error condition is reached. This error might carry the message 'More than one decimal point in number'.

Use the state table to analyse the following numbers:
a) 796
b) 5·2
c) +59
d) +7·3−6
e) ++8

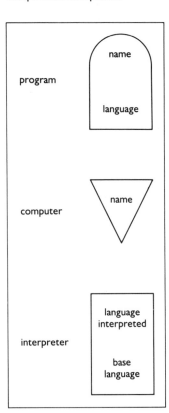

Figure 18.3
Additional symbols used with T
diagrams

f) –

g) Supply suitable messages for the other error conditions.

☐ h) Extend the state table to recognise floating point numbers like 3·6E9 and 4·7E−5.

7 Generate code in AMC or some other suitable assembly language for the following segments of
Basic programs:

a) `100 LET L = J + K`

b) `50 IF C > 10 THEN 200`

c) `100 FOR K = 1 TO 20`
`110 LET J(K) = J(K) + 1`
`120 NEXT K`

8 Consider the following portion of code, written in Basic and in AMC assembly language:

Basic	AMC assembly language	
`500 FOR J = 1 TO 27`	`LOA X N +1`	Use index register as loop counter, initial value 1.
	`NXT CMP X N +27`	Compare index with 27.
	`BGT OUT`	Exit loop if greater than 27.
`510 LET W(J) = 100`	`LOA A N +100`	Load 100 to accumulator.
	`STB A D W`	Store contents of accumulator in W+ index.
`520 NEXT J`	`INC X`	Increment index register.
	`BRN NXT`	Continue loop.
	`OUT`	

Optimise the AMC assembly code so as to speed up the execution of the loop.

9 Write a short program in Basic language and test it until it is free of errors.

Run your program a number of times, in each case introducing a single, simple error. For each
run, make a note of the error you have introduced and the diagnostic error message you obtain.
Comment on your findings.

If possible, repeat the process using exactly the same errors, on a different computer, or on a
different Basic translator on the same computer. Compare the error messages you receive in
each case.

10 Some additional symbols used in conjunction with T diagrams are shown in Figure 18.3.

Figure 18.4 shows how these symbols may be combined to depict the compilation and
running of a program. The example chosen uses a source program in Pascal being compiled and
run on a PDP-11 computer.

Draw similar combinations of these symbols for the following situations:

a) Compiling and running a Fortran program on an IBM 370.

b) Interpreting a Basic program on a Z80 based microcomputer.

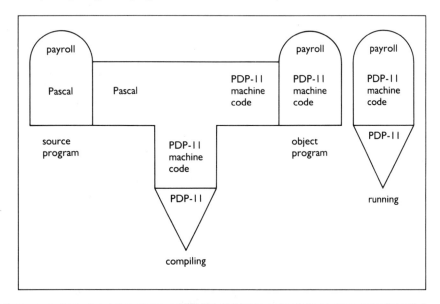

Figure 18.4
Compiling and running a Pascal
program on a PDP-11 computer

c) Assembling a Basic compiler written in Z80 assembly language to produce a compiler written in Z80 machine language. Note that a T diagram can also be used for an assembler.

d) A Pascal compiler for an Intel 8086 based microcomputer is written in Pascal. It is **cross-compiled** on a PDP-VAX, using a Pascal compiler written in VAX machine code, producing 8086 machine language.

11 A number can be recognised by a procedure which uses a device called a 'state table'. The procedure used in a computer program is as follows:

i) at the start of the recognition process the table is entered at state 1;

ii) a character appearing on the input causes a change in state as specified by the state table (e.g. if the process is in state 3 and the character + appears the recogniser changes to state 6 (entry 3 in column '+ or −') and proceeds to consider the next character on the input);

iii) successful recognition is achieved if an EXIT position is reached;

iv) a blank entry signifies non-recognition;

v) the symbol ∇ is used to signify any other character which is not an integral part of the number and is therefore used as a number terminator (e.g. space).

State name and number	Symbol				
	+ or −	Digit	.	E	∇
1 ⟨root⟩		4	2	3	
2 ⟨dec⟩		5			
3 ⟨exp⟩	6	7			
4 ⟨int⟩		4	2	3	EXIT
5 ⟨frac⟩		5		3	EXIT
6 ⟨exp-1⟩		7			
7 ⟨exp-2⟩		7			EXIT

Given the state table above:

a) indicate which of the following numbers will not be recognised and the state at which non-recognition occurs:

(i) 21·3   (ii) −12   (iii) 2·3E-2

(iv) 3·4E6   (v) 97·

b) define the syntax of numbers which can be recognised;

c) draw a program flow chart for the recognition process described above.

UL 79 I

12 A particular computer system **compiles** Basic programs into executable code. Describe the effect of the following Basic statements on (a) the storage requirements of the program (executable code and data), and (b) the likely execution time of the program.

i) REM

ii) DIM

iii) FOR ... ... NEXT

iv) END

In the light of your answers, why is the number of lines in a Basic program compiled by this system a poor guide to the amount of storage used, and/or the execution time?

What are the advantages of compiling a Basic program, as opposed to interpreting it? What are the advantages of interpreting?

UL 80 I

19
Operating systems

This chapter provides a brief introduction to a difficult and sometimes controversial area of computing, namely operating systems. The nature and objectives of operating systems are discussed, together with some of their desirable features. The bulk of the chapter is an overview of the structure of a typical operating system.

This chapter describes one of the most important pieces of software which transforms the hardware of a computer into a useful machine. A few of the concepts introduced in earlier chapters are developed here. Many of the ideas introduced in this chapter pave the way to an understanding of data processing and computer applications, which form later chapters in this book.

It must be emphasised that this chapter is only a very brief introduction to the topic. Although the principles of operating systems are now fairly well understood, they are still the subject of intense research and development work.

19.1 Some Background Information

Before commencing a study of operating systems, it is necessary to provide some background information to the topic. This is in the form of a second look at the nature of a computer and a brief survey of the way in which computers can be operated.

19.2 A Second Look at the Nature of a Computer

At the beginning of this book, a computer is defined as follows:

A computer is a collection of resources, including digital electronic processing devices, stored programs and sets of data, which, under the control of the stored programs, automatically inputs, processes and outputs data, and may also store and retrieve data.

Since that definition was given, the ideas of hardware and software have been introduced, and developed to a considerable extent. For the purposes of this chapter, it is important to emphasise the view of a computer as a set of resources. These resources may be hardware, software or a combination of both. Together they provide such facilities as input, processing, output, etc. For example, a compiler is a software resource which provides the facility of language translation. This concept of a resource is used extensively in this chapter.

19.3 Types of Computer Operation

Computers vary considerably in size and capability. Similarly, there is a wide variety of ways in which they can be operated. This section examines some of these types of computer operation. Each type of computer operation requires a different type of operating system. Systems are reviewed in order from the simplest to the most complex.

Most microcomputers and some minicomputers can only process one program at a time. This is **single program operation**, and it requires only a simple operating system. The operating system supervises the loading, compilation and running of each program, and the input and output of data. Any errors occurring are reported.

Next in complexity is **batch processing**. A number of programs are batched together, and then run as a group. Although the programs are actually run one at a time, input and output from various programs can overlap to some extent.

Similar to batch processing, but much more sophisticated, is **multiprogramming**. At any one time, a number of programs are on the computer at various stages of completion. Resources are allocated to programs according to the requirements of the programs, and in order to maximise the usage of the different resources of the computer.

Both batch processing and multiprogramming can permit **remote job entry**, where programs are submitted for processing at sites remote from the computer.

The most sophisticated type of computer operation is **multi-access**, where a number of users can interact, via terminals, with their programs while they are running.

Looking at computer operation in a slightly different way, one can classify some computer applications as **real-time processing**. Real-time processing requires that the computer keep pace with some external process. In many real-time systems, computers interact directly with other equipment. A common example is computers controlling machines. Real-time processing is generally restricted to computers with multiprogramming or multi-access capability, though it is becoming more common in the case of microcomputers under single program operation. Real-time processing places an additional burden on an operating system, since there is a deadline associated with every action performed by the computer.

This section on types of computer operation is not to be confused with a later section on types of data processing systems, in Chapter 21. When this later section has been studied, it is a useful exercise to compare the two.

Having outlined the various ways in which computers can be operated, the scene has been set to confront the question, 'What is an operating system?'.

19.4   The Nature of an Operating System

Like the question 'What is a computer?', the question 'What is an operating system?' is surprisingly difficult. The answer is given here in several stages.

Firstly, an operating system is a program, or set of programs. Operating systems vary in size from very small to very large, but all are pieces of software. In the past, almost all operating systems were written in a low level language. Currently, many operating systems are partly or completely written in a high level language.

Secondly, an operating system is, by virtue of its name, a system. You will recall that a system is a collection of parts, working together towards some common goals. The goals, or objectives, of an operating system are discussed shortly.

Thirdly, you will recall that a computer may be regarded as a set of devices, or resources, which provide a number of services, such as input, processing, storage and output. The operating system of the computer may be regarded as the manager of these resources. It controls the way in which these resources are put to work.

Finally, an operating system is the lowest layer of software on a computer. It acts directly on the 'raw' hardware of the computer. It supports other layers of software such as compilers and applications programs. Part of the task of an operating system is to 'cushion' users from the complexities of direct use of the computer hardware.

In summary, then, an operating system is a program, or set of programs, driving the raw hardware of a computer, which manages the resources of the computer in accordance with certain objectives, providing higher layers of software with a simplified computer.

19.5   The Development of Operating Systems

Operating systems are as old as electronic computers. It was realised from the start that the hardware of a computer on its own is very difficult to use. Various **supervisor**, **executive** or **monitor** programs were written to make aspects of using a computer easier. As time went by, these programs became larger, more complex, and, unfortunately, more cumbersome and less reliable.

Gradually the objectives and functions of these supervisory programs became clearer, and the term operating system came into use. Better program design led to improvements in efficiency and reliability of operating systems. Sophisticated operating systems made very large computers and networks of linked computers a practical possibility.

Now operating systems face a new challenge, from cheap, plentiful microcomputers, which require only the simplest of monitor programs for their operation.

19.6   Objectives of Operating Systems

All operating systems have two major objectives. These are to make it possible for the resources of the computer to be used efficiently, and to obscure the difficulties of dealing directly with the hardware of the computer.

The first objective, of efficient resource utilisation, is made especially difficult by the fact that some devices of a computer work much more quickly than others. Part of the task of an operating system is to ensure that fast devices such as processors are not held up by slow devices such as input/output devices.

To achieve the second objective, of simplifying the use of the hardware of the computer, the operating system creates a **virtual machine**. A virtual machine is a simplified computer, with all difficult details taken care of by the operating system. People writing other software for the computer need only know about the virtual machine, and not about the actual hardware of the computer. Details of the idea of a virtual machine are explained in the sections on the structure of an operating system, later in the chapter.

19.7   The Functions of an Operating System

Having established what an operating system is, and what its objectives are, the next question is 'What does an operating system do?'. The answer to this question depends to some extent on the type of computer operation in question. The functions of a multi-tasking operating system on a large computer are somewhat different from those of a single program operation monitor on a microcomputer. Nevertheless some general points can be made. These apply to a greater or a lesser extent depending on the type of computer operation.

The functions of an operating system may be loosely classified as time allocation, resource control, input/output control, error handling and protection, operator interface and accounting. These are briefly discussed below, and again mentioned in the context of the structure of a typical operating system, later in the chapter.

Time allocation involves the scheduling of all the various activities going on in the computer. Resource control is the allocation of the resources of the computer in a rational way. Input/output control involves channelling data to and from the peripherals of the computer. Error handling and protection involves the detection and reporting of errors, and minimising their effect. The operator interface is the communication with the person operating the computer. Accounting involves charging users, according to a scale of costs, for their use of the resources of the computer.

This is indeed a diverse list of functions. At this stage it is worth remembering that they must all be performed in accordance with the objectives of the operating system, outlined in the previous section.

19.8 Desirable Features

Operating systems have certain objectives, and must perform a number of functions. In addition, they must have some desirable features. These desirable features include **efficiency, reliability, maintainability** and **small size**.

Efficiency implies that an operating system must carry out its tasks promptly. Time spent on operating system functions is productive computing time wasted. Reliability is crucial, as a major failure in an operating system can render the host computer useless. Maintainability means that modifications to the operating system are easy to make. A clearly written, well structured program is essential for this.

Finally, in spite of all the things it must do, and all the other desirable features it must have, the program for an operating system must be as small as possible. A small operating system does not occupy very much main or backing store on the computer, is less error prone, and runs more quickly. Other desirable features tend to increase the size of an operating system. In practice, a compromise has to be reached between them and the requirement of small size.

19.9 The Structure of a Typical Operating System

The remainder of this chapter is a description of the structure of the program for a typical, or perhaps ideal, operating system. It must be emphasised that in practice the program structure varies according to the size and complexity of the operating system. Nevertheless, the features mentioned here are all present to some extent.

The program structure is presented as a series of modules. The first module, called the **nucleus**, is a service module for the others. Each of the other modules performs one or more of the operating system functions mentioned previously. The other modules are **memory management, input/output control, backing store management, resource allocation and scheduling** and **protection**.

19.10 The Nucleus

The lowest level module of an operating sytem is known as the **nucleus**. It is supported directly by the hardware of the computer, and provides a number of services required by the other layers of the system.

Most computers have certain machine instructions whose use is restricted to the nucleus of the operating system. These restricted instructions generally include ones which transfer control from one program to another, and ones which access restricted registers. Restricting these instructions in this way is a very efficient means of controlling the overall running of the computer, and limiting the effects of errors.

Tasks carried out by the nucleus include handling interrupts, allocation of work to the processor and providing a communication mechanism between different programs.

As discussed in Section 10.23, an interrupt is an external event causing the running of a program to be suspended. See Section 17.7.10 for an example of the use of interrupts.

When the hardware of the computer detects that an interrupt has occurred, control is transferred to the interrupt handler in the nucleus of the operating system. The interrupt handler determines the cause of the interrupt and then takes appropriate action. This action may be to transfer control to another module of the operating system, to start up some other program, or to resume the program which was interrupted. As many interrupts are caused by requests for input or output, the input/output handler is one of the modules most commonly called.

In allocating work to the processor, the nucleus generally transfers control to the program which the scheduler has determined should be the next to run.

The communication function is generally achieved by maintaining a queue of messages waiting for each program in the system. The nucleus receives a message from a program, and adds it to the queue of its destination program.

19.11   Memory Management

The main store of most computers is far too small to handle all the programs and data on the computer at any one time. The memory management module of an operating system allocates main store to programs or parts of programs which need it most. Everything else is kept on backing store. When main store is allocated, it is done so in a structured, orderly way.

The commonest memory management policy is to create a **virtual memory**. This is the memory of the computer as seen by a particular user, and is often much larger than the actual main store of the computer. The operating system takes care of all transfers between main and backing store. Thus, to a user, main store and backing store are all part of the same thing, namely the virtual memory of the computer.

19.12   Input/Output Control

The problem with input and output is that different input/output devices have different characteristics, and run at very different speeds. For example, a line printer outputs characters one line at a time, whereas a paper tape punch outputs characters one at a time. A line printer works about one hundred times as fast as a paper tape punch.

The input/output control module of an operating system deals with these problems by making input and output **device independent** from the point of view of the user. To a user, all devices have the same characteristics, and are instructed in exactly the same way. The operating system deals with the irregularities of each type of device.

A very common technique, especially useful for output, is **spooling**. Data for output is held on a spool, or queue, on backing store, until the output device is ready for it. Figure 19.1 illustrates this procedure.

19.13   Backing Store Management

The backing store of a computer is where the bulk of the data and programs being processed are kept. The backing store management of an operating system has the

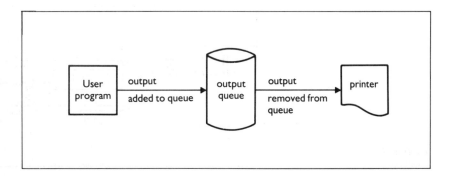

Figure 19.1
Spooling

task of maintaining the structure of all this information, and ensuring that the backing store of the computer is used efficiently.

Data and programs on backing store are kept in **files**. The backing store management supervises the creation, updating and deletion of files. A directory is kept of all the files on the computer at any time. The backing store management co-operates with the memory management during the transfer of data to and from main store.

The files on backing store have very different purposes. Some contain information which may be shared. Others are private, or even secret. Accordingly, each file has a set of **access privileges** which indicate to what extent the information in the file may be shared. The operating system checks that these privileges are not violated.

19.14 Resource Allocation and Scheduling

Most of the time that a computer is running, the demand for its resources is greater than their availability. To deal with this problem, an operating system generally has a **resource allocation policy** built into it. The resource allocation mechanism puts this policy into practice.

Matters would be very simple if a straightforward policy like 'first come, first served' could be used. The problem is that such policies can lead to a situation known as **deadlock**. This is when two programs prevent each other from continuing because each has claimed a resource which the other one possesses. Deadlock is analogous to the situation of two wide vehicles meeting half way across a narrow bridge, shown in Figure 19.2. Various resource allocation policies have been evolved, either to prevent deadlock, or to recover from it should it occur.

The **scheduler** is mainly concerned with the allocation of processor time to programs. This is done in accordance with some **scheduling policy**. Scheduling policies vary considerably from one operating system to another. Some involve the allocation of a level of priority to each program.

A very common scheduling policy on multiprogramming and multi-access systems is known as **time slicing**. Each program on the computer is allocated a short slice of processor time. If the program is not completed during its time slice, then it returns to a queue of programs waiting their turn. Figure 19.3 illustrates this method of scheduling. Scheduling policies cannot be too complicated, otherwise the computer spends far too much of its time deciding what to do next.

19.15 Protection

When a computer contains a number of items of software, accessing various stores

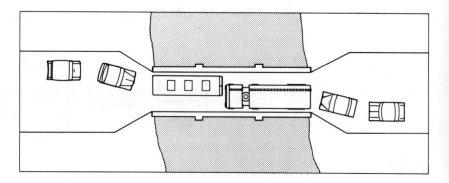

Figure 19.2
Deadlock

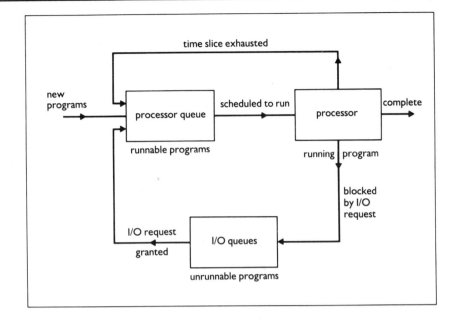

Figure 19.3
Time slicing

of information, these must be protected from each other. The most essential piece of software to protect is, of course, the operating system itself.

Protecting is generally against two eventualities, namely errors and deliberate abuse of the system. Although it is impossible to prevent errors, it is essential to detect and diagnose them as early as possible, and to limit their effects. Deliberate abuse of the system is rather more difficult to deal with. Although protection mechanisms are designed to prevent unauthorised activities from succeeding, few operating systems are regarded as foolproof.

Protection mechanisms are distributed throughout most operating systems, with most attention being paid to main store and backing store. Files on backing store are protected by the system of access privileges mentioned previously. Protection of main store is discussed below.

Main store protection is regarded as the most important aspect of the security of a computer, because everything that a computer does is via code or data resident in main store. The memory management system allocates portions of main store for various purposes, and then assigns these portions various levels of protection, depending on their nature. Checks are carried out to ensure that the protection of a portion of memory is not violated.

Some operating systems allocate **levels of privilege** to all programs on the computer. The nucleus of the operating system has the highest level of privilege, while applications programs have the lowest level. The use of certain machine instructions, and access to main store and backing store, is governed by the level of privilege of the program concerned. Some operating systems regard their protection mechanism as their most significant feature.

19.16 Accounting

One of the more mundane tasks that some operating systems must perform is to keep a record of the charges incurred by each user program. The most significant portion of the cost is generally for processor time. Information is passed to the accounting module from the scheduler, to establish how much processor time a program has used. Other charges are for the use of backing store media and printer paper.

The accounting module requires regular maintenance as prices of computer use change. In spite of inflation, price changes are quite often in the downward direction.

19.17 User and Operator Interface

Communication between an operating system and the outside world takes the form of two interfaces, namely that between the operating system and a user of the computer, and that between the operating system and the person operating the computer.

In a batch processing system, the user interface is the **job control language** (JCL). This is the language in which instructions to the operating system are placed at the front of each program. These instructions specify, among other things, the maximum running time of the program, how much main store is required, and what peripherals are to be used. In some cases the operating system may be instructed what to do if an error is encountered in the program. Certain job control languages permit the user to define **macro-instructions**. These are single instructions which are interpreted as a group of instructions, defined previously. An example of some job control instructions is shown in Figure 19.4. They instruct an operating system to compile and run a program written in Pascal.

In reply to these job control language instructions, the operating system outputs a series of messages, indicating the progress of various stages of the program.

In a multi-access system, communication between the user and the operating system is interactive. The user can issue **commands** to the operating system from a terminal. The operating system responds to these commands, and sends messages to the user.

The interface between an operating system and the person operating the computer is also one of commands and messages. Many of the functions of the operating system can be over-ridden by the operator if necessary. This applies particularly to scheduling and resource allocation. At all times the operator is in ultimate control of the computer.

A typical section of a **console log**, showing commands from the operator and messages from the operating system, appears in Figure 19.5

```
#job testprog umace07 lines 600 time 10
#password s021suf
#deck myfile pascal


    [program]


/*
pascal myfile
exec myfile print
#eoj
```

Figure 19.4
Job control language

```
1804 26 batch queue = 37
1804 51 job asp3 umach09 started
1804 53 job asp3 umach09 error 57
1804 55 job asp3 umach09 abandoned
1905 02 job testprog umace07 started
batch queue? 39
1905 12 job testlog umace07 time limit exceeded
1905 14 job testprog umace07 abandoned
1905 23 job at47 umach01 started
1905 25 disk vol 3721 allocated
1905 31 disk vol 3721 free
1905 37 job at47 umach01 ended
1905 39 batch queue = 38
disk vol 3721? free
```

Figure 19.5
A console log

19.18   An Assessment of Operating Systems

Having read this chapter, and reflected a moment, you will realise the magnitude of the task undertaken by the operating system on a medium or large sized computer. An operating system must perform a number of different tasks, in an integrated way, under very difficult circumstances. Some of the largest and most complex pieces of computer software ever written are operating systems.

Because operating systems evolved in a haphazard way, without clearly defined objectives or a respectable program structure, some of the early large systems were slow, clumsy and error prone. Job control language and operating system messages were almost incomprehensible.

Time and experience have brought about a new generation of smaller, simpler and more efficient operating systems, with much better user and operator interfaces. However, some of the habits from the bad old days still remain.

As mentioned at the beginning of this chapter, one of the biggest challenges to operating systems comes from microcomputers. Most microcomputers have a very small operating system permanently stored on read-only memory. Microcomputer salesmen never tire of pointing out the fact that medium and large sized computers spend a considerable proportion of time (often more than 30 per cent) running their operating systems. Their effective processing power is thus much less than it appears. A few microcomputers, at a small fraction of the price, would be just as powerful ... Over the next few years the marketplace will no doubt resolve this question.

19.19   Conclusion

This chapter has been a brief survey of a very large topic. Some of the main points in the chapter are summarised below:

- An operating system is a program, driving the raw hardware of a computer, which manages the resources of the computer in accordance with certain objectives. The two major objectives of an operating system are the efficient utilisation of the resources of the computer, and to conceal the difficulties of dealing directly with the hardware of the computer.
- The functions of an operating system include time allocation, resource control, input/output control, error handling and protection, operator interface and accounting. Desirable features include efficiency, reliability, maintainability and small size.

- The program for an operating system may be structured into the following modules: a nucleus, memory management, input/output control, backing store management, resource allocation and scheduling, protection, accounting and user and operator interface.
- In practice, operating systems attain their objectives with varying degrees of success. It remains to be seen whether microcomputers will erode the market for medium and large sized computers with sophisticated operating systems.

Exercise 19

1 The phrase 'running under an operating system' is used to describe a computer using a particular operating system. For example, one might say 'a 380Z microcomputer running under CP/M'.
   Use the concept of a virtual machine to explain the significance of this phrase for a person writing a program for the computer concerned.

2 Briefly describe what is meant by each of the following terms: resource; single program operation; batch processing; multiprogramming; remote job entry; multi-access; real-time processing; interrupt; spooling; deadlock; time sharing; job control language; console log.

3 In your own words, give a brief answer to the question 'What is an operating system?'.

4 Name a significant feature which modern microcomputers have in common with early electronic computers.

5 State some advantages of the concept of a virtual machine.

6 Operating systems are described in the text as 'some of the largest and most complex pieces of computer software ever written'. Explain why this is the case.

7 Summarise the structure of a typical operating system.

8 Why is the nucleus the most privileged part of an operating system?

9 Why is the concept of virtual memory so useful to a programmer?

10 A microcomputer has a single program operation monitor as its operating system. Summarise the objectives of this system and the features you would expect it to have.

11 Why is it essential for an operator to have ultimate control of a computer, rather than an operating system?

12 What is understood by the term **interrupt**? How may interrupts be used to make input/output processing more efficient in a multiprogramming system?
   In a particular computer system, those devices capable of causing an interrupt do so by means of a signal placed on an **interrupt-line** shared by all the devices. This signal causes the central processor to save the current contents of the sequence control register in a special register and to transfer control to an **interrupt service routine** provided by the programmer.
   In order that the device causing the interrupt may be identified, a flag is set at the same time as the signal is placed on the interrupt-line. There is a different flag for each device, and these flags may be tested by the interrupt service routine.
   The following assembly language instructions are provided for manipulating and testing the interrupt system.

DISABLE	sets the central processor to ignore any signals on the interrupt-line, and hence not to respond to any interrupts.
ENABLE	resets the central processor to recognise signals on the interrupt-line.
SKPFLG (device)	causes the next instruction in sequence to be skipped unless the flag associated with the **device** is set. Thus, if the flag associated with the line-printer is set, **SKPFLG (PRINTER)** will cause the statement immediately following to be executed, but otherwise to be skipped.
CLRFLG (device)	causes the flag associated with the **device** to be reset, regardless of its present status. Thus **CLRFLG (KEYBOARD)** resets the input keyboard flag.
RETI	returns from an interrupt by simultaneously **ENABLE**-ing the interrupt system and transferring control to the address held in the special register.

Among the remaining assembly language instructions are the following:

STORE address   stores the current contents of the accumulator in location **address**, overwriting anything already stored there. Thus **STORE RATE** stores the contents of the accumulator in the location with symbolic address **RATE**.

LOAD address   loads the accumulator with the contents of **address**, overwriting the present contents of the accumulator. Thus **LOAD TIME** loads the accumulator from the location with symbolic address **TIME**.

JUMP address   transfers control to the location **address**. Thus, after executing **JUMP LOOP**, execution continues sequentially from the instruction stored in the location with symbolic address **LOOP**.

Below are shown significant parts of an interrupt service routine, in a system where the disk-reading mechanism, the line-printer and the input keyboard can cause interrupts. The lines are numbered for ease of reference only, and symbolic labels are indicated by the use of a colon, as in line 10.

```
1                    DISABLE
2                    STORE SAFETY
3                    SKPFLG (DISK)
4                    JUMP DISKROUTINE
5                    SKPFLG (PRINTER)
6                    JUMP PRNTROUTINE
7                    SKPFLG (KEYBOARD)
8                    JUMP KBROUTINE
9                    JUMP ERROR
10   DISKROUTINE:CLRFLG (DISK)
     .. .. ..
19                   JUMP RETURN
20   PRNTROUTINE:CLRFLG (PRINTER)
     .. .. ..
30     KBROUTINE:CLRFLG (KEYBOARD)
     .. .. ..
40         RETURN:LOAD SAFETY
41                 RETI
```

   i) What is the purpose of the **DISABLE** instruction (line 1)?

   ii) What is the purpose of the **STORE** instruction (line 2) and the corresponding **LOAD** instruction (line 40)?

   iii) What sort of error has occurred if the **JUMP** in line 9 is executed?

   iv) What is the purpose of the **CLRFLG** instruction in line 10 and under what circumstances will it be executed?

   v) What would you expect the routine beginning at line 20 to accomplish?

   vi) What would you expect the last instruction to be in the portion of the routine beginning at line 20?

   vii) What might happen if the programmer had inadvertently inserted an **ENABLE** instruction before line 41?

   viii) What pair of instructions would test for a paper-tape reader interrupt (device code **PTR**) and branch to an appropriate routine?

   ix) Where should these instructions in (viii) above be placed in the sequence of instructions in lines 1 to 9? Give a reason for your answer.

UL 80 1

13 a) State how and why an operating system can be constructed so that programs can produce 'spooled' output in backing store which is later sent to output devices by a system routine.

   b) For this system routine

      i) show what tables of information would be required;

      ii) construct a flow diagram.

OLE 80 II

20
Operating systems case studies

This chapter presents very brief surveys of four operating systems currently in use. The intention is to consolidate the general ideas introduced in the previous chapter, and to give some idea of how the principles of operating systems are put into practice.

Each of the operating systems outlined here is designed for use on one of the computers whose hardware is investigated in Chapter 13. Like their host computers, these operating systems are representative of the range of systems currently available, and are generally regarded as being well designed. The names of the operating systems are as follows:

CP/M used by many microcomputers, including Z80 microprocessor-based computers.
Unix used by PDP-11 minicomputers.
VME/B used by ICL 2900 series mainframe computers.
COS used by Cray 1 large computers.

Each operating system is first described in general terms. Then some of the features of operating systems, introduced in the previous chapter, are discussed, as implemented by the particular system. Where possible, a brief assessment of the system is given.

20.1 CP/M

The **Control Program for Microprocessors (CP/M)** operating system is one of the most widely used operating systems on microcomputers. It first became available in 1975. CP/M is written in the high level language PL/M, discussed in Section 17.7.

20.1.1 General Features

CP/M is a general-purpose, single user operating system, supporting single program operation of the microcomputer. Its overall task is the management of the resources of the computer. It deals with incoming information from the keyboard, manages the information displayed on the screen, and allocates disc and memory space. It takes over control of the computer between the running of applications programs.

CP/M responds to a number of commands from the user of the computer. These commands enable files to be created, edited and copied, programs to be compiled and run, etc. Additional software can be added to the basic CP/M system, and incorporated into its list of commands.

20.1.2 Overall Structure

CP/M is made up of three modules, called **console command processor (CCP), basic input/output system (BIOS)** and **basic disc operating system (BDOS)**

CCP interprets commands from the keyboard, and supplies information to the user. BIOS contains a set of subprograms to control the various input and output peripherals attached to the processor. BDOS is in charge of the management of disc files. It relieves the user of all detailed work in this area.

20.1.3 Memory Management

CP/M supervises the allocation of memory space for various purposes. The concept of virtual memory is not implemented. Instead, the memory is partitioned into a number of fixed areas, each for a specific purpose. This is illustrated in Figure 20.1 (the term bootstrap loader is explained in Chapter 21).

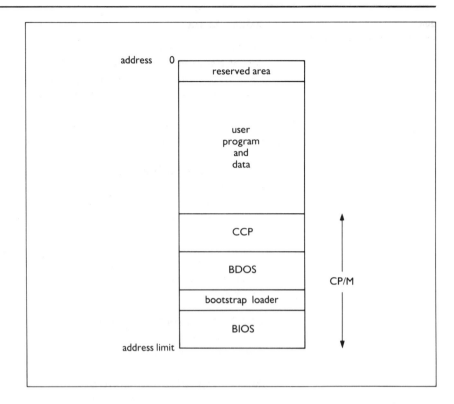

address 0

reserved area

user
program
and
data

CCP

BDOS

bootstrap loader

BIOS

address limit

CP/M

Figure 20.1
CP/M memory allocation

20.1.4   Input/Output Control

CP/M examines input from the keyboard, and manages the transfer of data to the display screen, printer or other peripherals of the microcomputer.

20.1.5   Backing Store Management

All the data and programs in the computer are structured as **files**. Various CP/M commands permit the storage and retrieval of these files, as well as editing, joining of two or more files into a single file, creation and deletion of files, and other file handling procedures.

20.1.6   User Interface

In most cases, as far as microcomputers are concerned, the user of the system is also the operator of the computer. The user interface of CP/M is designed with this in mind.

Instructions to CP/M are in the form of **commands**. Each command starts with a short English word (examples are Attach, Ed, Dump, Save), followed by further information providing the details required for the command to be carried out. Information passes from CP/M to the user in the form of **messages**, and **prompts** on the screen which invite the user to type further commands.

20.1.7   An Assessment of CP/M

CP/M has proved to be simple, robust and reliable. Its increasingly wide popularity is a tribute to its quality. It is being implemented on a wide range of 8 and 16 bit microcomputers. A multiprogramming version, called MP/M has been written, which is gaining popularity on the more powerful microcomputers which are becoming available.

20.2   Unix

The **Unix** operating system was originally designed for use with PDP computers. The version discussed here, designed for PDP-11 computers, first went into operation in 1971. It has subsequently been updated several times, and is in the process of being modified for use on a wide range of minicomputers, and some 16 bit microcomputers.

Although it is not the operating system supplied by the manufacturers of PDP computers, Unix is widely used on these computers, particularly at universities.

20.2.1   General Features

Unix is a general-purpose, multi-user, interactive operating system. It supports both multiprogramming and multi-access. An assembler, a number of compilers for high level languages and a text editor are among the items of systems software available under Unix. Unix itself is written in a high level language.

Unix is designed for a number of users accessing a single processor via terminals. No single user is regarded as the operator of the computer. All users may submit commands to the operating system in the course of their work. Responses to these commands are sent to the users by the system.

20.2.2   Memory Management

Unix implements the concept of virtual memory. Each user appears to have access to the entire memory of the computer.

20.2.3   Input/Output Control

Each peripheral device in the system is controlled via one or more **files**. These files are treated in exactly the same way as ordinary data files. In other words, to display an item of data, the data is written to the file associated with the VDU. This considerably simplifies the input and output of data, and obscures all the peculiarities of the various peripheral devices from the user. Facilities also exist for the spooling of output for a line printer.

20.2.4   Backing Store Management

All backing store space is regarded as being partitioned into **files**. The contents of a file may be structured according to the wishes of a user, but the relationships between files are controlled at system level by **directories**. Directories enable files to be grouped together, and permission to be given by a user for other users to share his or her files. The operating system maintains a **root directory** via which every file in the system may be accessed. The filing system is regarded as one of the most important features of Unix.

20.2.5   Protection

Protection within the system is achieved via protection bits associated with each file. These enable read, write and execute permission to be established for a file, both for its owner and for other users. Different users have different levels of privilege, which determine the extent to which they may access files, and thereby use the resources of the computer.

If an error is detected during the running of a program, the operating system jumps to a simple error handling subroutine. A facility is also available for a user to interrupt a program which appears to be going wrong.

20.2.6   User Interface

All commands to the operating system are interpreted by a program called the **shell**.

One notable feature of the shell is that it enables a user to control the extent of multitasking carried out by the computer. In normal circumstances, the operating system completes its response to one command before prompting a user to input another command. However, a user may instruct the system to start work on a command, and then accept another command straight away. Actions resulting from both commands are multiprogrammed together.

20.2.7   An Assessment of Unix

Unix combines the features of simplicity, ease of use and small size with considerable flexibility and power. It is a small, conventional operating system which has met with a wide measure of acceptance. Although it is some years old, its popularity is still on the increase.

Although it was originally designed for minicomputers, Unix is being implemented on some of the more powerful 16 bit microcomputers currently becoming available. One of its chief competitors in this area is CP/M or its derivative, MP/M.

20.3   VME/B

The **VME/B** (for **virtual machine environment**) operating system is used by most computers in the ICL 2900 series. It was designed and developed at the same time as the range of computers which support it.

20.3.1   General Features

VME/B is a sophisticated, general-purpose operating system, incorporating a number of advanced features. It supports transaction processing, multi-access and batch processing simultaneously. One of its prime objectives is to provide a simple, consistent high level interface to all users. It is flexible, in the sense that it can be tailored to the requirements of a particular installation.

VME/B is written in a high level language, specially designed for the purpose. Communication with VME/B is via a language called **system control language (SCL)** which is a block structured high level language.

20.3.2   Virtual Machine Concept

As its name implies, VME/B is centred on the virtual machine concept. The virtual machine available to each user includes that user's program and data, and all the operating system facilities and utility programs needed by the user. To a user, a virtual machine appears completely self-contained, yet VME/B allows certain segments of data and code to be shared, to prevent unnecessary duplication of software. A very sophisticated protection mechanism is used to ensure the security of each virtual machine, and of shared segments. This mechanism is discussed in a later section.

Figure 20.2 illustrates the idea of several virtual machines sharing certain segments.

20.3.3   Program Structure

Like many operating systems, VME/B is built up of a number of layers. These layers are shown in Figure 20.3. At the centre is the **kernel**, which transforms the hardware of the computer into a number of virtual machines. Next is a layer of systems software which manages the resources of the virtual machines. The outer layer contains applications programs.

Unlike older operating systems, VME/B does not have a completely rigid boundary between systems and application software.

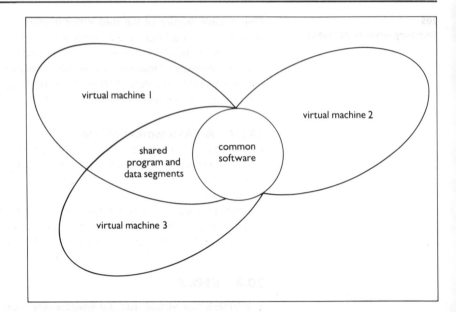

Figure 20.2
Virtual machines under VME/B

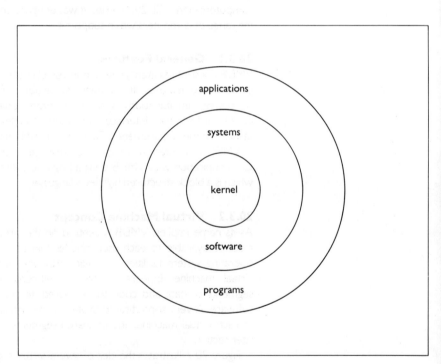

Figure 20.3
VME/B program structure

20.3.4 Memory Management

Each virtual machine is provided with a virtual store which can be much larger than the main store of the computer. VME/B manages all transfers of segments of programs and data to and from backing store in order to implement this policy.

Each virtual machine makes extensive use of a hardware driven stack. The stack considerably simplifies the processing of programs originally written in a high level language.

20.3.5   Communications Management

One of the overall objectives of the 2900 series is the efficient handling of data communications. On the hardware side, a number of input/output controllers are used to link peripheral devices to processing units and main store. On the systems software side, VME/B supervises and schedules all input and output. This relieves users of this burden, and makes the best use of the hardware resources.

20.3.6   Backing Store Management

All aspects of the use and security of files are handled by VME/B through the use of an integrated filestore. The user may be responsible for the placement of his or her files on backing store, or may choose to leave this task to the operating system.

20.3.7   Scheduling

Scheduling of work takes place at several levels within the software. At the highest level, there are separate schedules for the transaction processing, batch and multi-access streams. At an intermediate level there is a scheduler for virtual machine resources, and at the lowest level the scheduler allocates the real hardware resources of the computer.

20.3.8   Protection

One of the most important aspects of the VME/B operating system is its protection mechanism. It is based on the concept of **levels of privilege**. Every process in the computer has associated with it a level of privilege in the range 0 to 15, 0 being the highest level, and 15 the lowest. Levels 0 to 2 are reserved for the kernel, levels 3 to 9 are for other systems software, and levels 10 to 15 are for applications programs. See Figure 20.4.

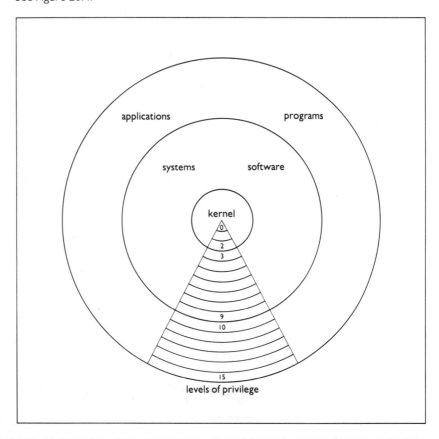

Figure 20.4
VME/B levels of privilege

When a process is running, a register called the **access control register** contains its level of privilege. Each segment of data that the process may wish to access contains a **read access key** and a **write access key**. Each key has a value between 0 and 15. Access is only permitted if the level of privilege in the access control register is less than or equal to that of the particular key. For example, a process with privilege level 11 may read from a segment with read access key 14, but may not write to a segment with write access key 8. Furthermore, each segment has an **execute permission bit**. Only if this bit is set may the code in the segment be executed.

This is an extremely powerful and versatile protection system. It enables portions of the operating system to be protected from other portions, and users to create levels of protection within their own applications programs. It minimises the damage caused by an error at any level, and prevents the kernel from being corrupted by an error at any other level of systems or applications software.

20.3.9   Software Supported by VME/B
Among the systems software supported by VME/B are a Basic interpreter, Fortran, Algol and Cobol compilers, and data management software.

The Basic interpreter is an interactive system which allows online syntax checking, editing and alteration of the flow of a program during execution.

The Fortran, Algol and Cobol compilers share a number of modules, and produce object code in the same format. High level language programs may be written in a mixture of these three languages.

The data management software is a flexible facility which allows a range of data structures to be constructed and developed by users. In particular, it provides a feature known as **data independence**, which is a vital property of all large stores of data. The concept of data independence is discussed in Chapter 24.

20.3.10   An Assessment of VME/B
VME/B is a large, complex and sophisticated operating system. Many of its design concepts are based on experience with the Atlas computer which, in its time, was the most powerful computing system in the world.

Although there have been some problems, it seems that the majority of users of VME/B are quite satisfied with the system. Many features, especially the protection mechanism and the high level system control language, are very highly regarded. In general, VME/B is considered to be a 'state of the art' system, and a model for the development of other operating systems.

20.4   COS

The **Cray operating system (COS)** has been designed specifically for Cray 1 computers. Its intention is to manage the work performed by a Cray 1 computer in such a way as to provide for the most efficient use of the resources of the system.

20.4.1   General Features
Cray computers are designed for the processing of fairly small numbers of very large programs. This simplifies the requirements of the operating system to a considerable extent.

COS provides a batch multiprogramming environment. As many as 63 programs can be in some stage of processing at any one time. COS is designed to be as simple and straightforward as possible, and to occupy only a small proportion of the main store of the computer. COS is written in Cray assembly language, CAL.

20.4.2 Structure

The Cray 1 operating system consists of four modules, namely executive, system task processor, control statement processor and utility programs.

Executive is responsible for overall control of the system. It performs scheduling, input/output and interrupt handling functions.

System task processor is responsible for the processing of all user requests to the operating system.

Control statement processor interprets all job control statements in user programs. In some cases this involves making a request to the system task processor.

Utility programs include a program loader, a source language maintenance program and copying and positioning routines. These programs are kept on backing store until they are needed.

Figure 20.5 shows the allocation of main store to COS modules and user programs.

20.4.3 Memory Management

Each program which is in some stage of processing is allocated an area of main store. When a program is complete, or is unable to continue for some reason, it is copied to backing store. Its memory area is freed for other use.

20.4.4 Input/Output Control

Almost all communication between a Cray 1 computer and peripheral devices is via a front-end processor. COS supervises the transfer of data between the Cray 1 and the front-end processor.

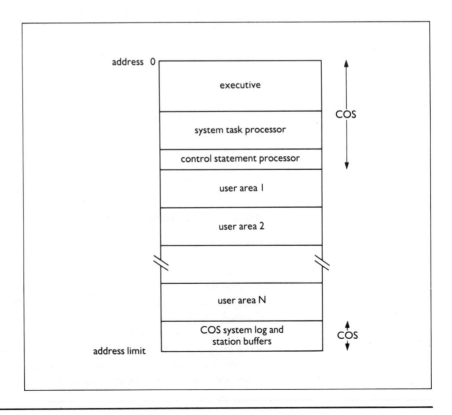

Figure 20.5
COS main store allocation

20.4.5 Backing Store Management

COS supervises the organisation of all data on backing store, and regulates the transfer of such data to and from main store. Backing store is accessed via a number of channels, and COS takes full advantage of this facility.

20.4.6 Resource Allocation and Scheduling

The majority of programs submitted to a Cray 1 computer require a compilation or an assembly, followed by the execution of the object program. COS supervises these steps, calling up a compiler or an assembler, and other utility programs as required.

Scheduling is deliberately kept very simple. Programs continue for a fixed period of time, or until a resource they require is not available. Then an **exchange mechanism** comes into action to switch execution from one program to another. Register values of the outgoing program are stored in a specially designated main store area.

20.4.7 Protection

The COS protection mechanism is very simple. Each program is allocated a single area in main store. Any attempt to address a location outside this area is not permitted.

Two registers, called **base address** (BA) and **limit address** (LA), define the area of main store which can be accessed by the program currently being executed. Some of the privileged portions of the operating system are not limited by these registers.

20.4.8 Accounting

Accounting records of each program are kept by the operating system.

20.4.9 User and Operator Interface

Instructions by users to the operating system are in the form of **job control information** supplied with each program. For each program run, COS creates a **log file** detailing the progress of the program. The log file includes each job control statement, together with messages indicating the success or otherwise of each step.

COS maintains communication with the operators of the computer, and collects information about the utilisation of the system, particularly the backing store facilities.

20.4.10 An Assessment of COS

COS is an excellent example of how an extremely complex hardware system can be effectively managed by a simple, straightforward operating system. COS is designed to 'keep out of the way' as much as possible, and permit the maximum use of the resources of the computer by the users.

20.5 Conclusion

Although few in number, the operating systems outlined in this chapter are representative of the range of systems currently in use. Each is designed for a particular type of computer, and a particular area of application. The systems vary considerably in size and complexity, from the sophistication of VME/B to the straightforward simplicity of both CP/M and COS. Nevertheless, they all have a number of features in common.

These operating systems represent some of the more successful attempts to write programs to the extremely demanding requirements outlined in the previous chapter. Each in its own way transforms the raw hardware of its host computer into a machine which can be put to useful work.

Exercise 20

1 Which of the case study operating systems support:
   a) Multiprogramming
   b) Multi-access?
2 Which of the case study operating systems implement the concept of virtual memory?
3 Compare and contrast the protection mechanisms provided by Unix, VME/B and COS.
4 Summarise the features provided by each operating system for the controlling of programs by users.
☐ 5 Multics, VM/370, RTL2, T.H.E. and George 3 are the names of a few more well-known operating systems. Investigate one of these systems (or another of your choice), and summarise its features, using the same headings as contained in this chapter.

21
Other systems software

The major items of software available on most computer systems, namely an operating system, an assembler and a number of compilers or interpreters, have been discussed in previous chapters. However, there are a number of other tasks performed by systems software in the majority of cases. These tasks, and the programs which perform them, are the topic of this chapter.

This chapter is the concluding chapter in the section of the book devoted to software. It relates fairly closely to other chapters in the section, and rounds off the picture of the layers of software which transform the raw hardware of a computer into a useful machine.

In this chapter, the emphasis is on the tasks performed by various items of software. Details of the way the various programs are written are deliberately avoided, as these vary considerably from one system to another. In some cases, tasks described here are performed by compilers, assemblers or operating systems. In other cases, they are performed by separate programs.

21.1   The Objectives of Systems Software

This is a useful point at which to summarise the overall objectives of systems software. These objectives apply as much to software which has already been introduced as to software which is introduced in this chapter. The two overall objectives, from the point of view of a user or applications programmer are:

assistance with program development
and
assistance with the running of programs.

Broadly speaking, assemblers and compilers work towards the first objective, while operating systems are dedicated to the second objective. The various tasks performed by other items of systems software are also directed towards one or other (or sometimes both) of these objectives.

The tasks carried out by other items of systems software are as follows: **linkage, loading, run-time diagnostics, editing** and various **utility** functions. It must be emphasised that this is not an exhaustive list, but it is adequate for the purposes of this course. Each of these tasks is now discussed under a separate heading.

21.2   Linkage

In many cases, the output from a compiler or assembler is a set of separate modules of machine code, often corresponding to subprograms in the source code. These modules relate to each other, generally via call and return instructions, and may also relate to other program modules from a previous compilation or assembly.

The task of a **linkage program**, sometimes rather misleadingly called a **linkage editor**, is to plant the appropriate addresses in all the call and return instructions, so that all the modules are linked together properly.

A linkage editor enables a single object program to be built up from sections which may be in various high level languages, or in a combination of high and low level languages. It also enables a program to be linked to various utility programs which are permanently stored in the system. These utility programs are discussed later in this chapter.

21.3   Loading

When a program has been compiled or assembled, and all the object code modules linked together, the resulting object code is seldom in the position in the main store

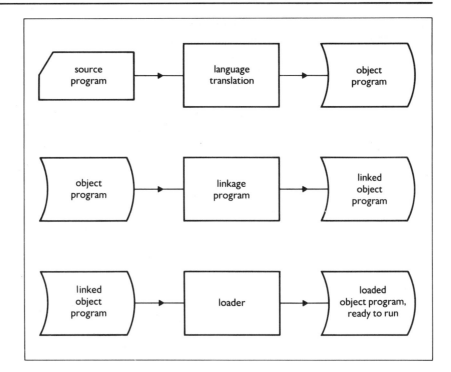

Figure 21.1
Language translation, linkage and
loading

of the computer in which it is to be run. In many cases, all the addresses in the program are relative to the start of the program. They do not yet contain the machine addresses of the store locations to which they refer.

A loading program thus performs two functions. It copies the object code of a program into the store locations in which it will reside during execution, and changes the addresses in program instructions to match the addresses into which the program has been loaded. This process is known as **relocation**. Execution of the program can then commence.

Many compilers and assemblers are called **load-and-go** systems because they include linkage and loading modules. As soon as language translation is complete, the machine language version of the program is linked, loaded and run. The language translation system remains in control throughout.

Figure 21.1 shows the process of language translation, linkage and loading. For an interpretation of the symbols used, see Figure 22.1.

21.4 Bootstrap Loaders

A very important program loader on every computer is the one which loads the first program into the computer after it has been started up. These programs have been given the name **bootstrap loaders**, from the phrase 'to pull oneself up by one's bootstraps'. The origin of this name is explained below.

In the early days of computing, a bootstrap loader worked in the following manner. Hand keys on the operator's console of the computer were used to load a very short, simple program into a few memory locations. This program was sufficient to activate a peripheral device, often a paper tape reader, and to load a longer, more sophisticated loading program. This loading program would then be run, to load other items of software, generally starting with the operating system.

Bootstrap leaders frequently used the technique of **self-modification**. This technique is demonstrated in the exercise at the end of the chapter.

The advent of semiconductor memories, containing portions of read-only store, has largely put an end to the early morning routine of hand keyed instructions and paper tape. In most modern systems, including microprocessor-based systems, a fairly sophisticated program loader is permanently stored in ROM. When the processor is switched on, control passes automatically to this loader. By the time that the visual display screen in the operator's console has warmed up, all systems software has been loaded, and the computer is ready to start work. Some computers include a **reset button** which may be pushed as a last resort when things have gone wrong. The initial loading program is again activated, and the system is able to start afresh.

21.5 Run-time Diagnostics

During the process of developing and testing a program, it is extremely useful to know precisely what is happening at various stages of the program. In a few computer systems, **run-time diagnostics packages** enable this to be achieved. The way these packages work is generally as follows.

The programmer creates a **breakpoint** at every stage where he or she wants to investigate the state of the program. This is done by inserting either a halt instruction, or some special instruction or directive at each breakpoint. The program is then compiled or assembled, and run. When a breakpoint is reached, control passes to the run-time diagnostics package. The program is suspended, but the contents of all registers is preserved. The diagnostics package enables registers and store locations to be displayed and altered if necessary. Execution of the program can then be continued from the instruction following the breakpoint. A run-time diagnostics facility can save one of the most expensive elements of a computing system, namely programmer's time.

21.6 Editing

One of the most useful facilities for program development is an **editor**. An editor permits the insertion, amendment or deletion of individual characters, groups of characters or entire lines of a program. Editing is generally done to the source code (i.e. the high level or assembly language) version of a program. When all the amendments have been made, the program is once again compiled or assembled, and then run.

Some assembler programs include a built-in editor. As soon as a line of program has been edited, it is translated into machine code, and any necessary amendments are made to the machine code versions of other program lines. In this way the program remains in an assembled state during editing. It is ready to run throughout the process.

Most computer systems have one editor which can be used on programs in any language supported by the computer. In some cases, the editor may be used more generally, on any program or data file in the system.

21.7 Utility Programs

Items of systems software which perform a variety of tasks on any particular computer generally go under the name **utility programs**, or occasionally **library programs**. These programs carry out such tasks as file creation, copying files, routing messages between users and analysis of the performance of the computer system. Scientific installations often have an extensive library of mathematical programs, particularly for the analysis of statistics.

These programs considerably reduce the length of applications programs, and relieve programmers of the task of writing large portions of identical code for different programs.

21.8 Conclusion

This chapter has introduced a few of the programs which are available on most computer systems to assist with the development and running of programs.

This chapter concludes the part of the book on computer software, comprising Chapters 14 to 21. It is a useful point at which to present a very brief summary of the main points made during these chapters. The summary is based on the view of a computer as a core of hardware, surrounded by layers of software.

The very centre of a computer is its **hardware**. From a programmer's point of view, the hardware may be regarded as a set of registers and functional units and an addressable main store. On its own, the hardware can only be programmed in its particular machine language, a task almost impossible for anyone except the designers and builders of the computer.

The layer of software which interfaces the hardware is the **operating system**. The operating system transforms the raw hardware of the computer into a **virtual machine**, by taking care of the awkward details of memory and backing store management, and input and output.

Interfacing the virtual machine is an outer layer of systems software. This layer includes **compilers, interpreters, assemblers** and various **utility programs**. These items of software enable the computer to be programmed in a variety of languages, and give a fair amount of assistance in the development of these programs.

Outside the layers of systems software is a layer of **applications programs**. These programs set the computer to do useful work. They are supported by the various layers of systems software, and, of course, by the hardware. The work done by these programs forms the topic of the remaining part of this book.

The 'surface' of the layer of applications programs is known as the **user interface** of the computer system. It is the computer, as it appears to a person using it – an integrated hardware and software system.

Exercise 21

1 Briefly define the following terms: linkage program; loader; load-and-go compiler; bootstrap loader; run-time diagnostics; breakpoint; editor; utility program; user interface.
2 Summarise the tasks performed by a load-and-go compiler.
3 An applications program, written in a high level language, requires the use of two utility programs for its execution. The utility programs are regarded as subprograms by the applications program. Machine code versions of the utility programs are kept on backing store.

  Describe in outline all the events which occur before running of the applications program can commence.
4 The program shown below is a simple bootstrap loader, written in AMC assembly language. It demonstrates the technique of self-modification.

```
        LOA  X  N  +2      Initialise index register to 2.
STR  IRQ  P                Request paper tape reader to input a character.
HRE  BIN        HRE        Branch to this instruction until input is complete.
        INP  A             Copy character from input register to accumulator.
        CPB  A  N  /*/     Compare character in accumulator with *.
```

```
         BEQ        GO      Branch to instruction labelled GO if equal.
    INS  STB  A     GO      Store accumulator contents at address labelled GO.
         LOA  A  D  INS     Load address part of instruction INS to accumulator (the index
                            register adds 2 to the value of INS to locate the address part).
         INC  A             Increase accumulator by 1.
         STO  A  D  INS     Store updated address in instruction INS.
         BRN        STR     Branch to instruction labelled STR.
    GO
```

Self-modification means that the program modifies one of its own instructions, namely the address part of the instruction labelled **INS**.

    This program inputs a string of characters from a paper tape.

    a) At which address is the first character from the tape loaded?

    b) At which address is the second character from the tape loaded?

    c) What character is used to mark the end of the tape?

    d) What happens when the end-of-input marker is reached?

    e) Briefly describe the overall effect of the program.

☐ f) The technique of self-modification is now regarded as obsolete. Rewrite the program so that the index register is used to achieve the same effect as the modified instruction.

5 Normally an assembler translates a reference to a label into a reference to a numeric address relative to the start of the segment being assembled. Why is this address *relative* to the start of the segment instead of being a physical address in immediate access memory? Your answer should include a brief explanation of relocation.

JMB 80 I

22
Principles of data processing

This is the first of several chapters concerned with the way in which computers are put to work, particularly in a commercial or industrial environment. This chapter describes the role of a computer in a practical data processing situation. Different kinds of data processing systems are described. The bulk of the chapter is concerned with the way in which a piece of work is prepared for a computer to carry out.

This chapter describes data processing in general terms. The next six chapters cover specific aspects of data processing in more detail. All these chapters depend on concepts introduced in this chapter.

22.1 The Nature and Objectives of Commercial and Industrial Data Processing

Data processing is a general term describing the work done by a computer. In practice its meaning is slightly more restricted. In a commercial or industrial context, data processing implies the use of a computer, or several computers, for part of the work of the company.

As is customary in computing, a **system** is set up to handle each data processing application. The system includes hardware, software, collections of data and the work of a number of people.

There are several reasons for introducing a computer into a company. The commonest are to reduce costs, to take advantage of the facilities offered by computers, and to increase the volume of business. In addition, computers can supply better management information, and enable long-term forecasts and plans to be made. Also, computers enable some operations to be carried out which would be impossible without them. These reasons for introducing computers are also the general objectives of a data processing system.

The background to commercial data processing requires a few words of description. A commercial environment is characterised by large quantities of data, usually requiring identical processing. The costs of various operations are important, and it is vital that deadlines are met. Computerised systems must run smoothly, with adequate backup if anything should go wrong.

22.2 Types of Data Processing Systems

Although no two data processing applications are quite the same, it is possible to identify a number of distinct types of data processing systems. The essential characteristics of the most important types are outlined below. The rest of this chapter concerns the way in which work is prepared to be done by a computer, and is equally applicable to all the types of data processing.

Unfortunately, there is no generally agreed classification of data processing systems, and types of data processing systems are often confused with types of operating systems. See Chapter 18 for a classification of operating systems. The types of data processing systems outlined here are a reflection of current practices in the computing industry.

Broadly speaking, data processing systems are of three types: systems where processing is done periodically; real-time systems, and database systems. Each type is described below.

22.3 Systems Where Processing is Done Periodically

These systems are characterised by large volumes of data of identical type. From time to time, batches of such data are processed in one operation. Because the data is stored in files, these systems may be called **file processing systems**. More details are given about files later in this chapter, and the whole of the next chapter is devoted to them.

The commonest example of file processing systems is payroll systems. Once a week or once a month, a payroll system is put into action to produce the payslips for all the employees of a company. The volume of data processed is large, and each employee receives identical treatment by the system.

File processing systems are now regarded as 'traditional' data processing systems. They closely resemble manual methods of data processing.

22.4 Real-time Systems

Real-time systems have no manual counterpart. They have only become available since the introduction of computers. Real-time processing is data processing 'while you wait'. In other words, the computer must keep pace with some external process. Small quantities of data are processed in one operation. The delay in processing the data, which varies from a fraction of a second to a couple of minutes, is acceptable to the user of the system.

Three types of real-time systems may be identified, though the distinction between them is fairly fine. The types are **process control**, **information storage/ retrieval** and **transaction processing**.

Process Control

Process control is an industrial application of computers. It is the continuous monitoring and controlling of an operational process by a computer. Measurements taken from the process are sent to the computer at frequent intervals, often many times a second. Control instructions are issued by the computer in response to this data. The time taken to process the data is generally very short.

One example of process control is the automatic control of several aspects of oil refining. The temperature, pressure and composition of substances in various reactor vessels are monitored, and control instructions are issued accordingly.

Information Storage/retrieval

This type of data processing is concerned with accessing and updating data stored in files. Fairly small quantities of data are handled in one operation, and calculations or other operations on the data are minimal.

An example of an information storage/retrieval system is a medical records system. The medical record of a patient can be accessed or updated by doctors, nurses or administrators from a terminal.

Transaction Processing

A transaction processing system is one which handles specifically defined transactions one at a time. Each transaction is processed to its conclusion before work on the next transaction commences. The amount of data supplied for a transaction is small, fitting into predefined categories. Processing may include a certain amount of calculation, as well as updating files.

The commonest example of transaction processing is airline seat reservations. All the information required to make a reservation is supplied to the system, which then checks whether one can be made. If so, various files are updated, and passenger totals are adjusted.

22.5   Database Systems

Database systems use one store of information (the database) to support all the data processing activities of a particular company. The database is independent of any individual application. Applications may be of any of the types of data processing described in the previous sections. Database systems are described in detail in Chapter 23.

22.6   Data Communications Systems

Several of the types of data processing systems mentioned in the previous sections involve the transmission of data from one place to another. This aspect of data processing is discussed in Chapter 25.

22.7   The Data Processing Cycle

The **data processing cycle** is the sequence of actions carried out during the development of a new data processing application. Depending on the application, the cycle can take anything from a few weeks to more than a year. The cycle has evolved from experience gained in the use of computers. It is fairly strictly adhered to in most cases.

The person, or team of people, most actively involved in all stages of the data processing cycle have the job title of **systems analyst**. A description of the data processing cycle is a description of the work of a systems analyst.

The next few sections of this chapter outlined the steps of a data processing cycle.

22.8   The Desire for Computerisation

In a variety of ways, and for various reasons, the need to computerise one aspect of the work of a company becomes apparent. Various reasons for the introduction of computerised working are outlined in Section 22.1.

The desire for computerisation is generally expressed by one of two groups of people within the company, namely the **management** or the **users**. Managers are concerned with profits, productivity and growth. The users are the people whose work will be done, partially or completely, by computer. They have detailed knowledge and experience of how the work is done at present.

The decision to investigate the possibility of changing to computerised working is generally taken at the appropriate level of management, in consultation with the users. But the way ahead is fraught with difficulties. How will the work be done by computer? What equipment will be needed? What changes will there be in staffing? What effects will the change to computers have on the company as a whole?

This is where a systems analyst comes in. The data processing cycle is a systematic process of answering these questions. The cycle may be terminated at several stages if it becomes obvious that it would be unwise to change to computers after all. Most of the detailed work forming the data processing cycle is undertaken by the systems analyst.

There are three overall phases in the data processing cycle. These are **system design**, **system development** and **system implementation**. Each phase consists of several steps. These are discussed in the sections which follow.

22.9   System Design

This phase is concerned with deciding whether it is feasible to do a piece of work by computer, and outlining a way in which the work can be done.

Feasibility Study

This is a preliminary survey, carried out by a systems analyst, to determine whether a full scale investigation should be carried out. The survey is generally conducted by consultation with management and users. A **feasibility report** is prepared, outlining the objectives and constraints of the proposed system, estimating some of the costs involved, and recommending whether or not to continue with the project.

System Investigation and Analysis

If the feasibility report is favourable, and approved by the managers, then a detailed **system investigation** is undertaken. This takes the form of interviews, surveys, questionnaires and sometimes the systems analyst working with the users for a while. The two objectives are to gain a thorough knowledge of the current way of working, and analyse, in a fair amount of detail, the steps involved in computerised working.

System Specification

The result of the system investigation is a detailed **system specification** of the proposed data processing system. This includes a summary of the overall working of the system, and more detailed sections on the files of stored data required, the input and output data and the various types of processing to be done.

The system specification generally includes a **systems flowchart**, which is a diagram showing the overall flow of data through the system, and the various operations carried out. The system specification is submitted to the managers for approval. It may be accepted, modified or rejected. When agreement has been reached, it marks the end of the system design phase of the data processing cycle.

22.10 Systems Flowcharts

This section leaves the data processing cycle for a moment, to provide a little more detail about **systems flowcharts**, and to introduce some common data processing operations.

Figure 22.1 shows some systems flowchart symbols in common use. Notice that there is one set of symbols for stored data, and another set for various types of processing.

Many data processing operations are concerned with **files**. A file is a large collection of data, with a definite logical structure, held on a physical medium such as magnetic tape or magnetic discs. Systems flowchart segments are discussed below for a few common operations on files. Files and file processing are discussed in detail in Chapter 23.

File Creation

Data is transferred from an external medium, such as punched cards, to a file on a magnetic tape or disc. In most modern systems, data is typed directly from data entry terminals to the file. See Figure 22.2.

File Validation

The data in a file is subjected to various tests. Incorrect data is printed on an **error report**, correct data is stored on another file. See Figure 22.3. This process is called **validation**.

Updating a File

A file of amendments is used to bring the data on another file up-to-date. A new file is produced of the **updated** information. See Figure 22.4.

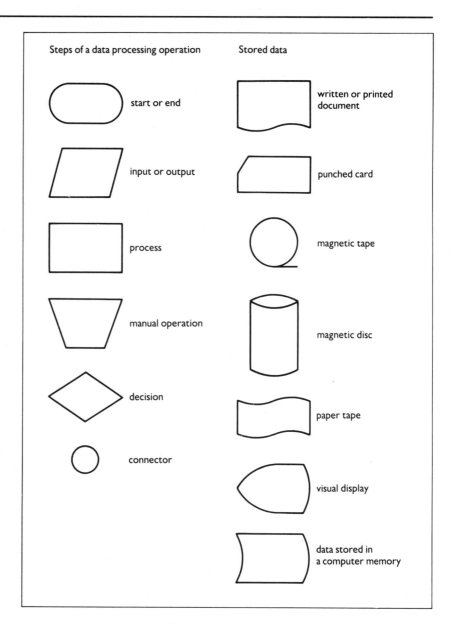

Steps of a data processing operation

- start or end
- input or output
- process
- manual operation
- decision
- connector

Stored data

- written or printed document
- punched card
- magnetic tape
- magnetic disc
- paper tape
- visual display
- data stored in a computer memory

Figure 22.1
Systems flowchart symbols

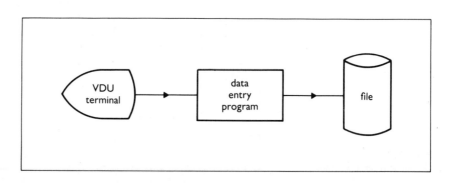

Figure 22.2
File creation

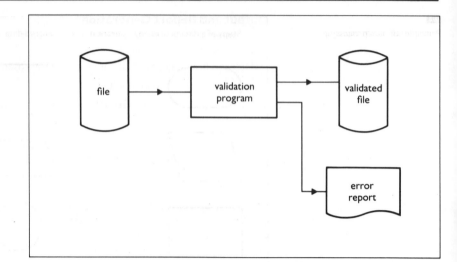

Figure 22.3
File validation

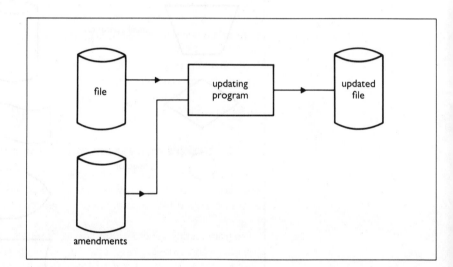

Figure 22.4
File updating

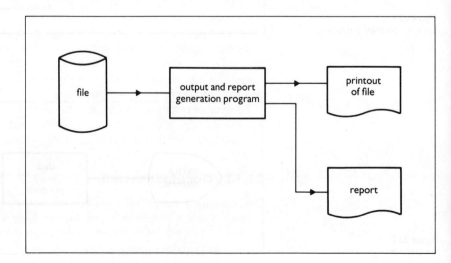

Figure 22.5
Output and report generation

Output and Report Generation

The contents of a file is output, and a **report** is **generated**, summarising the information contained in the file. See Figure 22.5.

After this brief digression, the next section returns to the data processing cycle.

22.11 System Development

Once the specification of a new data processing system has been accepted, the detailed work on the development of the system can begin. **System development** is concerned with specifying, writing, testing and documenting the programs for the new system.

Program Specification

Using the relevant portion of the systems flowchart, together with various file specifications, the objectives of each program required are set out in detail. Several programs are generally required, and these are further broken down into **modules**, each module performing a specific task.

It is usual to specify what must be done by each module of each program, without stating how it is to be done. The method used in each module is at the discretion of the programmer writing the module.

Program Writing

A team of **programmers** sets to work, writing each module of each program. Modules are generally written separately, often by different programmers, and combined at a later stage.

22.12 Program, System and Acceptance Testing

Experience has shown that it is very unlikely for a newly written program, no matter how carefully specified, to work correctly first time. All the modules of the new programs are tested separately, and then combined, or **built**, into complete programs.

Program testing generally uses specially prepared **test data**. This contains all the data errors and awkward cases that are likely to arise, and is designed to try to make the new programs fail. Testing continues in this way until all the errors in the programs have been identified and corrected, and the programmers and systems analysts are satisfied.

System testing is to try out the running of the data processing system as a whole. The programs are run in their intended sequence, and the various manual parts of the operation are carried out. The passing of data from one stage to the next is checked, as are security and backup features. When these tests are satisfactory, the system is ready to be tried out by the users.

Acceptance testing is carried out by the users. They see if the system performs to their satisfaction, and again try to 'break' the system with awkward cases and incorrect data. Modifications are made to the system until the users are satisfied.

22.13 Documentation

Documentation is a written description of how a program works, how it is to be used, or how it is to be run on a computer. Several types of documentations are prepared during the development of a data processing system.

Program documentation is a careful account of how each module of a program works. It is for the use of anyone who wishes to understand the detailed working of a program, in order to test it or modify it.

User documentation is an account of how a program is to be used. It is written in non-technical language, and does not contain any details of how the program works.

Operator documentation is a description of how a program is to be run on a computer. It states which devices are needed and which data files must be loaded, and any special stationery required. It also specifies what is to be done should the program fail. Operator documentation is referred to by computer operators.

At the acceptance testing stage, all the documentation associated with the system is checked by the users.

22.14 System Implementation

The final phase of the data processing cycle concerns putting the new system to work. Pilot running, with the new system doing part of the work, is often used. It is also common, though not always possible, to run the new and the old systems in parallel for a while.

Finally, often a year after the new system was proposed, it is in full productive operation. As can be imagined, the cost of the whole design, development and implementation process is considerable.

Not all firms use their own employees to design and develop data processing systems. Some firms, particularly small companies, commission software houses or computer bureaux to do the work. Other firms select and purchase applications packages, which are ready-to-run applications programs. Nevertheless, in all cases a modified form of the data processing cycle is carried out.

22.15 System Maintenance

Once a system is in operation, it is unlikely that it remains entirely satisfactory for long. On the one hand, experience in using the system brings to light shortcomings and suggests improvements. On the other hand, the requirements of the system change as time goes by. For these reasons, the system requires periodic **maintenance**. Maintenance requires re-specification of portions of the system, and amendments to programs and documentation accordingly. A certain amount of testing is also involved.

22.16 What Can Go Wrong?

The above description of the data processing cycle makes it sound like a textbook operation, with no problems likely to arise. In practice this is not always the case. A few of the commonest sources of problems are outlined below.

Changing Specifications

For a variety of reasons, it is often necessary to change the specification of a system while it is under development. Changes can arise from altered business circumstances, new hardware becoming available, or because someone has thought of an 'improvement' to the system. The amount of disruption caused by a change depends on the nature of the change. In some cases, considerable amounts of detailed work have to be done again.

Increasing Costs

At today's levels of inflation, it is certain that almost all costs will increase. Estimates of these increased costs are generally made at the start of a project, but they can never be totally accurate. Unforeseen costs almost always arise. Occasionally, increased costs lead to the abandonment of a new system. However, in most cases, cost increases tend to tip the balance in favour of computers, where hardware prices are still coming down.

Delays

The feasibility report generally contains estimates of the duration of the various stages of a data processing cycle. A series of deadlines is usually set up. Depending on the circumstances surrounding the project, these are or are not met. In general, the data processing industry has quite a good record for meeting deadlines. Delays can be a nuisance or a disaster, depending on how vital it is to have the new system in operation. Delays always have the effect of increasing the development cost of the system.

Resistance to Change

Changing to computerised working implies new work practices, new equipment to operate, and, in some cases, transfers to different jobs or redundancies. Most people, familiar with one way of doing a job, are reluctant to change their working habits. Very few people are happy about being made redundant.

Trade unions are likely to raise objections if the welfare of their members is being threatened. Inter-union disputes over new work practices are particularly difficult.

All these factors must be taken into account when a new data processing system is being planned. Unfortunately, lack of consideration of the welfare of employees, lack of consultation and inflexible attitudes have sometimes led to serious problems in this area.

22.17   Conclusion

This chapter is intended to give a 'feel' for the way in which computers are put to work in commerce and industry. It is worth stressing that data processing in this area is strongly influenced by business practices, and that a relatively small proportion of the data processing cycle is spent actually writing programs.

The main points raised during the chapter are as follows:

- Data processing systems are generally set up in order to reduce costs, increase the volume of business of the company and to take advantage of the facilities offered by computers.
- Data processing systems may be classified as file processing systems and real-time systems. Real-time systems include process control systems, information storage and retrieval systems and transaction processing systems. Some of these systems use databases, some involve data communication.
- The data processing cycle is the sequence of activities required to bring a new data processing system into operation.
- The overall steps of a data processing cycle are system design, system development and system implementation. Each of these steps can be broken down into more detailed steps.
- A systems flowchart is used to illustrate the overall steps of a data processing system.
- In spite of careful planning, a number of things can go wrong during a data processing cycle. Common problems include changing specifications, increasing costs, delays and resistance to change.

Exercise 22

1 Summarise the objectives of a data processing system.

2 What are the characteristics of the environment of a commercial data processing system?

3 Classify the following data processing systems according to the types of data processing described in the chapter:

a) An accounting system, where accounts are brought up-to-date once a month.

b) An order processing system, where each order is processed as soon as it is received.

c) A bank accounting system, where accounts are brought up-to-date every night.

d) The on-board navigation system on a rocket.

e) The book index at a library.

4 Summarise, in about 100 words, the most significant features of the data processing cycle.

5 At what stages may a data processing cycle be terminated before the new system is put into operation?

6 A small company, which already has a computer, intends to computerise another part of its operations. It intends to buy an applications package to run the new work on its computer. Outline the parts of the data processing cycle which the firm might follow.

7 Why is it not adequate to use sets of real data during program testing?

8 State some effects of delays in meeting deadlines during a project.

9 At which point in the data processing cycle is it most likely that resistance to change on the part of employees will become apparent?

Outline some approaches which could be used by managers in dealing with this problem.

10 A chain of retail shops wishes to implement a point-of-sale transaction recording system. The overall specification of the system is as follows:

1 Cash registers are to be replaced by data entry terminals, linked to a microcomputer within each shop.

2 When a sale is registered, the stock number for each item sold is entered. The price of the item is displayed. The total for the sale is displayed and the amount paid by cash, cheque or gift voucher is entered. The amount of change is displayed.

3 At the end of each day, the microcomputer produces a printout showing the total cash, cheques and gift vouchers collected at each till. A file is produced on a floppy disk, showing the number sold of each stock item. This file can be inspected on the display screen.

4 The file of stock movements is then transmitted via a telephone link to a central mainframe computer.

a) Draw one or more systems flow diagrams showing the overall steps of this system.

b) Identify the applications programs required for this system.

c) Write out a specification for each application program.

d) Identify any potential problems in the implementation of this system.

11 A stock control system is to be devised for a wholesale supplier of electrical goods. Suggest a suitable computer configuration and give reasons for your choice of equipment. Indicate how data capture will be organised and what files will be necessary. Draw outline system flow charts.

UL 78 II

12 A large hotel has installed a minicomputer to control the reservation of rooms. The management decide to implement an online system which enables the reception clerks to use terminals to access the system to make bookings, or cancellations, or enquiries. The management require reports on advance bookings, the present state of room occupation and a monthly report on the statistics of bookings.

Draw an outline system flow chart for the system.

Specify an appropriate hardware configuration and explain why each item was chosen.

How might the hotel protect itself against the breakdown of the computer or its inoperability due to a power cut?

UL 79 II

23
Files

This chapter introduces a number of ideas concerned with files, the way files are stored, different file structures and common techniques of file processing. It extends some of the ideas from the previous chapter, and provides essential material for a further study of computer applications, contained in the next four chapters.

23.1   Files, Records, Fields and Keys

This section clarifies some of the terms used in connection with files and file processing.

Computers inherited files and file processing from manual data processing systems. It is important to remember that many of the ideas and terms used in this area are common to both types of system.

Whether it is stored in a filing cabinet, on a magnetic disc or on any other form of storage, a **file** is an organised collection of data. Files are generally large, contain related items of information, and are strictly arranged according to some structure. Common file structures are discussed later in the chapter.

The unit of data which makes up a file is a **record**. A record contains a number of data items, and each record in a file generally has the same structure. The structure of a file is determined by the way in which the records are arranged within the file.

Individual data items occupy **fields** within a record. A field may be of fixed or variable width. The term **field width** refers to the number of characters in a field.

The commonest way of identifying a record is by means of a chosen field within the record. This field is referred to as the **key** of the record. The only restriction on keys is that all the records in a file have distinct keys. For this and other reasons, more than one field is sometimes used as the key of a record. The fields are then called the **primary key, secondary key**, etc.

For example, consider the information in a telephone directory as a file. A record is the entry for one person. A record comprises three fields, namely surname and initials, address and telephone number. The primary key is the surname and initials field, and the secondary key is the address. The two keys together are sufficient, for practical purposes, to identify each person uniquely, whereas a surname and initials on its own is not always enough.

It is important to realise that files, records and fields are logical entities. Different terms are used for groupings of data on physical media, such as punched cards, magnetic tapes and magnetic discs. These are discussed in the next section.

23.2   File Storage

The next few sections concern the way in which files are stored on physical media, in particular punched cards, magnetic tape and magnetic discs. Some of the terms used in connection with these media are introduced, together with some of the limitations imposed by the media.

23.3   Punched Cards

Every now and then, the imminent death of punched cards is confidently predicted by some prominent person within the computer industry. Although the relative importance of punched cards has declined in recent years, they are still an important method of data storage. Ideas associated with punched cards often outlive the cards themselves – the notion of a **card image** is quite common in data processing systems which use visual display terminals.

When a deck of cards is used to store a file, it is quite common, though not always

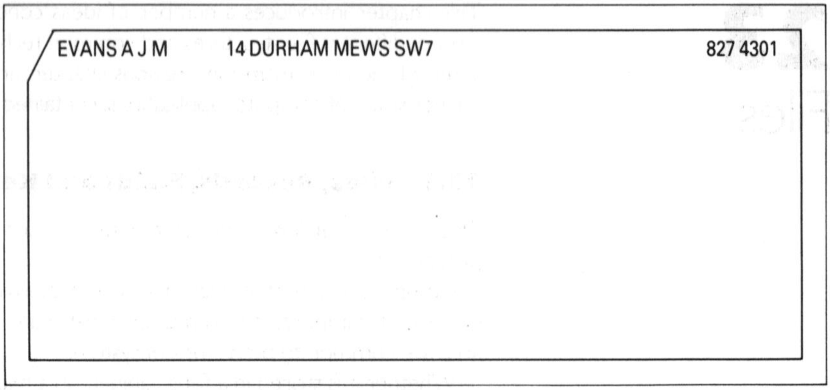

| EVANS A J M | 14 DURHAM MEWS SW7 | 827 4301 |

Figure 23.1
Data on a punched card

the case, to have one record stored on each card. This restricts a record to the number of characters which can be stored on one card, in most cases 80.

Under this arrangement, fields are generally of fixed width, and occupy fixed positions within a card. Figure 23.1 shows a punched card being used to store a record of a telephone directory file. The first 22 characters are for the surname and initials field, the next 50 characters are for the address field, and the last 8 characters are for the telephone number field.

It can be seen that punched cards offer a restricted and somewhat old fashioned method of storing files. However, they are very useful for computers which can only process one record of a file at a time.

23.4 Magnetic Tape

Magnetic tape is currently the cheapest method of storing large quantities of data for access by computer. It is second only to magnetic discs in popularity.

The unit of transfer of data to and from a magnetic tape is a **block**. Between successive blocks on a tape is a blank area known as an **inter-block gap**. The reason for this arrangement is that data can only be read from or written to a tape when it is running at full speed. As an entire tape can store far more data than the capacity of most computer memories, the tape is divided into blocks. The inter-block gaps are for the tape to be started up, slowed down or reversed. Most magnetic tape units can read or write data with the tape running in either direction.

In most cases, the size of a block is somewhere between the size of a record and that of a file (a file may extend over several tapes). The phrase **blocking factor** refers to the number of records per block, for a particular file.

Compared with punched cards, magnetic tape places far fewer restrictions on the size of records and fields, and makes variable width fields a practical proposition. The major constraint introduced by magnetic tape on data access is that it is a **serial access** medium. That is to say, the time taken to access a block of data depends on its position on the tape. The quickest way to access all the data on the tape is in the order in which it occurs on the tape. This has a number of implications as far as the structure of files which can be stored on magnetic tape is concerned.

23.5 Magnetic Discs

Magnetic discs are the commonest way of storing data for access by computer. Although discs are more expensive than tapes, for the same amount of data, their price is decreasing, while storage capacities are increasing.

Magnetic discs can generally store data on both surfaces. A number of discs are

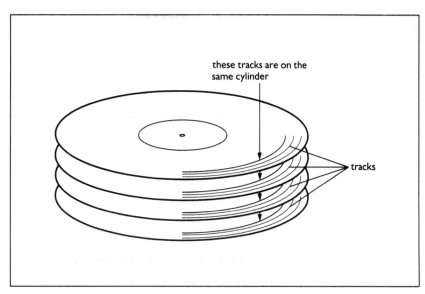

these tracks are on the same cylinder

tracks

Figure 23.2
Data layout in a magnetic disc pack

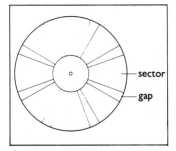

sector

gap

Figure 23.3
Sectors in a magnetic disc

often combined to form a **disc pack**, as shown in Figure 23.2. On each surface, data is arranged in concentric rings, or **tracks**. Corresponding tracks, directly above and below each other in a disc pack, form a **cylinder**. All the data in a cylinder can be reached without moving the read – write head of a magnetic disc drive.

For the same reasons as apply to magnetic tapes, data on a magnetic disc are divided into units called blocks or **sectors**. The gaps between the sectors allow for movement of the read – write head. See Figure 23.3.

To locate a block of data on a disc, it is necessary to know which surface it is on, which cylinder it is in, and the position of the block around the circumference of the disc. This information, generally expressed as a sequence of numbers, forms the **address** of the block. This disc address is very similar to the idea of an address in the main store of a computer.

Magnetic discs are called **random access** devices. That is to say, blocks of data can be accessed equally quickly, regardless of their positions on the disc. This is not completely true, as data items in the same cylinder can be accessed more quickly than data items in different cylinders. Many disc access systems have ways of minimising the movements of the read – write heads, which speeds up the transfer of data. However, it is true to say that any block of data on a disc can be accessed in an acceptably short time for most purposes.

The random access nature of discs, and the fact that blocks of data can be located by addresses, means that files of a far more complex structure can be stored on magnetic discs than on magnetic tape or punched cards.

23.6 File Structures

In the early days of computing, the structure of a file was largely determined by the storage medium available. Today the situation has been reversed. The nature of the computer application determines the structure of the files, which in turn determines the type of storage medium used.

The commonest types of file structure are **serial** files, **sequential** files, **indexed sequential** files and **random** files. The following four sections discuss these types of files.

23.7 Serial Files

A serial file is one in which the records are in no particular order. Serial files are mainly used for temporary storage of data, until a more highly structured file is created. Magnetic tapes and magnetic discs are equally suitable for storing serial files, and punched cards may be used.

23.8 Sequential Files

A sequential file is one in which records are in order of one or more keys. The order may be numeric or alphabetic. For example, a file of examination results may be sorted in order of class of pass (primary key) and, within each class, alphabetic order of surnames (secondary key).

Sequential files may be stored on magnetic tapes or magnetic discs, and are the backbone of the 'traditional' file processing systems mentioned in the previous chapter.

23.9 Indexed Sequential Files

Indexed sequential files are the commonest types of files in current use. As their name suggests, indexed sequential files are ordered files which also have an index. The **index** is a set of data which enables the key of a record to be associated with its address. It is very similar to the index of a book, which relates words and phrases to page numbers. The index of a file is generally stored at the beginning or the end of the file. If more than one level of index is used, as is often the case, different parts of the index are stored throughout the file.

Since indexed sequential files require that data items be located by addresses, they must be stored on magnetic discs. A number of different indexing techniques are in use, but only one is discussed here. It is the simplest, and relates directly to the structure of a magnetic disc pack. It is called **cylinder – surface – sector** indexing.

For each disc pack of the file, there is a **cylinder index**, which relates each cylinder number to the highest key value stored in that cylinder. Once a cylinder has been selected, its **surface index** is used. This index relates each surface of the cylinder to the highest key value in that surface. Once a surface has been selected, its **sector index** is used. This relates each sector number to the highest key value within the sector. The required sector is then copied from the disc, and the required record located.

For example, consider a file which stores records of motor car parts. Each record concerns one part, with the part number being the key. Part numbers are in the range 00001 to 99999. The following table contains a portion of the cylinder index of the file, together with one surface and one sector index.

Cylinder index		Surface index for cylinder 106		Sector index for surface 4	
Cylinder	highest key	Surface	highest key	sector	highest key
1	00 396	1	41 177	1	41 179
2	00 785	2	41 124	2	41 186
...		3	41 171	3	41 194
105	41 027	4	41 223	4	41 200
106	41 421	5	41 269	5	41 207
107	41 803	6	41 318	6	41 214
...		7	41 368	7	41 219
256	99 999	8	41 421	8	41 223

Suppose it is required to access the record for part number 41 192. Inspection of the cylinder index shows that this record is in cylinder 106. The surface index for this cylinder is then accessed. Inspection of this index shows that the record is on surface 4. The sector index for this surface is then accessed. This index shows that the required record is in sector 3. This sector is then copied from the disc, and searched for the required record.

It can be seen that accessing this record required four accesses to the disc, once for each of the three indexes, and one for the data sector. After each disc access, the index or data sector is searched, in the memory of the computer.

One advantage of indexed sequential files is that it is easy to leave spaces in sectors, surfaces or cylinders for the insertion of new records. This allows a file to grow without having to be copied onto another disc, and re-indexed, too frequently.

23.10 Random Files

Random files are ones in which records are scattered at random on the storage medium. In order to access a record, there is a function which relates the key of the record to its address on the storage medium. This process is known as **address generation**. As in the case of indexed sequential files, this requires that magnetic discs be used to store the data.

It is occasionally possible to use the backing store address of a record as its key. In this case, accessing the record is extremely simple. More frequently, some calculation or manipulation must be carried out on the key of the record in order to produce its backing store address. One technique for this is called **hashing**, and the file structure is called a **hash table**. Problems arise when two different key values produce the same backing store address. Address generation techniques are investigated in more detail in the exercise at the end of the chapter.

Random files are most suited to applications where rapid access is required to individual records. If access to groups of records with consecutive keys is required, then indexed sequential files are much more useful. Random files are much less common than indexed sequential files.

23.11 File Processing

This section outlines the steps of some of the commonest file processing operations, namely **validation, sorting** (both in a computer memory and on backing store), **merging, searching** and **updating** files. To conclude the section, some techniques to ensure the security of data are introduced.

The techniques are described in general terms, and implementation-dependent features are avoided. This helps to keep the process as simple as possible. It must, however, be borne in mind that when these techniques are put into use, matters can become extremely complicated.

23.12 Validation

Validation is the process of checking input data, before storing or processing it. A number of checks can be carried out; the ones used in each case depend on the application. Validation is one of the most important and time-consuming steps in many data processing systems.

The simplest checks are **type** and **range** checks. Type checks determine whether the data is of the correct type (alphabetic or numeric). Range checks determine whether numeric data is within an acceptable range.

Various totals can be used to check input data. If batches of data are input, items in each batch can be added up, and the **batch total** input. The total is re-calculated by the program, and compared with the one input. If the totals are different, an error has occurred. The same principle applies to **hash totals**, which are totals of data items within the same record.

Numeric data items of particular importance, such as the keys of records, often have **check digits** attached to them. The value of the check digit can be determined from the other digits in the number. The check digit is tested from time to time, to see if an error has arisen during copying of the data item.

There are several ways of calculating check digits in common use. Some of them are introduced in the exercise at the end of the chapter.

23.13 Sorting (in Main Store)

Sorting is a very common data processing technique. Some programming languages, notably Cobol, have a single instruction to cause a file of data to be sorted. Much attention has been devoted to discovering efficient ways of sorting, as it can be an extremely slow process.

For a set of data to be sorted, all the data must be in the main store of a computer. If the set of data is too large for this, it must be sorted in portions, each of which can be accommodated in the available main store. This section is concerned with the part of the process which takes place in the main store of a computer, using data which has already been loaded into the main store. A later section examines the problem of sorting larger sets of data.

An informal algorithm for a common sorting technique is now introduced. The technique is called **quicksort**, as it is one of the fastest sorting methods.

Algorithm for Quicksort
If the set contains more than one record
then   select the first record,
        partition the remaining records into two subsets:
           a **left subset**, with keys less than that of the first record
           a **right subset**, with keys greater than that of the first record,
        place the first record between the two subsets,
        quicksort the left subset,
        quicksort the right subset.
else   the set is sorted.

Notice that the algorithm is recursive, in other words it calls itself repeatedly, for smaller and smaller subsets of the set of data.

The example below shows the steps of quicksort applied to the keys of eight records in a file. The square brackets show which elements have not yet been sorted.

Original order of keys:
   [11 9 23 7 31 5 2 17]

Select first key (11) and partition the set:
   [9 7 5 2] 11 [23 31 17]

Quicksort left subset:
   Select first key (9) and partition the set:
   [7 5 2] 9 11 [23 31 17]

Quicksort right subset:
   Select first key (23) and partition the set:
   [7 5 2] 9 11 [17] 23 [31]

Quicksort the first remaining subset:
     Select first key (7) and partition the set:
     [5   2]   7   9   11   [17]   23   [31]

Quicksort the first remaining subset:
     Select first key (5) and partition the set:
     [2]   5   7   9   11   [17]   23   [31]

All remaining subsets are of length one element, and are therefore already sorted:
     2   5   7   9   11   17   23   31

Although this process appears anything but quick, it is in fact better than most of its rivals for larger sets of data. It is not, however, the only method in use.

23.14   Merging

Merging is the process of combining two ordered files of data to produce a single ordered file. The method is very simple, and is outlined in the algorithm below.

Algorithm for Merging

Records from ordered files A and B are to be merged to form ordered file C.

Repeat
     if all records from A have been removed
         then copy remaining records in file B to file C
     else if all records from B have been removed
         then copy remaining records in file A to file C
     else compare next records in files A and B,
         copy the record with lower key to file C
Until all records from files A and B have been merged.

The important fact about this process is that it does not require that all the data be in the main store of the computer. One record from each input file is, in fact, sufficient. Thus files can be merged which are much larger than the capacity of the main store of the computer doing the merging.

Although merging is a process in its own right, its most common application is to form part of a sorting process for files which are much larger than the capacity of the main store of the computer which is sorting them.

23.15   Sorting Large Files

A number of techniques are used to sort files which are too large for the main store of the computer. They are all based on combinations of sorting and merging.

The file which is to be sorted is divided into **strings**, each of which can be accommodated in the main store of the computer. Each string is sorted, and the sorted string copied to backing store. These strings are merged, creating successively larger strings, until the whole file has been merged into a single string.

The following sequence of merges illustrates this technique, though it is not actually used in practice. Consider a file which has been divided into eight strings. The strings have been sorted, and copied onto two magnetic tapes, as follows:

Tape A: | String 1 | String 3 | String 5 | String 7 |

Tape B: | String 2 | String 4 | String 6 | String 8 |

The strings are merged in pairs, the resulting strings being placed alternately on two further tapes.

Tape C:

| String 9 (String 1 + String 2) | String 11 (String 5 + String 6) |

Tape D:

| String 10 (String 3 + String 4) | String 12 (String 7 + String 8) |

These strings are again merged in pairs, and the resulting strings copied onto alternate tapes.

Tape A:

| String 13 (String 9 + String 10) |

Tape B:

| String 14 (String 11 + String 12) |

These two strings are merged to form a single string, which is the entire file, in order. The merging techniques used in practice are more complicated. They reduce the number of merges needed for a given number of strings. Nevertheless sorting a large file on a small computer is an extremely tedious affair. It is frequently the slowest step of the entire data processing operation.

23.16 Searching

Searching is the process of locating a record in a file, given the key of the record. If the file has an index, then the index is used to locate the record. If the file is randomly organised, then the process used to load a record is also used to access it. Otherwise, the file must be searched. Two common file searching techniques are discussed here, namely the **sequential search** and the **binary search**.

Sequential Search
A sequential search involves examining every record in a file until the required one is found. It is only used if a small number of records are present, or if the file is not ordered. On average, half the records in the file have to be examined before the required record is located.

Binary Search
A binary search involves partitioning the file into smaller and smaller subsets, each of which is known to contain the required record, and each of which is half the size of the previous subset.

An informal algorithm for a binary search is as follows:

Algorithm for Binary Search
If the set contains at least one record
    then   select the middle record,
            partition the remaining records into two subsets:
                a **left subset**, with keys less than that of the middle record
                a **right subset**, with keys greater than that of the middle record,
                if the middle record is the required record
                    then **the required record has been found**

else if the key of the required record is **less than** that of the middle record
then **binary search** the left subset
else **binary search** the right subset
else **the required record is not in the set**.

Notice that this algorithm is very similar in structure to that for a quicksort. Once again, it is recursive.

The example below shows the steps of a binary search applied to the keys of eight records in a file. The required record has key value 7.

Initial situation:
2   5   7   9   11   17   23   31

Select middle record (key 9), partition set:
[2   5   7]   9   [11   17   23   31]

Required key is less than that of middle record, so binary search left subset:
2   5   7

Select middle record (key 5), partition set:
[2]   5   [7]

Required key is greater than that of middle record, so binary search right subset:
7

Select middle record (key 7), which is the required record.

It can be seen that the process of dividing the set into two subsets is carried out three times to locate the required record. In general, the maximum number of steps, for a file of N records, is $\log_2 N$. A binary search is considerably quicker than a sequential search.

A binary search does not require that all the records of a file be in the main store of the computer. The backing store addresses of records can be used to locate the middle element of each set. This element must be copied into main store for examination. However, the requirement of backing store addresses does rule out the use of magnetic tapes.

23.17   Updating

Updating a file involves amending, deleting and inserting records so as to bring the information in the file up to date. A file to be updated is generally a sequential file. The amendments data is sorted into the same order as the ordering of the sequential file.

The systems flow diagram, Figure 22.4, in the previous chapter shows the process of updating a file. The process forms a cycle, since the up-to-date file produced on one occasion forms the file to be updated on the next occasion.

23.18   Report Generation

Most active files in a data processing system contain large volumes of data. In order to provide an accurate, up-to-date picture of the state of the system, it is important to generate **reports** at regular intervals. These reports summarise the data on one or more files, and are intended for the information of managers at various levels of the organisation. A program language, called RPG, intended for the generation of reports, is discussed in Chapter 17.

As an example, consider a file containing records of all the sales by a particular company. A report might be generated from this file once a week, showing the total number of sales, the total value of the sales, and breakdowns of these figures by salesman, product group, area and method of payment. This report could be used by the sales manager. The total sales figures could be included in reports to managers at higher levels.

23.19 Data Security

The files used by most data processing systems are vital to the system. Any loss or corruption of data can lead to delays, loss of business or legal action being taken against the company. For these reasons it is essential that files be guarded against computer failures, program errors, human errors and malicious interference.

If files are stored on magnetic tapes, and updated regularly, it is common practice to keep the previous two versions of the file, together with the amendments used to update them. This is called the **grandfather–father–son** principle, each version being a **generation** of the file. If the current generation of the file is lost, it can be re-created from previous generations.

If magnetic discs are used to store a file, then these are periodically copied, or **dumped**, onto another magnetic disc or magnetic tape. All the data used to update the file since the last dump is kept. Dumping is often done as part of a **housekeeping** process, during which the file is 'tidied up', with out-of-date records being dated and gaps closed up.

It is essential to keep a **log** of all operations carried out on a file. The log shows the dates on which various updates and dumps took place, and included identification numbers of the various discs and tapes used. Additional security precautions include keeping magnetic discs and tapes in fireproof safes, and storing copies at different sites, away from the computer.

Protection against deliberate data corruption is much more difficult, as it ultimately involves the trustworthiness of staff members. Some of the security precautions in this area include restriction of access to computer and data preparation rooms, the use of passwords when logging on at terminals, and strict job segregation – programmers may not operate the computer, etc.

Good data security is achieved by constant vigilance, and strict adherence to specified procedures, in other words, 'working by the book'. Unfortunately, this tends to make some computing jobs rather tedious.

23.20 Conclusion

This chapter has outlined some of the essential ideas of files, file storage, file structure, file processing and data security. This material relates closely to the next chapter, on databases, and to a later chapter on data processing case studies.

Having studied the chapter, you will probably realise how much effort goes into designing files for various applications, and to keeping these files accurate and up-to-date. You will also realise that computerising a task does not automatically solve all the problems associated with the task.

Exercise 23

1 A word processing system includes a file of letters sent by the user of the system. There is a record for each letter, containing the name and address of the person to whom the letter was sent, the date and the text of the letter.
   a) Suggest one or more keys for a record. Justify your choice.
   b) Suggest a suitable structure for organising the file. Consider likely uses of the file in making your choice. Include these uses in reasons for your choice of structure.
   c) State, with reasons, the storage medium you would use for the file.

2 Distinguish between the terms **record** and **block**.

3 Explain why individual data items cannot be accessed from a magnetic tape.

4 A monthly payroll program requires the input of the following data for each employee: name, employee number, days worked, days on leave, days ill and days absent for any other reason.
   a) Suggest a suitable field layout for the input data, if it is to form one line on a VDU screen.
   b) Which data item is likely to include a check digit?
   c) What additional check(s) can be carried out on the data as it is input?

5 The batch total of a set of data is checked after the data has been input, and is found not to match the batch total which was input with the data. Later checks show that all data items are in fact correct.

   Explain where the error must be, and discuss the limitations on the usefulness of batch totals imposed by this situation.

6 A common method of calculating check digits is as follows: multiply each digit of the number, including the check digit, by a **weighting factor**, and add up the products. The check digit is chosen so that the total thus formed is exactly divisible by a suitable number, usually 11. For example:

number:	3	7	4	6	5	check digit
weighting factor:	9	5	3	7	1	
products:	27	+35	+12	+42	+5 = 121, exactly divisible by 11.	

Using the same set of weighting factors, calculate the check digits for the numbers 6297 and 5116. Use the symbol X if a check digit of 10 is required.

7 A form of index sometimes used on indexed sequential files is called a **hierarchical index**. Like cylinder–surface–sector indexing, this has several levels of indexing. However, each level of index does not correspond to a physical aspect of the layout of the file on the disc.

   The top level index relates each index number of the next level of indexes to the highest key value contained in that index. Each of the next level of indexes has a similar structure, relating to a third level of indexes. Each of these indexes relates a set of block addresses to the highest keys within the block.

   For example:

Top level index		Second level index 11		Third level index 531	
Second level index number	Highest key	Third level index number	Highest key	Block address	Highest key
1	12509	501	125 254	26501	132 504
2	25038	502	125 517	26502	132 510
...	...	...	...	...	...
11	137 503	531	132 758	26543	132 712
12	150 063	532	133 047	26544	132 719
...	...	...	...	...	...
50	625 341	550	137 503	26550	132 758

   a) Describe the steps in locating the record with key 132 714, using these indexes.
   ☐ b) Suggest why this method is slightly slower than cylinder–surface–sector indexing.

8 A technique for calculating the backing store address from the key, in random files, is called **folding**. For example, if the key is 9 digits long, then the three sets of three digits are added up to obtain the backing store address, as follows:

Key: 396 421 608

```
    396
    421
 +  608
 ───────
   1425
```

Backing store address: 1425

   a) Use this technique to calculate the backing store addresses of these keys: 492 117 503, 625 417 902.
   b) If the address thus calculated is already occupied, then the next available address is used instead. This principle is called **open hashing**. Assuming an initially empty file, use this principle to load records with the following keys: 462 803 906, 341 915 916, 638 702 831, 594 913 666.
   c) Load the records from part (b) in a different order. Comment on your findings.

9 Carry out the steps of a quicksort on the following sets of numbers:
   a) 6   14   18   23   5   9   11   12,
   b) 5   9   11   3   14   19   2   27,
   c) 18   16   10   11   8   4   3   7,
   d) 8   15   9   16   10   17   11   18.
   Comment on any effects of initial ordering, or partial ordering, on the steps of the process.

10 Assume that a computer memory can only contain four records of a particular file. Use the method outlined in the text to sort a file with key values as follows:
   12   4   9   21   8   5   20   2   7   11   15   6   3   1   19   13.

11 Outline the steps of a binary search to locate the record with key 19 from a file with keys as follows:
   4   7   8   10   11   19   23   31.

12 During the updating of a file, stored on magnetic tape, a power failure occurs. Both copies of the file are corrupted. Outline the steps involved in re-creating the up-to-date version of the file.

13 During the updating of a file stored on a magnetic disc, a **disc crash** occurs. The read–write head comes into contact with the surface of the disc, destroying the disc and damaging the disc drive. Outline the steps involved in re-creating the file.

14 Outline some of the measures taken to protect data from deliberate interference. Give your opinion on the effectiveness of these measures, and the wider implications of their use.

15 A suite of programs has been designed to maintain a file of credit accounts for a large number of bank customers. Each customer is allowed a specified amount of credit and the system keeps a record of his balance by processing transactions nightly.
   Give a list of the programs required and their functions in the system.
   Describe what procedures would be built into the programs to validate the input data.
   Suggest how the file would be stored and justify your choice.

UL 78 II

16 a) Finger-prints can be classified in terms of less than ten characteristics such as the number of lines between two principal features. Discuss the use that could be made of a computer system to assist the police with the identification of finger-prints. Explain what information would be stored, how a user of the system would make an enquiry and how the system could increase the effectiveness of retrieval of information.
   b) Describe a way in which files on finger-prints could be organised so as to facilitate the methods of retrieval.

OLE 79 I

17 a) Explain why the sorting of computer files of data is a process which may be frequently encountered in a data processing system.
   b) Describe a procedure for the sorting of data on magnetic tape, assuming that two additional tape decks are available for the sort.
   c) A generalised sort package has been written to sort data on magnetic tape. List the parameters which you would expect to supply in order to use such a package.

18 A gas board has about one million customers, each with a gas meter identified by a unique code of 8 digits; the code includes a check digit. The meter readings are of 6 figures, and readings are taken every 3 months. If a meter cannot be read an estimated reading is calculated. Describe how you would set about designing a computer system for the gas board, for the input of meter readings and the production of bills. Your description should contain:
   a) a diagram showing the main activities within the system and their interrelationships;
   b) a list of the files used with details of their structures, their expected sizes, the media on which they would be held and the arrangements for back-up copies;
   c) the reasons for the choice of input medium;
   d) details of the types of validation to which the input data is subjected;
   e) a brief list of the items to be covered in the documentation for the operators, for the management and for the programmers who are responsible for the maintenance of the system's software.

UCLES 81 Specimen I

24
Databases

This chapter introduces a relatively new, but rapidly developing area of computing, namely **databases**. The chapter explains the nature of a database, and discusses some of the advantages of using one. After introducing a few essential concepts, the structure of a database system is described. The three commonest approaches to the structuring of the data used in a database are outlined. The chapter concludes with a brief assessment of databases.

The topic is presented in broad outline only, as a detailed study requires some difficult concepts, and is beyond the scope of this course. This chapter is a brief introduction to the essentials of the topic.

One example is used to illustrate several of the points raised in the chapter. This example concerns a potential user of a database, namely a mail order retailer, selling a wide variety of goods from a number of warehouses to customers throughout the country. Although this example is not a case study, it is nevertheless a very realistic application of a database.

24.1   What is a Database?

This question is first investigated in an informal way, before a precise definition of a database is given.

Most organisations which use a computer do so for more than one application. In the case of the mail order retailer, applications might include customer accounts, stock control and payroll systems. Each of these applications requires a considerable volume of stored data.

The traditional approach to the storage of this data is to use files, as described in the previous chapter. Each application has its own set of files, containing the data it needs, and structured according to its method of processing.

In most cases, because all the applications are for the same organisation, there is a large degree of overlap of data between the files for the various applications. If these files are replaced by a single, large, suitably organised collection of data, accessed by all the applications, then this collection of data is a database. In the case of the mail order retailer, the database is a single collection of data used for customer accounts, stock control and payroll applications. A concise definition of a database is as follows:

A database is a collection of stored operational data used by all the application systems of an organisation.

The general idea of a database is illustrated in Figure 24.1.

24.2   Some Advantages of Databases

Using a single, centralised store of data for all applications has a number of advantages. The most significant of these are now discussed.

1   *Consistency of data:* when a data item is updated, its up-to-date value is available to all users. This ensures that the data used by all the applications is consistent.
2   *Less data proliferation:* because only one copy of each data item is kept, duplication of data is eliminated.
3   *Ease of setting up of new applications:* when a new application is contemplated, much of the data it needs is probably already on the database. Extending the database and providing a new interface is generally quicker than starting the new application from scratch.
4   *Easier security monitoring:* because all access to data is via a centralised system, a uniform system of security monitoring can be implemented. In most cases this is more effective than a number of separate security systems.

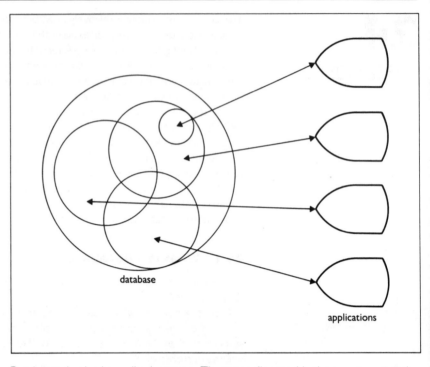

Figure 24.1
The general idea of a database

Databases do also have disadvantages. These are discussed in the assessment at the end of the chapter.

To get a more concrete idea of the advantages of using a database, consider again the example of the mail order retailer. Before the introduction of the database, every sale of goods to a customer required both stock control files and customer account files to be updated. This involved a duplication of effort, and any errors could lead to inconsistencies between the two files. With a database, only one update is required.

24.3 Some Concepts Related to Databases

Some essential concepts relating to databases are introduced in the next two sections. These are the ideas of **data models** and **data independence**.

24.4 Data Models

Although a database is a single collection of data, the data must appear to be different when viewed from different parts of the database system. Each user of the database must see a set of data suited to the particular application. Furthermore, the logical structure of the data might be different from the way it is physically represented on backing store media.

The way around these problems is the idea of a **data model**. A data model is the logical structure of the data as it appears at a particular level of the database system. Each user of the database has a different data model. For the example of the mail order retailer, consider the stock control and accounting applications.

The data model for the stock control application might be a set of item records, each containing an item number and a supplier. Associated with each item record is a set of stock movements, each comprising a date and a quantity supplied or dispatched. This data model is illustrated in Figure 24.2.

item record	item number	supplier
	N 423 961 X	A. M. Jones

stack movements	date	quantity	
	03/08/80	4801	s
	03/08/80	5	d
	04/08/80	11	d
	05/08/80	7	d
	06/08/80	23	d

s = supplied
d = dispatched

Figure 24.2
Mail order retailer's database: stock control data model

On the other hand, the data model for the customer accounting application might be a set of customer records, each containing a customer number and customer details. Associated with each customer record is a set of transactions Each transaction includes a date, item number, quantity and price. This data model is illustrated in Figure 24.3.

In addition, there is the data model associated with the data base as a whole. This model depicts the ideal, logical structure of the data, independent of the media on which the data is stored. All other data models are derived from this central model. The structure of a central data model is discussed later in the chapter.

It is the task of the various layers of the database system software to create and maintain these data models. The words **transformation** or **mapping** are used for the process of creating one data model from another.

customer record	customer number	customer details
	C 491 267 4	P. Sharp 4 Elm Street Ashton

transactions	date	item number	quantity	price
	04/08/80	N 436 215 4	1	10.45
	04/08/80	N 391 204 9	1	23.16
	05/08/80	N 423 961 x	3	9.95
	10/08/80	N 104 723 5	2	38.47

Figure 24.3
Mail order retailer's database: customer accounting data model

24.5 Data Independence

You will recall that a database is a large store of operational data. Because it is operational, it is changing all the time. Data items are constantly being updated, and new data is being added. In most cases, the total volume of data is increasing. On the other hand, new and improved data storage media are constantly becoming available. These are generally cheaper, more compact and quicker to access than before.

For these reasons, it is necessary from time to time to replace the media on which the data is stored. If applications referred directly to the storage media, this would require amendments to every applications program. These amendments would be slow, error-prone and costly.

Accordingly, the central data model of the database, and all user data models derived from it, are independent of the physical storage of the data. One level of the database system software is devoted to mapping the central data model onto the physical representation of the data. If the storage media are changed, only this layer of software needs to be altered.

This discussion gives rise to the idea of **data independence**. Data independence is when the logical structure of the data, i.e. the central data model, and associated user data models, are distinct from the arrangement of the data on any particular backing store medium. The data models are unaffected by any changes in techniques of storing the data.

24.6   A Database System

In common with most aspects of computing, a database is part of a system, namely a **database system**. A database system consists of the stored data, the various data models, a piece of software called a **database management system**, and a person called a **database administrator**. Figure 24.4 illustrates the overall structure of a database system. Various aspects of it are discussed below.

The **users** of a database system are the various applications which put the data to work in different ways. Each application program may be written in a different language, and 'sees' a different model of the data. As shown in Figure 24.4, more than one application may use the same data model.

The **database management system** (DBMS) is a large and complex piece of software, responsible for all aspects of the creation, accessing and updating of the database. Tasks it performs include transforming or mapping the data from one model to another, or between the central data model and the stored database. All interactions between users and the database are dealt with by the DBMS. This includes carrying out various security checks. A database management system is a real-time system, and has quite a lot in common with an operating system.

The **database administrator** (DBA) is the person in charge of the overall running of the database system. Duties of a database administrator include deciding on the information content of the database and the structure of the various data models, deciding how the data is to be stored, liaising with users, and defining a strategy for back-up storage and recovery from breakdown. This job requires a combination of software and managerial skills.

24.7   Structuring the Data Model

The central decision in the design of a database system is the structure of the data model. Almost every other aspect of the database system depends on this structure.

Because the database is large, and there are many relationships existing between individual data items, a satisfactory structuring of the data is very difficult to achieve. Objectives of a well structured data model include efficiency of storage, ease of transformation to other models, speed of access to data and ease of modification of the model.

Three approaches to the structuring of data models are discussed. These are the **hierarchical**, **network** and **relational** approaches. Historically, these approaches have been developed in this order, with relational databases still being in their infancy.

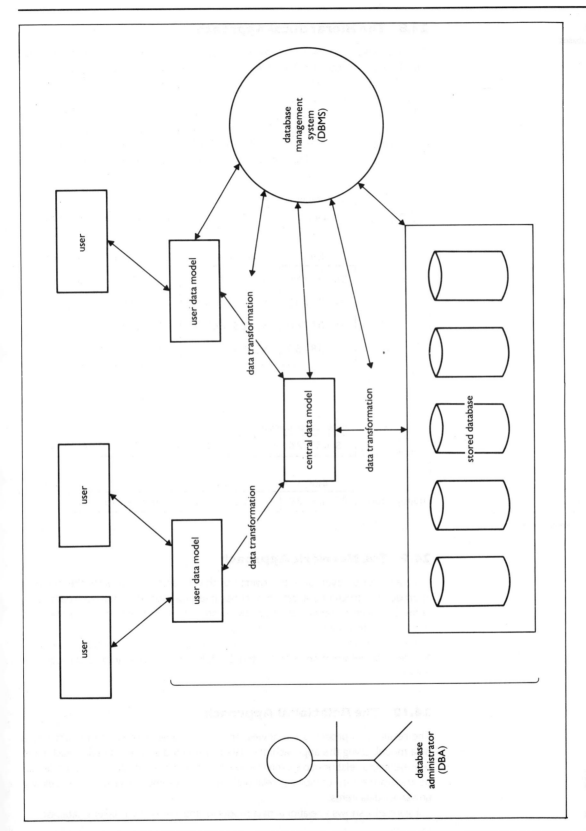

Figure 24.4
A database system

24.8 The Hierarchical Approach

The hierarchical approach involves creating a tree structure for the data. Different data items are stored at different levels, with some levels being 'below' others in the tree. The problem with the hierarchical approach is that not all data bases fit naturally into a tree structure.

Figure 24.5 shows an attempt to create a hierarchical model of the data for the mail order retailer's database. Two levels of the hierarchy are shown, namely the customer/supplier record level, below which is a level of trading records. Each customer/supplier record has one or more trading records associated with it.

	identification number		details		
customer supplier record	C 491 267 4		P. Sharp 4 Elm Street Ashton		

	date	item number	quantity	price	p = purchased
trading records	04/08/80	N 436 215 4	1	10.45	p
	04/08/80	N 391 204 9	1	23.16	p
	05/08/80	N 423 262 X	3	9.95	p
	20/08/80	N 104 723 5	2	38.47	p

	identification number		details		
customer/ supplier record	S 437 261 5		A.M. Jones PO Box 194 Ely		

	date	item number	quantity	price	s = supplied
trading records	03/08/80	N 423 961 X	480	9.95	s

Figure 24.5
Mail order retailer's database: hierarchical data model

24.9 The Network Approach

In an attempt to overcome the rigidity of the hierarchical approach, the network approach to structuring a data model has been developed. In this approach, data items are linked to other data items by pointers, forming a network. Information is extracted by traversing the network in various ways.

Figure 24.6 shows a network data model for the mail order retailer's database. Notice how information is extracted by following various arrows through the network.

24.10 The Relational Approach

The relational approach is the newest and most promising method of structuring a data model. Using this approach, the data is presented as a set of tables, each table representing a relationship existing between two or more data items. The model can be transformed by combining relationships via a common data item and deleting unwanted data items.

Figure 24.7 shows a relational data model for the mail order retailer's database.

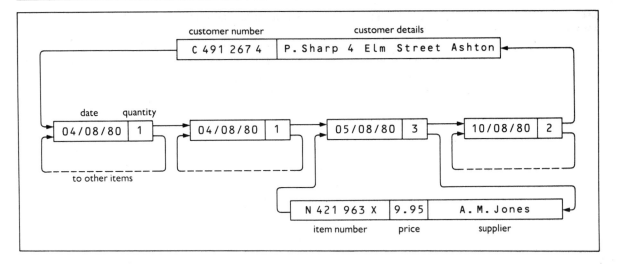

Figure 24.6
Mail order retailer's database:
network data model

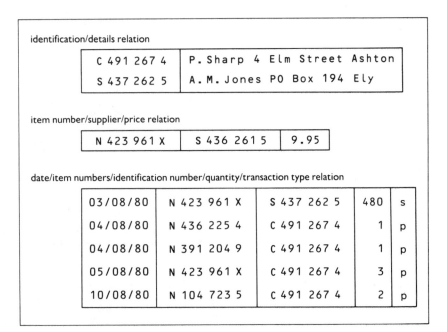

Figure 24.7
Mail order retailer's database:
relational data model

24.11 An Assessment of Databases

This chapter has outlined how large centralised data structures can be constructed to contain all the operational data of an organisation. The advantages of these databases were discussed earlier in the chapter. Experience has shown that databases do indeed have the advantages mentioned earlier, but they also have two major disadvantages.

The first disadvantage is that a database requires a large software system to create and maintain it, and a fairly large computer to support it. This is in contrast to the current tendency towards small, cheap microprocessor-based computers with small software overheads, and distributed processing.

The second disadvantage is that a database is an example of putting all one's eggs in the same basket. A failure of a database system, through an accident, deliberate damage or industrial action, can have serious consequences for an organisation with all its data processing dependent on the database.

Exercise 24

1 Briefly define the following terms: database; data model; data independence; database system; DBMS; DBA

2 You will recall that a system is a collection of parts working together towards some common objectives. List the objectives of a database system.

3 Explain, in your own words, the significance of the concept of data independence.

4 Summarise the advantages and disadvantages of the use of databases.

☐ 5 A news reporting agency uses a database system to store the text of all news items. News reports are supplied, by telex, by a number of correspondents, and then purchased by a number of newspapers and magazines.

The model of the data, from the correspondents' point of view, is as follows:

Correspondent record

Identity	Name
K 347 P	JOHN GREGGOROWSKI

News items supplied

Date	Text
05/11/80	TODAY RUSSIAN TANKS....
07/11/80	STRIKES IN POLAND....
08/11/80	URGENT DISCUSSIONS ARE....
11/11/80	THE SITUATION IS DETERIORATING....
12/11/80	NO SIGN OF AN END....

The model of the data, from the newspapers' point of view, is as follows:

Newspaper record

Identity	Name
N 417 W	WASHINGTON STAR

News items purchased

Date	Correspondent Identity	Text
04/11/80	K 007 L	LONDON EXPERIENCED....
07/11/80	K 347 P	STRIKES IN POLAND....
07/11/80	K 007 L	MISS WORLD....
09/11/80	K 291 A	ARGENTINA'S DICTATOR....
12/11/80	K 347 P	NO SIGN OF AN END....

a) Using either the relational or the hierarchical or the network approach, draw up a central data model for this system.

b) Explain how your data model can be used to determine which newspapers have bought any particular news item.

☐ 6 Design a suitable simple database system of your own. State the data model for each application, and also the central data model of the system.

7 RAPPORT is a relational database system marketed by Logica Limited. It can be used on a wide variety of mini and mainframe computers. Find out about the system, specifically how concepts introduced in this chapter are implemented.

25
Data communication

Over the past century, a number of communications networks have been developed, to the stage where they now encircle the globe and reach deep into space. Radio, television and telephone links enable hundreds of millions of people to keep in contact with each other, often over distances of thousands of miles.

Although the earliest forms of communication systems used a digital code (the Morse code) for information transmission, the bulk of the development of these networks has been for voice and picture transmission (with the important exception of the telex system). With the advent of computers, the situation is changing again. Information is being sent, in digital form, in increasing quantities, as more and more computers are being linked to local and global communications networks. The combination of computers and communications systems is one of the major areas of technological development at present. It may yet have as profound an impact on the lifestyles of millions of people as the advent of computers, or of telephones, radio or television had in their time.

This chapter is a brief introduction to the field of data communication. The topic is discussed from several angles. The first part of the chapter concerns the way in which data is transmitted between two computers, or between a peripheral device and a computer. The second part of the chapter outlines some of the hardware configurations which can be built up around a data communication network. The use of computers as exchanges in communications network is also discussed. The chapter concludes with two case studies of data communications systems.

In many ways the study of data communications is a subject in its own right. Accordingly, this chapter does not relate very closely to material in adjacent chapters. Indeed, it may be studied out of sequence if desired, or glossed over very lightly without much loss of continuity. It is included at this stage because it does depend to some extent on material introduced earlier in the book, and data communication is an application area of computers.

25.1 Concepts of Data Transmission

The first part of the chapter concerns some concepts relating to the transmission of data, in digital form, along a communications medium. These concepts are much the same whether the communication medium is a wire, a radio or a fibre optics link.

25.2 Bit Serial Transmission

Just as data is always stored and processed in a computer in binary form, so is it transmitted between computers in a binary form. Individual bits are grouped together to code characters, and characters are grouped together to form larger data structures.

If two digital devices are very close to each other, it is possible to connect them by a multi-strand cable which can transmit a number of bits simultaneously. This is **parallel** data transmission. In the majority of cases, where data is to be transmitted over any distance, a single carrier is used. In these circumstances, only one bit at a time is transmitted. This is called **bit serial** transmission.

It is possible to transmit the binary values 0 and 1 over short distances using the presence or absence of a voltage, or a positive and a negative voltage to represent these values. For long distance communications, whether by wire or by radio, a more sophisticated technique is required. In most cases, signals of two frequencies are used, one for a 0 and the other for a 1. The details of such techniques are beyond the scope of this course. It is sufficient to know that an **interfacing** device is placed at each end of the transmission line, to transmit and receive the appropriate signals for 0 and 1. Interfaces generally deal with the conversion of parallel data from the computer or peripheral device to serial data for the transmission line.

One of the commonest types of communications interfaces is called a **modem** (for **mod**ulator/**dem**odulator). Another device, which links with an ordinary telephone, is called an **acoustic coupler**. Both transmit and receive serial data along telephone lines.

The serial transmission of a set of characters is illustrated in Figure 25.1. Notice how the beginning and end of the bits for each character is marked.

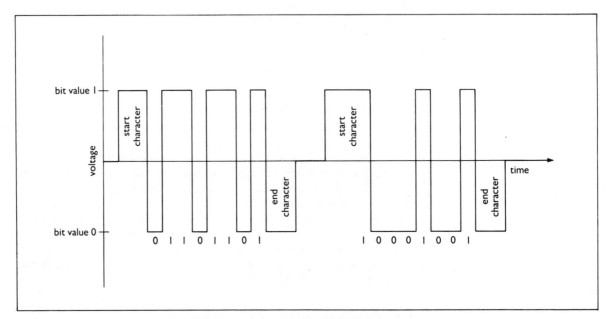

Figure 25.1
Serial transmission of a set of characters

25.3 Simplex and Duplex

Verbal communication between people is not possible if both talk at once, or each waits for the other to speak. Similarly, in data communication, there must be ways of establishing in which direction transmission is taking place at any one time. There are three approaches to this problem, as outlined in the following paragraphs.

Simplex communication is where transmission is in one direction only. This may be used, for example, for transmission of data from a remote input device to a processor.

Half duplex communication is where transmission may be in either direction, but not in both directions simultaneously. In other words, at any given instant, transmission is in one direction only. Ways of indicating that transmission is complete, and that the direction may therefore be reversed, are dealt with in the next section.

Full duplex communication is where transmission may proceed in both directions at the same time. This is the most sophisticated form of data communication.

25.4 Data Transmission Codes

Data transmission is an area where standardisation is very important. Any two items of equipment which adopt the same standards of data communication can be linked together.

One of the most essential standards in data communications is a code for the binary representation of characters. Fortunately there has been a very wide measure of agreement on this matter. Only a few character codes are used in data transmission, and one code, the **American Standard Code for Information Interchange (ASCII)**, is gaining increasing prominence. An increasing proportion of data communication is in this code. (As mentioned in Chapter 3, this code is becoming increasingly popular for the internal representation of data in computers.)

Data transmission codes include representations of letters, digits and punctuation marks, as well as a number of **control characters**. These characters only have relevance to the transmission of data, and are not used for the storage or processing of data. For example, there are characters to signal the end of transmission, or the start of a block of data. The codes for some of the ASCII control characters are shown in Figure 25.2.

hexadecimal	binary	interpretation
01	00000001	start of header
02	00000010	start of text
03	00000011	end of text
04	00000100	end of transmission
05	00000101	enquire, who are you?
06	00000110	acknowledge
07	00000111	ring bell
08	00001000	backspace

Figure 25.2
Some ASCII control characters

25.5 Speeds of Data Transmission

Speeds of data transmission vary considerably, depending on the application, and the data communication medium. The unit of measurement of data transmission rates is the **baud**. The precise definition of a baud is rather complicated, but it may, for practical purposes, be regarded as one bit per second.

On an ordinary telephone line, a data transmission rate of 110 baud is generally used. On special lines, this rate may increase to 9600 baud (9·6K baud). Even higher rates are possible on other communication media.

25.6 Packets

When one writes a letter, the pages are placed in an envelope, which is generally of a standard size. A similar principle is used in data communication. Data is transmitted, not in single characters, or groups of characters, but in packets.

A packet is a set of transmitted data, enclosed by strings of control characters. The control characters at the start and end of the packet follow a strict set of rules. Many of them are the same for all packets. The data within the packet is of a standard structure.

A packet is the unit of transmission and reception within a particular data communication network. All devices connected to the network send and receive data in packets of the same type.

25.7 Communication Protocols

When one sends a letter, one must follow a number of rules imposed by the Post Office. For example, the address must be set out in a certain way, and the stamp must be in the top right hand corner of the envelope. Similar rules apply in the case of data transmission. These rules are called communication **protocols**.

Among other things, a protocol specifies the structure of a packet of data, what control characters are used and what procedures are followed for the transmission and reception of data. For half duplex transmission, the protocol specifies the procedure for changing the direction of transmission.

The advantage of a communication protocol is this: any two devices which use the same communication protocol can be linked together. For this reason, communication protocols are designed very carefully, in order to be as widely applicable as possible. At present, there are only a small number of protocols in widespread use.

Many communications protocols permit the data in packets to be **compressed**. Compression aims to reduce the number of characters which actually need to be transmitted, for example, by representing repeated characters as a counter followed by the character.

25.8   Errors in Data Transmission

We all have experience of bad telephone lines, poor radio reception and erratic television pictures. These are all caused by interference, or **noise**, in the communications medium. Although careful design and higher quality (and more expensive) equipment can reduce the amount of noise, it can never be eliminated entirely.

Data communication is not immune to the problem of noise, although the situation benefits from the nature of digital transmission. As long as the signal for a 0 can be distinguished from that for a 1, a bit is correctly received. However, there is always a small probability that noise will cause the wrong bit value to be detected.

As it is impossible to prevent bits from being detected wrongly, the best that can be done is to try to detect when an error has occurred, and, in some cases, locate and correct the error. Most data transmission codes incorporate checks on the data transmitted. The commonest check is the inclusion of a **parity bit** in the code for each character. The question of parity is discussed in Chapter 3. Other checks include the insertion of **check characters**, or groups of check characters, as discussed in Section 12.19. One type of error correcting code, called the **Hamming code**, is discussed in the exercise at the end of this chapter.

25.9   Communications Networks

The next few sections outline some of the types of networks which can be constructed for data communication. The first of these sections concerns a single processor linked to a number of terminals. Subsequent sections discuss various aspects of **distributed processing**, where processing is done at a number of places in a network. The last section introduces the topic of **message switching** by computer.

The different types of network introduced here are not to be regarded as rigid stereotypes, but merely as examples of common communications configurations.

25.10   Central Processor with Terminals

A large central processor linked to a number of remote-access terminals is the 'traditional' approach to data communication. This arrangement is illustrated in Figure 25.3.

A refinement of this idea is to collect the lines to a number of terminals together at a suitable point, and connect this point to the processor by a single high volume data link. The device at the linking site is called a **multiplexer** or **cluster adaptor**. This technique is illustrated in Figure 25.4.

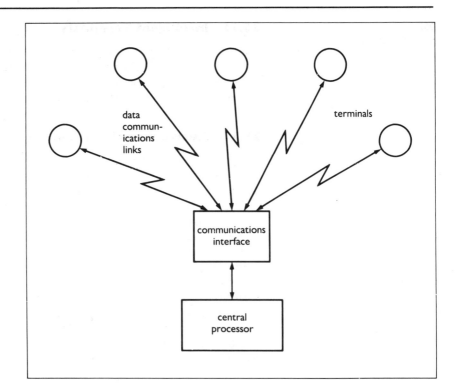

Figure 25.3
A central processor with remote
access terminals

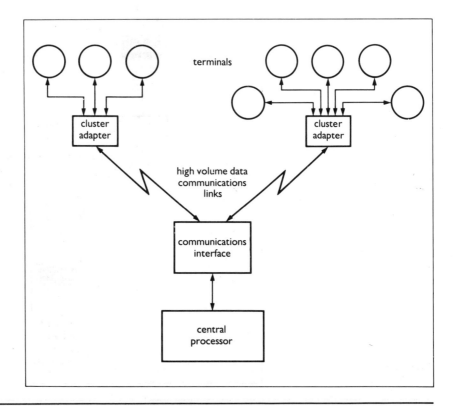

Figure 25.4
Terminals linked by cluster adapters

25.11   Intelligent Terminals

Instead of centralising all the processing in a computer network at one site, an increasingly common configuration makes use of **intelligent terminals**. The structure of the network is the same as that shown in Figures 25.3 and 25.4, but processing is shared between the CPU and the terminals.

25.12   Networks of Processors

Computer networks can include more than one processor, as shown in Figure 25.5. The processors can be long distances apart, connected by radio, telephone or satellite communication links, or they can be close together, often in the same building. The latter situation is known as a **local area network**. Local area networks are an increasingly popular computer configuration.

There are several advantages of processors linked in this way. The processing load is shared evenly between the processors. This is particularly significant if the processors are in different time zones, where off-peak times at one processor correspond to busy periods at others. The other major advantage is that a breakdown at one processor does not put the whole system out of action.

The major disadvantage of such a network is the size and complexity of the operating system required to control the network. A significant proportion of the time of each processor is spent doing 'housekeeping' tasks, in order to keep the network as a whole functioning smoothly.

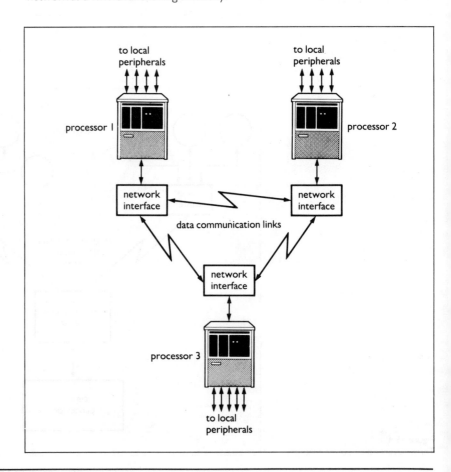

Figure 25.5
A network of processors

25.13 Ring Architecture

A type of local area network currently under development is based on the idea of a **ring**. As illustrated in Figure 25.6, the ring connects all the processors and peripheral devices in the network. All data communication between any two devices is via the ring.

The intention of a ring architecture is to combine the low cost of microprocessors with the flexibility and power of a multiprocessor computing system. Each processor

Figure 25.6
A ring network

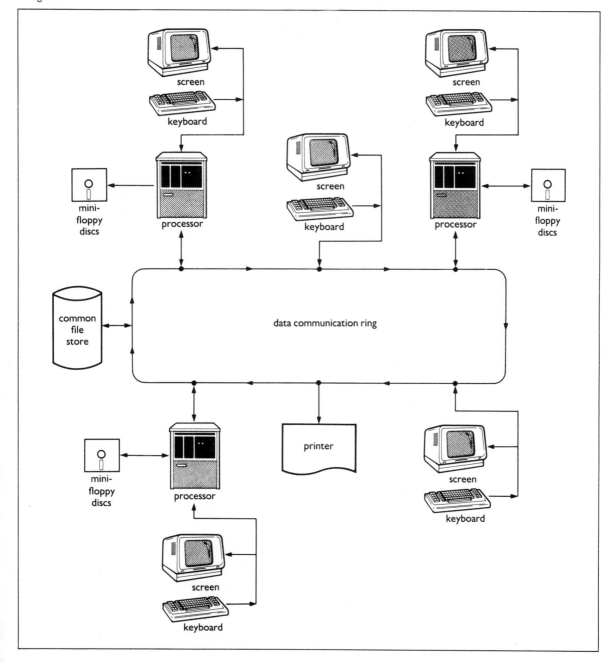

on the ring is a single-chip microcomputer. Yet the ring as a whole, with its shared backing store and input/output peripherals, is more powerful than a much more expensive system based on a single minicomputer. The ring architecture is also more resilient. It is not too adversely affected by the failure of any one unit. A case study of a local area network based on a ring is included in Section 25.16.

25.14   Message Switching

Message switching is the work performed by a telephone exchange. The switching involves establishing a link between the originator of a call and the receiver of the call.

In the early days of the telephone system, message switching was carried out by hand. In a few areas this is still the case today. The equipment in most common use at telephone exchanges at present is mechanical. The machinery interprets the digits of a dialled number by setting a series of switches. When all the switches have been set, the call is linked to its destination. This mechanical apparatus is slow, cumbersome and requires extensive maintenance to keep it in operation.

The most modern technique of message switching involves the use of computers. Using specially designed hardware and software, these computers can link calls extremely rapidly, keep records of which numbers have been connected, and supply the information necessary for the preparation of telephone bills.

Message switching computers, or electronic exchanges, as they are sometimes called, are gradually being introduced into telephone systems. They are also being used extensively in private data communication networks. As packets of data are transmitted on these networks, the work performed by the switching computers is called **packet switching**. Figure 25.7 illustrates a data communication network using a packet switching computer.

One significant advantage of a packet switching computer over an electronic telephone exchange is that the packet switching computer can store data if the destination processor is not ready to receive it. Such systems are known as **store and forward** systems.

25.15   Case Study 1: The Pixnet System

A Pixnet data communication system consists of a set of units, each with associated software, which control all aspects of data communication within a network. The system is independent of any host computer, and works in such a way that all devices linked to the network appear to be local to each other. The Pixnet equipment handles such matters as data compression and re-routing of messages in the event of a line failure.

Brief descriptions of key devices in a Pixnet network are included below. Figure 25.8 shows a typical network configuration using these devices.

Network control units (NCU) are located at switching points in the network. These enable any device in the network to be linked to any other device. An NCU can also route data along alternative communication lines in the event of a line failure, or to minimise transmission costs. Attached to an NCU is the **network administrator's console** which provides overall network control, and supplies information on the current status of the network.

Local control units (LCU) provide the interface between processors and the data communications network. All data is presented by the LCU to the processor as if it originates from a local device.

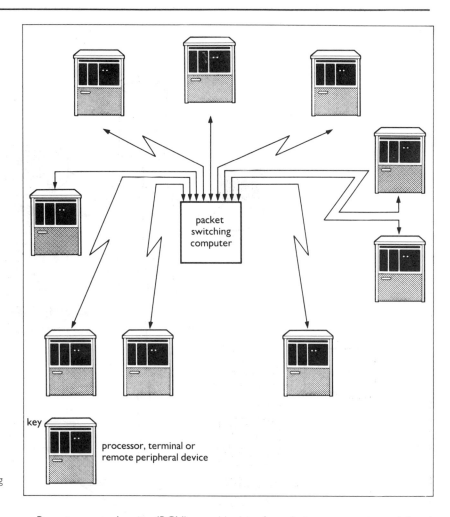

key processor, terminal or
remote peripheral device

Figure 25.7
A data communication network using
a packet switching computer

Remote control units (RCU) provide interfaces between remote peripheral devices and the data communication network.

The actual communication links can be telephone lines, radio links, fibre optics connections, satellite links, or any combination of these.

25.16   Case Study 2: The Cambridge Ring

The **Cambridge Ring** is the basic design for a local area network based on a data communication ring. It was first developed at Cambridge University in 1974, and versions of it are currently being marketed by several companies.

Principles of Operation

Figure 25.9 shows the arrangement of a typical ring. It consists of a number of **ring stations**, joined by a cable in a continuous loop. Each station has storage for a few bits of data, and signal delay in the cable creates storage for additional bits in transit. The stations and the cable may be thought of as a circular shift register, around which bits circulate at high speed, generally 10 megabits per second.

The circulating bits are organised into one or more **slots**, and a gap. Slots generally comprise about 40 bits. Any station may insert a **mini-packet** of data into a free slot as it passes. The mini-packet contains the address of the sending station, the address

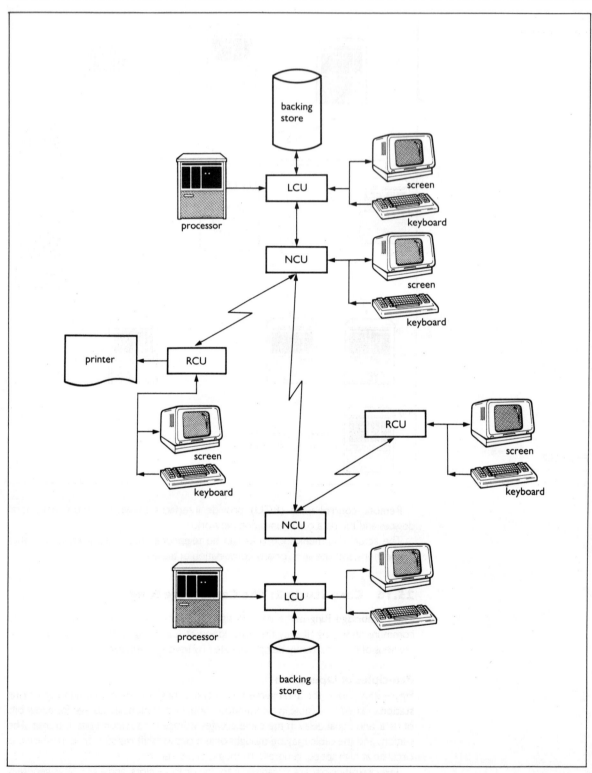

Figure 25.8
A Pixnet data communication network

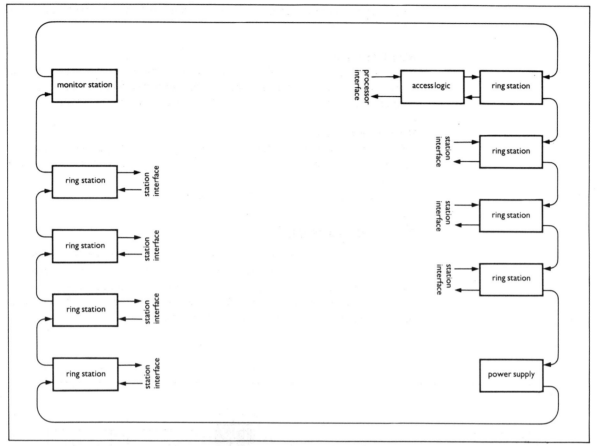

Figure 25.9
A Cambridge Ring

of the receiving station, two bytes of data, some control bits and a parity bit.

The mini-packet circulates around the ring until it reaches the station to which it is addressed. If the station is ready to receive, it copies the mini-packet into its internal registers, and marks the packet as accepted. The mini-packet continues around the ring until it again reaches the station which transmitted it. The station notes whether or not the mini-packet has been accepted, and marks it as free. To prevent one station from dominating the ring, a station must skip a slot before it can use another slot.

The Monitor Station

The monitor station is responsible for starting up the ring, determining the number of slots in circulation and detecting and recovering from errors.

Each station checks the parity of all passing mini-packets. If a parity error is noted, an error mini-packet is sent to the monitor station. The monitor station fills all empty slots with random bits, and checks them if they return still empty. If the ring breaks, the first station 'downstream' of the break sends a continuous stream of fault packets to the monitor station. In these various ways, a number of error checks are built into the ring. The monitor station plays an important part in the error detection process.

Power Supply

Power for the running of the ring itself is supplied from the monitor station and from one or more **ring power supply stations** in the ring. Each ring station requires local power for its registers, but the ring itself is not affected if the local power is switched off.

Ring Interfaces

A ring station provides a simple interface between the ring and a wide variety of connected devices. More sophisticated interfaces to certain processors are provided by **access logic**, which is placed between the ring station and the processor.

Ring Applications

A Cambridge Ring is suitable for a wide variety of local area applications. Distances between stations can be up to 100 m. A complete ring can thus measure several kilometres.

A typical ring application is illustrated in Figure 25.10.

25.17 Conclusion

This chapter has provided a brief introduction to the field of data communication. It must be emphasised that this is currently one of the major growth areas of computing. For example, during the next ten years it is intended to replace all the mechanical telephone exchanges in Britain with electronic equipment. Local area networks are another area poised for rapid development.

Figure 25.10
A Cambridge Ring application

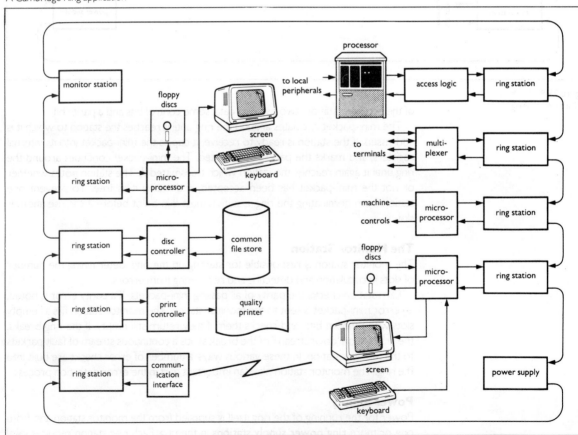

Exercise 25

1 Briefly define the following terms: serial and parallel data transmission; modem; simplex; half duplex; full duplex; control character; packet; protocol; noise; local area network; packet switching; interface.

2 Why is standardisation important in data communication?

☐3 The screen of a visual display unit shows 20 lines each of 40 characters. Data is transmitted to the VDU in packets, each packet containing the characters for one screen display, in order from the leftmost character of the top line, line by line, to the rightmost character of the bottom line. New-line characters are not required after each line.

Data is compressed by representing repeated characters as a counter (occupying one byte, with most significant bit 1), followed by the character. For example, a blank line is represented as follows:

	first byte		second byte	
Binary	1010	1000	0110	0000
Hexadecimal	A	B	6	0
ASCII	Count = 40		space	

a) Write down, in binary, hexadecimal and ASCII, the string of characters needed to transmit a screen display containing the following characters:

A row of dots (Hexadecimal 2E) on the second and nineteenth lines.
The characters **MESSAGE ENDS** starting at the left side of the fourth line, the rest of which is blank.
All other lines blank.

b) Count the number of bytes transmitted, and comment on the effectiveness of the compression system.

(Use Figure 3.1 for the ASCII codes of the characters.)

4 In addition to the Pixnet system, and networks based on the Cambridge Ring, there are a number of data communication systems currently available. Most large computer manufacturers market a system. Investigate one of these systems and compare it with the case study in this chapter.

5 A cluster adaptor combines a number of 110 baud lines into a single 9·6K baud line. If multiplexing information accounts for 10 per cent of the data on the high speed line, how many low speed lines can the cluster adaptor accept?

6 The Prestel data communication system, marketed by British Telecom in the UK and a number of other countries, is a system which is likely to have a considerable impact.

The user interface of the system is a specially adapted television set which connects to an ordinary telephone line. The system is supported by a number of minicomputers, one in each major population centre. Having dialled into the system, users can access 'pages' of information on a wide variety of topics, using a simple hand-held keypad for control.

a) Find out more about the services provided by the Prestel system.
b) Draw a diagram showing the configuration of the Prestel network.
c) Find out how information is supplied to the system.
d) Write a report on your findings, and comment on likely development areas of the Prestel system.

7 A code which will detect and correct single-bit errors is the **Hamming code**. This code requires a number of even parity check bits in a data item. They are distributed in such a way that they do not check on each other.

Three check bits are required for a four bit data item, as shown in the table below:

Data bits:				B1		B2	B3	B4
Check bits:	C1	C2		C3				
Digit numbers:	D1	D2	D3	D4	D5	D6	D7
Example	1	0	1	1	0	1	0
Check 1	*		*		*		*
Check 2		*	*			*	*
Check 3				*	*	*	*

In the example, the data bits are 1010 and the check bits are 101.

The digits are numbered from left to right, and the checks are determined by the binary equivalent of these digit numbers, expressed in the pattern of asterisks in the last three lines.

Each row of asterisks starts with a check bit. The remaining asterisks in the row indicate the data bits whose parity is indicated by the check bit. For example, check bit C2 tests the parity of data bits B1, B3 and B4.

If a single bit error occurs, the three checks are sufficient to locate and thus correct the error.

For example, if the data is corrupted to 1011110, the checks are as follows:

```
Data:        1 0 1 1 1 1 0

Check 1:     1     1   1   0   fail (value 1)
Check 2:       0 1       1 0   pass (value 0)
Check 3:           1 1 1 0     fail (value 1)
```

If a check fails, it is given the value 1, and if it passes, the value 0. The binary number thus formed indicates the position of the digit which is wrong. In the above example, the number is 101, indicating that the fifth digit is in error, which is in fact the case.

a) Locate and correct the errors in each of the following data items, with Hamming check digits as above.

```
1011101
0011000
1111101
```

□ b) An eight bit data item requires four Hamming check bits. Draw up a table, similar to the one above, showing the positions of the data and check bits, and the four checks to be carried out. (Hint: Start by drawing the binary pattern of asterisks.)

c) Write down some correctly encoded eight bit data items. In each case, introduce a single-bit error. Then perform the four checks, to ensure that they locate the error.

d) Repeat part (b) and (c) for 16 and 32 bit data items.

9 A local area data communication network which is arousing considerable interest is the **Ethernet** system, being developed jointly by Intel, Rank Xerox and Digital Equipment Corporation.

The structure of a simple Ethernet is shown in Figure 25.11. It consists of a single passive conductor, its 'ether', to which all communicating computers and peripheral devices are attached.

Any device may claim the 'ether' at any time, provided that it is not already in use. A simple mechanism exists for resolving contention between two devices which simultaneously try to transmit.

Data is sent in packets of variable length, addressed to a receiving device. Transmission is bit serial, at a rate of up to 10 megabits per second.

a) Find out more about the design of Ethernet.

b) Compare and contrast its design principles with those of the Cambridge Ring.

10 a) Describe the structure of a network of computers which is such that a user at a console can gain access to and use any of the computers, however remote from him they may be.

b) What problems arise when large volumes of data need to be transferred from one computer to another in such a system?

c) Discuss one problem which you would expect to arise in using a terrestrial computer to control one in a space vehicle at a distance of several light-minutes.

OLE 80 II

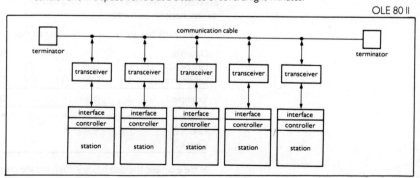

Figure 25.11
An Ethernet

26
Applications case studies

This chapter introduces a number of case studies of computer applications. As it is impossible within the space of one chapter to give an idea of the complete range of applications of computers currently in operation, these case studies have been chosen with a limited, but nevertheless important, set of objectives in mind.

The intention here is to present a few applications, in a certain measure of detail, which reflect current trends in computing. In particular, the use of distributed processing, data communication and minicomputers and microcomputers is emphasised. All the case studies are real-time systems.

An additional objective of this chapter is to give a more concrete form to many of the ideas introduced elsewhere in the book. These case studies show how many concepts of computing are being put into practice.

Each case study is examined from the same angles, namely the objectives of the system, the functions performed, the hardware and software used, and an assessment of the performance of the system.

26.1   Case Study 1: CBS European Manufacturing System

26.1.1   CBS

CBS is a worldwide organisation, dealing in a wide range of products and services. These include radio and television broadcasting, marketing records, cassette tapes, musical instruments and other leisure products, and publishing. CBS operates in a very large, but very competitive market, where demands change extremely rapidly. An efficient, flexible business approach, capable of rapid response to changing circumstances, is essential.

CBS UK carries on the operations of the company in Britain, and is closely linked to the company's European operation. One of the major aspects of its work is record production. In addition to producing records and tapes carrying their own labels, CBS UK does the production and packaging for a number of other record companies. Production takes place at a large factory in Aylesbury. Planning and overall management of the production is centred at the company's UK headquarters in London.

26.1.2   Computers in CBS

Computers play a vital part in the work of CBS. There is a large mainframe configuration in London, linked to two minicomputers, a microprocessor and other peripheral equipment at Aylesbury, and to a number of peripheral devices at the manufacturing plant in Haarlem, Holland. In addition, there are terminals at several of the other record companies for whom CBS produces records. The computer system is designed for continuous operation, and supports a number of real-time, transaction processing applications.

The application area chosen for this case study is the **European Manufacturing System.** This system monitors all aspects of record and cassette production in the UK and Holland, and will eventually be extended to Spain, to complete its coverage of CBS's European manufacturing plants.

The detailed study of the system, presented in the following sections, refers to the computer applications centred at the Aylesbury manufacturing plant.

26.1.3   Objectives of the System

The system has a number of objectives, many of which are inter-related. The most significant objectives are as follows:

1 Providing an up-to-the-minute picture of the manufacturing situation, at a number of levels of detail:

in broad outline, for central management and marketing personnel;
at an intermediate level of detail, for production plant managers;
in great detail for plant operators.

2 Monitoring the progress of each batch of records through the various stages of production.

3 Monitoring the performance of a number of key items of equipment, notably record presses.

4 Providing a comprehensive information service for the parts warehouse, which stores labels, posters, bags, inserts and sleeves for the records. This information enables all the parts required for a particular batch of records to be collected together as efficiently as possible.

26.1.4 Manufacturing Order Flow

In order to understand the role of the computer in record production, it is necessary to gain some idea of the operation as a whole. Figure 26.1 shows the overall flow of events during the manufacture of a batch of records or cassette tapes. Notice that each product consists of a number of **parts** such as the sleeve, the record label and any special promotional material, etc.

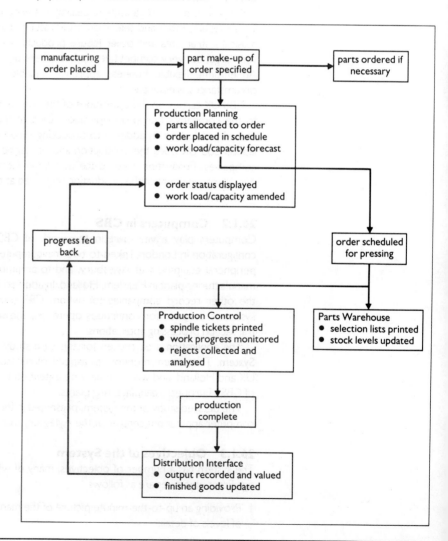

Figure 26.1
CBS manufacturing order flow

26.1.5 Stages of Record Production

Figure 26.2 shows the stages of the production of a record. The unit of production is a **spindle** of records (60 seven inch singles or 30 LPs). A batch consists of a number of spindles.

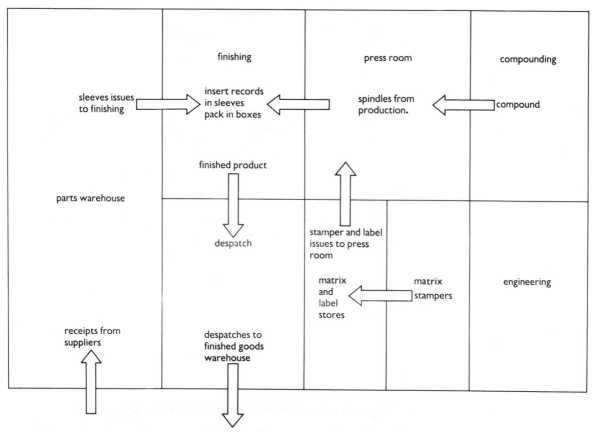

Figure 26.2
CBS stages of record production

26.1.6 An Overview of the System

The role of the computerised monitoring system is shown in Figure 26.3. Corresponding to the three levels of information mentioned in the objectives of the system, there are three aspects of the operation of the system. There are referred to as the Management Reporting Systems, the Plant Operational Systems and the Plant Application Equipment Systems in the diagram.

Four aspects of this system are discussed in more detail. These are the printing of spindle tickets (part of the production control operation), press monitoring (the Dextralog system), warehousing, and collating and lane selection.

26.1.7 Printing Spindle Tickets

When a batch of records is scheduled for pressing, a set of spindle tickets is printed for the batch. These tickets contain items of information which identify the batch, and fields for information to be entered manually as the spindle progresses through the various stages of production. They also contain the bar code used in collating the spindles into batches before finishing.

Spindle tickets are the means of recording all the data relating to the production of a record. They are an essential element in production planning, monitoring and control.

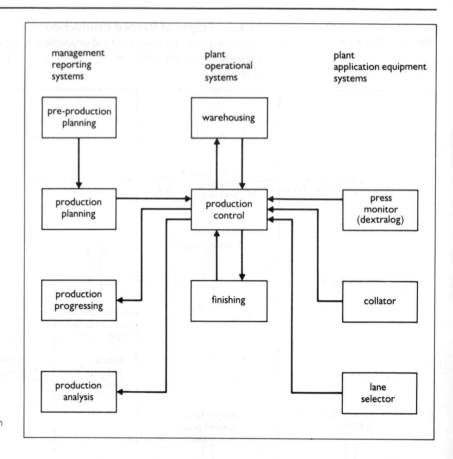

management
reporting
systems

plant
operational
systems

plant
application equipment
systems

Figure 26.3
CBS integrated manufacturing system
overview

26.1.8   Record Press Monitoring: The Dextralog System

The Dextralog press monitoring system provides a number of services, including:

1 the allocation of batches to record presses;
2 counting the records produced by each press;
3 if a press is idle, recording the reason for its stoppage;
4 forecasting when the end of a batch will be reached;
5 receiving information about rejected records, and updating pressing quantities accordingly;
6 providing real-time statistics on the progress of batches and the status of presses.

The hardware of the system includes sensors in each record press, a device on each press for entering the reason for stoppages, a colour monitor in the production control room showing the status of each press, 9 terminals with simple keypads for displaying real-time statistics, and two multiplexers. Processing is carried out on a dedicated Nova 3 minicomputer, with 32K of main store. The Nova 3 has a data link to a CTL 8040 minicomputer, which acts as a communications processor at the manufacturing site. The CTL is in turn linked to the central IBM mainframes.

Software consists of a module for each function of the system, synchronised by a simple transaction processing operating system. Each record press is polled by the operating system once every 20 seconds, to determine its status and whether is has pressed a record since it was last polled. Various modules are then invoked to process the data thus obtained.

Requests from the terminals are treated as interrupts. Modules are invoked to deal with these requests, and to display the required information on the screen. All 9 terminals work together, in other words a request from any terminal alters the display on all of them.

In general, the Dextralog system works extremely well. Its only shortcoming is the lack of data validation built into the system.

26.1.9 Warehousing
The real-time warehousing system provides the following services:

1 allocating rack positions to stocks;
2 locating stock items;
3 producing lists of stocks to be dispatched for a particular batch of records, in such a way as to minimise the movements of the unloading hoists;
4 updating stock levels;
5 reporting all stock movements to the mainframe computers.

The system is based on a CTL 8040 minicomputer, and includes terminals and a ticket printer as well as data communication links to the IBM mainframes.

The software is built up around a CTL operating system called TAD, transaction application driver. TAD allows a **foreground** of fully interactive transaction programs, and a **middleground** of 'batch' programs.

The foreground programs control data entry and validation. They produce a **logfile** of valid data, which is used by the batch programs. Foreground programs are specified by means of a program generating language (like RPG) which calls up standard routines, mostly written in Coral.

The middleground programs accept validated information from the logfile and process it. These programs are concerned with such matters as stock level updating. There are two such programs, both written in Cobol. The warehousing system generally works very well, though if a failure occurs, processing must be started again from the beginning of the current logfile.

26.1.10 Collating and Lane Selection
When spindles of records have been pressed, they are loaded onto a ski-lift type conveyor belt to be transported to the finishing area. When the spindles arrive, they are **collated** (all the spindles of the same batch are collected together) and diverted to a lane for finishing.

Collating and lane selection is done on an automated racking system, together with controls on nearby conveyor belts. The control panel of this racking system is connected to a dedicated microprocessor, which controls the allocation of batches to racks, and the routing of incoming spindles accordingly, as well as the allocation of finishing lanes to batches, and the routing of outgoing spindles. Identifying data is read from the bar codes on the spindle tickets.

26.1.11 Overall System Hardware
Figure 26.4 gives an overview of the hardware used by the CBS European manufacturing system, as well as by all the other CBS applications.

The hardware is designed for uninterrupted 24-hour-per-day operation. Accordingly, several essential components, including the central processing units and many communications links, are duplicated. This spreads the processing load more evenly, and enables the system as a whole to continue to operate in the event of a failure of any single element.

As can be seen from the diagram, the hardware can be grouped into three

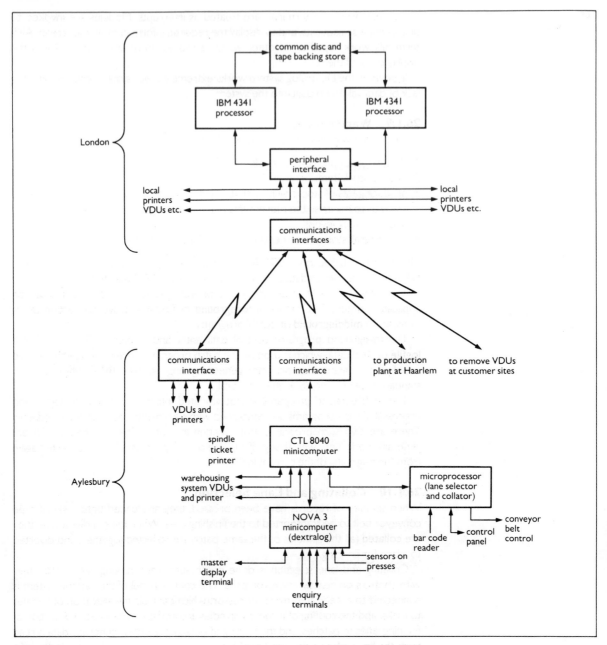

Figure 26.4
CBS overall hardware configuration

functional elements. These are the central processing unit, mass backing storage and local peripherals in London, the data communications network linking the central configuration with a number of remote sites, and the equipment at remote sites such as Aylesbury.

26.1.12 An Assessment of the System

The computer system is an integral part of the workings of CBS. Should the system fail completely, there is no manual backup. In this event, record production and a number of other activities of the company are severely curtailed.

The record of the computer system in this matter is very impressive. The system as a whole has been operational for considerably more than 99 per cent of the time over the last few years.

The computer system enables CBS to maintain an extremely rapid, flexible and efficient record production process. The productivity per worker is very high. The computer system plays an essential part in maintaining CBS's leading position in a highly competitive field.

26.2 Case Study 2: Greater London Council Wide Area Traffic Control System

26.2.1 Background

Moving people and goods around Greater London is a major problem. With a sprawling city centre containing thousands of historic buildings, strict pollution laws and conflicting needs of business people, shoppers, workers and tourists, a completely satisfactory road system is impossible to achieve. In recent times the prohibitive cost of major roadworks has been an additional limiting factor.

The Greater London Council Wide Area Traffic Control System is an attempt to make the best of the existing road network, by bringing the majority of the traffic lights in the inner part of the city under the control of a central computer system.

Development of the system started in 1968, when an experimental area in West London, containing some 70 sets of traffic lights, was brought under centralised control. As soon as it became obvious that the experiment was successful, Phase I of the scheme, encompassing the central area, commenced. In the period 1971 to 1975, approximately 500 sets of signals, as well as 100 pedestrian crossing controls, were linked to the control network. From 1975 to 1980, an additional 450 sets of signals, and 400 pedestrian crossing controls (including the original 70 experimental signals) were incorporated as Phase II of the scheme. In 1980, it was decided to replace the computer hardware of the system, as well as changing to a new basis of traffic control. As this transition will take a number of years to complete, this account of the system describes both the old and the new versions.

See Figure 26.5 for a map of the areas covered by the various phases of the system.

26.2.2 Objectives of the System

Broadly speaking, the traffic control system has three objectives, namely:

1 minimisation of the journey times of all vehicles in the controlled area;
2 provision of real-time information on the state of the system to a central control room, staffed by police officers;
3 continuously monitoring the performance of all the traffic lights in the network, and reporting any failures as soon as they occur.

From these objectives it can be seen that the system is not completely automated. Ultimate control of the traffic is in the hands of the staff of the control room. From here, computer control of each junction can be changed, or the junction released to local control.

26.2.3 Principles of Operation

As the principles on which the system operates are in the process of being changed, both the old and the new versions are described.

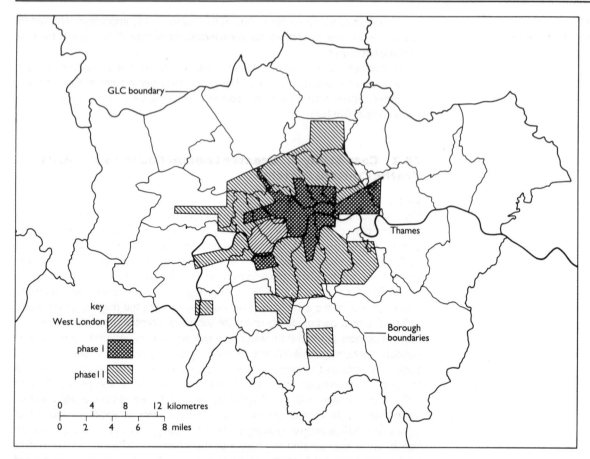

Figure 26.5
GLC traffic control areas

key
West London
phase I
phase I I

0   4   8   12 kilometres
0   2   4   6   8 miles

GLC boundary

Thames

Borough
boundaries

26.2.4 Fixed Timetable Control

The original principle of operation of the system is one of control by a number of **fixed timetables**. These are derived as follows.

The junctions controlled by the system are divided into **groups**. Within each group, control of traffic is synchronised. Control is not always synchronised across group boundaries. The basic unit of control is the **subgroup**. A subgroup is a single isolated junction, or a number of adjacent junctions which must be controlled together.

A **timetable** specifies the duration of each phase of each traffic light in a subgroup. Timetables are computed from the configuration of each junction, the distances between junctions and traffic volumes in various directions. They are then adjusted manually on the basis of observation of traffic behaviour.

A set of timetables is produced for each subgroup of junctions, for each expected type of traffic conditions. For example, there are morning and evening peak hour timetables, a night timetable, and various timetables for emergency conditions and ceremonial occasions. Working on a weekly cycle, the computer automatically selects the timetable of each subgroup, depending on the time of day and the day of the week. Under normal circumstances, all the junctions in a group are on the same timetable.

However, the timetable for any particular subgroup can be changed from the control room, should the situation demand it. The control room has closed circuit TV monitors fed by cameras at all significant intersections. The lights can also be released to local control if necessary.

26.2.5 Adaptive Control

Unlike fixed timetable control, adaptive control is designed to take into consideration the traffic situation at the time. The control system adapts to the situation in its phasing of traffic signals.

An adaptive control system requires a set of detectors to monitor vehicle movements at significant points in the network, and sophisticated software to perform the optimisation calculations, which determine traffic light phase lengths, in real time. The technique which has been chosen for use in the central part of the GLC network is called the **Scoot** system.

Adaptive control is being introduced into the central part of the system. It is not considered necessary to change the whole system to adaptive control.

26.2.6 Operation of the System

The traffic control system consists of a central computer installation, an adjacent control room, a data communication network, and a number of **outstations** in control of each subgroup of traffic lights.

The detailed control of the lights in a subgroup is carried out by its outstation. This control includes interlocking of the individual lights. Thus a computer or data transmission error cannot cause simultaneous green lights in conflicting directions, for example. If communication with the computer is lost, the outstation provides local control of the lights.

The data transmission network carries control signals from the computers to the outstations, and sends monitoring information in the opposite direction. Lines leased from British Telecom are used for this purpose.

The computer installation is designed for continuous, 24-hour-a-day operation. Accordingly, there is a considerable amount of parallelism in the system, including standby processors. The hardware and software used are described in later sections.

The traffic control room includes a number of **control stations**. At each station there is a visual display unit and several television monitors. A wide selection of information can be called up at a VDU. This includes information on the overall state of the network, as well as graphical displays of individual subgroups of junctions. The staff at the control room are in radio contact with all police cars and motor cyclists in the area. These can be called on to observe and report on the traffic situation where problems are occurring, or deal with a problem (such as a parked vehicle obstructing traffic) if necessary.

26.2.7 Hardware

As the hardware of the system is in the process of being replaced, both the old and the new configurations are described. The old hardware (Figure 26.6) is based on three Siemens central processing units. One controls the inner Phase I signals, another controls the outer Phase II signals, and the third is a 'hot standby' processor, ready to take over if either of the others should fail. A set of common peripherals can be switched to any one of the three processors. There is also a set of peripherals dedicated to each operational processor, including the interface equipment to the data communication links.

The new hardware (Figure 26.7) consists of a network of distributed processors. One processor (Master Subsystem A) is in overall control of the fixed timetable area, while another (Master Subsystem B) is in overall control of the Scoot adaptive control area. Connected to these processors are a number of **cells**. Each cell contains a processor, which controls approximately 50 subgroups of junctions. The outstations will eventually be replaced by solid-state microprocessor-based control units.

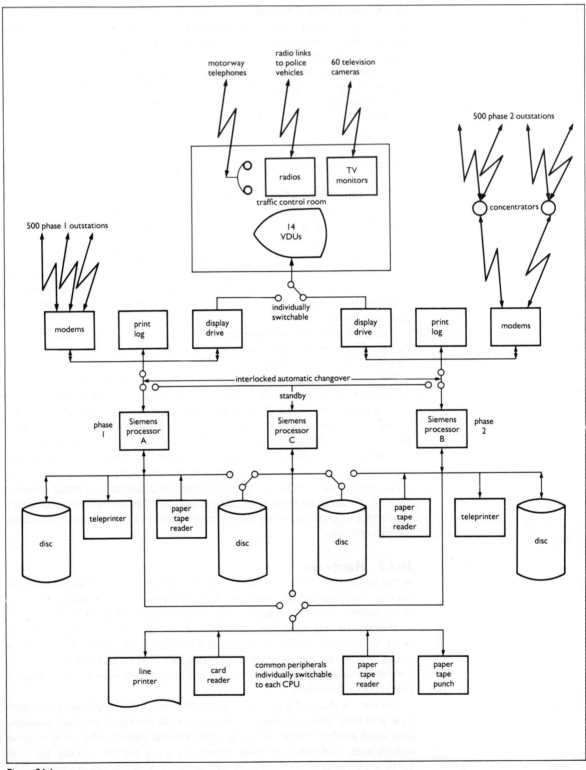

Figure 26.6
GLC wide area traffic control: phase 1 and phase 2 hardware

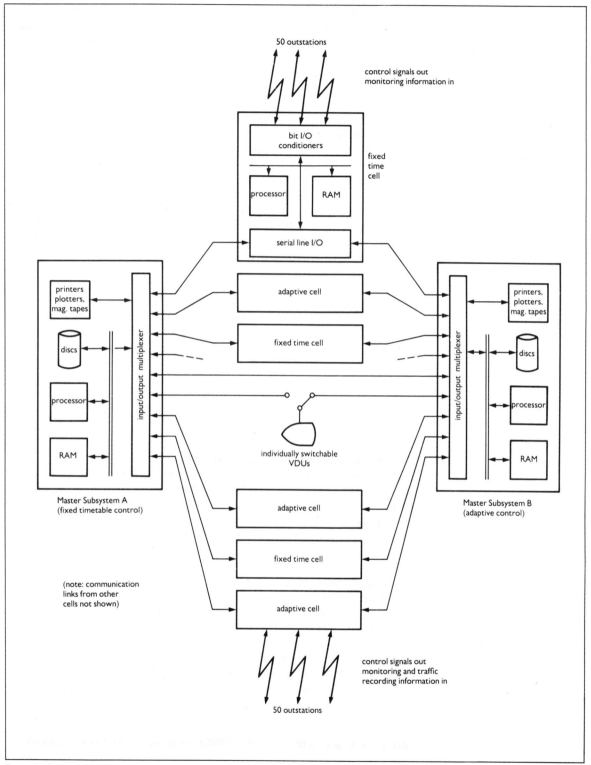

50 outstations

control signals out
monitoring information in

bit I/O
conditioners

fixed
time
cell

processor

RAM

serial line I/O

printers
plotters,
mag. tapes

input/output multiplexer

discs

processor

RAM

adaptive cell

fixed time cell

individually switchable
VDUs

Master Subsystem A
(fixed timetable control)

(note: communication
links from other
cells not shown)

printers,
plotters,
mag. tapes

input/output multiplexer

discs

processor

RAM

Master Subsystem B
(adaptive control)

adaptive cell

fixed time cell

adaptive cell

control signals out
monitoring and traffic
recording information in

50 outstations

Figure 26.7
GLC wide area traffic control:
eventual hardware configuration

The master subsystems exercise overall control of the system, such as the selection of timetables. Cells exercise more detailed control, such as the timing of phases.

The new system is designed to take advantage of the latest developments in microprocessor technology. Magnetic bubble storage devices are also used. The use of distributed processing gives the system a high degree of resilience in the event of component failures.

26.2.8 Software

Three different types of software are used by the system. There is the software for preparing the timetables, the fixed timetable control software and the adaptive control software.

Two programs, called COMPRESS and TRANSYT, are used to prepare traffic light timetables. This is done offline, using an IBM 370 computer belonging to the GLC. These programs are supplied with data specifying the layout of the road network, distances between junctions, expected (or desired) traffic speeds, and volumes of traffic in various directions. Some extremely complex calculations are carried out in order to produce timetables which minimise the expected transit time of all the vehicles in the network.

The fixed timetable control programs use the timetables produced offline to generate signals to all the outstations, and monitor the information coming from these outstations. Commands from the terminals in the control room are interpreted, and information is sent to these terminals in response to the commands. These commands can also cause a change in the timetable being used at any particular subgroup of junctions.

The adaptive control programs receive monitoring information of the current traffic situation. Optimising calculations are carried out in real time, and the phasing of the traffic signals is adjusted accordingly.

26.2.9 An Assessment of the System

The effectiveness of a traffic control system can be measured in a variety of ways. In addition to travel time, there are considerations of safety, fuel economy, pollution, ease of pedestrian movement, noise, adaptability to special circumstances, such as emergencies or ceremonial occasions, and the cost of the system. In a traffic network as large and complex as London's, only part of which is under central control, many of these yardsticks are very difficult to apply.

However, where measurements have been made, the results are extremely encouraging. On average, transit time is reduced by not less than 28 per cent, compared with the same traffic signals under local control. Comparative figures of road accidents are not available, but the safety record with the controlled area is regarded as being good.

On the question of cost, the traffic control system scores extremely well. The most expensive element in the system is neither the hardware nor the software, but the lease of the data communication links. Furthermore, the cost of installing and maintaining the whole system is less than the construction and maintenance costs of half a mile of motorway.

26.3 Case Study 3: ITN VT80 Graphics Display System

26.3.1 Background

As television coverage of newsworthy events has become more sophisticated there has been an increasing demand to be able to broadcast precise, up-to-the-minute information, in graphical form. This is particularly important in the coverage of elections and budgets, but is also very useful for news broadcasts.

Early attempts at graphical displays required skilled signwriters, who would quickly write the required lettering before it was held up in front of TV cameras. Later, computerised character generators came into use, enabling captions to be superimposed on pictures.

Currently, a number of television companies are turning to fully electronic means of generating graphics displays. The **VT80** system, developed by Independent Television News, is one of the first of these electronic graphics systems. It is the subject of this case study.

26.3.2 Objectives

The objectives of the ITN VT80 system are as follows:

1 to provide computer-generated graphics displays which can be injected directly into a TV signal transmitter;
2 to enable these displays to be updated in real time;
3 to permit a certain degree of animation in the displays;
4 to be simple enough to be operated by the presenter of the TV programme.

26.3.3 Operation of the System

There are two aspects of the operation of the system, namely the preparation of the displays, and the broadcasting of the displays.

26.3.4 Preparation of a programme

During the planning of a television programme, decisions are taken as to what displays are to be provided by the graphics system. Each display is a complete television picture, in colour.

The displays are then constructed from lines of text, columns of figures, graphs (particularly histograms) and other symbols. These symbols include maps, simple portraits of people and silhouettes of buildings. Symbols are input into the system by drawing them on special grids, and then specifying the contents of each area of the grid. A table of figures is then keyed in to define the symbol.

A certain amount of animation can be provided. For example, symbols can be coloured in after they have been displayed, histograms can 'grow' to their final size, and columns of figures can appear one line at a time.

Displays can include variables whose value is updated while the programme is being broadcast. These variables include numeric quantities, or the colour to be assigned to a certain symbol.

When all the displays have been prepared, a list of them is prepared for the presenter of the programme. This list shows the number of each display, together with a control key which calls it up, and in some cases one or two further control keys which initiate stages of animation of the display.

26.3.5 Broadcast of a Programme

During the broadcast of the programme, the presenter has the list of displays, a simple keypad and a monitor screen. The presenter calls up and animates the displays as they are required.

The producer of the programme sees the graphics display together with the pictures from the cameras. At any time, either the graphics display or one of the camera pictures can be selected for transmission.

While this is happening, information is arriving at the broadcast centre all the time, chiefly by telephone. Up-to-the-minute values of variables in the displays are entered at terminals.

26.3.6   Example of a Display Guide

Some of the material used for the coverage of the 1980 USA presidential election is presented here. Figure 26.8 shows the display guide used by the presenter of the program.

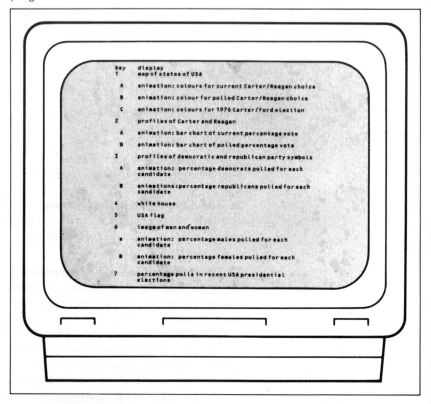

Figure 26.8
ITN VT30 presenter's guide

26.3.7   Hardware

Figure 26.9 shows the hardware used by the system. The processor is a PDP VAX minicomputer, a successor to the PDP-11 series.

The most important device is the interface between the processor and the broadcasting system. This device is the VT80 which gives the system its name.

The VT80 links to the main store of the processor using direct memory access (DMA). It accesses the data for a display, in digital form, and creates the electronic form of this display as a standard television signal. While the display is being broadcast, this signal is linked directly to the transmitter. The only other special hardware in the system is the simple keypad used by the presenter to select the display he or she requires.

26.3.8   Software

During the preparation of a display, a number of software routines are used. These create various parts of the display, such as characters of different sizes, outlines and shaded areas. These routines are written in Pascal or Macro, a PDP assembly language. Basic is also used for the preparation of 'rough' displays. These routines are then compiled, assembled or interpreted (in the case of Basic) to produce the machine code program for each display.

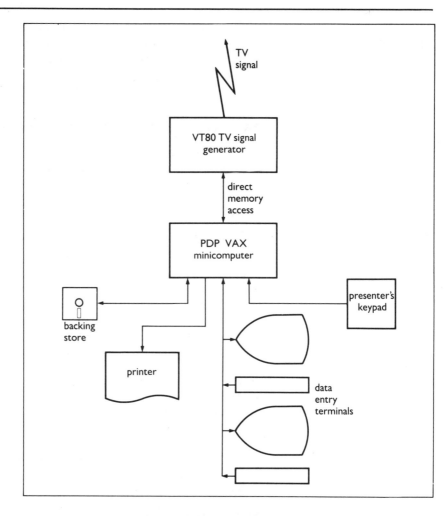

Figure 26.9
ITN VT80 hardware

The data structure for each display is a **display file**. It consists of a set of data describing each portion of the screen, specifically the character, position, colour and priority. There are 8 levels of priority. Characters with higher priority will supersede characters with lower priority at the same screen position. Any position on the screen not defined in this way is assumed to be background. The background colour of various portions of the screen is also defined in the display file.

During a broadcast, all the display files are loaded into main store. When a particular display is selected, the VT80 is given the address of the start of its display file. The VT80 accesses the file and creates the TV signal for the display.

The operating system supporting these activities is the standard VMS system supplied with the VAX processor. Its most important feature is that it can be made to be **event driven**. In other words, once the operating system has initiated a particular routine, no interrupts are allowed until that routine is complete. This prevents the disruption of the animation of a display while it is being broadcast.

26.3.9 An Assessment of the System

The VT80 system is a 'home grown' product. All the software, as well as the special-purpose hardware (in particular the VT80 device itself), have been designed and implemented by ITN. It seems likely that the system will be sold to other television companies.

In addition to fulfilling the objectives stated at the beginning of the case study, the VT80 system has some wider benefits. It enables a higher standard of television presentation to be maintained, and simplifies the production of a number of television programmes. The system is simple, fairly cheap, and easy to use. It is an example of a successful combination of computer and communications technology.

26.4 Case Study 4: VTS 100 Word Processor

26.4.1 Product Overview

The VTS 100 is a stand-alone, microprocessor-based word processing system, manufactured by Logica VTS Limited. It provides a wide range of facilities to the user, including the following:

Basic typing. As text is typed, it appears on the screen, and is automatically stored on a data disc. Text is stored in documents, each of which has a name.

Editing. Characters or words can be erased by a single keystroke. In addition, blocks or strings of text can be manipulated, stored or copied. Text can be re-formatted between different margins.

Printing. Any document on a data disc can be printed when required. Printing can be on continuous stationery or on single sheets. Printing of one document can be taking place while another is being typed or edited.

Copying and backup. Individual documents may be copied, either onto the same data disc or onto another disc. Entire discs may be backed up onto other discs.

Forms design. A form is a predetermined layout for typing. Standard forms provided by the system include paper of various sizes (A4, A4 landscape etc.). In addition, users can define their own forms for memos, letters on company letterhead paper, invoices etc.

The VTS 100 is an example of a dedicated computing system. Its hardware, although constructed from standard components, is specially designed to suit its requirements. Its software, at both system and application levels, is tailored to its hardware, as well as to its design aims of ease of use, versatility and high performance.

26.4.2 Unit Structure

The VTS 100 consists of four functional units, namely a control unit, keyboard, screen and printer. These are illustrated in Figure 26.10.

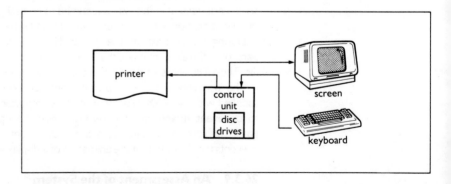

Figure 26.10
VTS 100 word processor: units

The **control unit** houses the processor and two 8 inch mini floppy disc drives, and, in some versions, the communications interface. It has connections for the power supply, and links to the screen, printer and keyboard.

The **printer** is a daisy wheel character printer, which prints alternate lines in alternate directions.

The **screen** displays green characters on a dark background. It shows 24 lines of 80 characters.

The **keyboard** is based on a standard typewriter keyboard, with additional groups of keys for control functions.

26.4.3 Hardware

As shown in Figure 26.11, the VTS 100 hardware consists of a **processor board** to which a number of external systems are attached. The board has three separately controlled interfaces.

The system is based on an **Intel 8080A 8 bit microprocessor**. This is driven by a clock generator, and interfaces the system bus via a system controller. 4K of ROM are used for system initialisation and low-level software.

The **Multibus I/O controller** is the interface to the external memory (48K bytes), dual floppy disc system and screen driving hardware.

The **Parallel I/O controller** supports the programmable peripheral interface, to which the printer and keyboard are attached.

The **Serial I/O controller** (a USART) supports the serial interface. This is used in some versions of the VTS 100 for data communication.

26.4.4 Software

VTS 100 software includes both system and application levels. Most of the software is written in PL/M, and compiled externally. All the software in use while the system is running is in object code, i.e. Intel 8080 machine language.

Software is stored in three different places in the system. Low-level routines which provide operating system facilities are stored in the 4K ROM. Higher level processes are resident in internal or external memory, with **overlays** being transferred to and from backing store. All software, apart from that stored in ROM, resides on a **system disc,** from which routines are copied at power-up. The system disc is also used for the transfer of overlays. However, it may be removed during such operations as backing up a data disc onto another disc.

In designing the software, a top-down approach was used, based on what a user (i.e. a typist) is doing at any time. Various low level activities, such as input/output procedures, were also taken into account. These considerations led to an overall software structure as shown in Figure 26.12.

Application Level

The application level software is partitioned into a number of **processes,** several of which are resident in main store at any time. As the software is too large for the main store, a system of overlays is used, controlled by an **overlay manager**. The overlay manager copies overlays from backing store (i.e. the system disc) to main store whenever they are required.

Each process has a controlling main program, generally based on a loop, which transfers control to various service routines as required. Routines from lower levels of software may be called. For example, the process VET handles basic typing and editing, responding to input from the keyboard and controlling the display on the screen. The process PRT controls the printer, queueing documents for printing, and passing lines of data to be printed as they are required by the printer.

Serving the applications processes, but above the system software level, are a number of **data input/output** routines. The code of these routines may be shared by a number of higher level processes. These routines have the task of mapping the

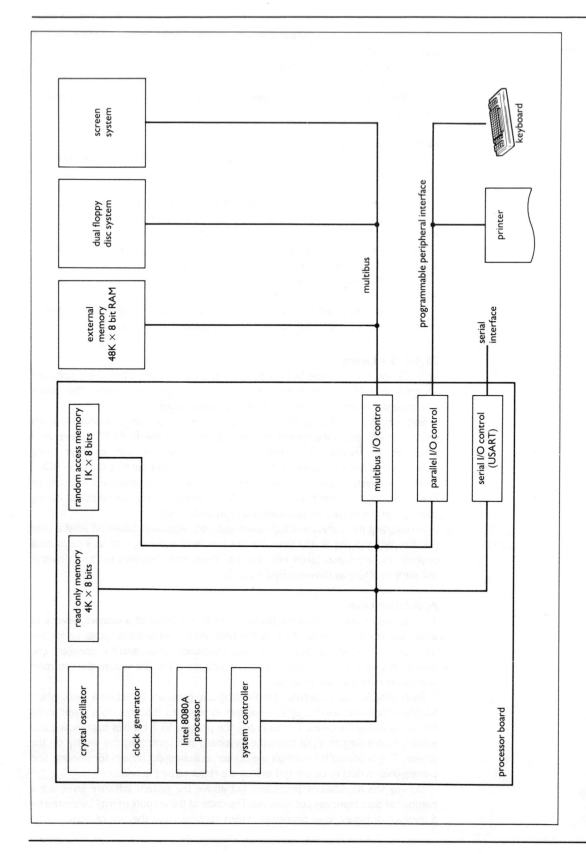

Figure 26.11
VTS 100 hardware block diagram

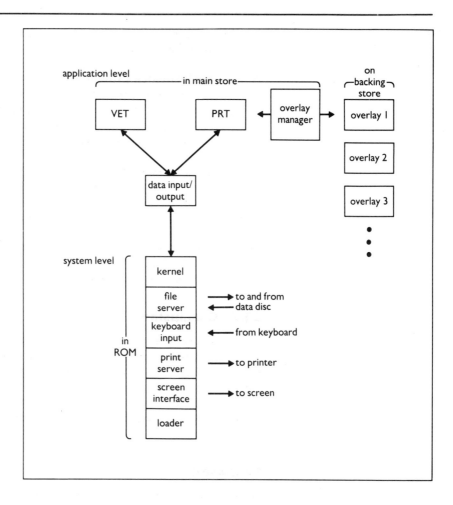

Figure 26.12
VTS 100 software structure

data structures required by the high level processes (documents, files etc.) onto the simpler structures required at a lower level (often individual bytes).

System Level

The 4K ROM contains all the system level routines used by the VTS 100. Much of this code is written directly at low level, in order to minimise its size and maximise its speed. This software provides a user program environment, dealing with such matters as scheduling, interrupt handling and low level input/output.

The main function of the **kernel** is to deal with scheduling. It maintains a queue of processes which are ready to run, in priority order, and a number of stacks of processes which are held up by various conditions. At any one time, one process is running, having been set in action by a procedure in the kernel.

A **file server** deals with transfers of data to and from the disc drives. One set of routines deals with the logical structure of the file, in terms of a string of bytes, another set deals with the physical aspects such as track and sector numbers.

A simple **keyboard input** routine waits for a key to be struck and then returns the input character. More sophisticated is the **screen interface** which sets up tables of data corresponding to lines on the screen, and transfers characters to the screen, advancing the cursor and scrolling up lines as required.

The transfer of characters to the printer is managed by a **print server** routine. The ROM sets up a pool of four buffers, which may be used for data in transit to or from any of the peripherals. Finally, the ROM contains a **loader** routine which supervises the loading of software into main store.

26.4.5 Performance Evaluation

The VTS 100, first marketed in 1978, was one of the earliest microprocessor-based word processors to become available. It contains a blend of simplicity and sophistication, and is designed for use by typists who may have little or no previous experience of word processors or computers.

In general, the VTS 100 has proved to be easy to use and reliable, and has been put to work in a variety of situations. Problems do occur from time to time, particularly with mechanical components like the printer. Occasionally, data on a disc becomes corrupted, resulting in portions of documents which are unreadable.

However, the VTS 100 is regarded as a pioneer in its field. Its wide acceptance has paved the way for a new generation of word processors, using larger scale integration and incorporating many advanced features. Machines like these are playing their part in a revolution in office practices, which had remained almost the same since the advent of the typewriter.

26.5   Conclusion

This chapter has presented four case studies of up-to-date, real-time computer applications, based on distributed processing, and using minicomputers and micro-computers. Although it is almost impossible to give a representative picture, within the scope of such a small number of case studies, of the number and variety of computer applications, nevertheless it is hoped that these case studies have provided some insights, and given a realistic view of current activities within the computing industry.

Exercise 26

1 Briefly describe the progress of a batch of records through the CBS manufacturing system. Mention each interaction of the batch of records with the computer system.
2 Describe the role played by data communication in the CBS manufacturing system.
3 Describe the role played by data communication in the GLC traffic control system. Mention the effects of errors in data transmission, and of failure of a data link.
4 Briefly compare and contrast the techniques of fixed timetable and adaptive traffic control.
5 Using the new hardware configuration, control of each traffic light in the GLC network is exercised at three levels. Identify these levels, and state what degree of control is exercised at each.
6 Outline the steps taken to include in a display a variable item of information, which can be updated in real time, using the ITN VT80 graphics display system.
7 Suggest some additional uses for a television real-time graphics system.
8 Comment on the degree of dependence of the organisations mentioned in these case studies on their computer systems.
9 a) Give some reasons for the use of PL/M as the programming language of the VTS 100.
   b) Why are certain parts of the software not written in PL/M, but in Intel 8080 assembly language?
10 Suggest some possible applications of a VTS 100 if it could be used in conjunction with a local area data communication network. For each application, outline the additional software which would be required for the VTS 100.
11 Describe how the concept of a module is implemented in the hardware and software design of the VTS 100.
12 Using a computer application of your choice, conduct a study of the workings of the system. Use the same general approach as in this chapter, and write a report of your findings.

27
The computing industry

It has been widely predicted that by the year 2000, computing will have become the world's largest single industry. As a whole, the computing industry encompasses a wide range of activities. It provides employment for a large number of people, and is becoming an increasingly important element in the economy of many developed countries. Computing appears to be one of the few industries which is successfully weathering the storms of inflation and recession.

This chapter describes, in outline, the current state of the computing industry. As far as possible, a worldwide perspective is maintained. Various aspects of the manufacture and use of computers are covered, as well as some of the service industries which have grown up around computing. Mention is made of some of the professional associations in the computing field. The chapter concludes with a look at the activity which keeps the whole industry moving forwards so rapidly, namely research.

27.1   The World Computing Situation

This section examines, in very broad outline, the worldwide picture of the computing industry. The most significant trends and activities in each region are described.

27.2   The USA – the Centre of Gravity

The centre of gravity of the computing industry is undoubtedly the United States of America. Here, computers are designed, produced and used in the greatest numbers. The USA has by far the largest number of computers in use per person. It is the home of a number of multinational computer manufacturing companies.

The USA is the world leader in one of the most important aspects of computer development, namely the design and production of large scale integrated circuits. Most of this activity is centred in California, in an area known as Silicon Valley.

27.3   The UK and Europe - Software Expertise

Although a certain amount of computer design and manufacture takes place in the UK and Europe, the strength in this region is in the software area. Program language design, systems software development and applications programs are the subjects of intense activity at universities, software houses, computer manufacturers and even some user installations.

27.4   Japan – Significant Growth

Japan's proven capability to produce large volumes of high quality manufactured goods is extending into the computing field. A number of Japanese manufacturers are now producing a wide range of computing equipment. Production of electronic components for computers is an extension of the country's established electronics manufacturing capability. However, Japan has not dominated the computer market in the way it has dominated the hi-fi, camera, motorcycle and motor car markets. It seems unlikely that it will do so in the foreseeable future, although its share of the world computer market is increasing.

27.5   OPEC Countries – Rapid Implementation

The massive shift of wealth to oil producing countries over recent years has led to many of these nations embarking on very ambitious development programmes. Many of these programmes include the importation of large, sophisticated computing systems, usually from the UK, Europe or the USA. Particularly strong application areas include defence, civil administration, hospitals and industrial production. The oil industry itself is a major user of computers.

Many computer workers have been enticed to these areas by large, tax-free salaries and extremely attractive fringe benefits. However, the political and social instability in these regions is a major hindrance to their development, both in the computing field and in other areas.

27.6   Developing Countries – A Slow Start

Most developing countries have made an extremely slow start in the use of computers. The point has been made that computers are helping to widen the gap between industrial and developing nations.

There are a number of reasons for the lack of widespread use of computers in the Third World. The most significant reason is a lack of applications. Most work in developing countries is labour-intensive, and little would be gained by the use of computers. Other reasons include a lack of expertise, minimal service and support facilities, political and social factors which lead to a distrust of Western products, and a chronic shortage of finance.

How this situation will change in the near future is the subject of much debate. It seems fairly likely that a number of factors will combine to keep the spread of computers in these countries to a very slow pace. However, should this pace increase, the Third World will become an enormous market for the whole range of computer products and services.

27.7   The USSR, Eastern Europe and China – Closed Doors

Although there has been a considerable amount of computer development in Communist countries, there is very little co-operation between these countries and the West in the field of computing.

The USSR and Eastern Europe have a policy of producing a unified range of computer equipment, with each country responsible for the development and production of certain units in the range. It appears that hardware development in these countries is several years behind that in the West. Microprocessors are just beginning to be produced. However, on the software side, particularly in scientific and mathematical programming, these countries are second to none.

Since the breakdown of relations between the USSR and China in 1961, China has pursued an independent course in computer development. For a variety of reasons, including political pressure, development has been slow. Emphasis is on scientific, military and industrial applications.

There are a number of reasons for the lack of co-operation between East and West in the field of computers. By far the most prominent is mutual distrust, as computers are a vital part of modern military systems, particularly nuclear weapons systems. Computer sales from most Western nations to Communist countries have to be approved by government agencies. In a number of recent cases, permission has not been given. In addition, there is a desire in Communist countries to develop their own high technology products, and not to be dependent on imports from the

West. Finally, there is a lack of Western currency with which to pay for the computers.

27.8   The Computing Industry by Activities

Having completed a very brief survey of the world computing situation, this chapter continues with an examination of the various activities within the computing industry.

27.9   Computer Manufacture

One of the most significant activities within the computing industry is the manufacture of computer equipment. The next few sections examine various aspects of computer manufacture, and identify some of the most significant companies engaged in this work.

27.10   Original Equipment Manufacture

The raw materials of computers are integrated circuits and other electronic components, cathode ray tubes for VDU screens, keyboards, plugs, casings and a host of other components. Companies which make these components are called **original equipment manufacturers** (OEMs). There are a very large number of these firms, but the most significant of them are the manufacturers of microprocessors and other large scale integrated circuits. Among the leading companies in this field are Motorola, Intel, Zilog, Rockwell and Texas Instruments in the USA, and Ferranti, Mullard and Inmos in the UK.

27.11   Mainframes

The largest corporations in the computing industry are those engaged in the design, development and manufacture of mainframe computers and associated software. Some computer manufacturers rank among the largest corporations of any kind in the world.

The leading company in this area, in terms of income, number of computers sold, number of employees and profit, is International Business Machines, more commonly known as IBM. With branches all over the world, including agencies in Moscow and Peking, IBM has built up a sales and support network second to none.

When electronic computers were first developed, during and after the Second World War, IBM was already an established manufacturer of office equipment. Although it was fairly slow in moving into computers, once it entered the market, it soon reached a position of dominance which has never been challenged. One of the most significant influences which IBM has on the computer market is its pricing policy. IBM keeps prices as low as possible, spreading the development cost of a product over its whole lifetime. Other manufacturers generally have little option but to follow IBM's lead.

Other prominent USA-based mainframe manufacturers are Burroughs, Honeywell, Cray, NCR, Amdahl, Control Data Corporation and Univac. The leading British firm in this field is International Computers Limited (ICL). In Japan there are Fujitsu, Hitachi and Nippon Electric Company (NEC).

Although the strength of the companies mentioned in this section is in mainframe manufacture, many of them also supply minicomputers and microcomputers, as well as systems and applications software. The tendency is also increasing to sell a computer as part of a hardware-plus-software package.

27.12   Minicomputers

In spite of the pressure from microcomputers, the market for minicomputers does not appear to be declining at the present time. Minicomputers are also benefiting from the availability of cheap large scale integrated circuits. Many are now able to provide facilities which a few years ago were confined to mainframes.

As in the case of mainframes, the most significant manufacturers of minicomputers are based in the USA. Digital Equipment Corporation (DEC), producer of PDP computers, is the most prominent. Hewlett-Packard (USA) and Digico (UK) are other important minicomputer manufacturers.

27.13   Microcomputers

Undoubtedly the fastest growing area in the field of computing is the microcomputers area. Performances are increasing and prices are tumbling, as a number of manufacturers compete in a potentially huge market. Rather surprisingly, at the time of writing, none of the manufacturers of minicomputers or mainframes has made much impact in this area. All the companies engaged in this area are far too numerous to mention. A few of the more significant ones are as follows: Commodore, manufacturers of the Pet, Apple, and Radio Shack, producers of the TRS-80, in the USA; Research Machines (380Z), Acorn Computers (Atom, the BBC microcomputer, and Econet) and Sinclair (ZX80) in the UK; and Sharp (MZ-80K) in Japan. A number of these microcomputers use the Zilog Z80 microprocessor.

27.14   Dedicated Microprocessors

In addition to being used in microcomputers, microprocessors are being incorporated into a growing number of other products. These products include calculators, watches, cameras, automatic production equipment, industrial robots, word processors, banking terminals, motor cars, aircraft, railway locomotives and juke boxes. A few of these products are produced by computer manufacturers. The rest are helping to keep a large number of other companies in business.

This is a very rapidly expanding field, with enormous potential for further development. However, it is also the field which is causing considerable concern in some areas. Particular problems are the possible massive increase in unemployment, and the lifestyle which would evolve in a world of chips with everything.

27.15   Peripherals

In the early days of computing, it was the usual practice for all the units of a computer system to be produced by the same manufacturer. These days it is becoming increasingly common for a computer installation to be assembled from units made by a number of different manufacturers. The peripherals used in these systems are **plug-compatible** with the processors. In other words, they can be connected directly to the processors, without any interfacing adjustments needing to be made.

The continued growth of computing, and the introduction of new types of peripherals, is creating a very large market for peripheral equipment. A number of manufacturers are currently engaged in this area. Among the most prominent are Memorex, the USA-based magnetic disc manufacturer, and Westrex, a producer of terminals.

27.16　Computer Services

Computer manufacture is the branch of the computing industry primarily concerned with the supply of hardware. Computer services is the branch more concerned with software. A large number of companies are engaged in some form of computer services. These companies are also known as **software houses**, **systems houses** and **computer bureaux**. Although the individual companies tend to be smaller than manufacturers, together they form a substantial industry in their own right.

These companies provide a wide range of services, including standard software packages, consultancy in a number of areas, custom-built software, combined hardware and software packages and the hire of computing equipment. The phrase **turnkey contract** is used to describe the arrangement whereby a computer service company provides a complete, ready-to-use computer system, designed to the specifications of a customer.

Consultancy is provided in such areas as computer systems design, management of projects, program design, purchase of computer equipment, marketing and the forecasting of future trends.

27.17　Users and User Groups

The majority of industrial and commercial organisations in the Western world are computer users. Most of these organisations are irrevocably committed to computers. In other words, they would be unable to continue to operate without their computer systems.

Many computer users are members of **user groups**. Each group generally represents the users of a particular type of computer. These groups enable users to discuss problems of mutual concern, and enable them to bring pressure on computer manufacturers to rectify faults which the users have found with their systems.

27.18　Computer Media Suppliers

The computing industry supports a large number of suppliers of computer media. Traditional media such as punched cards, paper tape and printer paper are still in demand, though their market is beginning to dwindle. However, there is an increasing demand for magnetic discs and tapes, microfiches, OCR stationery, pre-printed stationery for computer output, and a large number of other products. As new devices come into use, the need is created for media to supply these devices.

27.19　Professional Associations

As computing has spread to involve the work of more and more people, a number of associations have been formed to represent the interests of people who work with computers in various ways. Most prominent of these organisations are the **British Computer Society (BCS)** and **National Computing Centre (NCC)**, in the UK, the **Association for Computing Machinery (ACM)** in the USA and the **International Federation for Information Processing (IFIP)**.

Although each of these organisations has a unique character, their activities cover similar areas. Their most significant activities include the following:

1 Holding conferences, meetings and seminars on a very wide variety of topics

relating to computing. Some of these topics are very specialised, others are much broader issues, such as computers and privacy.

2 Publishing journals, weekly and monthly bulletins and newsletters, as well as books and pamphlets on matter relating to computers. Some of these publications are the accepted means of communicating new developments in computer research. Others contain news, editorial comments, product advertisements and advertisements of job vacancies in the computing field.

3 The creation and maintenance of standards and codes of practice for the computing industry.

4 Promoting debate on issues relating to the use of computers, such as privacy and unemployment, and giving evidence to Commissions of Enquiry into these issues.

5 Providing an informal meeting place for their members.

These organisations have helped to enhance the status of the computing industry, and provide an invaluable internal safeguard against abuses of the power of computers.

27.20 Research

It has been said that, in computing, yesterday's research is today's product is tomorrow's museum piece. Although this is somewhat of an overstatement, it does establish two points. Firstly, the pace of computer development is very fast, and, secondly, the leading edge of computing is research.

The importance of research to computing can be seen by the amount of money allocated to it, both by governments and by companies. All computer manufacturers, and many computer service companies, have research divisions. A large proportion of the income of these companies is allocated to these divisions. Some of the research is at the most fundamental level of semiconductor technology and computing theory, looking many years into the future.

Most universities, colleges and polytechnics have computing science departments. These departments have both a teaching and a research function. Unlike the situation in many other fields, there is generally very close co-operation between the academic world and the industrial and commerial world in the field of computer research. This has proved very fruitful in the past, and will no doubt continue to be so.

27.21 Conclusion

This chapter has provided a very brief survey of the most significant aspects of the computing industry. As you will now realise, it is an industry which includes a number of different activities. Indeed, much of its strength is in its diversity. Although it has reached the age of maturity, it retains its youthful optimism, and is still growing vigorously.

Exercise 27

1 Briefly define the following terms: OEM; plug-compatible; turnkey contract.
2 Compare and contrast the computing situations in the USA and the USSR.
3 Suggest some reasons for the emergence of the USA as the world leader in computer manufacture.
4 Suggest some reasons for the lack of Japanese penetration into the computer market.
5 Give your views on the role of computers in Third World countries.
6 Summarise, in about 100 words, the most significant activities in the computing industry.

7 Give your own views on the importance of research to computing.

8 Investigate one or more of the professional associations mentioned in Section 27.19. Write a report listing its activities, publications and areas of interest.

9 Select a major industrial activity such as motor car production, steel making or nuclear energy. Write an overview of the industry, using similar categories to the ones in this chapter. Then compare the industry with the computing industry, mentioning in particular relative rates of growth and future prospects.

28
Data processing personnel

This chapter concerns the people who work with computers. It covers both the manufacture and applications of computers, as well as some of the services associated with computing. Descriptions are given of the commonest jobs done in the various fields. It must be remembered that job definitions in computing are not always very rigid. Working practices differ considerably from one organisation to another.

This chapter relates closely to the two previous chapters, concerned with computer applications and the computing industry. It gives an added dimension – the human factor – to the study of the applications of computers.

This is the last chapter in the part of the book concerned with computer applications. It provides a link to the concluding chapters of the book which consider computing in a broad perspective.

28.1 Computer Manufacture

As described in the previous chapter, there are two overall stages in the manufacture of computers, namely original equipment manufacture, and the design and assembly of complete computer systems.

28.2 Integrated Circuit Manufacture

One of the most important raw materials of modern computers is integrated circuits, often containing complete processors. These are designed and developed by **electronics engineers**, and fabricated by highly skilled workers using extremely sophisticated equipment. Computers are used in the design, manufacture and testing of these circuits.

28.3 Computer System Manufacture

The complete process of designing and constructing a computer is extremely complex, and involves the work of a number of people. The stages are generally as described in the following sections.

28.4 Research

Most computer manufacturers have a research department, investigating new devices, new software techniques and new computer applications. **Research engineers**, **technicians** and **scientists**, and highly skilled **software writers** are among the staff of these departments. A more detailed discussion of computing research is to be found in Section 27.20.

28.5 Design

The overall design of a new computer, or series of computers, is in the hands of **computer architects**. Modern computers are designed from both the hardware and the software point of view. Accordingly, **systems programmers**, who write the systems software for the computer, are also involved in the design process.

28.6 Construction

Highly skilled production workers are responsible for the various stages of construction and assembly of units. Production lines are not used. Generally, a team of workers is assigned to take a unit through all the stages of construction and exhaustive testing.

28.7 Sales

One of the highest paid jobs in computing is that of **computer salesman**. Salesmen operate in an intensely competitive environment, where their level of pay depends to some extent on their sales figures. The process of selling a large computer system can take a considerable period of time.

28.8 Installation and Maintenance

Field engineers are responsible for the installation and commissioning of new computer units, and the maintenance and repair of systems in operation. With many computers running 24 hours a day, this type of work often involves calls at extremely unsocial hours.

28.9 A Data Processing Department

Traditionally, an organisation which uses a computer has a **data processing department**, containing all the staff who work directly with the computer. As discussed later in this chapter, this method of structuring an organisation is becoming less common. Other departments and individuals in an organisation relate to the data processing department as **users** of the computing equipment.

In overall charge of a data processing department is a **data processing manager**. Responsibilities of a data processing manager include the overall policy of the department, approval of projects, staff recruitment and the relationship of the department with the rest of the company.

The work of a data processing department has two aspects, namely the program development aspect, and the operations aspect. On the program development side, **systems analysts** are responsible for steering each project through the data processing cycle, as described in Chapter 22. **Programmers**, more properly called **applications programmers** in this context, are responsible for writing, correcting and maintaining programs, and producing various items of documentation, explaining how programs are used. This work is described in more detail in Chapter 27.

On the operations side, there is generally an **operations manager** in charge of scheduling the use of the computer, arranging for maintenance and ordering supplies. A team of **operators** man the computer room, often working in shifts under **shift leaders**. More about the work of a computer operator is to be found in Section 19.17.

The flow of data to and from the computer is sometimes supervised by **data controllers**, who ensure that the right data is available at the right time. **Data entry staff** operate data entry terminals, or, in older installations, card punches, to keep up the supply of data to the computer. In many large computer systems, **file librarians** are responsible for the large numbers of magnetic tapes and magnetic discs used.

If the computer supports a database, then a **database administrator** is in charge of this aspect of the work. The responsibilities of a database administrator are discussed in Section 24.6. If a data communication network is used, this is often under the overall charge of a **network administrator**.

28.10   New Directions in Job Definitions

In many organisations, computers have become such an integral part of their operations that a separate data processing department is not required. The majority of the workers in such organisations make some use of the computer. Programming and systems design is generally contracted out to software houses, or software packages are purchased.

An expanding computer application generally involving firms in this category is word processing. In many modern offices, all clerical, accounting and communications work is done on word processing systems. Most of the people working in these offices use a word processing work station to some extent.

28.11   Software Houses

Situated between computer manufacturers and computer users are **software houses**, or **computer service bureaux**. These provide a wide range of services, including consultancy on computer projects, supplying software to a customer's specifications, selling software and supplying complete computer systems. These organisations are described in more detail in Section 27.16.

Many software houses have extremely flexible working arrangements. Most of their workers are skilled in a variety of areas, including systems and applications programming, systems analysis, project management and computer design. A team of workers is assigned to each project which is undertaken. Work is shared among the members of the team according to their interests, capabilities and experience. There is no strict demarkation of jobs.

When a project has been completed, the team is disbanded. Workers are assigned to other projects. People who work in this manner are sometimes known as **software engineers**.

28.12   Conclusion

This chapter has provided a very brief survey of the commonest jobs created by the use of computers. It must be emphasised that, in spite of rising unemployment in many areas of work, there is generally a shortage of workers in the computing industry. Salaries in the computing field are, in the majority of cases, extremely attractive.

Exercise 28

1 Outline the work done by each of the following: electronics engineer; systems programmer; computer architect; field engineer; data processing manager; systems analyst; applications programmer; operations manager; data controller; database administrator; software engineer; network administrator.
2 Suggest one or more possible career paths for someone who starts working in the computing field as an applications programmer.
3 Compare working arrangements in a software house with those in a car assembly plant.
4 The list of data processing jobs mentioned in this chapter is not exhaustive. By studying the computer press, or some other suitable source, identify some jobs not described here. Write brief accounts of the nature of these jobs.
5 Comment on the fact that there are virtually no unskilled jobs in the computing industry.
6 One of the prime requirements for a job in the computing field is experience. This makes it difficult for new graduates, or people transferring from other areas of work, to obtain their first job in computing. Investigate this situation and comment on it.

29
Computing in perspective

This chapter takes a step back from the subject of computing, in order to view it in a broader perspective. To be able to do this, some of the ideas introduced in previous chapters are restated in more general terms. In addition, the social, economic and political background of computing is investigated. All this is in an attempt to give a rounded picture of computing. Where possible, a worldwide point of view is maintained, though the situation in Britain is often used as an example.

Some of the material introduced here is contentious, and will become increasingly so in the near future. It is impossible to be completely unbiased in presenting such material. The best that can be done is, wherever possible, to present both sides of the argument. Several questions in the exercise at the end of the chapter invite you to form and clarify your own opinions on some of the topics presented.

This chapter relates to all the material in the rest of the book. It should help to clarify some of the concepts introduced earlier, and show how certain of these concepts are related.

29.1   A Second Look at the Question 'What is a Computer?'

Much of the early part of this book is devoted to the question, 'What is a computer?'. Having studied the working and applications of computers, it is appropriate at this point to return to the original question.

A computer is a tool. Like a hammer, washing machine or car assembly plant, it is an extension of a person's capability to carry out a task. Although a computer is a very general-purpose tool, all the tasks it can help to perform are in one field of activity, namely information processing.

A computer has two major aspects, namely its hardware and its software. The hardware, increasingly comprising large scale integrated circuits, gives a computer its general-purpose information processing capability. Hardware is small, very reliable, uses very little electrical power, and is very cheap.

The software of a computer dedicates it to performing specific tasks. The software, in the form of stored instructions to the computer, is generally structured in layers. The innermost layers are closest to the hardware of the computer, whereas the outer layers form the interface with the user. Software is expensive, and, relative to hardware, somewhat error-prone.

However, with the increasing tendencies to store software on read-only memory, to control computers at the very lowest level by micro-instructions, and to include circuits in computers dedicated to specific tasks, the boundary between hardware and software is becoming blurred.

Although a very wide variety of computers is now available, the designs of all digital electronic computers are based on a few principles set out just after the Second World War. These principles include the storage of data and instructions together in the main store of a computer, and the idea of an instruction cycle to process one instruction at a time. Many contemporary computers have modified these principles, but the modifications are still variations on the same basic theme.

A computer is a system, a set of components working together to achieve some common objectives. In use, computers are components of larger systems, including the social, economic and political systems of modern society.

Finally, computers have been called 'intelligent'. This description must be treated with caution. A computer is more intelligent than a hammer, but less intelligent than a person. For example, unless the design principles of computers are radically changed, a computer will never be able to understand input in a natural language like

English. Computers cannot take initiatives, respond to unforeseen circumstances or make moral judgements.

29.2 Computers at work

Wherever there is a need to process information, computers can be put to work. Information processing includes storing and accessing information, creating and updating data structures, sorting and selecting information, performing calculations and controlling machinery. Computers can accept input from their environment, and in turn supply output to their environment. Computers are being linked to data communications networks to an increasing extent.

But the work done by computers can also be seen in a wider context. Computers create jobs for a large number of people who work with them, but put others out of work by taking over their jobs. The information processed by computers is sometimes sensitive personal information. Computer applications include such contentious areas as the guidance of nuclear weapons and the filing systems of secret police forces.

The next few sections of this chapter are a very brief exploration of the wider implications of the use of computers.

29.3 Implications of Computing

Computers have already had a profound impact on the economic and social fabric of the societies in which they are used. With the increasing availability of cheap microprocessors, an even wider impact is predicted. Some alarming prophecies have been made in this connection.

However, computers cannot be judged in isolation. Together with inflation, recession, war, famine, prejudice, and the effects of other technologies, computers are just one of the factors influencing the nature and direction of contemporary societies. To further complicate the situation, computers interact with these other factors.

The social implications of the use of computers is a very large, complex and controversial subject. All that can be done within the confines of this book is to outline the specific issues where concern has already been expressed, and give a broad overview of the pressures which are affecting the course of modern societies, showing the place of computers among these pressures.

29.4 The Areas of Concern

There has been unease about the effects of computers ever since they were first introduced. Misleading and exaggerated accounts in books, films and newspapers, and in television and radio reports have made the situation worse. But the biggest problem is the ignorance, on the part of the majority of people, of the nature, capabilities and limitations of computers.

This general unease has gradually focused on three major areas of concern about the implications of computers. These issues are employment and unemployment, privacy of personal information, and the use of computers in establishing and maintaining political control. Each of these issues is now briefly discussed.

29.5 Employment and Unemployment

It is an inescapable fact that computers and microprocessors in other devices put people out of work. But on the other hand, computers create jobs, both directly and indirectly. Jobs created directly include all the people who design, construct, program and operate computers. This is an enormous, prosperous and growing industry. By their contribution to efficiency and productivity, computers create and preserve jobs in an indirect way.

The net effect of all this is that computers are changing the nature of employment. Jobs are lost in manual and semi-skilled areas, and created in skilled and professional areas. This implies that a shift in training patterns, and considerable retraining of displaced workers is necessary, as one attempt to cope with the problem.

In the present economic climate, computers are not the only cause of unemployment. The recession currently affecting most Western nations, and the consequent drop in demand for such products as steel, motor cars and chemicals, are far bigger causes. For these reasons, studies of the unemployment that has been caused by computers, and projections of the unemployment that computers will cause, are contradictory. Very few firm conclusions can be drawn from them. This is not, however, a cause for complacency.

It seems that each application of computers must be judged on its merits, from the point of view of employment and unemployment. In all cases, it is necessary to take a broad view of the situation, in an attempt to see the long term effects, and the wider implications, of the introduction of computers at a particular place.

29.6   Privacy

The issue relating to the use of computers which affects the greatest number of people is the privacy of personal information stored by computers. Who should have access to this information? How safe is this information against unauthorised disclosure?

Although manual methods of storing personal information have been in operation for a long time, the widespread use of computers for this purpose makes the problem potentially far worse. In theory, it is now possible to obtain millions of items of information in a few seconds.

There are in fact two aspects to this problem, namely the deliberate disclosure of information by the people or organisations which store it, and the 'theft' of this information by outsiders.

With regard to the first aspect of the problem, a number of countries now have legislation regulating the storage and dissemination of personal information. These countries include the USA, France, Sweden and Canada. In spite of several committees of enquiry, and a White Paper on the subject, Britain has, at the time of writing, no legislation to protect stored information.

Concerning the second part of the problem, various attempts have been made to provide adequate security for stored confidential data. These include 'scrambling' the data into a code, limiting access to computers and terminals, and systems of passwords for people 'logging on' to the system. Just how effective these measures are, remains to be seen.

One fact must be stressed in this context. The pressure for privacy legislation, and for better security systems for stored data, has come mainly from within the computing industry. Although discontent has been expressed by the public at large, there has been no major public outcry on this issue.

29.7   Computers and Political Control

One of the most sinister applications of computers is their use by the security forces of a number of states, to store and process information about terrorists, spies, subversives and other 'persons of interest' to these forces. Indirect evidence suggests that this is a very widespread computer application, though official confirmation of the existence of these computers is very rare.

The problem is that there are no public safeguards on the use of such computers Most people would agree that every available resource needs to be used against spies and terrorists, but where does one draw the line? There is also evidence that so much information is gathered by some of these systems that it is impossible to sort out the vital from the trivial.

29.8   Computers in a World of Change

It has been pointed out since the days of ancient China that the only constant fact about civilisation is that it is changing. This section is an attempt to give a very brief assessment of the forces of change which are currently in operation in industrial societies, and identify the place of computers among these forces.

It seems that the pressures for change currently at work fall into five very broad categories. These are political and religious pressure, resource pressure, population pressure, pollution pressure and technological pressure. Each of these is now very briefly discussed.

29.9   Political and Religious Pressure

Both religious and political views incline people to have visions of the kind of society in which they want to live. In some countries, these pressures have their outlet in the political institutions of the state. Changes occur from time to time, but without too much dislocation or upheaval.

However, there are also numerous instances where political and/or religious motivation has led to terrorism, civil wars, forcible changes of government and conflicts of all types between states. Many such conflicts remain unresolved today, and in many parts of the world, no stable solutions are in sight. The ever-increasing power of available weapons, including nuclear weapons, is an additional factor which compounds the seriousness of these problems.

Political and religious pressure is the oldest and most visible force for change at present in operation. But it must now take its place among other pressures, and be affected by them.

29.10   Resource Pressure

Over the last decade it has become apparent that a number of the earth's natural resources are becoming seriously depleted, and will be completely used up in the foreseeable future if present trends in the consumption of these resources continue.

The most obvious resource in this category is oil. Oil producing countries have realised the degree of dependence of industrialised nations on their output, and the fact that their reserves are limited. Accordingly, the price of oil is being pushed higher and higher, with a number of consequences for both producers and consumers.

Other minerals, including a number of metals, are being depleted at an alarming rate. Renewable resources like timber and fish stocks are being used up faster than they can replenish themselves. Species of plants and animals are becoming extinct, depleting once and for all the 'pool' of genetic material available on earth.

Resource pressure is forcing a change in the way of life of many people. Its worst effects are being felt by poor and underprivileged individuals and nations at the present time, but it will begin to affect everyone in the near future.

29.11   Population Pressure

In spite of a number of efforts to control it, the global population is increasing at a disturbing rate. The largest increases are occurring in the poorest countries. It is almost impossible for food production to keep pace with population growth. The result is that North America and Europe have grain surpluses, wine lakes and butter mountains, while much of the rest of the world has malnutrition and famine.

Population pressure is a factor in the miserable way of life of a significant proportion of the people of the world. It may yet demand a change in the way of life of the rest before a more satisfactory state of affairs is reached.

29.12   Pollution Pressure

It is becoming increasingly clear that harmful substances are being released, by a number of industrial processes, into the air, water and ground which are beyond the capacity of the environment to dispose of. In spite of considerable success in some areas, notably the control of air pollution in certain cities, the problem of pollution is becoming worse. Certain enclosed seas such as the Baltic and the Mediterranean are in danger of losing their capacity to support marine life. An increasing number of poisons are present in air, water and food supplies. The percentage of carbon dioxide in the atmosphere is slowly but steadily increasing.

Most pollution is being caused by industrial nations. Pollution pressure is forcing these countries to change in a number of ways. Industrial, agricultural and domestic practices are having to adjust to increasingly stringent regulations. If pollution is not brought under control in the fairly near future, the consequences could be extremely serious.

29.13   Technological Pressure

Ever since the industrial revolution, technology has been the driving force in the evolution of Western societies. Each major breakthrough has had profound social repercussions. Furthermore, it appears that the pace of technological innovation is quickening.

Since the Second World War, we have seen jet engines revolutionise long distance transport, transistors lead to a multiplicity of cheap, high quality electronic devices, television create a global village, nuclear energy provide a significant proportion of electric power, nuclear weapons transform war into a potential global catastrophe, and computers become an essential aspect of industrial and commercial activity. Each of these changes has had beneficial and detrimental effects. One of the disadvantages is the upheaval caused by constant change, a phenomenon becoming known as future shock.

Computers must take their place amongst the technological innovations which are propelling societies forward. Although computers are a major influence, they are not the only influence in this field. Technological pressures must, in turn, take their place amongst the other pressures mentioned in previous sections. It very seldom happens that all these pressures are acting in the same direction. One reason for the complexity and lack of cohesion of contemporary societies is that they are at the mercy of a number of different forces, none of which is very clearly understood, pushing the societies in different directions.

29.14 Conclusion

This chapter has presented, in a very condensed form, a retrospective overview of the nature of computers, the work they do, and some of the effects they are having on the societies in which they are used. The place of computers among the many pressures determining the course of these societies has also been discussed.

This chapter has skirted round the question 'Are computers a good thing?' Occasionally, rather extreme answers, in one direction or the other, are given to this question. This chapter makes the case that the answer to this question must lie between the two extremes.

On the one hand, consider the situation where computers are used to the maximum extent which is technically possible. The result would be an economic and social disaster, with massive unemployment, widespread discontent and disorder amongst large sections of the population, a highly regimented way of life and repressive governments.

On the other hand, consider the situation where computers are phased out completely. This would result in the collapse of the financial systems, and of most industrial and commercial organisations in all developed countries. Supplies of food, gas, electricity and water would be adversely affected. Standards of local and national administration, policing and medical services would suffer. The high standard of life which we have come to expect would no longer be possible.

The sane alternative is to steer a middle course, judging each computer application on its merits, and taking into account both the immediate and the wider implications of the situation. In the forseeable future, the further spread of computers will probably become a political issue. The more people there are who know something about computers, the better are the chances of reaching a satisfactory consensus on these issues.

Exercise 29

1 Put the question 'What is a computer?' to a number of people, particularly people not concerned with computing. Make a note of the answers you receive.

In the light of your findings, discuss any common misconceptions about the nature of computers you observe. Discuss the significance of these misconceptions in relation to the further acceptance of computers, and suggest ways in which these misconceptions might be reduced.

2 Identify the design principles of computers which have remained the same since the Second World War.

□ 3 Identify the most significant aspects of computing which may be described as systems. State briefly the objectives of each system, and mention any major subsystems.

4 Comment on the use of the word 'intelligent' in relation to computers.

5 In the light of your knowledge of computers, identify one or more accounts of the impact of computers in a book, film, newspaper, or television or radio programme which may be described as 'exaggerated and misleading'. Justify your choice(s).

6 Give your views on the issue of computers and unemployment. Include your comments on the following topics:

Whether computers are in any way related to other major causes of unemployment, such as declining industries like steel making and motor car manufacture.

Whether you think that the increased job opportunities created by computers offsets the unemployment they cause.

What the effect of computers on unemployment will be in the future.

7 Name some areas in which you think computers should not be introduced because of the unemployment which would be caused.

8 Find out the attitude of some Trade Unions towards the introduction of computers.

9 Give your views on the issue of computers and privacy. Include your comments on the following topics:

The extent to which privacy is already being abused by various computer applications.

The potential for abuse of privacy in the future, by computer applications.

Whether legislation should be introduced in this area, and, if so, what form the legislation should take.

10 Find out about the privacy laws existing in some countries. Briefly describe each situation you investigate, and identify similarities and differences between them.

11 Give your views on the issue of computers and political control. Mention what (if any) safeguards you think should be placed on the use of computers in this area.

☐ 12 Outline some of the most significant changes which, in your view, have been brought about by the introduction of the following technologies:

telephone;
radio;
television;
motor cars;
jet passenger aeroplanes;
nuclear weapons.

13 Give your own views on the most significant factors causing change in societies today. Identify the relative importance of computers among these factors.

30
The future of computing

The problem with writing about the future of computing is that events catch up with prediction at an alarming rate. Almost the only thing that can be said with certainty is that computing has a future, playing an increasing role in almost every walk of life in industrial countries.

An additional problem is the great number of potential future applications in the field of computing, far too many to be discussed in any detail here. The best that can be done is to mention the most significant trends, and identify a few particular developments which seem likely to be especially important.

This chapter looks at the future of computing in four areas, namely concepts of computing, hardware, software and applications, though it is realised that developments in these areas are to some extent interconnected. Accordingly, the chapter concludes with a section on general development areas.

30.1   Concepts of Computing

Electronic digital computers are based on a small number of fundamental concepts which have remained unchanged since the Second World War. These concepts include the binary representation of data and instructions, the idea of an addressable store, the idea of a stored program, and the use of registers. Although such concepts as pipelining, content-addressable store and parallelism have come into use more recently, they enhance, but do not replace, the original concepts.

These simple concepts determine both the strengths and the limitations of computers as we know them today. On the one hand, they give rise to the speed, reliability and precision of computers. But on the other hand they place a limit on the 'intelligence' of computers. For example, no computer based on these principles will ever be able to 'understand' a natural language like English. Although these principles will no doubt continue to be further enhanced, it seems unlikely that they will be fundamentally altered in the foreseeable future.

One area of development is worth mentioning in this context, as it relates to the fundamental concepts of computing. This area is the field of **artificial intelligence**. Artificial intelligence is the subject of intensive research, notably at a few leading universities. Some of the results achieved so far have been used in such areas as chess playing programs. It remains to be seen whether any major breakthroughs will emerge from this work.

30.2   Hardware

Computer hardware is the area in which development is most rapid, and most spectacular. It is fairly certain that the recent trends towards smaller, faster, more reliable and cheaper hardware elements will continue. No doubt limits of size and performance will be reached, but these limits are not in sight at the moment.

It is also fairly certain that new materials and new techniques will come into use. For example, the next few years should see the first applications of **magnetic bubble memories** and **Josephson junctions**.

Magnetic bubble memories store bit patterns of data by means of tiny 'bubbles' of magnetism, which are made to move along a magnetic material by the creation of new bubbles behind them. When they reach the edge of the material the bubbles are read, and, if necessary, re-written onto the other end of the material.

A Josephson junction is a solid-state switch which works at a very low temperature, close to absolute zero. It is the basic building block of an integrated circuit which operates many times faster than the highest speed possible with conventional technology.

One hardware area where there is scope for completely new devices is computer peripherals. Possibilities include flat liquid crystal display screens, and a variety of input/output devices for graphics, speech synthesis and voice recognition. There will probably be a proliferation of special purpose peripherals, following the lead of banking terminals.

30.3 Software

Far less visible than hardware developments, but none the less crucial, are developments in the software field. Here, the main area of progress seems to be an increasing clarity as to what is required of a high level programming language. Accordingly, the rate of proliferation of new programming languages will probably slow down, as attention focuses on the few more successful ones.

The old favourites, Cobol and Fortran, still have plenty of life in them. Increasing competition is developing between Basic and Pascal in certain areas such as higher education. It is doubtful whether either language will replace the other, but their respective 'territories' will probably become more clearly defined. Much attention is being centred on Ada as it becomes operational. It remains to be seen whether it will fulfil its design objectives of being suitable for large software projects, particularly systems software and real-time applications.

Progress will no doubt continue in the background areas of software, particularly language design and abstract data types. The field of proving the correctness of programs, as if they were mathematical theorems, is still in its infancy. Hopefully, work in these areas will lead to better structured, more correct programs.

Current research in programming languages is directed towards a level of languages 'above' high level languages. These languages are becoming known as **specification languages**. It is felt that, although high level languages are problem oriented, they are still too closely tied to the structure and functioning of computers. A specification language is aimed at providing a user-oriented way of specifying the requirements of a task or problem. This specification is then translated into a program, in a high or low level language.

30.4 Applications

Three major trends are apparent in computer applications. The first is the increasing popularity of real-time systems. The second is the emergence of computers from guarded, air-conditioned rooms into offices, factories, schools and homes. The third is the increasing tendency to link computers to communication networks. Local area networks seems likely to be one of the most significant growth areas in computing in the forseeable future.

These tendencies are steadily altering the range of services which are offered by computers, and are giving rise to thousands of potential new applications. Many established computer users are introducing real-time methods, and replacing large, costly equipment with newer, cheaper but usually more powerful models.

Adverse economic conditions do not appear to be having much effect on the continued spread of computers. Hardware prices continue to run counter to inflation, though software costs are generally tied to wages, and increase accordingly. In some cases it seems that companies are being faced with a choice between two alternatives: using computers to become more efficient, or going out of business.

30.5 General Tendencies

There are a few general trends in computing which cannot be classified as hardware, software or applications developments. These are discussed here.

One of the more obvious trends is the move away from general-purpose computers, to dedicated systems, where the hardware is tailored to a specific task, and the software is thus much simplified. Examples already in operation are electronic telephone exchanges, word processors and the microprocessors used in some cameras. With the price of hardware continuing to fall, this promises to be a very big growth area in computing.

Another of these trends is a tendency to a much more sophisticated user interface in many systems. Graphics and voice recognition play an important part in this. This tendency stems from the realisation that computers are there to serve the needs of the user, and not vice versa.

A third tendency, which has already been mentioned briefly, is the increasing use of data communication. This will affect both hardware and software design, and open up many new areas of applications. Local area networks, enabling resources such as large backing stores to be shared by a number of microprocessors, are particularly promising.

30.6 A Case Study of the Future: The Intel 432 micromainframe

An outstanding example of the direction of computing in the 80s is provided by the **Intel 432 micromainframe**. Using only three chips, it has the following significant features:

> 32 bit processing;
> a high level instruction set;
> a silicon operating system;
> an architecture tailored to the support of high level languages such as Ada.

The Intel 432 is superior in processing power to many mainframe computers in use during the 70s. Although it is a general-purpose device, its main applications area is the support of real-time, multi-function activities. The processing chips can be configured in a number of different ways, to support various degrees of multi-processing and communication between processors.

Instructions are implemented in microcode. The instruction set supports all four arithmetic operations on integers and floating point numbers of several different lengths. Operating system functions are also included in the instruction set.

The fact that the operating system is an integral part of the hardware means that the time spent carrying out operating system functions is kept to a minimum. The operating system supports an extremely sophisticated virtual store mechanism, with a virtual address space of 2^{40} bytes. Extensive use is made of cache stores for the rapid transfer and processing of data and instructions. Associative stores are also used.

The software philosophy of the Intel 432 is based on a hierarchy of **objects**. Objects include processors, processes, contexts, static and dynamic data structures and blocks of code. Code and data are always stored as separate objects. One of the objectives of the design of the Intel 432 is the reduction of software costs.

When the Intel 432 goes into volume production, it is hoped that a price of $200 per processing chip will be achieved.

30.7 Conclusion

This chapter has provided a very brief survey of the most significant trends at present evident in the field of computing. A few individual developments of particular significance in the forseeable future have been identified.

In conclusion, it seems appropriate to devote a few words to the limits to the growth of computing, in each of the areas mentioned in the chapter.

From the conceptual point of view, unless there is a major breakthrough, computers will continue to be constrained by the limitations of the fundamental principles which form the basis of their design. In hardware, physical limits of speed, size and storage capacity will eventually be reached. In software, the situation is less well defined. Various common techniques such as sorting and searching seem to be approaching the limits of their efficiency already. The gulf between high level languages and machine architecture is another limiting factor.

In computer applications, the rate of growth seems at the moment to be almost unchecked. However, it seems certain that, if technical and economic factors do not begin to moderate this growth, then social and political considerations will become the deciding factors.

In the short and medium term, the future of computing as a growing, thriving activity seems assured. In the longer term, provided that the transition from expansion to a state of stability and consolidation can be accomplished smoothly, the prospects for computing seem very promising indeed.

Exercise 30

1 Using the material from this chapter, as well as your own observations, identify the five current developments in computing which, in your opinion, will have the most significant impact in the near future.
2 Give your own views on the possibilities of fundamental changes in computer design in the near future.
3 Comment on the trend from general purpose towards special purpose computers.
4 Give your views on the future of 'traditional' programming languages like Fortran, Cobol and Algol.
5 List some application areas of computers which you think will develop in the near future.
6 Give your opinion on the effects of adverse economic conditions on the future expansion of computers.
7 Give your opinion of the limits to growth of computing.

31
Revision exercises

All the questions in this exercise are taken from past examination papers in Computing Science. In most cases, questions cover material in more than one chapter of the book.

1 a) Explain the difference between an **operand** and an **operand address** as used with reference to an assembly language. State *four* ways in which the address part of a machine level instruction may be used *and* give an example of each.

b) Describe *one* method of representing alphanumeric characters for storage in a fixed word length of 24 bits. State *two* machine code operations which are desirable for the internal manipulation of such characters.

c) Describe, with the aid of a diagram, *one* method of storing data items based on the principle of **last-in – first-out**. Draw flow diagrams to show how an item of data can be removed from the store you have described and how an item of data can be input, incorporating tests to examine whether the store is full or empty as necessary.

AEB 79 I

2 a) Explain, with the aid of a block diagram, how the major functional units of a simple computer are interrelated with respect to the flow of information (i.e. instructions and data) and the flow of control commands.

Note: Use firm lines to show information flow and dotted lines to show flow of control commands.

Draw a flow diagram to represent the basic process of the **fetch – execute** cycle in the control unit of a typical computer, naming and stating the functions of any special registers involved. Your diagram should show how the cycle takes account of jumps, address modification and indirect addressing.

Note: You are not required to discuss or represent the electronic circuitry of the control unit.

AEB 79 I

3 a) Describe the operation of *either* (i) a key to disc encoder, *or* (ii) a key to tape encoder.

b) Describe the principle of operation of **one** output device with which you are familiar. State **one** advantage and **one** disadvantage of the device. Explain briefly how the design and operation of the device may be influenced in the future by advances in computer technology.

c) Discuss the relative merits of punched paper tape and punched cards as data preparation media making particular reference to the detection of errors, speed and cost.

AEB 79 I

4 a) Explain how multiprogramming assists in maximising the use of the central processor.

b) Discuss the term **interrupt** making particular reference to **peripheral interrupts** and **error interrupts**.

AEB 79 I

5 a) What is meant by the term **operating system**? State *four* of the functions of an operating system.

b) Describe what is involved when an assembly language program is translated into machine instructions including in your discussion reference to **labelled instructions**, **jump instructions** and **directives**.

AEB 79 I

6 An engineering company manufactures components using numerically controlled machine tools. The main computer users in the company are:
a) Accounts and Finance Section who are responsible for administrative tasks
such as invoicing, orders and payroll.
b) Operational Research Section who investigate how processes may be
made more efficient.
c) Development Section who produce programs for the machine tools.
i) For each of the above sections, name a high level language that would
be suitable for their applications, describing the features that make it
appropriate.
ii) All programs submitted to the Computer Section are run under an
operating system. Give a brief description of a control language for an
operating system and explain how it assists the user.

AEB 79 II

7 In relationship to computer systems, explain the meaning and purpose of the
following:
i) feasibility study;
ii) system flowchart;
iii) source document and turnaround document;
iv) system maintenance.

AEB 79 II

8 Variables declared in a routine which is called recursively cannot be allocated
fixed storage space.
a) Explain why this is so.
b) Describe briefly, by means of diagrams or otherwise, how storage could
be allocated and released as required.

UCLES 81 Specimen I

9 a) The truth table for the NOR operation is as follows:

P	q	p NOR q
0	0	1
0	1	0
1	0	0
1	1	0

(0 represents zero)

The NOT operation may be defined in terms of the NOR operation, by

NOT $p = p$ NOR p

Define the AND operation in terms of the NOR and NOT operations.
b) The assembly language for a certain computer has only a single logical
instruction, NOR, as described below.

NOR A forms the bit by bit logical NOR of the content of the
accumulator with the content of address **A**, and places the
result in the accumulator.

Some other instructions in the assembly language are as follows:

LOAD A   loads the accumulator with the content of address **A**.
STORE A   stores the content of the accumulator in address **A**.
INCR A   increments of the content address **A** by 1.
JUMP A   the next instruction to be executed is at address **A**.

JSUB   A stores the link address (the address of the **JSUB** instruction + I) in address **A** and jumps to address **A + 1**.

If **! A** is written instead of **A**, the address which is the content of address **A**
is used.

If an operand is not preceded by an instruction the line represents a data
word whose initial content is the value of the operand (a constant or the
address associated with an identifier).

The rest of the line following a ★ is treated as a comment.

A subroutine to perform the NOT operation on the content of the
accumulator could be written

```
★SUBROUTINE NOT:  ACC:= NOT ACC
NOTWS:          Ø           ★WORKING STORE
NOT:            Ø           ★ENTRY POINT
        STORE   NOTWS
        NOR     NOTWS       ★P NOR P IS NOT P
        JUMP    !NOT        ★EXIT
★END OF NOT
```

and it would be called in the following sequence which sets the content of
B to the logical NOT of the content of **A**.

```
        LOAD    A
        JSUB    NOT  ★ACC:= NOT ACC
        STORE   B
```

The sequence

```
START:  LOAD    A
        JSUB    AND  ★ACC:= ACC AND PARAMETER
                B    ★ADDRESS OF PARAMETER
        STORE   C
```

(in which the third line forms a word containing the address **B**) is used to
set the content of **C** to the logical AND of the contents of **A** and **B**.

Write the subroutine AND. You may, if you wish, make use of the
subroutine NOT.

Assuming that at execution time the labels **NOT**, **AND** and **START**
are addresses **103**, **120** and **180**, and that **A**, **B** and **C** are addresses
200, **201** and **202**, copy and complete the following table up to the
state after the instruction **STORE C**.

Instruction address	ACC	A (200)	B (201)	C (202)	NOT (103)	NOTWS (102)	AND (120)	....
180	5	5	3	unknown	0	0	0	
181								182
121								

10 a) Explain with the aid of diagrams how data records can be deleted from and inserted into a linked list. Describe from a programmer's point of view how to set up a linked list and how to manage the free storage.

A list of identifiers is stored as follows:

 i) the character codes of the first and the last characters of the identifier are added to the length of the identifier and the result is divided by 16, the remainder providing a hash value;

 ii) the entry in a hash table corresponding to the hash value contains either zero, indicating no identifier with this hash value, or a pointer to an identifier;

 iii) associated with the identifier is a value of either zero, indicating no further identifiers with this hash value, or a pointer to another identifier with this hash value.

b) Show this structure in a diagram, and describe how a new item may be added to the list.

c) What is the purpose of the type of calculation described above in (i)?

UCLES 81 Specimen II

11 Figure 31.1 is a block diagram of a parallel adder that can add 3-bit binary 2s complement numbers $a_2 a_1 a_0$ and $b_2 b_1 b_0$. (Each block marked FA in the figure is a full adder.)

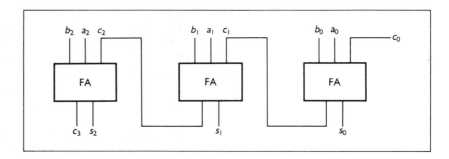

Figure 31.1

a) i) Write a truth table for c_2 as a function of a_1, b_1 and c_1.

 ii) Minimise this function and draw a minimal logic circuit that has inputs a_1, b_1, c_1 and output c_2.

b) Draw the figure again but now with extra gates needed for computing

$$b_2 b_1 b_0 - a_2 a_1 a_0$$

using three full adders. State the value that should be applied to c_0 when subtraction is required, but do not show internal details of any full adder.

c) Draw a circuit that has as inputs a control signal d and two binary numbers $b_2 b_1 b_0$ and $a_2 a_1 a_0$.

If $d = 1$ the output of the circuit is to be $b_2 b_1 b_0 - a_2 a_1 a_0$. If $d = 0$ the output of the circuit is to be $b_2 b_1 b_0 + a_2 a_1 a_0$. Subtraction must be achieved by using three full adders. Your diagram should show how c_0 is determined by d. Do not show internal details of any full adder, but represent each full adder by a block marked FA, as in the figure.

JMB 79 1

12 Below is an assembly code fragment. Each instruction is followed by a semicolon and an explanatory comment, in which 'ac' stands for the accumulator (the contents of ac are unchanged by instructions such as **SA GVN** and **JZ PRIN**). **NEXT, NOCH, PRIN,** and **FINIS** are labels.

Execution of this fragment starts at the first instruction. Locations 100 to 127 contain the following integers which remain unchanged. All values are decimal.

location	contents	location	contents	location	contents	location	contents
100	63	101	1093	102	104	103	112
104	42	105	217	106	108	107	120
108	19	109	486	110	0	111	0
112	69	113	3211	114	116	115	124
116	66	117	7298	118	0	119	0
120	45	121	556	122	0	123	0
124	96	125	188	126	0	127	0

i) After this fragment has been executed once, with input 45, what value is printed? Show clearly the working by which you obtain your answer.

ii) After this fragment has been executed again, with input 66, what value is printed?

iii) Locations 100 to 127 contain a data structure that facilitates access to data. Name this structure and draw a diagram of it, showing the contents of all locations in this structure.

```
        RA                  ; read an integer into ac
        SA   GVN            ; store ac in location GVN
        LN   100            ; load value 100 into ac
        SA   CRN            ; store ac in location CRN
NEXT:LA@CRN                 ; load into ac contents of location whose address
                              is stored in CRN
        SB   GVN            ; subtract contents of GVN from ac, leaving result
                              in ac
        SA   RES            ; store ac in location RES
        JZ   PRIN           ; jump to PRIN if contents of ac equal zero
        LA   CRN            ; load contents of CRN into ac
        AN   2              ; add 2 to ac leaving result in ac
        SA   CRN            ; store ac in CRN
        LA   RES            ; load contents of RES into ac
        JG   NOCH           ; jump to NOCH if contents of ac greater than 0
        LA   CRN            ; load contents of CRN into ac
        AN   1              ; add 1 to ac leaving result in ac
        SA   CRN            ; store ac in CRN
NOCH:LA@CRN                 ; load into ac contents of location whose address
                              is stored in CRN
        JZ   FINIS          ; jump to finish if contents of ac equal zero
        SA   CRN            ; store ac in CRN
        JU   NEXT           ; jump unconditionally to NEXT
PRIN:LA   CRN               ; load contents of CRN into ac
        AN   1              ; add 1 to ac
        SA   CRN            ; store ac in CRN
        LA@CRN              ; Load into ac the contents of the location whose
                              address is stored in CRN
        WA                  ; print contents of accumulator
FINIS:                      ; the rest of the program need not concern you.
```

13 Order processing is implemented in both batch and real-time mode. Describe briefly two applications to illustrate respectively each mode of implementation.

For each application give details of the method of data collection and conversion to machine readable form. Explain why the data collection methods are appropriate.

In both cases there will be a need for data validation. Suggest ways in which this validation can be done.

UL 79 II

14 a) What is an **interrupt**? Give three examples of situations which can lead to interrupts.
   b) Why do different interrupts have different priorities? Illustrate your answer by discussing a situation in which two interrupts of different priority have to be dealt with together.
   c) Describe how input and output can be carried out under system (rather than program) control and indicate the advantages of this.

OLE 78 I

15 a) Define the terms **pointer, linked list, tree, first-in – first-out list**.
   b) Explain how pointers can be used (i) to add a new item to a linked list, (ii) to remove an item in the middle of such a list, (iii) to join two such lists to form a single list.
   c) Show how storage in terms of linked lists could be used to hold information about distances between towns.

OLE 78 I

16 a) Describe the structure of the files which would be needed by a regional health authority to contain a computer record of the medical history of patients living in its area.
   b) What computing equipment would be necessary if such files were to be used by hospital staff and general practitioners?
   c) What benefits might be secured by such a system?
   d) Discuss the safeguards for confidentiality which would be desirable in such a system, and explain how they could be provided.

OLE 78 II

17 a) Explain why, for tables of information held alphabetically, as in a dictionary, it is not usually possible to compute the exact address at which a given entry will be found.
   b) Explain three methods of constructing and using such a table in which the searching time for an entry is respectively:
      i) proportional to the length of the table;
      ii) increasing with length of table, but less than proportionally;
      iii) independent of table length, but dependent on the proportion of storage filled by the table.
   c) Give one example in each case to illustrate situations in which each of these methods would be appropriate.

OLE 80 I

18 a) Show how the logical function NOT-Equivalent (Exclusive OR) can be constructed from AND and NOT *only*.
   b) Construct a truth table for
   (A AND (NOT C)) AND (B OR C) AND (NOT ((NOT B) AND C)) and so simplify the expression.
   c) Two three-bit binary integers *abc* and *def* are added together. Explain why a four-bit number *ghij* may result. Write down logical expressions for each of *j, i, h* and *g* in terms of *a* to *f*.

d) Explain why **shift characters** are required to represent the decimal digits and letter of the alphabet on 5-hole paper tape, and show how this can be done.

OLE 78 I

19 Draw a diagram to represent a linked list held in immediate access storage, where it is required to hold both forward and backward links.

Draw a similar diagram to show how the list is represented when it is empty of data items.

Give an algorithm, diagrammatically or otherwise, for the insertion of a new item at the end (tail) of the list.

Would this linked list structure be suitable for the storage of a **stack**? Give reasons for your answer.

UL 80 I

20 Describe how the following data structures may be organised when used by a program in an assembly language, indicating how data is placed in and retrieved from each structure:
a) an array,
b) a stack,
c) a tree.

UL 80 II

21 Explain how a multiprogramming system functions.

A time-sharing system with many terminal users is using a multiprogramming operating system. Describe the way in which the file system can be arranged so that users can share files. What is meant by security and reliability in the context of file processing?

UL 80 II

22 Software is to be used to convert any given 6-bit character code, by reference to immediate access memory, into a corresponding 12-bit punched-card character code. State in words a very fast method for this code conversion, assuming that the stored data is appropriately organised and that there is sufficient immediate access memory with at least twelve bits per word.

JMB 80 I

23 A particular index-sequentially organised file has only one level of indexing and only one index, which has already been read into immediate access memory. The file is subdivided into blocks and the index has one entry per block. There is no overflow. Omitting low-level details, give an alogorithm, either in words or with the help of a flowchart, for efficiently retrieving one record from this file, given the key.

JMB 80 I

24 a) Simplify the logic circuit in Figure 31.2.
b) The arithmetic and logic unit (ALU) of a particular computer has eight

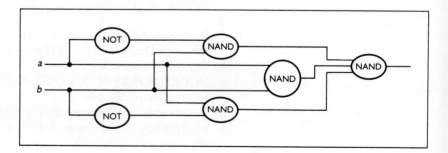

Figure 31.2

functions such as **ADD, SUBTRACT, NEGATE, ADD COM-PLEMENT,** and so on. The ALU function is selected by a three-bit function code. One of the control inputs to the ALU should be set equal to zero for functions **ADD, AND, SUBTRACT,** and **ADD COM-PLEMENT,** and should be set equal to one for the other four functions. Design a minimal logic circuit whose output is this control input to the ALU and whose input is the three-bit function code. The function codes for **ADD, AND, SUBTRACT** and **ADD COMPLEMENT** are respectively 001, 010, 101 and 110.

c) A simple multiplexor circuit has six binary inputs a, b, c, d, x, y and one output p. Inputs a, b, c, d are data bits and x and y are control inputs. Draw a logic design for this circuit such that:

> if $x = 0$ and $y = 0$ then $p = a$;
> if $x = 0$ and $y = 1$ then $p = b$;
> if $x = 1$ and $y = 1$ then $p = c$;
> if $x = 1$ and $y = 0$ then $p = d$.

JMB 80 I

25 a) The minimum unit of data transferred between immediate access memory and disc is normally a block, whereas the minimum unit of data transferred between central processor unit and paper tape reader is normally one character. Account for this difference.

b) Draw a diagram, with annotations, to show clearly how one disc surface is physically divided into blocks.

c) In a particular installation a specific random access file is physically held entirely within one cylinder of a magnetic disc unit. Explain why this may be better than distributing the file over more than one cylinder.

d) Explain what is meant by peripheral transfer.

e) i) Explain what is meant by double-buffering.

ii) Give one example of a situation where double-buffering would be appropriate.

iii) Give one example of a situation where double-buffering would not be appropriate.

JMB 80 II

26 a) Using *either* address modification *or* indirect addressing, write an assembler language program to read thirty characters and output them in the reverse order. Beside each instruction write an explanatory comment to say what that instruction does.

b) Write an assembler language program to read one character into an accumulator, and either print letter E, if the parity of the character code now in the accumulator is even, or print letter O, if if it is odd. Use shifting and counting to determine parity. Beside each instruction write an explanatory comment to say what that instruction does.

JMB 80 II

27 Various systems are available that enable a user at home to receive computer data via a television set.

Assuming that such systems were developed to enable home users to receive and transmit information and to create and use data files, suggest, with reasons,

a) the facilities which such a service should provide for the user;

b) how this service could be used to manage household and personal affairs;

c) how this service could change the nature of data processing industry.

JMB 80 II

28 A large retail organisation, having department stores in a number of large towns, wishes to install a central computer at the head office, with on-line terminals at each store and at a central warehouse in order to control stock.
   a) Suggest, with reasons, a configuration for the computer system and clearly describe the use of the terminal devices.
   b) Construct systems flowcharts that show both the functions of the system as well as the use of files.
   c) Explain what benefits the organisation might reasonably expect from the installation of the system.

JMB 80 11

29 Explain the functions of the following personnel in a computer installation, clearly identifying any inter-relationships between them.
   i) Systems Analyst
   ii) Programmer
   iii) Computer Operations staff
   iv) Job control clerk

JMB 80 11

Glossary of terms

This glossary contains brief explanations of the technical terms introduced and used in the book. In a few cases, a word or phrase has more than one meaning depending on the context. When this occurs, the alternative meanings are clearly marked.

absolute address   an address which identifies a store location without any modification being required.

acceptance testing   testing of a computer, item of software or data processing system by its intending users.

access privileges   an indication, on a file, of the extent to which the information in the file may be shared.

accumulator   a register storing a data item during processing.

acoustic coupler   a device used for data transmission and reception which interfaces with a telephone handset.

address   a number which locates a particular storage space in main store or on certain types of backing store.

address generation   the process of obtaining the address of a record in a random file from the key of the record.

address modification   indexed, indirect or relative addressing.

addressing mode   the method of addressing used in a particular machine instruction.

algorithm   a description of the steps needed to carry out a task.

alphanumeric   characters which may be letters or digits.

American Standard Code for Information Interchange (ASCII)   a code very commonly used for data transmission, and becoming increasingly popular for data representation on storage media.

applications programmer   a programmer whose work is concerned with applications software.

arithmetic and logic unit (ALU)   the part of a processor where arithmetic and logical operations are performed.

array   a fixed number of data items of identical type, stored together.

assembler   a program which translates from the assembly language to the machine language of a particular computer.

assembly language   a programming language whose data structures correspond to the physical structure of the registers and main store of its host computer, and whose instructions are closely related to the machine instructions of the computer.

assignment   the process whereby a variable takes on a value.

associative store   a cache store which, when supplied with the value of a data item, returns the address of the item.

backing store   storage for large quantities of data, accessible to a processor.

backing store control unit   a unit which controls the flow of data to and from a set of backing store devices.

bar code   a character code in terms of patterns of thick and thin stripes.

base language   the language in which a compiler is written.

batch processing   the running of a number of programs in succession, in a batch.

batch total   the total of various numeric items in a batch of input data.

baud   a rate of data transmission which is approximately equal to one bit per second.

beat   the time interval for one stage of a pipelined operation.

binary   base two.

binary coded decimal (BCD)   a numeric code in which each decimal digit is coded separately in binary.

binary search a method of searching a file involving partitioning it into successively smaller subsets, each of which is known to contain the required record.

binary tree a tree in which each node may have at most two subtrees.

bistable see **flip-flop.**

bit a binary digit, a 0 or a 1.

bit serial data transmission the transmission of data one bit at a time.

block (1) the unit of data transferred to or from a magnetic tape or disc in one operation, and stored as a physically separate entity.

block (2) a structural element in programs in certain high level languages.

blocking factor the number of records per block for a file stored on a magnetic tape or disc.

block-structured language a high level programming language which allows programs to be structured in blocks.

BNF a notation for writing syntax rules.

Boolean algebra a system of notation for Boolean logic.

Boolean logic the theory of mathematical logic, first investigated by George Boole.

Boolean operation an operation which transforms one or more Boolean variables, producing a Boolean variable as a result.

Boolean variable a variable which can have either of two values only.

bootstrap loader a program which, with minimal assistance, loads itself onto a computer and then enables other programs to be loaded.

branch a transfer of control from one part of a program to another.

breakpoint an instruction which causes the running of a program to be suspended.

buffer a storage area for data in transit to or from main store or a peripheral device.

build to construct a program from its constituent modules.

bus a passage for the transmission of data, address and control signals within a computer.

byte a set of bits containing the code for one character, generally eight bits.

cache store a small, fast store between a processor and a large main store.

call to transfer control to a procedure, function or subprogram.

card image a unit of stored or displayed data having the same characteristics as a punched card.

carry bit a bit which is set if there is a carry out of the most significant place during addition.

carry prediction circuits logic circuits used in fast parallel adders to determine the value of each carry directly from the inputs.

central processing unit (CPU) the unit of a computer system in which processing takes place.

character code a code in which each character is coded separately as a set of binary digits.

character printer a printer which prints one character at a time.

character set (1) the set of characters which can be represented in a particular character code.

character set (2) the set of all characters which may be used by a particular computer or programming language.

check digit a character appended to a data item (generally numeric) which enables the validity of the item to be checked.

check sum a data item appended to a transmitted block of data, containing the sum of the other bytes or words in the block.

chip a common word for integrated circuit.

circular buffer   a fixed area of store containing a queue, in which the rear of the queue 'wraps around' to the top of the area whenever it reaches the bottom.

circular list   a list in which items are linked in a closed loop.

clock pulse generator   a device which generates timing pulses for a processor.

cluster adaptor   see **multiplexer**.

code generation   the production of object code during the compilation process.

communications processor   a processor handling the communications traffic between another processor and a communications network.

compiler   a program which accepts a source program in a high level language and translates it into an object program in a machine language.

compression   a technique for the reduction of the number of characters transmitted in a data communication system.

computer   a collection of resources, including digital electronic processing devices, stored programs and sets of data, which, under the control of the stored programs, automatically inputs, processes and outputs data, and may also store and retrieve data.

computer architect   a person responsible for the overall design of a computer.

computer operator   a person who operates a computer.

computer output on microfilm (COM)   reducing displayed output onto microfilm.

condition codes   bits which indicate the current status of a processor.

Conference on Data Systems Languages (CODASYL)   the overall steering committee for the maintenance and development of Cobol.

console log   a record of all the commands to an operating system, and messages from the system, in chronological order.

constant   a data item which retains the same value throughout the running of a program.

content-addressable store   see **associative store**.

control character   a character used in data transmission to perform some control function.

control memory   memory (generally ROM) in which microcode is stored.

control switch   a solid-state switch which regulates the passage of data on a bus.

control unit   the unit which controls the step-by-step operation of a processor.

cross assembler   an assembler which runs on a different computer from the one for which it is assembling programs.

cylinder   a set of tracks, vertically above each other on a magnetic disc pack, which can be accessed with the read-write head in the same position.

data   information in a coded form, acceptable for input to, and processing by, a computer system.

data channel   a pathway for the passage of data inside a computer.

data controller   a person who controls the flow of data to a computer.

data entry staff   people who operate data entry terminals.

data highway   see **data channel**.

data independence   the separation of the (logical) data model of a database from the (physical) structure of the stored data.

data model   the logical structure of the data as it appears at a particular level of a database system.

data processing   a general term describing the work done by a computer.

data processing cycle   the sequence of actions carried out during the development of a new data processing application.

data processing department   the division or section of a company with direct responsibility for data processing.

data processing manager (DPM)   the person in charge of a data processing department.

data structure   a set of data in which individual items are related in a particular way, and on which certain precisely specified operations can be performed.

data type   a data item or data structure having certain properties.

database   a collection of stored operational data used by all the application systems of an organisation.

database administrator (DBA)   the person in charge of the overall running of a database system.

database management system (DBMS)   the software responsible for all aspects of the creation, accessing and updating of a database.

deadlock   the situation arising when two programs prevent each other from continuing because each holds a resource needed by the other.

deck   a set of punched cards.

declaration   a statement of the name and type of a variable in a program.

decoder   a logic circuit which selects one of a number of outputs according to the code of an input signal.

dedicated computer   a computer designed for a specific task or narrow range of tasks.

dedicated register   a register with one specific function.

device   a physical unit which carries out some operation.

diagnostic error message   a message output by a computer, indicating the location and cause of an error in a program.

diagnostics   the process of locating an error and determining its cause, carried out by a computer.

diagnostics program   a program which examines the current state of a computer, displaying the contents of various registers and store locations.

dictionary   a set of information created and accessed during the compilation process.

digital   the representation of data in discrete quantities.

digital plotter   an output device which draws maps, plans, engineering drawings, etc.

dimension   the number of indices associated with an array.

direct data entry (DDE)   data entry directly onto backing store.

direct memory access (DMA)   direct access by peripheral devices to main store, bypassing processor registers.

directive   an assembly language instruction which does not have a counterpart in machine language.

disable interrupts   to make a processor unreceptive to interrupts.

disc cartridge   an enclosure containing a single exchangeable disc.

disc crash   a read–write head coming into contact with the surface of a magnetic disc.

disc drive   a device which reads from and writes to a magnetic disc.

disc pack   a set of magnetic discs on a common shaft.

distributed array processor (DAP)   a processor with parallel elements which can carry out an operation on all the elements of an array simultaneously.

documentation   a written description of how a program works, how it is to be used, or how it is to be run on a computer.

dump   to copy an entire file onto another storage medium, generally from a magnetic disc onto a magnetic tape.

dynamic data structure   a data structure which changes in size while in use.

dynamic memory   solid-state storage in which data 'leaks away' and must be refreshed periodically.

editor a portion of systems software which allows programs or data files to be edited.

emulate to simulate the behaviour of one computer, at machine language level, on another computer.

enable to activate a logic circuit or component.

enable interrupts to make a processor receptive to interrupts.

even parity see **parity bit**.

exchangeable disc pack a set of magnetic discs which can be removed from a disc drive.

execute to carry out a machine instruction or a program.

exponent the power of two of a floating point number.

feasibility study a preliminary study of a proposed data processing application, which indicates whether or not further investigation and development should take place.

ferrite core a small ring of soft iron which can be magnetised in one direction or the other to store a 0 or a 1.

fetch the phase of an instruction cycle in which a machine instruction is fetched from store.

field the place allocated for a particular data item, on a data storage medium, or in a data structure such as a record.

FIFO first-in–first-out, describing a queue.

file a collection of data, structured in a particular way, used for a particular purpose.

file librarian a person responsible for the magnetic tape and magnetic disc files at a computer installation.

file processing system a type of data processing application where the emphasis is on the periodic updating of files.

firmware software permanently stored on read-only memory.

fixed point a number in which the binary point occupies a fixed position.

flag a single bit register used in the control and synchronisation of peripheral devices.

flip-flop a logic circuit which has two stable output states. An input signal can cause it to 'flip' from one state to the other.

floating point a number expressed as the product of a fraction of magnitude between $\frac{1}{2}$ and 1 and an integral power of two.

floppy disc a small flexible magnetic disc.

format the layout of input or output data.

frame the coding area for one character on paper or magnetic tape, being a row of bit coding positions across the width of the tape.

front panel the front surface of a unit, generally containing switches and indicator lights.

front-end processor a processor which controls the flow of data into and out of another processor.

full adder a logic circuit which adds two bits, together with a previous carry, to produce a sum and a carry.

full duplex describes data transmission in both directions simultaneously.

function a portion of a program which carries out the task of evaluating a function, and which is invoked from any point in the program at which the function is used.

gate a functional element for a Boolean operation in a logic circuit.

gate delay the time interval between a change in the input signals at a gate and the stabilisation of its output signal in its new state.

general-purpose computer   a computer capable of a wide range of applications.

general-purpose language   a programming language, in most cases a high level language, suitable for a wide variety of applications.

general-purpose register   a register which can fulfil a number of functions.

global variable   a variable whose scope is the entire program.

grandfather – father – son principle   a method of ensuring the security of data by keeping three generations of a file, as well as the information needed to update the generations.

graphics terminal   a VDU capable of graphics displays.

half adder   a logic circuit which adds two bits, producing a sum and a carry.

half duplex   describes data transmission in alternate directions, but not in both directions simultaneously.

Hamming code   a data code with sufficient built-in checking for a single bit error to be corrected and a multiple bit error to be detected.

hardware   the physical components, solid-state and otherwise, which make up a computer.

hard-wired control   the execution of machine instructions directly by hardware.

hash total   the total of various numeric items within a record.

hashing   an address generation technique, where the address of the first possible location of a file is generated.

hexadecimal   base sixteen.

hierarchical model   a database structure based on a tree configuration.

high level language   an application-oriented programming language, one which is a convenient and simple means of describing the information structures and sequence of actions required to perform a particular task.

high order digits   a group of digits in a number with the highest place values.

high resolution graphics   graphics displays with a fine level of detail.

immediate access store   storage in which each location can be written to or read from immediately.

immediate operand   a data item located in a machine or assembly language instruction.

implementation   the putting into practice of a design or concept, under a particular set of circumstances.

index   a variable which indicates the position of an element in an array.

index register   a register which contains an offset to be added to a base address.

indexed address   an address to which the contents of an index register must be added in order to obtain an absolute address.

indexed sequential file   a sequential file which includes an index relating the key of each record to its address.

indirect address   an address which locates the address of a data item.

information processing   a general term used to describe the work done by a computer.

information storage/retrieval   a type of data processing application where one or more large stores of information are continuously kept up to date, and may be accessed at any time.

input   data supplied to a computer from its environment.

input device   a device which supplies input data to a processor.

instruction cycle   the sequence of actions require to carry out one machine instruction.

instruction decoder   a set of logic circuits which interpret an instruction as a sequence of control signals.

instruction register (IR)   a register which contains the current program instruction.

instruction set   the set of machine language instructions for a particular type of computer.

integrated circuit   a single solid-state unit, containing a number of transistors and other components, which performs one or more logic operations.

intelligent terminal   a terminal which incorporates a certain amount of processing capability.

interface   a point of contact between one module and another, or between a module and its environment.

interpreter   a program which enables a computer to run programs in a high level language, statement by statement.

interrupt   an external signal causing the execution of a program to be suspended.

interrupt line   a signal line used to generate an interrupt.

interrupt service routine   a program module which provides the initial response of a processor to an interrupt.

inter-block gap   a gap left between successive blocks on a magnetic tape or disc.

job control language (JCL)   the language in which instructions to an operating system are written.

Josephson junction   a solid-state switch, working at a temperature close to absolute zero, which forms the basis of a logic circuit.

K   a unit of stored data, $1K = 2^{10} = 1024$.

key   a data field which identifies a record.

large scale integration (LSI)   the inclusion of thousands of transistors and other components on a single integrated circuit.

level of privilege   a figure which determines the degree of access to system resources of a program.

lexical analysis   the first stage in the analysis of a source program by a compiler.

LIFO   last-in – first-out, describing a stack.

line printer   a printer which prints all the characters in an entire line in one operation.

linkage editor   a portion of systems software which links all the modules of a program.

linked list   see list.

list   a set of data items, stored in some order, where data items may be inserted or deleted at any point within the set.

loader   a portion of systems software which copies a machine language program into the store it will occupy during execution, and adjusts any relative addresses contained in the program.

local area network   a data communication system connecting a number of computers and other devices in the same vicinity.

local variable   a variable whose scope is limited to one block of a program.

location   the storage space for one data item.

logic circuit   a circuit, resembling an electrical circuit, connecting a number of logic elements.

loop   a portion of a program which is repeated.

low level language   a machine or assembly language.

M   a unit of stored data, $1M = 2^{20} = 1\,048\,576$.

machine language   a programming language which controls the hardware of a particular type of computer directly.

macro   a single instruction in an assembly language or a system command language, which represents a group of instructions.

magnetic bubble memory   a random access store made up of a substance in which small zones of magnetism move, each zone storing a 0 or a 1.

magnetic disc   a data storage medium comprising a metal or plastic disc coated with a magnetisable substance.

magnetic ink character recognition (MICR)   recognition of characters printed in a magnetic ink.

magnetic tape unit   a device which reads from and writes to magnetic tape.

main store   solid-state storage directly accessible to a processor.

mainframe   a large computer, consisting of a number of free-standing units.

mantissa   the fraction part of a floating point number.

mark sensing   detection of shaded areas in a document.

mask   a logic circuit which selects certain bits of a data item.

medium   a means of storing data.

medium scale integration (MSI)   the inclusion of hundreds of transistors and other components on a single integrated circuit.

megabyte   one million bytes.

memory address register   a register, connected to a main store via a decoder, which holds the address currently being accessed within the store.

memory cycle   the sequence of steps to read a data item from, or write a data item to main store.

memory data register   a register which holds a data item during transfer to or from a main store.

merging   the process of combining two ordered sets of data to produce a single ordered set.

message switching   the routing of a message from its origin to its destination.

microcode   instructions which carry out the steps of a machine instruction at the level of opening and closing gates.

microcomputer   a computer based on a single-chip microprocessor.

microfiche   a small sheet of film containing approximately 100 pages of microfilm.

microprocessor   a single chip containing most of the processing circuits of a computer.

microsecond   millionth of a second.

minicomputer   a small computer, generally with a number of functional devices mounted in a rack in a single unit.

mnemonic   a group of letters, generally representing an operation code in an assembly language.

modem   a modulator/demodulator, a device used to interface a telephone line used for data transmission.

module   an interchangeable unit, performing a specific function, and having a specific interface with its environment.

most significant digit   the digit in a number with the highest place value.

multiplexer   a device which interleaves communication from a number of data channels onto a single data channel.

multiprogramming   a method of computer operation where a number of programs are in various stages of running at any time.

multi-access   the simultaneous access of a number of users, via terminals, to a computer.

multi-port memory   a memory which has a number of input/output ports.

nanosecond   thousand millionth of a second.

network architecture   a computer configuration containing a number of communicating processors and other devices.

network model   a database structure based on a series of links between data items, forming a network.

node   a data item in a tree.

noise   interference in a data communication channel.

normalisation   adjusting the binary point in a floating point number so that the magnitude of the fraction part is between ½ and 1.

nucleus   the lowest software level of an operating system, providing a small number of essential services to higher levels.

null pointer   a pointer which does not point to anything.

object program   a program in a machine language, produced by a compiler from an equivalent source program in a high level language.

octal   base eight.

odd parity   see **parity bit**.

ones complements   a binary code in which the most significant bit represents one less (in magnitude) than the corresponding twos complement value.

operand   the data item referred to by a machine instruction.

operating system   a program, or set of programs, driving the raw hardware of a computer, which manages the resources of the computer in accordance with certain objectives, presenting higher levels of software with a simplified virtual machine.

operation code   the part of a machine instruction which determines the type of operation to be carried out.

operation table   a table which shows, for a particular logic operation, the values of the output variable resulting from all possible combinations of the input variable.

operations manager   the person in charge of the running of a computer installation.

operator documentation   an account of the operator procedures needed to run a program.

operator's console   the device which enables the person operating a computer to interact with it.

optical character recognition (OCR)   recognition of printed characters by a light scanning process.

ordered list   a list in which items are in numerical or alphabetical order.

original equipment manufacture (OEM)   the manufacture of components such as integrated circuits, switches, casings, etc. for computers and associated devices.

output   data supplied to its environment by a computer.

output device   a device which supplies data from a computer to its environment.

overflow   the occurrence of a numerical result which is outside the limits imposed by the number representation used.

overflow bit   a status bit which is set when overflow occurs.

overlay   a portion of the code of a program which is held on backing store and copied into main store when needed.

packed decimal   a BCD code using four bits per decimal digit.

packet   a unit of transmitted data, enclosed by strings of control characters.

packet switching   the routing of data packets from their origin to their destination.

parallel adder   a logic circuit which adds all the bits of two input numbers at the same time.

parallel data transmission   the transmission of a number of data bits simultaneously, generally by means of multi-strand cable.

parallelism   the performance of several actions simultaneously inside a processor.

parity   a method of self-checking involving the use of a parity bit.

parity bit   a bit in the code for a data item which is set to a 0 or a 1 so that the total number of 1s in the data item is even, for even parity, or odd, for odd parity.

parity check   a check to determine whether the parity of a data item is correct.

parsing   the application of a set of rules of syntax to a source program by a compiler.

peripheral   a device, linked to a processor, which performs an input, output, storage or data communication function.

pipelining   a processing technique using an independent unit for each stage of an operation, the units being connected in sequence via buffers.

place value   the weighting assigned to a digit in a number, depending on its position.

plug compatible   describes items of computer equipment which can be connected together directly.

pointer   a data item which contains the address of another data item.

pop   to remove a data item from a stack.

portable   describes programs which can be run on more than one type of computer.

precedence   the order in which operations in an expression are carried out.

precision   a measure of how closely a number can approximate its exact value.

procedure   see **subprogram**.

process control   the continuous monitoring and/or controlling of an operational process by a computer.

processor   a unit, printed circuit board or single chip in which processing takes place.

program   a set of instructions to a computer.

program counter (PC)   a register which stores the address of the current program instruction.

program documentation   an account of the structure and workings of a program.

programmable read-only memory (PROM)   read-only memory which can be loaded under program control.

programmer   a person responsible for designing, writing, testing, correcting, maintaining and documenting computer programs.

protocol   a set of rules, used in data communication systems, which specify the packet structure and the procedures to be followed for transmission and reception.

pseudo-operation   see **directive**.

push   to add item to a stack.

push-down list   see **stack**.

push-down stack   see **stack**.

queue   a data structure in which items are added at the rear and removed from the front.

quicksort   a particularly efficient method of sorting data.

random access   describes a data storage medium where the time taken to access a data item is independent of its position on the medium.

random access memory (RAM)   solid-state storage, in which data can be accessed from any location.

random file   a file in which records are not in any order, but are located by an address generation technique.

read-only memory (ROM)   solid-state storage which can be read from but not written to.

read–write head   a device which detects or creates magnetised areas on a disc or tape.

real-time processing   processing which must keep pace with some operation which is external to the computer.

record   a set of data items which are related in some way, generally forming the unit of data in a larger structure such as a file.

recursion   the capability of a procedure or function to call itself.

register   a storage element for one data item, for a particular purpose such as control, processing or data transmission.

relational model   a database structure based on a set of tables which define relationships between data items.

relative address   the offset of a data item from the machine instruction containing the address.

relocatable code   instructions and data which can be moved in main store without the need to change any addresses within the code.

remote job entry (RJE)   the submission of programs for processing at sites remote from the computer.

report generation   the process of summarising the information in a file and generating a report containing this summary information.

reserved word   a word which has a defined meaning in the context of a programming language.

reset   (1) the input to a flip-flop, a signal on which causes the flip-flop to change its 0 state.

reset   (2) the updating of a program counter so that it contains the address of the next machine instruction.

resource   a functional unit, program or set of data within a computer.

result register   temporary storage for the output from logic circuits.

ring   a local area network based on a closed loop of cable.

root   the node at the 'top' of a tree.

scheduler   part of an operating system which determines the sequence in which programs are run.

scope   the part of a program in which a particular variable can be used.

searching   the process of locating a record in a file, given the key of the record.

sector   a unit of stored data on a magnetic disc.

self-checking code   a code which contains enough information within the coded form of the data item to determine whether the data item has been coded or transmitted correctly.

sequencing   the flow of control from one program instruction to the next.

sequential file   a file in which the records are in order of one or more keys.

sequential search   a method of searching a file by accessing each record in turn until the required record is found.

serial access   describes a data storage medium where the time taken to access a data item depends on its position in the medium.

serial adder   a logic circuit which adds the bits of two input numbers one pair at a time.

serial file   a file in which the records are in no particular order.

set   the input to a flip-flop, a signal on which causes the flip-flop to change to its 1 state.

shift register   a register which enables bits of a data item to be shifted from one position to the next.

sign-and-magnitude code   a code in which the sign of a number and its magnitude are represented separately.

sign extension   copying the sign of a low order byte into all the bits of the high order byte of a word.

simplex   describes data transmission in one direction only.

single program operation   a type of computer operation where only one program is run at a time.

slave store   see **cache store**.

software   the programs which direct the operation of a computer.

software engineer   a person skilled in a wide area of software and systems design.

software front panel   software which displays the contents of processor registers on the screen of an operator's console.

software house   a company whose activities are centred on the production of computer software.

source document   an original document containing data for input into a computer system.

source program   a program, in a high level language, which forms the input for a computer.

specification language   a programming language, above the level of high level languages, for stating the specifications of a task.

spooling   maintaining a queue, on backing store, of data for output, generally by a printer.

stack   a collection of data items which may only be accessed at one end.

stack base   the fixed end of a stack.

stack pointer   (1) a pointer which indicates the current position of the top of a stack.

stack pointer (SP)   (2) a register which contains the current address of the top of the system stack.

static data structure   a data structure which stays the same size once it has been created.

static memory   solid-state storage which retains data as long as power is switched on.

status bits   see **condition codes**.

store and forward   a type of packet switching where data is stored at intermediate points while in transit.

string   (1) a set of characters stored together.

string   (2) a subset of a file which is small enough to be accommodated in a computer main store.

subprogram   a portion of a program, which carries out a specific task, to which control can be transferred from any point in the program, and from which control returns to the point from which it was called.

subroutine   see **subprogram**.

subsystem   a part of a system which accomplishes a part of the goals of the system.

subtree   a portion of a tree, itself having a tree structure.

symbolic address   a group of characters which represents the address of a data item or instruction.

syntax   the rules which govern the structure of a program in a particular language.

syntax analysis   the determination of the structure of a source program by a compiler.

syntax error   a violation of a syntax rule of a programming language by a program written in the language.

system   a collection of parts working together towards some common goals.

system maintenance   the periodic alteration of some aspect of a data processing system in the light of experience or changing requirements.

system specification   an outline of a proposed data processing application, including a statement of the objectives of the system, and a summary of the overall working of the system.

systems analyst   a person responsible for the analysis and overall design of a data processing system.

systems flowchart   a diagram showing the overall structure of and flow of data through a system.

systems programmer   a programmer whose work is concerned with systems software.

systems software   the layers of software, generally comprising operating systems, assemblers and compilers which transform the hardware of a computer into an application-oriented machine.

target language   the language into which programs are translated by a compiler.

teletype   a terminal comprising a keyboard and a character printer.

terminal   a general-purpose input/output device.

terminal node   a node at the 'bottom' of a tree.

test data   data which is specifically designed to test the working of a program.

time slicing   a scheduling policy in which each program is in turn allowed a short interval of processor time.

top of stack   the point at which data items may be added to or removed from a stack.

track   (1) a circular path on the surface of a magnetic disc, on which consecutive bits of data are recorded.

track   (2) a row of bit coding positions along the length of magnetic tape.

track   (3) a row of punching positions along the length of paper tape.

transaction processing   a type of data processing application where transactions are processed in real time.

transistor   an electronic component, one or more of which can be made to carry out a logic operation.

tree   a hierarchical data structure, in which each element is linked to one element above it, and zero, one or more elements below it.

truncation error   an error which occurs when bits of a number are discarded, without any rounding taking place.

truth table   see **operation table**.

turnkey contract   a contract for the supply of a complete, ready-to-use computer system, including hardware and software.

twos complements   a binary code, using the usual place values, except that the most significant bit represents a negative quantity.

underflow   the occurrence of a numerical result which is less than the lower limit imposed by the number representation used.

uninterrupted power supply   a unit which ensures a constant power supply to a computer.

update   to bring a file or other collection of information up to date.

user documentation   an account of how a program is to be used.

user group   a group of people or organisations which are users of the same make of computer equipment.

utility programs   programs for various 'housekeeping' tasks as file creation, copying files, routing messages and providing mathematical facilities.

validation   the process of checking input data before storing or processing it.

variable   a data item which can change its value during the running of a program.

very large scale integration (VLSI)   the inclusion of tens of thousands of transistors and other components on a single integrated circuit.

virtual machine   the image of the hardware of a computer created by various layers of software, especially an operating system.

virtual memory   the image of a computer memory presented by an operating system to higher levels of software.

visual display unit (VDU)   a terminal comprising a keyboard and display screen.

Winchester disc   a small high-capacity hard disc.

word   a set of bits which can be manipulated by a computer in one operation.

wordlength   the number of bits in one word.

work station   a terminal, intelligent terminal or microcomputer at which certain tasks are carried out.

wrap-around carry   a carry from the most significant to the least significant bit of a number.

Teachers' notes

These Notes are intended for the guidance of a teacher of Computing Science at Advanced level or equivalent. They indicate some of the ways in which this book can be used, and provide brief answers to selected questions in the exercises. It must, however, be emphasised that the best preparation for the use of this book as course material is a familiarity with its contents; one of the intended uses of the book is as a 'briefing text' for teachers about to start a course in Computing Science at Advanced level or equivalent.

Use of the Book

Computing is a broad, many-faceted subject, with complex inter-relationships between its constituent topics. Accordingly, the structure of this book has been chosen with considerable care, in order to provide a logical path through the topics, and a cumulative flow of information. However, not every chapter in the book depends on all its predecessors, as shown in Figure 32.1. There is considerable scope for selection of material, and variation in the order of presentation, depending on circumstances.

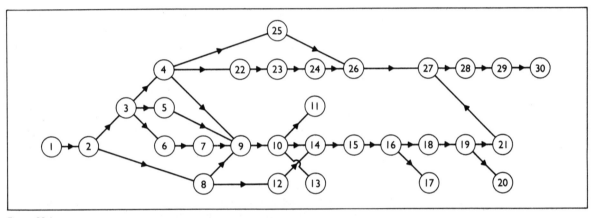

Figure 32.1
A-level Computing Science: chapter dependencies
The numbers in the circles are chapter numbers.
The material in each chapter depends on *all* the paths leading to the chapter.

For a computing science course, it is recommended that the chapters be followed more or less in sequence. If pressure of time is great, then the case study chapters, Chapters 13, 17 and 20, can be glossed over lightly, or left for pupils to peruse in their own time. It is certainly not recommended that all the high level case studies in Chapter 17 be 'ploughed through'. A selection must be made according to circumstances. Similarly, chapters on databases (Chapter 24), data communication (Chapter 25) and social effects of computers (Chapter 28), can be treated fairly lightly, as they contain material which is not (yet) in many Advanced level Computing Science syllabuses. Nevertheless, the material they contain is vital for any pupil who intends to further his or her studies in computing, or plans a career in that direction.

If this book is intended for a Computer Appreciation Course, then the essential material is the principles of computing (in particular Chapters 1 to 3) and the applications and implications of computers (Chapters 22 to 30). The more technical chapters on hardware and software can be treated lightly or omitted.

Answers to Exercises

Answers to exercises have been selected for inclusion here on the basis of the following criteria:

- If a question requires a brief, specific answer then it is included. The only exception is the questions which require definitions of terms; answers to these are to be found in the Glossary of Terms.
- Where questions require discussion, in selected cases a few relevant points are included. In most cases, conclusions are not drawn, as the merit of an answer lies in the logic of its argument, and not in the 'correctness' of its conclusion.
- Answers to questions from past examination papers in computing science are not included.
- If a question is a 'comprehension' question, with the answer contained in the text, a reference is given to the section of the text containing the answer.

Exercise 2

2 Systems: central and local government; automatic pilot; any organ of the body; solar system, etc.
Non-systems: crowd of looters; shuffled pack of cards; components of an engine before assembly, etc.

3 Slide rule: No, not automatic or programmable.
Automatic washing machine: No, does not process information.
Programmable pocket calculator: } No, only performs part of the work of a computer, or
Television game: } Yes, but only a dedicated computer.
Motor car electronic ignition system: No, does not contain a stored program.

4 In many cases, the distinction between the device and a computer is very fine, based on the nature of the 'processing' carried out by the device. Examples include robots, electronically controlled cameras, multi-function digital watches, etc.

7 Examples include many modern buildings (particularly of the Portakabin type), almost all electrical apparatus, plumbing systems using plastic pipe, telephone systems, the lens systems associated with many modern cameras, etc.

8 Advantages include:
- ease of replacement of faulty modules
- ease of expansion by adding more modules
- ease of understanding of design principles
- ease of planning for future enhancements.

Exercise 3

1 The essential electronic components of computers are all bistable devices. Advantages are simplicity and wide tolerances.

2 Roman numerals.

3 Each character is coded separately as a set of binary digits.

4 Add the binary codes of the two digits, and the carry bit.

If the sum exceeds nine (1001),
    then subtract ten (1010) from the sum, and set the carry bit to 1.
    else set the carry bit to 0.

☐ **5** Assuming that one of the numbers has been 'padded' with leading zeros if necessary, so that both numbers are of the same length:

> Set carry bit to zero
> Repeat, for each digit of the numbers, from the right
> > Add a pair of digits and the carry bit, as outlined above.
> Create an additional digit for the sum, containing the carry bit.

6

	four bits	six bits	eight bits
3	0011	000011	00000011
−3	1101	111101	11111101

Duplicate the leftmost bit of the number to fill the new bit positions. This process is called **sign extension**.

7

	four bits	six bits	eight bits
3	0011	000011	00000011
−3	1100	111100	11111100

Same process as with twos complements.

8

	Bits	twos complements range	ones complements range
a)	4	−8 to 7	−7 to 7
b)	6	−32 to 31	−31 to 31
c)	8	−128 to 127	−127 to 127
d)	16	−32768 to 32767	−32767 to 32767
e)	n	-2^{n-1} to $2^{n-1}-1$	$-(2^{n-1}-1)$ to $2^{n-1}-1$

9

	−1	$\frac{1}{2}$	$\frac{1}{4}$	$\frac{1}{8}$	$\frac{1}{16}$	$\frac{1}{32}$
$\frac{3}{8}$ =	0	0	1	1	0	0
$-\frac{5}{16}$ =	1	1	0	1	1	0
$-\frac{17}{32}$ =	1	0	1	1	1	1
$\frac{1}{5}$ =	0	0	0	1	1	0

10

$$11000 = 0{\cdot}11 \times 10^{101} \quad \text{(written entirely in base two)}$$
$$0{\cdot}011 = 0{\cdot}11 \times 10^{-1}$$
$$-10{\cdot}11 = -0{\cdot}1011 \times 10^{10}$$
$$0{\cdot}101 = 0{\cdot}101 \times 10^{0}$$

11

$$0{\cdot}110 \times 10^{11} = 110$$
$$-0{\cdot}1011 \times 10^{110} = 101100$$
$$0{\cdot}1101 \times 10^{-111} = 0{\cdot}0000000110 1$$

12

	decimal		sign	$\frac{1}{2}$	$\frac{1}{4}$	$\frac{1}{8}$	$\frac{1}{16}$	$\frac{1}{32}$	$\frac{1}{64}$	$\frac{1}{128}$	$\frac{1}{256}$	$\frac{1}{512}$	$\frac{1}{1024}$
a)	10	=	0	1	0	1	0	0	0	0	0	0	0
	15360	=	0	1	1	1	1	0	0	0	0	0	0
	−1	=	1	1	0	0	0	0	0	0	0	0	0
	$\frac{7}{128} = 0{\cdot}0547$	=	0	1	1	1	0	0	0	0	0	0	0
	$-\frac{5}{1024} = -0{\cdot}0049$	=	1	1	0	1	0	0	0	0	0	0	0
b)	80	=	0	1	0	1	0	0	0	0	0	0	0
	−3072	=	1	1	1	0	0	0	0	0	0	0	0
	$\frac{5}{512}$	=	0	1	0	1	0	0	0	0	0	0	0
	$-\frac{1}{2}$	=	1	1	0	0	0	0	0	0	0	0	0
	1.5	=	0	1	1	0	0	0	0	0	0	0	0

decimal		sign	8	4	2	1	
a) 10	=	0	0	I	0 .	0	
15360	=	0	I	I	I	0	
−1	=	0	0	0	0	I	
$\frac{7}{128} = 0.0547$	=	I	0	I	0	0	
$-\frac{5}{1024} = -0.0049$	=	I	0	I	I	I	
b) 80	=	0	0	I	I	I	
−3072	=	0	I	I	0	0	
$\frac{5}{512}$	=	I	0	I	I	0	
$-\frac{1}{2}$	=	0	0	0	0	0	
1.5	=	0	0	0	0	I	

c) From $\frac{1}{2} \times 2^{-15} (= \frac{1}{65536})$ to $\frac{1023}{1024} \times 2^{15} (= 32736)$

13 a) 8

b) 16

c) Suggestions in the region of Mantissa: 56 bits, Exponent: 8 bits.

14

decimal	binary	octal	hexadecimal
45	101101	55	2D
21	10101	25	15
32	100000	40	20
4097	1000000000001	10001	1001

15 a) Parity error in 5th byte.

b) Parity error in 7th column.

c) 7th bit in 5th byte (should be 0).

16 a) No – the parity bit might have been copied incorrectly.

b) No – two bits might be in error.

c) Parity will detect that a single bit error most probably has occurred.

Exercise 4

2 Data structures enable large, potentially unwieldy collections of data to be managed by relatively simple operations. Concepts associated with data structures have led to advances in computer architecture. Data structures have improved the design of programs.

3 a) Indexes in books, filing systems, maps, etc.

b) Possibilities include: casual conversations; modern 'classical' music (John Cage etc.); clues in a crime, etc.

4 See Section 4.1.

☐ **5** a) Array, stack, tree.

b) Each is fairly easy to implement in a computer memory, using pointers where necessary. Each is extremely important for a wide range of computer applications.

6 To mark an empty stack, the end of a list and a terminal node of a tree.

7 Split the string at the point of insertion, obtaining <leftstring> and <rightstring>.

Form a new string by joining <leftstring>, <newstring> and <rightstring>.

8 a) 1: Let index $I = 1$
2: If $I > 10$, halt
3: Let $Z(I) = X(I) + Y(I)$
4: Increase I by 1
5: Go to step 2.

b) 1: Let total $T = 0$
2: Let index $I = 1$
3: If $I > 10$, halt
4: Let $T = T + X(I)$
5: Increase I by 1
6: Go to step 3.

☐ **c)** 1: Let product $P = 0$
2: Let index $I = 1$
3: If $I > 10$, halt
4: Let $P = P + X(I) . Y(I)$
5: Increase I by 1
6: Go to step 3.

9 a) A(1, 1) into B(1)
  A(1, 2)   B(2)
  A(1, 3)   B(3)
  A(2, 1)   B(4)
  A(2, 2)   B(5)
  A(2, 3)   B(6)
  A(3, 1)   B(7)
  A(3, 2)   B(8)
  A(3, 3)   B(9)

☐ **b)** If $A(I, J)$ goes in $B(K)$
  then $K = 3(I - 1) + J$

☐ **c)** A(0, 0) into B(0)
  A(0, 1)   B(1)
  A(0, 2)   B(2)
  A(1, 0)   B(3)
  A(1, 1)   B(4)
  A(1, 2)   B(5)
  A(2, 0)   B(6)
  A(2, 1)   B(7)
  A(2, 2)   B(8)
  If $A(I, J)$ goes into $B(K)$
  then $K = 3I + J$

10 a) $21 - 10 \div 5$ stack 21

| 21 |

stack 10

| 10 |
| 21 |

stack 5

| 5 |
| 10 |
| 21 |

Divide 10 by 5, stack result

| 2 |
| 21 |

Subtract 2 from 21, stack result

| 19 |

d) $6 \times (4 + 5) \times 3$ stack 6

| 6 |

stack 4

| 4 |
| 6 |

stack 5

| 5 |
| 4 |
| 6 |

Add 4 and 5, stack answer

9
6

Multiply, stack answer

54

stack 3

3
54

Multiply, stack answer

162

11 c) Disadvantage: The queue 'moves' in the memory of the computer.

12 a) See Figure 32.2.
   b) See Figure 32.2.
   c) Pointers A2 and C1 point to the new data item B.
      Pointer B1 points to data item A.
      Pointer B2 points to data item C.

13 See Figure 32.3.

Figure 32.2
Exercise 4, Question 10

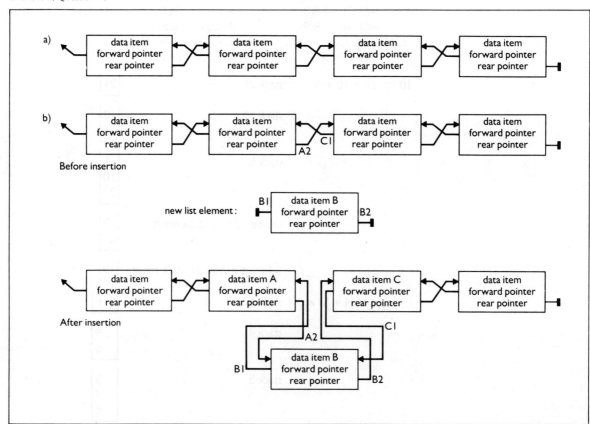

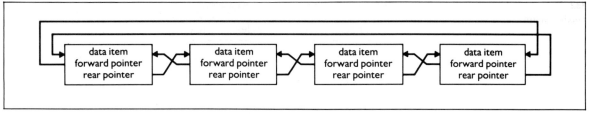

Figure 32.3
Exercise 4, Question 13

14 Insertion

If there is at least one free element in the array,
Then repeat, starting from the front of the array
   Compare element to be inserted with current array element
Until element to be inserted is earlier in alphabetical order than current array element.
Mark current array element.
Repeat, starting from rear of array, to marked array element
   Move element one place down in array
Insert new element in front of marked element.

Deletion follows a similar pattern, to locate element to be deleted and move remaining elements up one place, inserting a free space at the end.

Comment: Storing ordered data in an array involves a lot of movement of array elements during insertion and deletion.

15 See Figure 32.4.

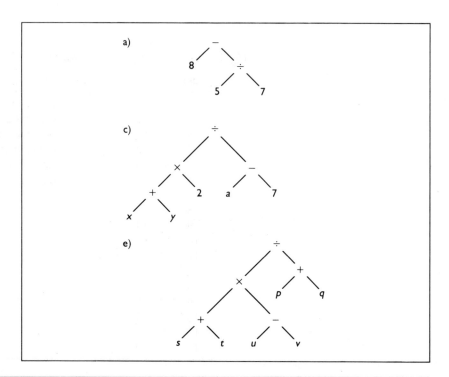

Figure 32.4
Exercise 4, Question 15

b)

pointers array		data array	
index	item	index	item
1	1	1	+
2	5	2	×
3	9	3	p
4	0	4	q
5	2	5	−
6	13	6	r
7	15	7	s
8	0		
9	5		
10	17		
11	19		
12	0		
13	3		
14	0		
15	4		
16	0		
17	6		
18	0		
19	7		
20	0		

Note that these are by no means the only correct answers.

16 a)

pointers array		data array	
index	item	index	item
1	1	1	control module
2	6	2	input module
3	8	3	processing module
4	12	4	output module
5	0	5	calculation module
6	2	6	backing store transfer module
7	0		
8	3		
9	14		
10	16		
11	0		
12	4		
13	0		
14	5		
15	0		
16	6		
17	0		

17 a)   array   b)   array

index	item
1	+
2	×
3	–
4	p
5	q
6	r
7	s

index	item
1	a
2	–
3	b
4	–
5	–
6	c
7	d
8	–
9	–
10	–
11	–
12	e
13	–
14	–
15	–

c) Regular binary trees, such as Figure 4.20, are best stored by this method, but skew binary trees, such as Figure 4.21 are better stored by the method of Question 16.

18 a) Figure 4.20: $p \times q + r - s$.
Figure 4.22: a e c b d.
b) Interchange lines 'output node' and 'traverse right subtree'.
c) Figure 4.16: 7 4 9 × +.
Figure 4.20: p q x r s − +.
Figure 4.22: e c d b a.

19   Enumeration literal   values
a) month   Jan, Feb . . . Dec
b) peak   Skiddaw, Ben Nevis, etc.
c) station   Capital, LBC, BBC1, etc.
d) Advantages: Clarity and ease of understanding.
Disadvantages: Very 'wordy'.

Exercise 5

3

		−8	4	2	1
2 + 5:	2 =	0	0	1	0
	+5 =	0	1	0	1
	7 =	0	1	1	1

            ↙ ↖ ╱
           0   0
Carry in = 0, carry out = 0, answer correct.

		−8	4	2	1
6 + 3:	6 =	0	1	1	0
	+3 =	0	0	1	1
	−7 =	1	0	0	1

            ↙ ↖ ╱
           0   1
Carry in = 1, carry out = 0, answer incorrect.

$4 - 5$:

	0	1	0	0
$4 =$	0	1	0	0
$-5 =$	1	0	1	1
$-1 =$	1	1	1	1

↙ ↖ ↗
0   0

Carry in = 0, carry out = 0, answer correct.

$-2 - 7$:

$-2 =$	1	1	1	0
$-7 =$	1	0	0	1
$7 =$	0	1	1	1

↙ ↖ ↗
1   0

Carry in = 0, carry out = 1, answer incorrect.

4

	−31	16	8	4	2	1
$14 + 9$ $14 =$	0	0	1	1	1	0
$9 =$	0	0	1	0	0	1
$23 =$	0	1	0	1	1	1

↙ ↖ ↗
0   0

Carry in = 0, carry out = 0, answer correct.

$25 + 18$ $25 =$	0	1	1	0	0	1
$18 =$	0	1	0	0	1	0
$-20 =$	1	0	1	0	1	1

↙ ↖ ↗
0   1

Carry in = 1, carry out = 0, answer incorrect.

$17 - 13$ $17 =$	0	1	0	0	0	1
$-13 =$	1	1	0	0	1	0
	0	0	0	0	1	1

↙ ↖ ↗
1   1

        1   add carry out

$4 =$	0	0	0	1	0	0

Carry in = 1, carry out = 1, answer correct.

$-8 - 31$ $-8 =$	1	1	0	1	1	1
$-31 =$	1	0	0	0	0	0
	0	1	0	1	1	1

↙ ↖ ↗
1   0

        1   add carry out

$24 =$	0	1	1	0	0	0

Carry in = 0, carry out = 1, answer incorrect.

Conclusion: Same overflow rule as for twos complements.

5 Product = 10110110.

☐ **6** Use a working area layout as in Figure 5.1, except that area C is not used.
Algorithm:

1 Initially, B contains zeros, A the divisor and D the dividend.
2 Repeat, for each bit of the numbers:
Shift the bits in B and D together one place to the right.
If the contents of B is greater than the divisor in A
then subtract A from B, placing the result in B
place a 1 in the least significant bit
position of D
else place a 0 in the least significant bit
position of D.
3 When the process is complete, the quotient is in D and the remainder in B.

7

		mantissa					exponent		
	sign	$\frac{1}{2}$	$\frac{1}{4}$	$\frac{1}{8}$	$\frac{1}{16}$		sign	2	1
$A + B =$	0	1	0	0	1		0	1	1
$B + C =$	0	1	0	0	1		0	1	0
$A \times B =$	0	1	0	0	1		0	1	1
$A \times C =$	0	1	1	1	1		0	0	1

8 Range of positive numbers: $2^{-32}(= 2.829 \times 10^{-10})$ to $2^{31}(= 2\,147\,483\,648)$.

9 a) 0111
1000
100110

b)

		mantissa					exponent			
	sign	$\frac{1}{2}$	$\frac{1}{4}$	$\frac{1}{8}$	$\frac{1}{16}$		sign	2	1	
$A + B =$	0	1	0	0	1		0	1	1	no change
$B + C =$	0	1	0	0	1		0	1	0	no change
$A \times B =$	0	1	0	1	0		0	1	1	more accurate
$A \times C =$	0	1	1	1	1		0	0	1	no change

Exercise 6

2 Inputs

A	B	C	AND	OR	NAND	NOR
0	0	0	0	0	1	1
0	0	1	0	1	1	0
0	1	0	0	1	1	0
0	1	1	0	1	1	0
1	0	0	0	1	1	0
1	0	1	0	1	1	0
1	1	0	0	1	1	0
1	1	1	1	1	0	0

3 See Section 6.1.

4 a) $D = (\bar{A} = B) . C$

b) $H = (\overline{E + F}) \oplus (\overline{F . G})$

c) $L = (I . \bar{J} . K) + (\bar{I} . J \bar{K})$

5 See Figure 32.5.

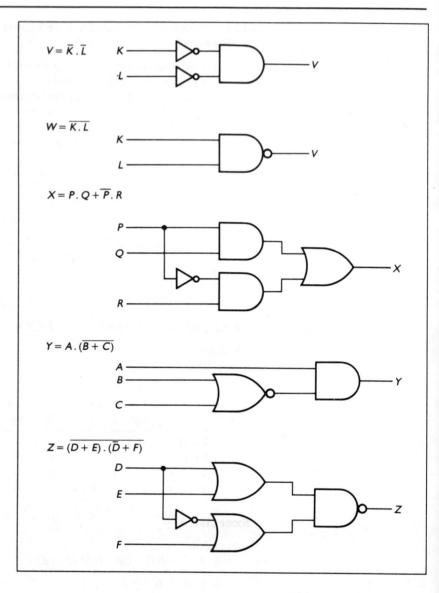

$V = \bar{K} . \bar{L}$

$W = \overline{K . L}$

$X = P . Q + \overline{P} . R$

$Y = A . (\overline{B + C})$

$Z = \overline{(D + E) . (\overline{D} + F)}$

Figure 32.5
Exercise 6, Question 5

□ **6** $A \oplus B = (A + B) . (\overline{\overline{A} . \overline{B}})$

7 b) $K = \overline{\overline{A} + \overline{B}}$ simplifies to $K = A . B$.

$L = (C + \overline{D}) . (C + \overline{E})$ simplifies to $L = C + \overline{D + E}$.

$M = (P . (\overline{Q} . \overline{R})) + (P . (Q . R))$ simplifies to $M = P . (\overline{Q + R} + Q . R)$.

□ **8** $D = \overline{A} . B . C + A . \overline{B} . \overline{C}$

9 $A . B = \overline{A} = \overline{B}$

10 a) See Figure 32.6.
b) See Figure 32.6.
c) Any combination of logic operations can be expressed in terms of the NAND operation only.

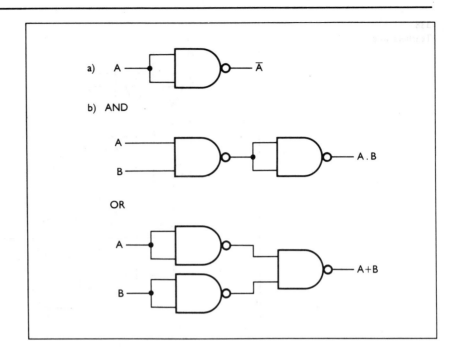

a) $A \rightarrow \overline{A}$

b) AND

A, $B \rightarrow A.B$

OR

A, $B \rightarrow A+B$

Figure 32.6
Exercise 6, Question 10 a) and b)

Exercise 7

2 a) 10101000
   b) 10001000

3 a) 8
   b) 2^n

☐ **4** a)

Inputs			Outputs	
A	B	C	S	T
0	0	0	0	0
0	0	1	1	0
0	1	0	1	0
0	1	1	0	1
1	0	0	1	0
1	0	1	0	1
1	1	0	0	1
1	1	1	1	1

   c) See Figure 32.7.

☐ **5** See Figure 32.8.

☐ **6** Relevant points:
   ● A logic circuit can be thought of as a module, connected to other logic circuits by inputs and outputs.
   ● Many logic circuit modules are constructed as integrated circuits.
   ● A logic circuit module can be replaced by another, with a different but equivalent arrangement of logic gates.

8 See Figure 32.9.

☐ **9** See Figure 32.10.

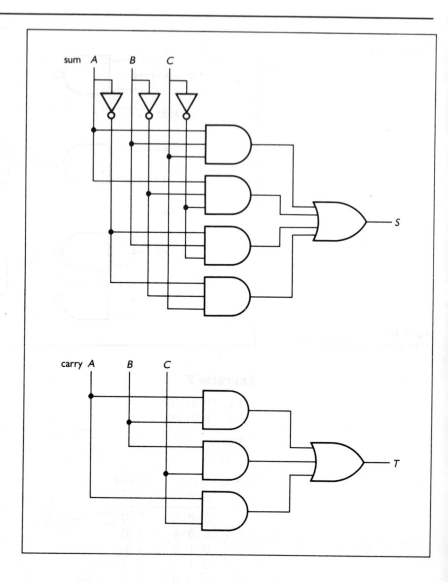

Figure 32.7
Exercise 7, Question 4 c)

Exercise 8

1 Relevant points:
- The concept of modularity enables the structure of a computer system to be expressed at a number of different levels of detail.
- Most computers are constructed as separate modules.
- Modular construction simplifies the design of processors and peripherals.
- Modular construction enables units to be interchanged, allowing a system to grow as required.

5 Prominent plug-compatible equipment manufacturers include Memorex (particularly disc drives) and Westrex (terminals).

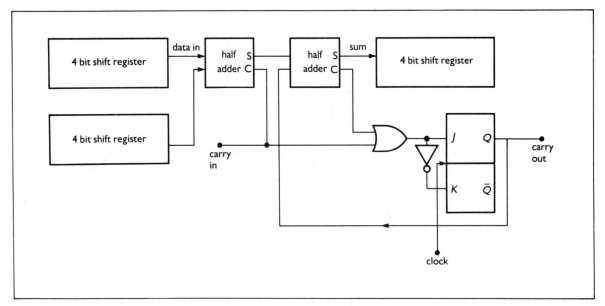

Figure 32.8
Exercise 7, Question 5

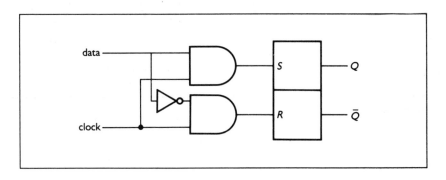

Figure 32.9
A D type flip-flop

Exercise 9

2 See Section 9.5.

3 a) $2^{24} = 16\,777\,216$
 b) 16M
 c) $1M = 1024K$

4 Relevant points:
 ● The concept of modularity enables the structure of a processor to be explained in relatively simple terms.
 ● Each module of a processor may be implemented as a single chip.
 ● The same processor design may be implemented by different but equivalent chips.

5 See section 9.9.

6 See Figure 32.11.

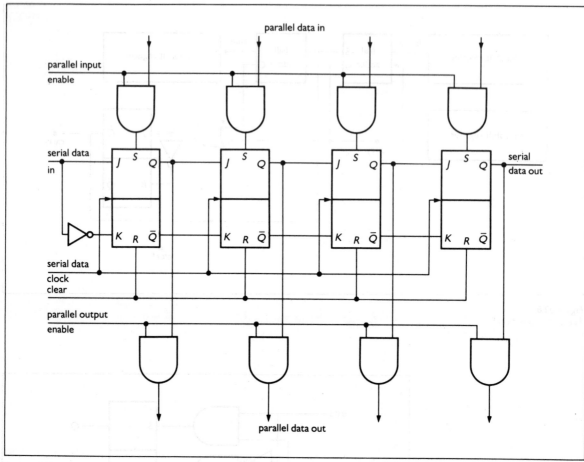

Figure 32.10
A USART

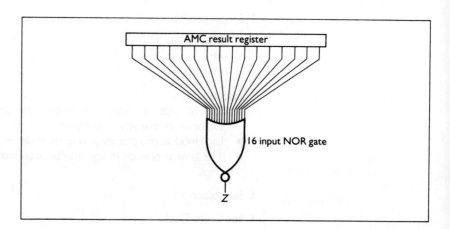

Figure 32.11
Exercise 9, Question 6

Exercise 10

2 Absolute address: to access individual data items stored at a known location.
Indexed address: to access the elements of an array.
Indirect address: to access data items from a structure such as a list or tree.
Relative address: to access relocatable data or code.
Immediate operand: to store a constant.

3 The data item whose address is located at address **49B6** is loaded into the accumulator. Since the address at location **49B6** is **3521**, the data item at this address, **AB02**, is loaded.

4 a) Comment: For positive and negative numbers:
   - Arithmetic shift left has the effect of multiplication by 2.
   - Arithmetic shift right has the effect of division by 2.

5 **0046, 0116**

6 Stack: **CCDD**   Stack pointer: **01FC**
       AABB

7 As an eight bit twos complement number, **80** $= -128$.
As a sixteen bit twos complement number, **FF80** $= -128$.
The process of sign extension preserves the value of both negative and positive quantities.

8 a)

Address	Instruction		Comments
0000	08		Length of arrays, 8 bytes or 4 words.
0001			Array 1, assumed to be
to 0008			already loaded.
0009			Array 2, assumed to be
to 0010			already loaded.
0011			Array 3
to 0018			

Start of program

0019	2122	0000	Load byte at address 0000 to index register.

Start of loop to add each pair of numbers

001D	0320		Decrease index register by 1.
001F	0320		Decrease index register by 1.
0021	670E		Branch to address **0031** if negative.
0023	1114	0001	Load first array element.
0027	1314	0009	Add second array element.
002B	1214	0011	Store in third array.
002F	61EC		Branch to address **0010**.

End of loop

0031	8500		End of program.

b) **FFFE** $(= -2)$

c) The start addresses of the arrays (**0001, 0009** and **0011**) will change, as will the location of the program. Branching instructions, being relative, are not affected.

d) The instruction at address **0027** becomes **1514   0009**.

9

Address	Instruction		Comments
0000	001F		Address of first character, later of current character.

Start of program loop

Address	Instruction		Comments
0002	2113	0000	Load character at address in location **0000** to accumulator.
0006	2A11	7E	Compare character with end marker.
0009	6212		Branch if equal, to address **001D**.
000B	7410		Copy character from accumulator to output register.
000D	7310		Signal output device to unload output register.
000F	6DFE		Branch back to this instruction if output not complete.
0011	1112	0000	Load address of current character to accumulator.
0015	0210		Increase contents of accumulator by 1.
0017	1212	0000	Store address of next character in location **0000**.
001B	61E5		Branch to address **0002**, to output next character.

End of program loop

Address	Instruction	Comments
001D	2500	Halt.
001F		First character.

Exercise 11

2 The functional units and buffers for the pipeline are shown in Figure 32.12. During each 'beat', data passes from a buffer, through a functional unit, to the next buffer. The hardware used by each buffer is physically separate from that used by the other buffers.

Problems
- The duration of each 'beat' is the same. Several stages take a variable amount of time, depending on the instruction.
- Branch or jump instructions can result in the wrong instructions being loaded into the pipeline.

Comment
The AMC architecture does not lend itself to a simple instruction pipeline.

3 All the instructions in the loop are loaded into the cache while the loop is being executed. This considerably increases the processing speed of the computer.

4 a) 320 microseconds.
   b) 630 microseconds.
   c) $320 + 10(n - 1)$ microseconds.

5 They emphasise the shortcomings of the 'elementary' view of a computer, as an 'automatic, electronic information processing machine' (Section 1.4) and give credence to the view of a computer as a 'collection of resources' (Section 2.3). Advanced CPU features do not, however, contradict either of these views.

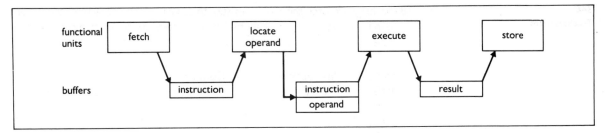

Figure 32.12
An AMC instruction pipeline

Exercise 12

2 Two of the most significant reasons are the shift in the nature of computing from a remote to a real time, interactive operation, and the advent of microcomputers.

☐ **3** Computers based on currently understood design principles will never be able to interpret input in a natural language. Continuous passages of spoken input will only be intelligible if they conform to some command language, similar to a high level programming language.

4 a) 20 000 cards.
  b) 150 000 seconds, approximately 42 hours.
  c) 50 minutes.
  d) 12 000 seconds, or 3 hours and 20 minutes.
  e) 120 000 seconds, approximately 33 hours.
  f) 6000 seconds, or 1 hour and 40 minutes.

5 1200 characters per second.

6 a) 20 000 blocks.
  b) 2 microseconds.
  c) 50 microseconds.
  d) 67 microseconds × 20 000 blocks = 1340 seconds, approximately 22 minutes.

7 a) Flag A goes from 1 to 0
      Flag B goes from 1 to 0
      Character loaded into buffer
      Flag B goes from 0 to 1
      Flag C goes from 0 to 1
    Then
      Flag C goes from 1 to 0
      Flag B goes from 1 to 0
      Character copied from buffer
      Flag B goes from 0 to 1
      Flag A goes from 0 to 1
  b) Flag A indicates that the peripheral is ready for the transfer of another data item.
    Flag C indicates that the processor has completed a transfer of data.
  c) Most of the delay will occur waiting for flag A to be set to 1 by the peripheral.

☐ **8**The program uses the index register to 'count in' the characters, and assign them to successive store locations. The characters are added to a running total as they are input. This total is then compared with the checksum characters.

Address	Instruction		Comments
0000	0000		Running total of characters, initially zero.
0002			
0003			
0004			
0005			
0006			Space for input characters.
0007			
0008			
0009			
000A			Space for check sum.
000B			

Start of program

000C	0120		Clear index register.

Start of loop to input characters

000E	7110		Signal peripheral device to load input register.
0010	6CFE		Branch back to here if input not complete.
0012	7210		Copy character to accumulator.
0014	2214	0002	Store character at address (**0002** + index).
0018	1312	0000	Add running total into accumulator.
001C	1212	0000	Store new value of total.
0020	0220		Increase index register by 1.
0022	1A21	0007	Compare index with **0007**.
0026	66EG		Branch if less than or equal, to **000E**.

Start of loop to input check sum

0028	7110		Signal peripheral device to load input register.
002A	6CFE		Branch back to here if input not complete.
002C	7210		Copy character to accumulator.
002E	2214	0002	Store character at address (**0002** + index).
0032	0220		Increase index register by 1.
0034	1A21	0001	Compare index register with **0009**.
0038	66EE		Branch if less than or equal, to **0028**.

End of input loop

003A	1112	000A	Load check sum to accumulator.
003E	1A22	0000	Compare with running total.
0042	6204		Branch if equal, to **0048**.
0044	0110		Clear accumulator (check fails).
0046	6104		Branch to **004C**.
0048	1111	0001	Set accumulator to 1 (check succeeds).
004C	7410		Copy to output register.

004E	7310	Signal peripheral device to output character.
0050	60FE	Branch back to here if output is not complete.
0052	8500	Halt.

Exercise 13

1 A general-purpose register may be used for a number of functions, such as accumulator, index register, stack pointer, program counter etc. Computers which use general-purpose registers are the Z80 microprocessor and the PDP-11.

A special purpose register is used for one function only. Computers which use special-purpose registers are the ICL 2900 series and the Cray 1.

2 One-address: Z80, ICL 2900, Cray 1.
Two-address: PDP-11.

4 ICL 2900, Cray 1.

5 a) 7
   b) AMC: 80 clock periods per loop cycle, 2560 for entire process
      Cray 1: 35 clock periods.
   Comment: The AMC takes about 7000 times as long as the Cray 1.

6 ICL 2900 series. It is designed to be a 'high level language processor', which involves extensive use of a stack.

Exercise 14

```
2 a) CLR  A
      STO  A    DT1
  b) LOA  A  N  +16291
      STO  A    CS1
  c) LOB  A    CTR
      INC  A
      STB  A    CTR
  d) LOA  A    AB1
      CMP  A    AB2
      BZE       EQU
  e) LOA  A  N  /EF/
      PSH  A
      LOA  A  N  /CO/
      PSH  A
      LOA  A  N  /AB/
      PSH  A

3 RTA  WRD
  NM1  WRD

  Start of subprogram
  SBP  POP  A
       STO  A    RTA
       POP  A
       STO  A    NM1
       POP  A
```

```
                          CMP  A    NM1
                          BGE       LT2
                          LOA  A    NM1
                   LT2    PSH  A
                          LOA  A    RTA
                          PSH  A
                          RTS
```

End of subprogram, start of main program

```
       STR    LOA  S  N  +127
              LOA  A  N  +16693
              PSH  A
              LOA  A  N  +25252
              PSH  A
              JSR        SPB
              POP  A
              HLT
```

```
 5 a)   HI1  WRD    +10000    High-order word of integer 1.
and b)  LI1  WRD     +8763    Low-order word of integer 1.
        HI2  WRD    +20000    High-order word of integer 2.
        LI2  WRD    +14261    Low-order word of integer 2.
        HSM  WRD               High order word of sum.
        LSM  WRD               Low-order word of sum.
```

Start of program

```
        LOA  A  LI1    Load low-order word of integer 1.
        ADD  A  LI2    Add low-order word of integer 2.
        STO  A  LSM    Store in low-order word of sum.
        LOA  A  HI1    Load high-order word of integer 2.
        ADC  A  HI2    Add high-order word of integer 2
                       plus previous carry.
        STD  A  HSM    Store in high-order word of sum.
        HLT            Halt.
        END            End of program
```

c) Unless a loop is used, the program structure is as above, with the addition of **LOA**, **ADC** and **STO** instructions.

☐ d) Twos complement subtraction always results in the correct bit pattern for the low-order word, even if the low-order word of the second number is larger than that of the first. However, in the latter case, the high-order word of the difference is too large by 1, since this should be 'borrowed' for the low order subtraction. This situation is indicated by the overflow bit being set during the low order subtraction.

Using data areas as for part a), the program is as follows:

```
             LOA  A   LI1    Load low-order word of integer 1.
             SUB  A   LI2    Subtract low-order word of integer 2.
             STO  A   LSM    Store in low-order word of difference.
             STC             Set carry bit.
             BVS      NXT    Branch if overflow set by subtraction.
             CLC             Clear carry bit.
       NXT   LOA  A   HI1    Load high-order word of integer 1.
             SBC  A   HI2    Subtract (high order word of integer 2 + carry).
```

```
            STO  A       HSM   Store in high order word or difference.
            HLT                Halt.
            END                End of program.
```

6 The program uses a subset of the instructions in Example Program 14.2.

```
PTR  WRD           LE1   Address of first list item, later of current list item.
```

Start of program loop

```
NXT  LOA  A       PTA   Load address of current list item to accumulator.
     INC  A             Increment accumulator, to become address of
                        pointer part of list item.
     STO  A       PTR   Store address of pointer part of list item.
     LOA  A  I    PTR   Load pointer part of list item to accumulator.
     BZE          OUT   Branch out of loop if it is zero.
     STO  A       PTR   Store address of next list item.
     BRN          NXT   Branch to instruction labelled NXT to continue.
```

End of program loop

```
     LOA  A       PTR   Load address of pointer part of last list item.
     DEC  A             Decrement accumulator, to contain address of
                        last list item.
     HLT                Halt.
LE1  BTE          /A/   First list item.
     WRD          +0    Pointer part of first list item.
     END                End of program.
```

7 The program below uses the same data as Example Program 14.5, except that 'sum' is interpreted as 'difference', and 'carry' as 'borrow'. A 1 in the borrow digit of the difference indicates that the difference is negative, and should be subtracted from 100000 to obtain the magnitude.

```
     LOA  X  N    +14   Initialise the index register to 4, one less than the
                        number of digits in each number.
```

Start of subtraction loop

```
AGN  LOB  A  N    /0/   Load the code for 0 to the accumulator.
     ADB  A  D    NM1   Add digit of first number, using indexed addres-
                        sing.
     SBB  A  D    NM2   Subtract digit of second number.
     SBB  A       CRY   Subtract borrow from previous subtraction.
     CPB  A  N    /0/   Compare difference with code for 0.
     BLT          LTN   Branch if less to instruction labelled LTN.
     STB  A  D    SUM   Store digit in difference, using indexed addres-
                        sing.
     CLA  A             Clear accumulator.
     STB  A       CRY   Store zero in borrow byte.
     BRN          NXT   Branch to instruction labelled NXT.
LTN  ADB  A  N    +10   Add 10 to accumulator.
     STB  A  D    SUM   Store digit in difference, using indexed addres-
                        sing.
     LOB  A  N    +1    Load 1 to accumulator.
     STB  A       CRY   Store 1 in borrow byte.
NXT  DEC  X             Decrease index register by 1.
     BGE          AGN   Branch if greater than or equal to zero, to
                        continue loop.
```

End of loop, deal with borrow digit of difference

```
            LOB  A  N   /0/   Load the code for O to accumulator.
            ADB  A      CRY   Add borrow byte.
            STB  A      CDS   Store result in borrow digit of difference.
            HLT               Halt.
            END               End of program.
```

9 The version of the program written below uses a third working area, **WA0**, to allow for a possible double length product.

```
  IN1  WRD      +2647    Integer 1.
  IN2  WRD      +3159    Integer 2.
  WA0  WRD      +0       High-order word of product.
  WA1  WRD      +0       Low-order word of product.
  WA2  WRD               Working area.
```

Start of program

```
            LOA  A      IN2   Load integer 2 to accumulator.
            STO  A      WA2   Store integer 2 in working area.
```

Start of multiplication loop

```
  NXT  BZE          OUT   Branch to end of program if number in
                          accumulator is zero.
       LOA  A       WA1   Load low-order word of product.
       ADD  A       IN1   Add integer 1.
       STO  A       WA1   Store new value of low-order word of
                          product.
       LOA  A       WA0   Load high-order word of product.
       ADC  A  N    +0    Add carry from previous addition.
       STO  A       WA0   Store new value of high-order word of
                          product.
       LOA  A       WA2   Load working area to accumulator.
       DEC  A             Decrease accumulator by 1.
       STO  A       WA2   Store new value of working area.
       BRN          NXT   Branch to continue loop.
```

End of multiplication loop

```
  OUT  HLT               Halt.
       END               End of program.
```

11 A store instruction with an immediate operand makes no sense.

Exercise 15

3 Checking the assembly language program for errors, and reporting the nature and position of any encountered.

4 A label can only be associated with one absolute address in the symbolic address table of an assembler.

5 An additional entry in the table of mnemonic and machine operation codes, and routines to carry out any special assembly operations required by the new instruction.

6 AMC Machine Language

Address	Instruction	
0000	1121	<u>0001</u>
0004	1A21	<u>001B</u>
0008	65<u>0C</u>	
000A	1111	<u>0064</u>
000E	2214	<u>0018</u>
0012	0220	
0014	61<u>EE</u>	
0016	8500	

7 Use the AMC Simulation Program to check these.

Exercise 16

2 See Section 16.1.

3 See the first paragraph of Section 16.2.

4 See Section 16.4.

5 Similarities: Use of character symbols, words and constructions based on rules of syntax.
Differences: Natural languages are not precisely defined. A valid program in a high level language has only one interpretation, whereas natural languages can be vague or ambiguous, or have several levels of meaning.

6 a) Some valid sentences:

John sings
John sings and John eats and John sleeps

Some invalid sentences:

John and George eats
Ringo eats or sleeps

b)

461·31	valid
·734	valid
4325	invalid
45·6·7	invalid
846·	invalid

c) Rule 1 becomes:
<decimal number> : : = <decimal point> <number> | <number>
<decimal point> <number> | <number> |
<number> <decimal point>

d) <signed integer> : : = <sign> <integer>
<sign>   : : = + | −
<integer>   : : = <digit> | <digit> <integer>
<digit>   : : = 0 | 1 | 2 | 3 | 4 | 5 | 6 | 7 | 8 | 9

7 a) x: lines 2 to 19
count: lines 3 to 19
v: lines 10 to 14

b) Yes.
c) No.
d) local variables: w, v, y, z
global variables: x, count.
e) line 17.

8 a) $Y = 4, X = 4$
b) **LET T = X**
LET X = Y
LET Y = T

9 a)   **READ (1, 200) I, J, K, L, M, N**
200 FORMAT (I2, 1X, I2, 1X, I2, 1X, I4,
1X, I4, 1X, I4)
b) **3614 2915 23 79 63725498**
c) Advantages: precision, ability to check data as it is input.
Disadvantages: tedious, error-prone, difficult to program.

10 a) $y = 5$
b) $y = 10$
c) $y = 10$
d) $y = 9$
e) $y = 0$
f) Using 'elementary' Basic:
100 IF X < 0 THEN 120
105 IF X > 9 THEN 120
110 LET Y = 9 – X
115 GO TO 125
120 LET Y = 10
125 REM CONTINUE
The logic of this program segment is not nearly as easy to follow as the Pascal statement.

11 See Section 16.12.

Exercise 17

2 The three strongest reasons are the theoretical emphasis of Algol, its poor input/output facilities and the increasing popularity of Pascal.

4 Algol's aim of being a 'universal programming language' is very lofty, and rather idealistic. Pascal's aim to be a simple, well-structured teaching language which is easy to implement on a wide range of computers, is much more realistic.

5 Reasoned cases can be made for Pascal, Basic and PL/M.

6 Possible reasons (for both languages) include their suitability for the type of work for which they are designed, and their ease of use by people working in the particular fields to which they apply.

9

Language	Relative emphasis on arithmetic
Fortran	strong
Algol	strong
Cobol	moderate
Basic	moderate
Pascal	moderate
RPG	weak
PL/M	weak

Exercise 18

2 See Section 18.2.

3 It is simpler than compilation, and only requires one copy of the program being interpreted.

4 See Section 18.4, second paragraph.

5 a) Valid
   b) Invalid.
   c) Invalid.
   d) Valid.
   e) 2. $<$condition$> ::= <$variable$> <$relation$> <$constant$> |$
          $<$variable$> <$relation$> <$variable$>$

6 a) Valid.
   b) Valid.
   c) Valid.
   d) Invalid – error 2.
   e) Invalid – error 2.
   f) Invalid – error 3.
   g) Error 1: No number present,
      Error 2: Duplicate sign in number,
      Error 3: No digits in number,
      Error 4: Duplicate decimal point.

   ☐ h)

State	+	−	digit	.	E	∇
1	2	2	3	4	error 5	error 1
2	error 2	error 2	3	4	error 5	error 3
3	error 2	error 2	3	4	5	exit
4	error 2	error 2	4	error 4	5	exit
5	6	6	7	error 6	error 7	error 8
6	error 2	error 2	7	error 6	error 7	error 8
7	error 2	error 2	7	error 6	error 7	exit

Next character (column header above +, −, digit, ., E, ∇)

   Error 5: Invalid number before exponent,
   Error 6: Decimal point in exponent,
   Error 7: Duplicate exponent symbol,
   Error 8: Incomplete exponent.

7 a) Basic   AMC Assembly Language

```
a) 100  LET  L = J + K                LOA  A      J
                                      ADD  A      K
                                      STO  A      L
b) 50  IF  C > 10  THEN  200          LOA  A      C
                                      CMP  A  N  +10
                                      BGT         XXO
c) 100  FOR  K = 1  TO  20            LOA  X  N  +1
                                 NXT  CMP  X  N  +20
                                      BGT         OUT
   110  LET  J(K) = J(K) + 1          LOB  A  D  J
                                      INC  A
                                      STB  A  D  J
   120  NEXT  K                       INC  X
                                      BRN         NXT
                                 OUT
```

9 One instruction is placed outside the loop, which is repeated 9 times, with three operations per repetition:

```
                        LOA  X  N  +1
                        LOA  A  N  +100
                   NXT  CMP  A  N  +27
                        BGT        OUT
                        STB  A  D  W
                        INC  X
                        STB  A  D  W
                        INC  X
                        STB  A  D  W
                        INC  X
                        BRN        NXT
                   OUT
```

10 See Figure 32.13.

Exercise 19

1 The program is being written for the virtual machine produced by the operating system, and not for the raw hardware of the computer.

3 See Section 19.4.

4 Small main store.

5 See Sections 19.6, 19.11 and 19.12.

6 The control and resource management of a large computer system, comprising more than one processor, large numbers of peripherals and several data communication channels is an extremely complex task.

7 See Section 19.9.

8 It is the only part which has direct access to the 'real' resources of the computer, and all requests for these resources must be channelled through it.

9 The programmer is freed from the problems of store allocation, and does not have to resort to such techniques as overlay programming.

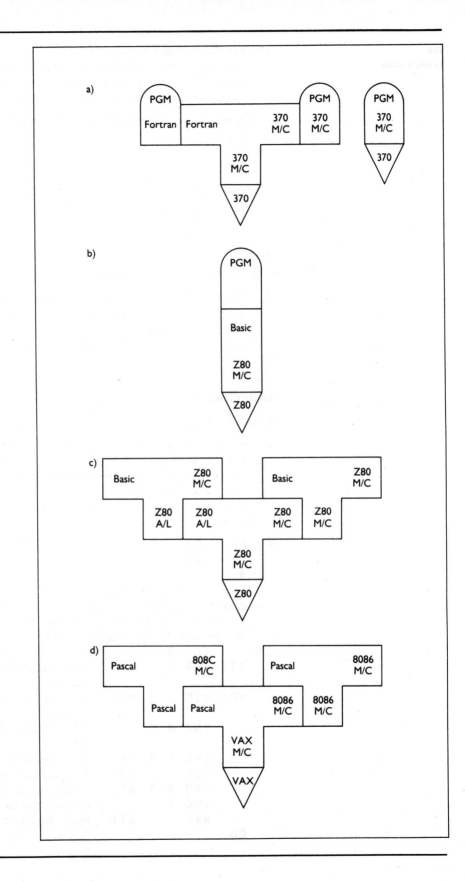

Figure 32.13
Exercise 18, Question 10

10 Objectives: efficient management of the resources (chiefly main store) of the computer, and simplifying the use of the peripherals.
Features: A simple main store manager, controllers for each peripheral and a mechanism to allow the user to interrupt an application program.

11 No software is infallible, and only an operator can respond to unforeseen circumstances.

Exercise 20

1 a) Unix, VME/B, COS.
  b) Unix, VME/B.

2 Unix, VME/B.

3 See Sections 20.2.5, 20.3.8 and 20.4.7.

4 CP/M and Unix provide facilities for interactive control by users, COS runs programs in batch mode, with control instructions included in the program, and VME/B can work interactively or in batch mode. VME/B system control language is a block structured high level language, unlike those of the other systems.

Exercise 21

2 See Section 21.3

3 The application program is compiled, with calls to the utilities regarded as unresolved external references. The utilities are copied from backing store, and the linkage editor deals with the unresolved external references in the calls from the main program and the returns from the utilities. Finally, the loading program places all the modules in their final positions for running, and transforms all addresses as required.

4 a) Address **G0**.
  b) Address **G0 + 1**.
  c) *****
  d) Control is transferred to the start of the program, at address **G0**.
  e) A machine code program is loaded, as a set of characters, from a paper tape, to main store, starting at address **G0**. When the end of the program is reached, control passes to the first program instruction.

□f)				
	CLA A			Clear index register.
	STR IRQ P			Request paper tape reader to input a character.
	HRE BIN		**HRE**	Branch to this instruction if input not complete.
	INP A			Copy character from input register to accumulator.
	CPB A N		**/*/**	Compare character in accumulator with *****.
	BEQ		**GO**	Branch to instruction labelled **G0** if equal.
	STB A D		**GO**	Store accumulator contents at (**G0** + index).
	INC X			Increase index by 1.
	BRN		**STR**	Branch to instruction labelled **STR**.
GO				

Exercise 22

1 See Section 22.1.

2 See the last paragraph of Section 22.1.

3 a) Periodic processing.
   b) Real-time system, transaction processing.
   c) Periodic processing.
   d) Real-time system, process control.
   e) Database system, or real-time system, information storage/retrieval.

5 Almost at any stage, but most common are after a feasibility study, system investigation or acceptance testing.

6 Feasibility study, system investigation, system specification, evaluation of possible packages against the system specification, choice of package, acceptance testing.

7 They are not an adequate test of the robustness of the system.

8 Increased costs, particularly wage costs, delays and loss of business, and the computer acquiring a bad reputation.

9 At system specification time, or when parallel running is commenced.
   Possibilities are: guarantee of no redundancies, inducements of free re-training for higher paid jobs, undertakings to improve working conditions and, above all, keeping employees adequately informed about what is going on.

10 The system outlined below is only one possible approach to the task as specified.
   a) See Figure 32.14.
   b) One each for sale recording, updating of stock sales file, updating of cash takings file and transmission of stock sales file.
   c) Sale recording program

      Set sale total to zero.
      Repeat, for each item sold
         Input stock number and quantity
         Access price from stock price file
         Display stock number, quantity, price and amount
         Print stock number, quantity, price and amount on sale slip
         Add amount to total.
      Print and display total.
      Input amount of cash, cheque and gift voucher tendered.
      Calculate change.
      Display and print amount tendered and change.

      Other program specifications in a similar amount of detail.
   d) Training of data entry terminal operators.
      Ensuring that the prices displayed on goods are always the same as those in the price file.

Exercise 23

1 a) Possible keys are: name and date, or reference allocated to each letter.
   b) One possibility is: fields for name, address, date and each line of text of the letter, each field starting with the tab position of the first character of the text in the field.
   c) Any medium other than discs will make editing very difficult.

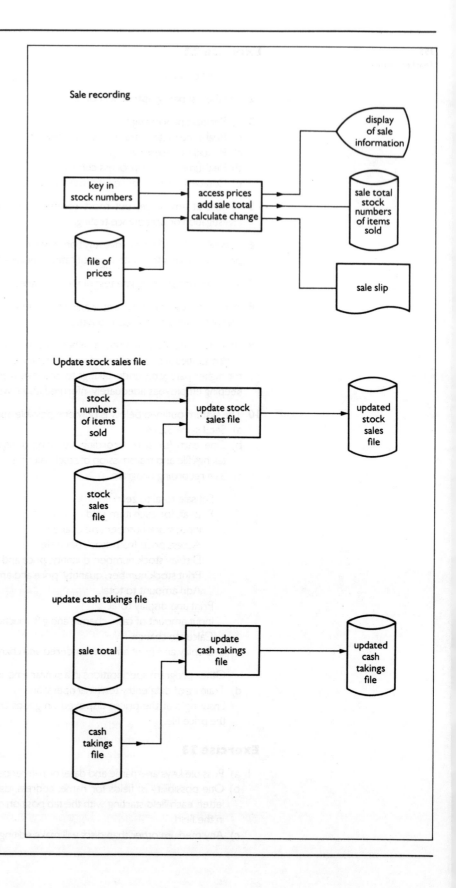

Figure 32.14
Exercise 22, Question 10

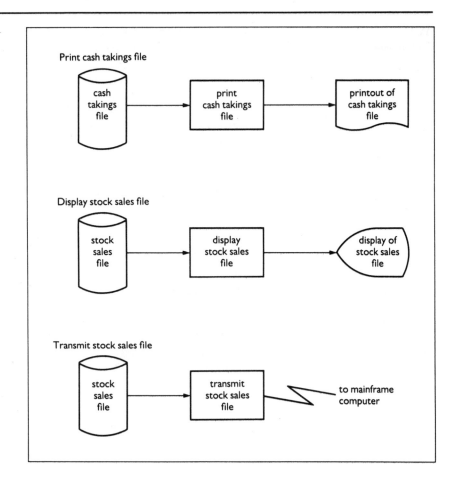

2 See Section 23.4.

3 Individual data items cannot be addressed on a magnetic tape.

4 b) Employee number
   c) A check on the total of the various categories of days.
       A check of the name against employee number on a reference file.

5 The batch total calculated before the data was input is wrong.

6 62973
   51164

7 a) Search the top level index for the first key greater than 132714.
       This corresponds to second level index 11.
       Search second level index 11 for the first key greater than 132714.
       This corresponds to third level index 531.
       Search third level index 531 for the first key greater than 132714.
       This corresponds to block 26544.
       Copy block 26544 to main store, and search it sequentially for key 132714.
   ☐ b) During cylinder – surface – sector indexing, the disc drive head is 'homing in'
       on the required sector. During hierarchical indexing, the location on the
       required block is only determined at the last step.

8 a) 412 117 503 has address 1112.
     625 417 902 has address 1944.
  b) 462 803 906 has address 2171.
     341 915 916 has address 2172.
     638 702 831 has address 2173.
     594 113 666 has address 2174.
  c) Loading in a different order will almost certainly result in different addresses for the records.

10 String 1: 17 4 9 21, sorted: 4 9 17 21
    String 2: 8 5 20 2, sorted: 2 5 8 20
    String 3: 7 11 15 6, sorted: 6 7 11 15
    String 4: 3 1 19 13, sorted: 1 3 13 19

    Tape A: String 1: 4 9 17 21   String 3: 6 7 11 15
    Tape B: String 2: 2 5 8 20   String 4: 1 3 13 19

    Merge in pairs:
    Tape C: String 1 + String 2: 2 4 5 8 9 17 20 21
    Tape D: String 3 + String 4: 1 3 6 7 11 13 15 19

    Merge to a single string:
    Tape A: 1 2 3 4 5 6 7 8 9 11 13 15 17 19 20 21

11 Initial situation:

    4 7 8 10 11 19 23 31

    Select middle record (key 10), partition set:

    4 7 8 10 11 19 23 31

    Required key is greater than that of middle record, so search right subset:

    11 19 23 31

    Select middle record (key 19), which is the required record.

12 Re-run the backup (grandfather) copy of the tape with the previous transactions to re-create the current version of the tape. Then update the current version with the current transactions, to re-create the new version.

13 The backup copy of the disc is re-run against all the transactions since it was backed up. The current updating is then repeated. Another backup copy of the disc is made either before or after updating.

Exercise 24

2 See Sections 24.1 and 24.6.

3 See Section 24.5.

4 See Sections 24.2 and 24.11.

□ **5** Specimen answer using a relational model.

a) **Table 1: Correspondent identities**

Identity	Name
K347P	JOHN GREGGOROWSKI

Table 2: Newspaper identities

Identity	Name
N417W	WASHINGTON STAR

Table 3: News items

Date	Correspondent identity	Newspaper identity	Text
04/11/80	K007L	N417W	LONDON EXPERIENCED...
07/11/80	K347P	N417W	STRIKES IN POLAND...
07/11/80	K347P	N327T	STRIKES IN POLAND...

Note that if an item is bought by more than one paper, then multiple entries are inserted in Table 3. A more efficient relational approach is to introduce a news item identity, and have a fourth table of this together with the text of the item. The third table would then contain the news item identity instead of the text.

b) Table 3 is used to locate the newspaper identities of all newspapers buying a news item with a given date and correspondent identity. Table 2 is then used to locate the names of the newspapers.

Exercise 25

2 See Section 25.4.

□ **3** a) **First row:**

	binary	1010	1000	0110	0000
	hexadecimal	A	8	6	0
	ASCII	Count = 40		space	

Second row:

	binary	1010	1000	0010	1110
	hexadecimal	A	8	2	E
	ASCII	Count = 40			

Third row:

	binary	1010	1000	0110	0000
	hexadecimal	A	8	6	0
	ASCII	Count = 40		space	

Fourth row:

	binary	0100	1101	0100	0101
	hexadecimal	4	B	4	5
	ASCII		M		E

... 8 characters ...

	binary	0100	0100	0101	0011
	hexadecimal	4	4	5	3
	ASCII		D		S

Rest of fourth to eighteenth rows:

	binary	1111	1111	0110	0000
	hexadecimal	F	F	6	0
	ASCII	Count = 127		space	

... repeated a total of 4 times

	binary	1101	0000	0110	0000
	hexadecimal	D	0	6	0
	ASCII	Count = 80		space	

Nineteenth row: See Second row.

Twentieth row: See First row.

b) Total characters transmitted: 28
Total characters (including blanks) displayed: 800.

5 78 lines.

□ **7** a) Data: 1   0   1   1   1   0   1

Check 1:	1		1		1		1	pass (value 0)
Check 2:		0	1			0	1	pass (value 0)
Check 3:				1	1	0	1	fail (value 1)

Error code 100, error in 4th digit.

Data: 0   0   1   1   0   0   0

Check 1:	0		1		0		0	fail (value 1)
Check 2:	0	1				0	0	fail (value 1)
Check 3:				1	0	0	0	fail (value 1)

Error code 111, error in 7th digit.

Data: 1   1   1   1   1   0   1

Check 1:	1		1		1		1	pass (value 0)
Check 2:		1	1			0	1	fail (value 1)
Check 3:				1	1	0	1	fail (value 1)

Error code 110, error in 6th digit.

□ b)

Data bits:			B1		B2	B3	B4		B5	B6	B7	B8
Check bits:	C1	C2		C3				C4				
Digit numbers:	D1	D2	D3	D4	D5	D6	D7	D8	D9	D10	D11	D12
Check 1:	*		*		*		*		*		*	
Check 2:		*	*			*	*			*	*	
Check 3:				*	*	*	*					*
Check 4:								*	*	*	*	*

Exercise 26

1 See Section 26.1.5.

2 See Sections 26.1.6 and 26.1.11.

3 See Section 26.2.6.

4 See Sections 26.2.4 and 26.2.5.
Local control: Interlocking of lights, and detailed light changes.
Subgroup control: In cell of central computer, implementation of timetable.
Top-level control: In Master subsystem, allocation of timetable.

6 See Section 26.3.4.

9 a) An important reason is that PL/M incorporates low-level features such as interrupt handling.
b) In these areas, speed of execution of code is of vital importance, and hand optimisation is essential.

10 Some possibilities include linking all the word processors to a large common filestore, a quality printer and a communications gateway.

11 See Sections 26.4.3 and 26.4.4.

Exercise 27

2 See Sections 27.2 and 27.1.

3 A significant reason not quoted in the text is the high degree of co-operation between universities and businesses in the field of computer research and development.

4 A major reason is the lack of Japanese experience in computer applications.

Exercise 28

2 The usual are:

Applications programmer – team leader – systems analyst – data processing manager.

Applications programmer – database administrator – data processing manager.

4 Other jobs include: components purchasers, technical authors, a wide variety of consultants, recruitment officers, network administrators, computer resources co-ordinators, database analysts, etc.

5 The most serious implication of this is the amount of training and re-training that is necessary if the computing industry is to absorb a significant proportion of people currently unemployed.

Exercise 29

2 See Section 29.2.

☐ 3 Major systems include: any computer application, a computer (with hardware and software as significant subsystems), the process of designing and manufacturing a computer. It is arguable whether the computing industry as a whole may be considered as a system.

Exercise 30

5 Possibilities to consider are applications centred around local area networks, speech recognition and synthesis and the use of magnetic bubble memory devices.

6 An area worth investigating is the 'traditional' manufacture of mainframe computers by large multinational companies.

Computing Science Software

AMC Simulation

Designed to accompany *Computing Science*
Available for a range of microcomputers
Accompanied by a detailed user guide
Supplied with two copies of the disk
Written by Peter Bishop
Produced by NELCAL

The A-level model computer (AMC) complements *Computing Science* and has been designed to illustrate three key areas in this book:

1. Processor architecture
2. Machine language
3. Assembly language

Further details and current price can be obtained from:
The Promotions Department
Nelson Computer Assisted Learning
Nelson House
Mayfield Road
Walton-on-Thames
Surrey KT12 5PL

Index